Praise for *This Ain't Rock 'n' Roll*

'In this important exploration of the relationship between pop music and the Third Reich, Daniel Rachel challenges the motivations of those artists who sought glamour and notoriety in exploiting Nazi imagery'

Billy Bragg

'Whilst it's slightly incredible nobody has before published a book on rock's periodic spasms of flirtation with Nazism, one could picture it as a dry, academic thesis rather than the absolute banger Daniel Rachel has written. It's hard to imagine there will be a more original book of non-fiction this year'

Emma Forrest

'A timely book exposing the complicated history of the use of Nazi symbols in popular music culture since the last world war. As the powers-that-be lurch towards a far-right future in 2025, there is no longer any hiding place for those pretending to be ignorant about the true meaning of Nazism, or using its emblems for their supposed subversive 'cool' factor. They have a choice, own their perverse fascination when exposed or apologise'

Pauline Black

Also by Daniel Rachel
Isle of Noises: Conversations with Great British Songwriters

Walls Come Tumbling Down: The Music and Politics of Rock
Against Racism, 2 Tone and Red Wedge

Don't Look Back in Anger: The Rise and Fall of Cool Britannia,
Told by Those Who Were There

The Lost Album of The Beatles:
What If The Beatles Hadn't Split Up?

Too Much Too Young, The 2 Tone Records Story:
Rude Boys Racism and the Soundtrack of a Generation

Co-authored by Daniel Rachel
When Ziggy Played the Marquee (with Terry O'Neill)

I Just Can't Stop It: My Life in The Beat (with Ranking Roger)

Oasis: Knebworth: Two Nights That Will Live Forever
(with Jill Furmanovsky)

David Bowie: Icon

One For the Road: The Life & Lyrics of Simon Fowler &
Ocean Colour Scene (with Simon Fowler)

THIS AIN'T ROCK 'N' ROLL

Pop Music, the Swastika and the Third Reich

Daniel Rachel

WHITE RABBIT

First published in Great Britain in 2025 by White Rabbit,
an imprint of The Orion Publishing Group Ltd
Carmelite House, 50 Victoria Embankment
London EC4Y 0DZ

An Hachette UK Company

The authorised representative in the EEA is Hachette Ireland, 8 Castlecourt
Centre, Dublin 15, D15 XTP3, Ireland (email: info@hbgi.ie)

1 3 5 7 9 10 8 6 4 2

A CIP catalogue record for this book is
available from the British Library.

ISBN (Hardback) 978 1 3996 3572 1
ISBN (Export Trade Paperback) 978 1 3996 3573 8
ISBN (Ebook) 978 1 3996 3575 2
ISBN (Audio) 978 1 3996 3576 9

Typeset by Born Group
Printed and bound in Great Britain by Clays Ltd, Elcograf S.p.A.

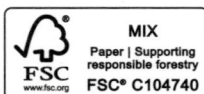

MIX
Paper | Supporting
responsible forestry
FSC
www.fsc.org
FSC® C104740

www.whiterabbitbooks.co.uk
www.orionbooks.co.uk

For Judith R. Rachel who died sometime during my own rock 'n' roll adventure. 'Look Mum, I write books now with an introduction by someone you once feared would brainwash me!'

For who would bear the whips and scorns of time,
Th'oppressor's wrong, the proud man's contumely,
The pangs of dispriz'd love, the law's delay,
The insolence of office, and the spurns
That patient merit of th'unworthy takes,
When he himself might his quietus make
William Shakespeare

Hamlet, Act 3, Scene 1

Nothing is more terrible than ignorance in action.
Goethe #231

Maxims and Reflections, translated by T. Bailey Saunders

A Holocaust survivor dies of old age, goes to heaven and tells God a Holocaust joke. God says, 'That's not funny,' and the survivor says, 'I guess you had to be there.'
Ricky Gervais to Jerry Seinfeld

Comedians in Cars Getting Coffee, Season 11, Episode 4

This ain't rock 'n' roll; this is genocide.
David Bowie

'Diamond Dogs'

Contents

Author's Note   xiii

Introduction by Billy Bragg   1

1 POP GOES THE SWASTIKA   5

Madalf Heatlump (Who only had one)   7
JOHN LENNON. THE BEATLES

Shouting the Blues   18
THE ANIMALS. JOHN'S CHILDREN.
THE ROLLING STONES

A Lousy Publicist   34
KEITH MOON. VIVIAN STANSHALL.
LED ZEPPELIN

Colour Me Pop   44
IGGY & THE STOOGES. BLUE ÖYSTER CULT.
SWEET

Rock Around the Bunker   56
SERGE GAINSBOURG. ROXY MUSIC

For those About to Rock   63
KISS. MOTÖRHEAD. ALEX HARVEY

Visions of Swastikas   75
DAVID BOWIE. QUEEN

Rivers of Blood   91
ERIC CLAPTON. ROCK AGAINST RACISM.
ANTI-NAZI LEAGUE

2 ROCK AND ROLL GAS CHAMBER   105

Too Fast to Live Too Young to Die   107
MALCOLM McLAREN. SEX PISTOLS

Deutschland Über Alles   127
SIOUXSIE & THE BANSHEES. LONDON SS.
THE CLASH

Blitzkrieg Bop   140
NEW YORK DOLLS. RAMONES. ELECTRIC
EELS. DEAD BOYS. RESIDENTS

Fascist in the Bedroom   148
THE DAMNED. *SALON KITTY. THE NIGHT
PORTER.* MADONNA. LADY GAGA

Fascinating Fascism   160
FETISH CLOTHING. SIOUXSIE SIOUX

Deutscher Girls   170
ADAM & THE ANTS. *RIPPED & TORN*

3 LOVE IN A VOID   187

Master-Racial Masturbation   189
2 TONE

An Ideal for Living   194
BLONDIE. SHAM 69. JOY DIVISION

Zyklon B Zombie   211
NEW ORDER. A CERTAIN RATIO.
THROBBING GRISTLE. FINAL SOLUTION

Welcome to the Cabaret   226
HUMAN LEAGUE. LOU REED. SPANDAU
BALLET. SPEAR OF DESTINY.

Olympia 233
THE SKIDS. OI! THE BIRTHDAY PARTY

Who Makes the Nazis? 241
THE EXPLOITED. THE FALL

4 NEVER MIND THE SWASTIKAS 247

This Way for the Gas, Ladies
and Gentlemen 249
WOODY GUTHRIE. RUSH. LEONARD
COHEN. PAUL WELLER. DEAD KENNEDYS

Arbeit Macht Frei 266
MANIC STREET PREACHERS. JANIS IAN.
INDIGO GIRLS

Sound of Drums 272
SKUNK ANANSIE. KULA SHAKER. U2.
MICHAEL JACKSON

Swastika Eyes 280
PRIMAL SCREAM. FAT WHITE FAMILY.
INTERPOL. BRYAN FERRY

Pretty as a Swastika 291
SLAYER. MARILYN MANSON. OZZY
OSBOURNE. NICKI MINAJ. JETHRO TULL.
LIBERTINES. NICO

Another Brick in the Wall 304
PINK FLOYD. ICE CUBE. KANYE WEST.
K-POP

Ghosts 315
TRUPA TRUPA

Epilogue   321

Acknowledgements   327

References   329

Image Credits   347

Index   349

Author's Note

In *Mein Kampf*, Adolf Hitler described the Nazi Party flag by its symbolic colours: red signified the social idea, white stood for nationalism, and the *Hakenkreuz* (swastika) represented the Aryan race and, by default, anti-Semitism. While flirting or indulging in Nazi imagery does not automatically equate to ideological endorsement, such symbols are inseparably linked to their historical context. Consequently, the artists discussed in this book can be broadly categorised into three groups: those who explicitly supported Nazi beliefs, those who appropriated Nazi imagery without clear political alignment, and those whose work actively opposes fascist ideas. All of these musicians have contributed to the legacy of rock 'n' roll, and any moral judgement is ultimately left to the discretion of the reader.

Introduction by Billy Bragg

In December 1992, BBC2 screened *Triumph of the Will*, Leni Riefenstahl's documentary film of the 1934 Nazi Party rally in Nuremberg. Almost two hours long, and featuring a Wagnerian soundtrack and striking visuals that have come to define totalitarianism, it promotes the supremacy of the Nazi Party and cult of Adolf Hitler.

Concerned by the reaction that such images of fascist iconography might provoke, the BBC scheduled the broadcast for five minutes past midnight and preceded it with a special programme in which a panel of experts struggled with the challenge inherent when viewing propaganda aimed solely at glorifying the Third Reich. Is it possible to admire Riefenstahl's film in aesthetic terms, without discounting the fact that this thrilling spectacle led directly to the Holocaust?

Nearly twenty years earlier, BBC2 had first screened *Triumph of the Will* in November 1973 as part of a series called World Cinema. Broadcast at prime time, between *The Money Programme* and a discussion about children's books, the BBC treated Riefenstahl's documentary as a historical curiosity. There was no special programme to alert viewers to the nature of what they were about to witness, nor any discussion after.

What changed in the ensuing two decades to make the screening of *Triumph of the Will* such a volatile issue?

Since its earliest years, pop music has been marked by a spirit of provocation. Few things are more rewarding to the emerging adolescent than annoying the grown-ups. Today's rebels sport tattoos and piercings, whereas for the sixties kids it was possible to provoke a reaction by simply growing your hair.

Despite the unprecedented success of the Beatles, John Lennon never lost the urge to provoke. As Daniel Rachel observes, he had a habit of responding to the mass hysteria that greeted the Beatles wherever they went by indulging in Hitler impersonations, arm in the air, forefinger on his top lip. While it is debatable whether this was a comment on the dangers of mass indoctrination or simply bad taste, we can be sure that it was not an endorsement of the Third Reich. Lennon was mocking Hitler, not glorifying him.

John Lennon was born during the Second World War, like almost all British pop stars of the sixties. When they were children, the Nazis were the people who bombed their streets. In the face of such a threat, mockery is a natural defence. As that generation took control of popular culture in the late sixties and early seventies, they tended to portray Hitler as a pantomime villain, a figure of fun, the butt of a joke the whole nation could laugh at because we won the war.

For those of us of the following generation, born in the late fifties, our initial experience of Nazis was derived almost exclusively from comics in which the British were plucky, the Americans were flashy and the Nazis were killed. The popular war movies of the time followed a similar path. There was death and glory in equal measure, but the fate of Europe's Jews was papered over by sympathetic German characters who were portrayed as soldiers, rather than Nazis.

While we were aware of the Holocaust, our conception of Nazism was still bound in our parents' experience of the Blitz. It wasn't until 1974, when footage of the liberation of Hitler's death camps was broadcast as part of ITV's *The World at War* series, that perceptions began to change. These graphic images of the victims of genocide, never before seen in such detail on British TV, changed the meaning of Nazism for my generation.

By the time punk rock came along three years later, it was hard to sympathise with claims that wearing a swastika was a homage to the movie *Cabaret*. Hitler was no longer a figure of fun. Joy Division weren't mocking the Third Reich when they named their band after brothels created by the SS in concentration camps. For all manager

Tony Wilson's disingenuous claims of postmodernist subversion in naming themselves Joy Division, the band were exploiting Nazism to make themselves look cool.

The only way to genuinely subvert the power of the swastika is to treat the Nazis as buffoons, as Mel Brooks did so successfully in *The Producers*.

Coolness, however, has no truck with buffoonery. It is the manifestation, in stylistic terms, of something deemed worthy of admiration.

So what was it that the pale coterie of Weimar-loving pop artists found so admirable in Hitler's regime? Was it the muscular construction of the autobahns? The thrill of Guderian's Panzer divisions sweeping through Belgium? The dream of a nation where the trains run on time?

Or was it that, by adopting Nazi style, using images, names, fashions, even haircuts lifted directly from the Third Reich, they found a simplistic way of suggesting that, despite their unprepossessing demeanour, they existed beyond good and evil, where objective morality means nothing and all that matters is the triumph of individual will?

It seems a lot of meaning to place on a pair of leather trousers, a brown shirt and a blond fringe shaved at the sides, but I've seen it tried, and been embarrassed for artists who should know better as I watched them stumbling over the Riefenstahl test, angrily defending their adoption of Nazi stylings while vociferously denying charges of anti-Semitism.

Utilising the darkest aspects of Nazism to confer an air of audacity and dispassion requires both poseur and admirer to share an understanding of the true meaning of the swastika. The thrill of pushing boundaries relies on everyone being aware of where the boundaries lie, and for Nazism, that place is the genocide of the Jewish population of Nazi-occupied Europe.

Triumph of the Will succeeds as spectacle because it relies on clean lines – of vision, of lighting, of swastikas and storm troopers. It contains none of the mud on the boots of the *Einsatzgruppen* as they systematically machine-gunned Jewish men, women and children in the ravine at Babi Yar. There is no smell of overdriven engines rising from hermetically sealed trucks converted to suffocate Jews with their exhaust fumes. You cannot hear the wailing as lethal Zyklon B pellets were dropped into the midst of those Jews deemed unfit for work at Auschwitz-Birkenau.

Yet the organisers – and doubtless some of the perpetrators too – of these crimes against humanity are present in Riefenstahl's film and the indelible stain that they left on history finds its most potent symbolism in the swastika.

In this important exploration of the relationship between pop music and the Third Reich, Daniel Rachel challenges the motivations of those artists who sought glamour and notoriety in exploiting Nazi imagery. In doing so, he raises once more the question that was put to Leni Riefenstahl after 1945, when she claimed that, while fascinated by Nazism, she was politically naive and ignorant of the fate of six million Jews:

How could you not know?

1

POP GOES THE SWASTIKA

Windows of a Jewish-owned store painted with the word *Jude* (Jew), Berlin, Germany, 19 June 1938.

Madalf Heatlump (Who only had one)

JOHN LENNON. THE BEATLES

It could have been a football match between Tottenham Hotspur and Arsenal, but as it is, this story begins with the English entertainer Tommy Steele at London's Finsbury Park Empire. In the audience that night was Jack Good, who thought to himself, 'This is the life!' Good would soon bring sex, energy and teenage music to British television as the producer of *Six-Five Special*, *Oh Boy!*, *Boy Meets Girls* and *Wham!!* 'I found the whole pop field fascinating,' Good told Maureen Cleave of the *Evening Standard* in 1963. 'I was mad about it. Hadn't been so excited since I saw a match between Spurs and Arsenal. You see I love excitement; I love to make people respond. I love a helluva hullabaloo. The theatre is for excitement, it's not for ideas – you get those in books.'[1]

Good introduced pop stardom into British living rooms, transporting a generation of teens into a world of fame and sexual promise. A former Royal Air Force pilot, Good described fighting against Nazi Germany as absolute hell. But in 1956, sitting in a darkened auditorium watching Tommy Steele, he made a disturbing connection, telling Cleave, 'Rhythm is in all of us. If we bottle it up, we are liable to respond to other things. Hitler, for example. Those rallies at Nuremberg must have been like the Hackney Empire. What a fantastic showman he was, all the music and the microphones. The microphone is the actor's magic wand . . . this dynamic quality is something you have, or you haven't.'

Jack Good may have been the first person to publicly draw a morbid comparison between a pop concert (or even a football match) and a Nazi rally, but the fascination was to endure.

In October 1958, Elvis Presley, whose maternal great-great-grandmother was Jewish, faced accusations of provoking his audiences 'not with music but a sex show'. After witnessing Presley's Hollywood debut at the Pan Pacific Auditorium, Dick Williams of the *Los Angeles Mirror* noted that the performance resembled 'one of those screeching, uninhibited party rallies the Nazis used to hold for Hitler'.[2] Five years later, as Beatlemania swept the nation, Maureen Cleave made a similar observation recording how the Fab Four would frantically shake their heads and emit trademark high-pitched OOOOHHHHs. It was a signal for an audience to scream and swoon as they sat on the edge of their seats in a state of amplified excitement. 'As an inducement to hysteria,' Cleave mused, casually, 'it's a wonder Hitler didn't think of it.'[3]

The theatre of the Third Reich needed little more in the way of staging. They were masterpieces of presentation, capable of reducing audiences to states of obedient rapture and enticing a civilised society to follow a path towards fascism and, ultimately, extermination. Similarly, pop music reflects on this dramatic art with a sense of awe and often without accountability. In the early days of rock 'n' roll, Adolf Hitler and the Nazis were easy targets for mockery, yet they also evoked a sense of wonder and reverence. This conflicting emotion sits at the core of rock history's flirtation with Nazism and this book is both a celebration of anti-fascist activism and a grim roll-call of culpable participants, and an attempt to ask the question, Why? Indeed, in 1964, John Lennon stood on the balcony of Liverpool Town Hall and gave a Nazi salute. Here, for the premiere of *A Hard Day's Night*, the Beatles looked out over a sea of adoring fans, wincing at the zealous antics of their leader, a twenty-four-year-old class clown. As a schoolboy, Lennon had drawn a self-portrait of himself, bespectacled and shaggy-haired, standing at a podium with his arm raised in rigid salute, writing 'HEIL JOHN' in block capitals across the page. In 2018, the self-portrait sold at auction for $54,000.

The ink drawing (8¾×11¾ inches) was part of a series created when Lennon was a student at Liverpool College of Art. The collection included a range of swastikas variously incorporated into hand-drawn badges, flags, and within the claws of a Nazi Party eagle (*Parteiadler*). One image recreated the distinctive lettering of a Hitler Youth membership badge, mandatory for German boys aged ten to thirteen years old, including the signature lightning bolt. In another, he outlined the upper torso of Hitler, characterised by his side parting and pencil-thin moustache. The underlined caption simply read: 'ALL YOU PEOPLE.'

Lennon's teenage doodlings were never intended for public view. They were private fantasies confined to his imagination. Yet how these secret drawings came to the attention of the public is an intriguing saga involving the death of Lennon's first wife, Cynthia Powell, and the sly manoeuvring of a Nazi sympathiser.

On 28 August 1991, Christie's auction house hosted 'The Cynthia Lennon Collection', offering forty-eight mementoes belonging to John Lennon, but not the Third Reich ink drawings. During an informal conversation with a member of the public on the first day of the auction, Cynthia disclosed details of her former husband's collection. A transcript of the conversation was later posted on a neo-Nazi website – authored by 'Mike & Earl'[4] – under the banner heading 'John Lennon's Adolf Hitler'.

'Halfway through my view [at Christie's],' the website text informed readers, 'I began chatting to a woman who was vaguely looking at the lots. "Do you know," I said, "the thing that immediately strikes you about all this is the very ordinariness of their lives?" "Oh, I don't know," she said, "at times it was very not ordinary." I looked at her; she was quite chubby, enhanced blonde hair, big smile, faded, but still very attractive looks. Smartly dressed. "Am I talking to Cynthia Lennon . . .?" I stumbled on. "Yes, you are," she confidently replied.'

As the conversation continued, the man (the webpage does not distinguish between Mike and Earl) explained to Cynthia how he had spent the morning 'examining fake Adolf Hitler paintings at an auctioneers at nearby New Bond Street'. 'So, you're a valuer, and you value Nazi items,' Cynthia asked, adding. 'I should come to you then, if I wanted any such items valued?' Then, continuing, she surprisingly revealed. 'John was absolutely fascinated by Adolf

Hitler. As a boy, he used to collect and swap Nazi badges, medals, daggers, and things. He used to call himself John "Adolf" Lennon, instead of Winston. I can remember him telling me that Hitler was like a modern-day Jesus Christ figure and how he took on the world . . . and nearly won . . .'

Evidently comfortable talking to the stranger, Cynthia further divulged Christie's refusal to auction Nazi memorabilia. 'It's not much,' she said, 'just some drawings John did of himself at college, you know . . . "in that guise" . . . and some medals he had left. They are still in the box he kept them in.'

An agreement was reached and one month later, Cynthia forwarded the assortment of drawings and medals to the interested party 'on the very strict understanding' that the items would sell only after her death. Thus, when Cynthia Lennon died on 1 April 2015, the collection sold online. It contained sketches drawn by John Lennon and other similar themed Third Reich ephemera including two Knight's Cross with Oak Leaves medals and a post-war Austrian commemorative medal celebrating the life of Hitler. The latter, John wore 'around his neck continuously,' Cynthia stated. 'It's a unique personal item of his which he had a deep attachment to in those youthful years.'[5]

As a Beatle, John Lennon actively campaigned for peace, writing anthemic songs such as 'All You Need Is Love' and 'Give Peace A Chance'. With his second wife, Yoko Ono, he planted acorns in Coventry Cathedral as an anti-war gesture and hosted 'bed-ins' as part of a global pacifist campaign. Yet, the latter-day public persona of a peace campaigner conflicted with his earlier private enthralment to Nazism. As Beatlemania spread rapidly across the world, Lennon increasingly saw a parallel between the adoration of screaming fans and the adulation German people bestowed upon Adolf Hitler.

On 17 August 1940, twenty years to the day before the Beatles played their first engagement in Hamburg, the Luftwaffe conducted the first of many bombing raids on Liverpool. Two months later, John Winston Lennon was born at the city Maternity Hospital, delivered during a brief respite in enemy aerial bombardment. On the back cover blurb of his idiosyncratic poetry anthology, *In His Own Write*, Lennon wrote, under the heading 'About the Awful'), 'I was bored on the 9th of Octover 1940 when, I believe, the Nasties were still booming us led by Madalf Heatlump (who only had one). Anyway, they didn't get me.'

Seven months later, the 'May Blitz' of 1941 subjected Liverpool to the most concentrated series of nightly air attacks on British soil outside London: killing 1,900 people, leaving 1,450 seriously wounded and 70,000 homeless. The Beatles grew up in the aftermath, which helps us to understand why John Lennon, and other musicians who became successful in the 1960s, obsessed over Nazism. 'Reminders of the war were all around,' says Paul McCartney. 'We played on bombsites a lot and I grew up thinking the word "bombsite" almost meant "playground". "Where are you going to play?" – "I'm going down the bombie."'[6]

On their first trip to Hamburg, the Beatles stopped en route to visit a war memorial and pose for snapshots. 'Driving through Holland, we stopped at Arnhem where all the people had parachuted out to their deaths (another little Winston Churchill trick),' George Harrison japed. 'There were thousands of white crosses in the cemetery.'[7]

Lennon refused to leave the van. Rather, he held back his feelings towards Germans until the Beatles' arrived in Hamburg. This the city where British and American bombers launched five major aerial attacks over a week in late July and early August 1943. The scale of devastation inflicted upon the northern port was unmatched by any other single Allied air attack in Europe during the Second World War. Albert Speer (Minister of Armaments and War Production) compared the devastation to the 'effects of a major earthquake . . . cyclone-like firestorms,' he wrote, 'people were suffocated in their cellars or burned to death in the streets'.[8] An estimated 45,000 German civilians died in the attacks and upwards of a million people, now homeless, fled the city and consuming conflagrations of fire. The death toll

was greater than the total British losses throughout the Blitz.*
Nevertheless, John Lennon relished the opportunity to exact
revenge as the Beatles prepared to entertain sailors on leave in
post-war Germany.

Impervious to his surroundings, the twenty-year-old Lennon
stepped onto a barely raised stage in Hamburg's Reeperbahn and
directed venomous abuse at the audience: 'We won the war,' he
taunted. 'Krauts!'

Next, Lennon bought a collection of Nazi memorabilia including
armbands, badges, Iron Crosses and medals from a street seller
at the harbour and shared them among the band. Then, during
the group's set at the Top Ten Club. and in blatant contravention
of German law, he goose-stepped across the stage, ranting, 'Sieg
Heil' and 'fucking Nazis'. One audience member, Rosi Heitmann,
recalled Lennon barracking the audience, shouting 'Nazi pigs' and
'Nazi swine'. 'The customers were bitter about it,' she determined,
'but the Beatles had their fun.'⁹

By the time the group secured a booking at the nearby Kai-
serkeller, word of Lennon's antagonistic behaviour preceded him.
The venue's owner, Bruno Koschmider, a former soldier in the
German Panzer division, instructed his staff to note inappropriate
onstage conduct. Lennon did not disappoint. Saluting the audience
and shouting, 'Heil Hitler', the singer placed a black comb across
his upper lip to represent a moustache. 'People laughed,' noted club
bouncer Horst Fascher.¹⁰ If the provocation unleashed flying beer
bottles and bar-room brawling, it did not make the public record.
However, the incident provided high drama in a fictionalised
account of the Beatles' Hamburg residency staged at the Royal
Court Theatre, London, in April 2001. Written by playwright David
Harrower, *Presence* explored the moment the group learn of Bruno
Koschmider's allegiance to the German army. 'The Beatles take on

---

* In the aftermath of the bombing, Karl Kaufmann, the *Gauleiter* of Hamburg,
dictated a letter to Adolf Hitler requesting the deportation of the Jewish population to clear housing for the displaced. In October 1941, the first transport of
Jews was sent to the Łódź Ghetto.

the Nazis', ran a *Guardian* headline, further informing readers that 'Paul's reaction [played by William Ash] is to go onstage, shout "Sieg Heil" and storm around in jackboots.'

This depiction was not far off the mark when Lennon and McCartney greeted fans in the maelstrom of Beatlemania. Following an extraordinary run of success with consecutive chart-topping releases worldwide, the Beatles formed an impenetrable bubble and, perhaps to maintain sanity, used humour as a defence against unprecedented levels of attention and demands on their time. In Melbourne, in June 1964, having landed on the other side of the world, the Beatles were in high spirits. Standing on the balcony of the South Cross Hotel, they looked down in wonder at the thousands of screaming fans gathered below. Laughing and fooling around, giddy with excitement, Lennon positioned his left finger across his top lip, in imitation of a Hitler moustache, and saluted the crowd. McCartney and Harrison followed suit amid shouts of 'Deutschland über alles' ('Germany above all') and peals of laughter. 'Greeting cheering crowds in Australia,' ran a caption in *Beat Publications*, 'whenever the Beatles appeared on a balcony, they couldn't resist giving Hitler-type salutes.'

Three weeks later, 200,000 fans gathered outside Liverpool Town Hall to celebrate the Beatles' return to Liverpool and the northern premiere of *A Hard Day's Night*. From the balcony, Lennon greeted the audience with his right arm firmly raised upwards. Unimpressed, Ringo told Lennon to, 'Cool it.' 'John got away with his Hitler bit on the balcony,' remarked Beatle roadie Neil Aspinall. 'Nobody seemed to pick up on it. John was always like that, a bit irreverent. Anybody in nerve-racking situations tends to do things to relieve the tension.'[11]

Irreverent Nazi gestures may be passed off as impulsive tomfoolery. But for lucky attendees with an invitation to watch the premiere of the Beatles' debut picture, more horseplay was on show. Increasingly annoyed by the relentless hectoring of Paul's onscreen fictional grandfather (played by Wilfrid Brambell), Ringo clicks his heels and makes a Nazi salute – albeit with his left arm. If the reflex reaction was typical of a young generation who vented their frustration at elders acting like 'Little Hitlers', then so too was the scene in which Lennon caricatures the torrent of war films flooding British and American cinemas. Sitting in a bath full of soap suds and surrounded by plastic warships, Lennon sinks a U-boat. 'Rule Britannia, Britannia rules the waves,' the semi-naked Beatle barks out. '*Guten Morgen, mein Herr. Wollen Sie noch einen Tee? Sie filthy Englander.*' He concludes the bilingual commentary with a hummed burst of the German national anthem.

For George Harrison, the nation's obsession with war functioned as a bulwark against the forward march of the modern age. 'We were the generation that hadn't been in the war,' he explained in 1971. 'We'd been born during the Second World War, and as we grew up, we became sick of hearing about it. To this day, the newspapers and television love the war and wars in general – they can't get enough of them. They keep putting programmes on about them. We were the generation who didn't suffer from the war, and we didn't want to have to keep being told about Hitler. We were more bright-eyed and hopeful for the future.'[12]

Indeed, while the Beatles were fooling around parodying the Führer, the world's media converged on Frankfurt am Main for the much-publicised Auschwitz trials. Between 20 December 1963 and 20 August 1965, twenty-two former high-profile Nazis working at Auschwitz-Birkenau extermination camp faced murder (or accomplice to murder) charges. Twenty received sentences of between three and ten years, and six life imprisonment. Two were acquitted. However, any suggestion of anti-Semitism in the Beatles was quashed on Sunday 21 April 1963 when the group performed at London's Pigalle Club to a predominantly Jewish audience, the concert having been advertised exclusively in the *Jewish Chronicle*. Then, the following year, during the Beatles' first visit to the US, a documentary film crew followed as John Lennon exited an elevator. 'Hey! Look at that!' he yelps, directing the camera operator towards a swastika daubed on the lift shaft wall. 'Stamp it out!'

Nonetheless, Lennon contradicted his show of outrage at the sight of the Nazi Party emblem three years later, when each of the Beatles presented a list of heroes to grace the cover of their 1967 studio album *Sgt. Pepper's Lonely Hearts Club Band*. Where Paul McCartney and George Harrison's wish list included Oscar Wilde, Marlon Brando, Ghandi and Bob Dylan, Lennon chose Hitler. 'Yes, he is on there,' artist Peter Blake revealed in 1997, 'you just can't see him,' adding, 'Hitler and Jesus were the controversial ones, and after what John said about Jesus* we decided not to go ahead with him – but we did make up the image of Hitler.'

Obscured on the finished artwork, contact sheets confirm Blake's recollection. 'If you look at photographs of the out-takes, you can see the Hitler image in the studio,' Blake continued, 'With the crowd behind there was an element of chance about who you can and cannot see and we weren't quite sure who would be covered in the final shot. Hitler was in fact covered up behind the band.'[13]

Third Reich notoriety continued in 1968 when the Beatles prepared to release their new single 'Hey Jude'. Surveying the group's newly launched Apple clothes boutique in central London, Paul McCartney looked at the paint-coated window and thought, 'Great opportunity. Baker Street, millions of buses going around . . .' and scraped 'Hey Jude' in the whitewash. The next day, the owner of a Jewish delicatessen in Marylebone phoned the Beatles' office and threatened to send his son to take care of Paul. 'This guy, Mr. Leon, who was Jewish, said, "What are you doing? How dare you do this,"' McCartney recounted in 2018. 'I had no idea it [Jude] meant "Jew", but if you look at footage of Nazi Germany, "Juden Raus" (meaning "Jews Out!") was written in whitewashed windows with a Star of

---

* 'Christianity will go,' Lennon told Maureen Cleave in March 1966 in an interview for the *London Evening Standard*. 'It will vanish and shrink. I needn't argue about that; I'm right and I will be proved right. We're more popular than Jesus now; I don't know which will go first – rock 'n' roll or Christianity. Jesus was all right, but his disciples were thick and ordinary. It's them twisting it that ruins it for me.'

David [to encourage boycotts and local hostility]. I didn't connect. I said, "No! No! No! Wait a minute. I swear to you, it's nothing like that." I calmed him down and he was cool. And his son didn't come around to beat me up!'[14]

The episode was deeply embarrassing, not only for McCartney but for the Beatles' manager, Brian Epstein. Born on Yom Kippur (Day of Atonement, 19 September 1934) to parents of Russian and Lithuanian descent, Epstein was an upstanding member of the Jewish community, a fact which John Lennon mercilessly exploited.

Spending time with the Beatles during their US tour in 1964, journalist Ivor Davis says Lennon never recoiled from needling Epstein about being both gay and Jewish. During a conversation with publicist and ghostwriter Derek Taylor, Davis recounted that Lennon and the other Beatles were drinking when Epstein disclosed that he had recently completed writing his autobiography. 'What is it called?' Lennon enquired, 'A Cellarful of Noise,' said Epstein. 'How about Cellarful of Boys?' Lennon countered. 'Cellarful of Goys,' replied Epstein, getting into the joshing spirit of things, and not sure whether the 'Goy' reference [among Jews: a non-Jew, a Gentile] would be understood by the other Beatles. 'No, no,' jibed Lennon, 'I've got the perfect title – Queer Jew.'[15]

Lennon's cruel humour often exploited other people's vulnerabilities. During the recording of the Beatles' 'Baby, You're A Rich Man' in June 1967, Lennon apparently sang the alternate lyric 'Baby you're a rich fag Jew'. 'People asked me whether I thought Lennon was anti-Semitic,' Ivor Davis reflected. 'I think not, although I did see him striding around his hotel suite, his finger to his lip, moustache-style, pretending he was Adolf Hitler. And from time to time Lennon would offer a Nazi salute to the crowd. It may have been his off-kilter way of relieving the crazy pressure of [touring] and poking fun at the public's endless adoration of the Beatles. Epstein, of course, castigated Lennon for his "Heil Hitler" act.'[16]

The Hitler 'act' was resurrected at Madison Square Garden, New York City on 30 August 1972. Now a solo artist, Lennon stood centre stage beside his wife, Yoko Ono.* 'I want to read you a statement by a well-known politician that you know of,' Ono said, addressing the 20,000-strong audience and holding a piece of paper in hand. 'The streets of our country are in turmoil; the universities are filled with students rebelling and rioting. Communists are seeking to destroy our country. Russia is threatening us with her might, and the Republic is in danger, yes, in danger, from within and without. We need law and order! Without law and order, our nation will not survive . . .' Pausing to survey the hushed arena, Ono revealed the identity of the speechwriter. A 'well-known politician,' 'this . . .' she said, '. . . is by Adolf Hitler, 1932.'

Film of the event shows a close-up of a young woman, mouth agape. It is an incredible moment. Words spoken forty years ago, highlighting the threat of Communism in Nazi Germany, have been translated to modern-day America, potentially undermining a generation's hope for a peaceful democracy. This was agitprop theatre. However, research indicates that Hitler did not speak the text; rather, it belonged to a collection of spuriously published quotes in the United States. It was immaterial; Ono and Lennon's message resonated: don't trust today's leaders spouting populist rhetoric.

---

* In the 1978 Rutles mocumentary, *All You Need Is Cash*, Ono is characterised as Hitler's daughter Chastity, dressed in SS uniform and introduced as 'a simple German girl whose father had invented World War Two'.

Shouting the Blues

THE ANIMALS. JOHN'S CHILDREN.
THE ROLLING STONES

'Born shouting the blues,' Eric Burdon proudly claimed of his birth in the industrial hub of Newcastle upon Tyne, northern England on 11 May 1941. 'Loud enough to be heard over the Nazi air raid, so it was always within me.'[1]

Targeted as an area of industrial production – shipbuilding, steelworks and coal distribution – Newcastle endured months of German bombing raids between July 1940 and December 1941. The memory of destruction stayed with Burdon who, like John Lennon and Animals bandmate Chas Chandler, collected souvenirs from the Second World War. In 1965, *NME* journalist Keith Altham visited Chandler's home and discovered a bedroom stacked high with Nazi armoury including sharpened swords, bayonets, guns, a green triangle pennant embroidered with a swastika sourced from a Nuremburg rally, and a dagger once owned by an SS (*Schutzstaffel*) general. 'Why do you and Eric collect all these sadistic weapons?' Altham enquired. 'Just a hobby,' Chandler replied nonchalantly, 'but at least it stops people from using them.'[2] A similar horde of Nazi artefacts clogged Eric Burdon's bedroom. 'Almost like a museum,' observed Genya Ravan, a Holocaust survivor* and renowned American rock singer and producer, 'books about Hitler everywhere, and uniforms, clothes, and war helmets hung on the walls.'[3]

---

* Born Genyusha Zelkovicz in Łódź Ghetto, Poland, 1940, Ravan was one of only four members of her Jewish family to survive the war.

Obsession with militarism would prompt the formation of Eric Burdon & War in 1969. 'The world is a ghetto,' Burdon declared, 'in need of music to fight racism and hunger and to promote hope and the spirit of brotherhood.' The sentiment is far removed from collecting Nazi memorabilia. But as we saw with John Lennon, private interests, harmless if they remain private, become problematic in public. Lennon paraded on stages in Hamburg shouting Nazi slogans, while members of the Animals invited journalists to inspect Third Reich artefacts. Displays of Nazi symbols are inevitably antagonistic and problematic and in both instances there was no accountability.

New groups thrive on controversy to boost record sales. But few would imagine a Jewish manager encouraging a lead singer to march onstage in Germany imitating a Nazi. Yet, in 1965, as the Rolling Stones waited side of stage in Berlin, it is exactly what Andrew Loog Oldham dared Mick Jagger to do, as 'a good laugh for me and Keith [Richards]'. Only, 'Mick took the suggestion one goose-step Führer,' Oldham quipped in his memoir, 2Stoned, 'and Sieg-Heil-ed his way around the stage to the kick and riff of "Satisfaction".' The young German crowd took Jagger's mockery at face value – 'not as a kind of Nazi camp like "Springtime for Hitler"' – and, recounts Oldham, 'turned on', the stadium transformed 'inadvertently into an impromptu Nazi rally'.[4] According to the NME, when the audience left the building 'they overturned 130 cars and every train leaving the city for the suburbs was wrecked completely'.[5]

Andrew Loog Oldham was born in Paddington General Hospital on 29 January 1944 as Germany mounted its final 'doodlebug' offensive over London. Having moved to Britain from Australia in 1923, his mother Celia hid her Jewish Ashkenazi heritage to avoid social stigma. His father Andrew Loog served in the United States Army Air Corps until shot down over the English Channel piloting an attack on Germany on 13 June 1943. Although circumcised, Oldham says it was not until researching his memoir in the 1990s that he discovered his Jewish ancestry. Nonetheless, mesmerised by Marlon Brando playing a disillusioned German officer in the 1958 picture

The Young Lions, the schoolboy Oldham bleached his hair with bathroom detergent and, say friends, assumed a German accent and became a 'blonde Nazi'.[6]

Mimicking Nazis was by no means exclusive to Jagger and Loog Oldham. Leatherhead rockers John's Children indulged in similar stage antics, cementing their reputation for outrageous live performances. Touring through the German cities of Nuremburg, Wuppertal, Herford, Düsseldorf and Ludwigshafen with the Who in 1967, singer Andy Ellison teased Pete Townshend in a hotel bar for stealing guitar riffs from his lead guitarist, Marc Feld.* 'There was a stony silence' recalled Ellison, 'then Keith [Moon] broke the atmosphere by goose-stepping around the table and doing a Nazi salute which he had seen us do on stage. Chris [Townson, drummer] joined in and I got up as well. Pete was in hysterics and it seemed to break the ice for a bit, although the hotel guests weren't impressed. The staff threw us all out of the bar, and we were still laughing as we went to our rooms.'[7]

Impersonating Nazis, with an exaggerated marching style and crisp tailored outfits, plays to a tradition of English vaudeville. The more shocking the costume and behaviour, the more triumphant the imitation. Thus, in 1966, when Rolling Stones founding member Brian Jones donned an SS uniform, a scandal erupted. That a German photographer, Werner Bokelberg, was responsible for the magazine image and the shoot happened in Munich added to the story's notoriety.

Photographed to promote Volker Schlöndorff's modern fairy tale *Mord und Totschlag* (*Degree of Murder*), for which he composed the soundtrack featuring Jimmy Page and Kenny Jones, Brian Jones stood erect, garbed in the all-black uniform of Heinrich Himmler's elite guard with an Iron Cross hung round his neck and a swastika wrapped around his upper left arm. In another image, Jones towers full-length trampling on a plastic doll crushed beneath his leather

---

* Recently recruited guitar player Marc Feld (later to become Marc Bolan of T. Rex fame) was Jewish.

boot. Crouched below, his then girlfriend Anita Pallenberg (born in occupied Italy in 1942 to German parents) looks directly into the lens, matching Jones' impassive stare. Viewed today, the set of photographs is shocking.

In late 1966, the Stones solidified their reputation as the 'bad boys' of rock. On the verge of a tenth straight top 10 hit, 'Let's Spend The Night Together', their next release expressed gratitude to fans and addressed the establishment following Mick Jagger and Keith Richards' brief imprisonment for cannabis possession. 'We Love You' featured Lennon and McCartney on backing vocals and the Beatles' influence was evident on the Stones' end-of-year release, *Their Satanic Majesties Request*. The Stones' devil-may-care attitude tied in with Jones gracing magazine covers around the world dressed as a Nazi. Norwegian magazine *Børge* presented a monochrome strip of the Stones' guitarist running down a third of the cover. Next to him, by contrast, a glamorous Nordic model smiled from the centre page, wearing a dazzling light-green sleeveless mini-dress that more appositely represented mid-sixties popular culture.

A month later, UK pop magazine *Rave* reported a new craze, the Teenage Express, describing a special excursion laid on by German Railways with rolling stock converted into a travelling dance hall. 'Another thing catching on in Germany is Nazism,' the magazine briefed. 'It seems unfortunate that controversial Stone Brian Jones should have picked this moment in time to pose for photographs in SS uniform and jackboots. Brian himself says, "The sense of it is that there is no sense in it at all!" But we must say,' *Rave*'s editorial blithely concluded, 'they aren't the best publicity pictures he could have had taken, are they? Ask yourself what you think, or better still, ask your dad.'

One disgruntled reader, Frances Lloyd of Middleton, Manchester, voiced disproval. 'I don't know why Brian Jones posed in uniform as an SS soldier, but to me it showed a sick side to Mr. Jones.' The complaint, printed on the letters page, sat beside a new image of Jones in German uniform. 'Don't get me wrong,' Lloyd continued, 'you see, I love and adore the Stones, but I have also seen documentaries about the Nazis and their camps. People were starved, assaulted, and brutally murdered by animals dressed in these uniforms. A nonsense pose. I'm sure I'm not the only one who feels like this,' Lloyd concluded.

The image of Jones continued to appear on the front pages of European publications (from the *People* in the UK to the *Hoja del Lunes* in Spain) provoking controversy and disgust in equal measure. According to director Volker Schlöndorff, who only became aware of the shoot after publication, 'Brian had a need to challenge people, challenge the public by showing up in a Nazi uniform. You could do that in London, but in Munich it was not very funny.'

Jones attempted to calm the escalating furore. 'The recent pictures of me taken in Nazi uniform were a put-down. Really, I mean with all that long hair in a Nazi uniform, couldn't people see that it was a satirical thing? How can anyone be offended when I'm on their side?' The note of surprise suggested he had been misunderstood and was being unfairly treated. Jones spelled it out. 'I'm not a Nazi sympathiser.' Then, on the offensive, he added, 'I noticed that the week after the pictures of me taken in that uniform appeared there were photographs of [actor] Peter O'Toole in the same newspaper wearing a German uniform for a film he's making. But no one put him down for wearing that!'[8]

On 5 July 1969, the Rolling Stones performed a free concert in London's Hyde Park to an estimated audience of half a million. They listened in reverential silence as Mick Jagger read a poem by Percy Shelley in memory of Brian Jones who died two days earlier.* Reviewing the events of a momentous week, the *News of the World* splashed the image of Jones in Nazi uniform across the front page, informing readers that the guitarist allegedly drowned

---

* In the same year, Mick Jagger, looking for an eye-grabbing image to personify the Rolling Stones' anti-authoritarian attitude, found inspiration in the Hindu goddess, Kali. Typically depicted as a four-armed woman in blue with a long tongue sticking out from red lips – or as the left-hand 'sauvastika' (swastika) – Kali was transformed by British designer John Pasche into the world-famous Stones logo.

during a party at his home at Cotchford Farm, East Sussex. 'Brian Jones in a mood of protest', the caption read. 'He bought this SS uniform from a Munich costume dealer. Brian was a pacifist. The pose, jackbooted on a crumpled doll, was a symbolic gesture against war-time German atrocities.'

In true British tabloid spirit, the tasteless commemorative image of Jones dressed in Nazi uniform contradicted the description of a pacifist. However, Jones was known to abuse women and subject them to psychological torture. In his memoir, Keith Richards described him as a 'women beater' and 'a kind of "schizo" who 'got aggressive and abusive'.[9] The wearing of a Nazi uniform was in line with a sadist whose overt cruelty compromised his position in the Rolling Stones and led to his dismissal shortly before he died.

Fifty years on, the image of Jones dressed in an SS uniform continues to both shock and, more disturbingly, inspire. Nick Reynolds, producer of the 2020 film *The Life and Death of Brian Jones* described its star as 'the original bad boy of rock and roll', marvelling that Jones was 'the Johnny Rotten and Sid Vicious of his day . . . all rolled into one'.[10] Having appropriated Jones' SS image on the cover of Gabinete Caligari's 1981 single 'Obedience', singer Jaime Urrutia explained, 'The aesthetic was beautiful and awesome and at that time you had to impress.' The Spanish rock group introduced live shows with the declaration, 'Hello, we are the Caligari Cabinet, and we are Nazis.' Today, Urrutia dismisses the offensive rhetoric. 'We wanted to shock,' he insists. 'We did it out of sheer provocation.'[11]

Nevertheless, the declamation had consequences. Encouraged by their intemperate zeal, far-right newspaper *El Alcázar* declared Gabinete Caligari 'Music for Mussolini's Blackshirts'.[12]

While Gabinete Caligari had little noteworthy influence on a wider European audience, the same could not be said of Belgian artist Guy Peellaert. He not only painted Brian Jones clothed in SS uniform but expanded the canvas to include all of the Rolling Stones. In 1973, *Rock Dreams* was hailed by its publishers Taschen as the '*Sgt. Pepper* of rock art'. Created by Peellaert and journalist

Nik Cohn, the book presented a fantasised history of rock 'n' roll, portraying stars like Tina Turner, Jerry Lee Lewis, Diana Ross, the Beach Boys and Jim Morrison in surreal, imagined settings inspired by their music.

In 1966, the Stones had presented themselves on the cover sleeve of their transatlantic top 10 single, 'Have You Seen Your Mother, Baby, Standing In The Shadow?' in Second World War military drag – 'a little frivolous in those frowning American times,' cautioned Andrew Loog Oldham.[13] Now, surrounded by prepubescent naked girls, Guy Peellaert painted Jones, Richards and Charlie Watts in full SS regalia, instruments in hand and drinking tea from a swastika-emblazoned saucer. Behind them, Mick Jagger poses semi-naked in women's lingerie, with SS jacket and Nazi armband hanging close by. As detailed in the accompanying text, Cohn described it as 'a palace of perpetual pleasures', noting that the members of the Stones dedicated their entire lives to recreation. 'Sometimes their games were nice, but mostly their games were naughty, nasty, or downright disrespectful and they pulled rude faces, stuck out their tongues or dressed in the strangest, the most disturbing costumes.'

With an estimated million copies sold, *Rock Dreams* was both a commercial success and a provocative cultural statement. When *Rolling Stone* asked Peellaert, 'How did Jagger feel about being portrayed as a corseted, super-realistic drag queen and a Nazi with a kink for pre-pubescent girls? "He liked it... of course," says Peellaert, with a sly smile.'[14]

After the artist's death in 2008, journalist David Hepworth called him 'one of the most influential people in the history of rock and roll music'. Reflecting on the controversial depiction of the Rolling Stones, – in Nazi uniforms, fondling naked pre-adolescent girls – Hepworth remarked, almost casually, 'Nobody batted an eyelid at the time,' perspicaciously adding, 'it challenged convention and effected change. It was dangerous.'

Far from taking offence, Jagger (some say Richards) requested a publication proof and, thereafter, invited Peellaert to join the Stones at a recording session in Munich. The premise was to design an album cover for their upcoming release, *It's Only Rock 'n' Roll.*

The meeting afforded Jagger the opportunity to ask Peellaert the meaning behind the portrayal of the Stones as Nazis and drag queens. 'It was Nik,' Peellaert squealed, attributing responsibility to his co-author. 'It was Nik!'[15]

The popularity of *Rock Dreams* speaks to a liberal-minded 1970s Britain. Images of Nazi uniforms and Third Reich symbolism raised little, if any, notable objection. Indeed, the association appeared to acknowledge Nazism as a cultural trend. In 1971, the Stones relocated to the south of France to record the follow-up to their fifth number 1 studio album, *Sticky Fingers*. Villa Nellcôte was a sixteen-room mansion built during the Belle Époque at Villefranche-sur-Mer on the Côte d'Azur. During the Nazi occupation, the property became the headquarters of a local Gestapo unit. When the Stones arrived to record what would become *Exile on Main Street*, they discovered remnants of gold swastikas engraved in the ironwork on the heating system and an unexpected historical relic unearthed in the cellar. 'I found a box down there with a big swastika on it, full of injection phials,' recalled acclaimed French photographer Dominique Tarlé. 'They all contained morphine. It was very old, of course, and our first reaction was, "If Keith found this box . . ." So, one night we carried it to the end of the garden. And threw it into the sea.'[16]

Keith Richards may have bemoaned the loss of ampoules of liquid morphine[17] but his lesser-known interest in Nazi regalia would cause greater consternation a year later. On 12 May 1971, Mick Jagger married the Nicaraguan-born political science student Bianca Pérez-Mora Macías in St Tropez. Several witnesses confirm Richards attending the ceremony attired in Nazi uniform. Musician Terry Reid is one such corroborator. He told David Hepworth that after the service Richards went to the nearby Hotel Byblos where guests could change before the reception. 'By and by we could hear a clanking noise growing ever louder,' Reid recounted. 'It was coming down the corridor towards us. Suddenly, it stopped right outside. The door swung open, and everyone did a double take. A man stood on the threshold. He was in full Nazi uniform. He seemed to be standing to attention, all SS tunic, with an Iron Cross or two dangling round his neck, and black jackboots. It was Keith.'[18]

Richards had previously worn the uniform in January 1967 when the Rolling Stones made their fourth appearance on the *Ed Sullivan Show* performing the stately 'Lady Jane'. During their last prime-time TV appearance, Mick Jagger had agreed to sing the revised 'let's spend some *time* together' instead of 'let's spend the night together' to appease the conservative sixty-five-year-old presenter. 'But when Ed asked them back and requested that they wear matching suits for a cleaner look, the group was ready for revenge', wrote Dick Clark in *The First 25 Years of Rock and Roll*. 'They showed up in rented Nazi uniforms. Sullivan threw a fit. The group had to change for the actual telecast [not a defiant Keith Richards who performed in an SS jacket], but they made their point.'[19]

Born on 18 December 1943, Richards remarked that whenever he heard the sound of sirens in old war films the hairs on the back of his neck would stand up and he would get goosebumps. 'It's a reaction I picked up in the first eighteen months of my life,' he said. 'I was born with those sirens.'[20] Raised in Dartford, Kent, his family home stood in 'Doodlebug Alley' where the German Luftwaffe's V-1 rockets ravaged southern England. Dramatising the experience, Richards commented, 'Hitler dumped one of his V-1s on my bed! He was after my ass!'[21] His fascination with Nazism endured in adulthood. According to biographer Victor Bockris, in May 1969, Richards purchased a '19-foot-long Nazi staff car rumoured to have been owned by [*Reichsmarschall* Hermann] Göring'.[22]

In his memoir, *Life*, however, Richards devotes several pages to his Jewish friend and surrogate 'second dad', Freddie Sessler. Twenty years his senior, Sessler lived through the German invasion of Poland, described by Richards as 'a story of horror and almost miraculous survival . . . Fifteen was when he watched his grandfather and his uncle being tortured and then shot by two Nazi officers in broad daylight in the main square of their town, while he held on to his terrified grandmother.'[23] Sessler later wrote an autobiographical memoir, dedicated to Richards, in which he recounts – quoted in *Life* – his arrest and escape from a labour camp. Yet, despite Richards' clear empathy for the victims of Nazi persecution, it is puzzling that his fascination with Third Reich memorabilia goes unmentioned.

Artefacts from Nazi Germany have been linked to members of the Rolling Stones' extended entourage, as well as certain segments of their fan base. When the Stones performed at Hyde Park on 5 July 1969, the group's tour manager Sam Cutler recruited so-called Hell's Angels to function as auxiliary security. The rough and ready motorcycle riders arrived with hand-embroidered 'Hells Angels' signs on the back of their jackets. 'They were a joke,' wrote Cutler in his memoir. 'Most of the bikers were no more Hells Angels than any young rock 'n' roller in England . . . just a bunch of risible wannabes who were barely old enough to know how to shave.'[24]

Young they may have been, but they were strong enough to attack members of the audience with chains and clubs. With swastikas emblazoned on their clothing, the biker gang intimidated crowd members and actively disrupted the peaceful gathering. A Metropolitan Police report on the concert judged that 'most of the arrangements' for security were successful but judged the provision of barriers and stewards around the stage as 'unsuccessful'. Moreover, a National Archive file damned the ad-hoc security provision as incompetent. 'The stewards, who were a group of motorcyclists dressed in Nazi type uniform and called "Hell's [*sic*] Angels" were totally ineffective despite their forbidding style of dress and general appearance.'[25]

Five months later – on 6 December – the Rolling Stones headlined another free concert at Altamont Speedway Park, California. Hired at the recommendation of the Grateful Dead, Hells Angels arrived on their customary motorbikes and drove directly through an aghast audience to the front of the stage. Fans scrambled either side of the procession and then, as the concert played out, were routinely intimidated and set upon by the leather-clad mob. As fights broke out at the foot of the stage, both Jagger and Richards appealed for calm. Pleas ignored, the Stones played on as eighteen-year-old Meredith Hunter pulled out a .22 calibre revolver. In the ensuing melee – documented by film-makers the Maysles brothers – a member of the Hells Angels, Alan Passaro, fatally stabbed Hunter.*

In the aftermath, the Stones severed all ties with the Hells Angels. Troubled not only by Hunter's death but an increased display of Nazi symbols, Ralph 'Sonny' Barger, a founding member of the Hells Angel Motorcycle Club, banned the use of Third Reich-related insignia and personally removed a swastika flag hanging outside the bikers' clubhouse, which was first raised to 'piss people off'. However, outraged by the Stones' rejection, a group of Angels organised a daring plot to murder Jagger. Locating the singer's home at the Hamptons, New York, the would-be assassins sailed across Long Island Sound only to encounter an unexpected storm. According to an FBI officer's statement in 2008, the assailants narrowly survived after being thrown overboard when the boat capsized.[26]

Lawless Hells Angels did not temper Mick Jagger's fascination with the history of the Third Reich. In 1974, the Rolling Stones' singer and his new bride Bianca posed for a *Sunday Times* magazine feature by photographer Leni Riefenstahl. The story of Riefenstahl and her personal relationship with Adolf Hitler defines not only her film career but plagued her life until her death in 2003, aged 101. Her work plays a central role in rock 'n' roll's relationship with the Third Reich and therefore makes it appropriate to study her background more closely.

Born in Berlin in 1902, Riefenstahl was a dancer and successful film actor before directing the definitive film of the Nazi regime, *Triumph des Willens* (*Triumph of the Will*, 1935). The recipient of gold medal awards in both Vienna and Paris, *Triumph of the Will* faced condemnation in the post-war era as a National Socialist propaganda film deifying a murderous regime. Respected historian Gitta Sereny is in no doubt that Riefenstahl was a devotee of Hitler. 'Having made some wonderful movies,' Sereny wrote, 'she

---

*   In 1971, a jury acquitted Passaro for acting in self-defence.

[Riefenstahl] put her immense talents to appalling use, in Hitler's service. It was for him and only for him that she made her two most famous films: in *Triumph of the Will*, her paean to the Nuremburg Party Congress and to Hitler, and in 1936 her hymn to physical perfection, considered by most a glorification of Hitler's aesthetic – her two-part film *Olympia*.'[27]

In 1932, Riefenstahl wrote to Hitler after watching him speak. She was granted a one-to-one audience, so beginning an intimate relationship that endured to 1944 – the same year, Riefenstahl married Peter Jacob, a major in the *Sturmabteilung*, a paramilitary wing of the Nazi party. Recognised by the Third Reich as the country's greatest film-maker, Riefenstahl's career subsequently benefitted, both financially and critically, from direct links to high-ranking Nazi officials including Josef Goebbels (Minister of Propaganda), Hermann Göring (Chief of Luftwaffe High Command), Martin Bormann (Chief of the Party Chancellery) and Hitler himself. Even before the Nazi Party's rise to power, Riefenstahl read Hitler's political manifesto *Mein Kampf* – telling the *Daily Express* in 1934 that it had made a 'tremendous impression' on her and the first page alone made her a 'confirmed National Socialist' – and enjoyed social and informal meetings with its author, stoking international speculation about the nature of their intimacy. 'What would happen if Adolf and Leni got married?' a popular joke of the era asked. 'Then Germany would have two Führers!'[28]

On 12 September 1939, Riefenstahl witnessed the massacre of a group of Polish Jewish civilians in the small town of Końskie close to the German–Polish border. Directing a 'Special Film Troop' and documenting the German army's invasion of Poland, Riefenstahl expressed horror at the atrocity to Hitler directly. Nonetheless, Riefenstahl continued her work, and filmed Hitler's victory parade in Warsaw. In May 1940, indicating her commitment to National Socialism, albeit as a non-member of the party, she telegrammed felicitations to Hitler after the occupation of France.

With indescribable joy, deep emotion, and filled with profound
gratitude, we share with you, my Führer, your and Germany's
greatest victory, the entry of German troops into Paris. Sur-
passing all other powers of the human imagination, you are
accomplishing deeds without equal in the history of mankind.
How shall we be able to thank you? Offering my congratula-
tions does far too little to convey to you the emotions that I
am feeling.[29]

Riefenstahl's knowledge of Nazi atrocities fascinates historians and
presented challenges for the judiciary. In 1952, the Berlin dena-
zification tribunal exonerated Riefenstahl of 'moral complicity'.
Unconvinced, the world's press pointed to knowledge of 'terrible
crimes'. Riefenstahl vigorously denied knowledge of the treatment
of the Jews in the face of researchers uncovering a curated web of
half-truths, lies and alternate versions of events. 'If she [Riefenstahl]
chooses to underplay her former allegiance to the Third Reich,'
Gitta Sereny determined, 'that is perhaps *her* way of "blocking"
the unbearable.'[30] Andres Veiel, director of the 2025 documentary
Riefenstahl, reached a similar conclusion. 'In the beginning, I was
the detective, looking for her guilt,' he recalled. 'Later on I realised
she does the job herself.'[31]

It was later revealed that Riefenstahl selected Roma and Sinti
extras (pejoratively labelled by the Nazis as 'Gypsies') from a forced
labour camp during the filming of *Tiefland*, which affected her
professional reputation. Based on the 1896 Catalan play *Terra
baixa* by Àngel Guimerà – and completed in 1954 – the majority
of the supporting cast were sent to Auschwitz-Birkenau in 1944 and
exterminated. Veiel's documentary also suggests that Riefenstahl's
direction at Końskie to 'get rid of the Jews' from the set indirectly
led to the deaths of twenty-two Polish Jews as they 'attempted to
flee as shots were fired'.

For a woman who described Hitler as 'the greatest man who
ever lived', the veneration of Riefenstahl by many of rock music's
aristocracy as one of the world's foremost film directors casts a
malignant shadow. One such champion was Mick Jagger, who

watched *Triumph of the Will* several times and, consequently, consented to the *Sunday Times* shoot with Riefenstahl. Whether Jagger's judgement was ill-conceived or even naive looks more questionable weighed against his actions later in the decade.

All the same, an appreciation of Riefenstahl's pioneering film work does not imply support for Nazi ideology. Far from it. Yet, it invites a more complex discussion regarding the reverence of Third Reich admirers in popular culture. This issue becomes particularly charged when artists display Nazi symbols, as Jagger did during the Rolling Stones' 1978 world tour, potentially trivialising their historical significance. Jagger took to the stage wearing a swastika T-shirt designed by Vivienne Westwood, originally purchased by Anita Pallenberg as a gift for Keith Richards. 'I bought a Destroy T-shirt for Keith, but he didn't like it,' Pallenberg later confirmed. 'Eventually Mick wore it onstage at an American show.'[32]

For survivors of Nazi persecution, the swastika is not merely a relic of history – it is a living symbol of oppression. Whether exhibited as a statement, a provocation or an attempt at subversion, it remains deeply painful. So when a public figure displays a swastika without explanation, how should we interpret it? Should we see Jagger's choice – given his status as the frontman of an anti-establishment band – as an attempt to devalue its significance? Or should we take its brandishing at face value, accepting its dark historical connotations? Ultimately, we each project our own meaning onto symbols. Perhaps Jagger and Westwood sought to reclaim the swastika, considering its origins as a symbol date back over 15,000 years.

In Germany, the swastika is known as the Hakenkreuz, literally hook (*Haken*) and cross (*Kreuz*). In the ancient Indian language of Sanskrit, swastika means 'well-being'. Indeed, a carved swastika can be seen on the outside wall of London's India House, set against two Bhodi trees to represent the provinces of Bihar and Orissa during the British Raj. For many cultures – Hinduism, Buddhism, Jainism, Odinism, Christianity and that of Native Americans – the swastika is a primordial sacred symbol of peace and prosperity. In Eastern

Europe, it signifies fertility. Before its adoption by the Nazi Party in 1919, the swastika was used to promote Western products such as Coca-Cola, Carlsberg beer and the Boy Scouts. Both the US army and the RAF also used it to decorate aircraft. The esteemed historian Laurence Rees records that German and Austrian nationalists began utilising the swastika as early as the 1890s. He further explains that, prior to the First World War, women in the German Gymnastics League (GGL) were known to wear this distinctive symbol. Emil Klein, a member of the GGL, recounted in Rees' *The Holocaust* that, 'The four F's – *frisch* (fresh), *fromm* (pious), *frohlich* (happy), *frei* (free) – formed a double swastika on the [bronze] badge that you wore as an insignia.' Additionally, *Völkisch* groups (a German ethno-nationalist movement active from the late nineteenth century and a precursor of National Socialism), who believed the ancient symbol of the swastika connected them with their early ancestors, also adopted this icon.

In 1918, the Jungdeutsche Bund (Young German League) promoted German nationalism and expansion, condemning 'Jewish capitalism' under the swastika symbol. Berlin-born historian and journalist Sebastian Haffner recalled 'a strange, repeated pattern; a few strikes combined in an unexpected, pleasing way to form a symmetrical box-like ornament.' Haffner asked a school friend what it was. '"Anti-Semitic sign," they said. The Ehrhardt Brigade [military group formed in 1919 to overthrow the Weimar regime] wore it on their helmets. Means "Out with the Jews". You ought to know it.' It was my first acquaintance with the swastika,' wrote Haffner.[33]

According to Hitler's autobiographical manifesto *Mein Kampf*, the Nazis adopted the swastika in 1919. Although proposed by Friedrich Krohn, a dentist and party member, Hitler claims to have modified the design to symbolise the struggle of the National Socialist crusade. Featuring a red background with a white disc and a black swastika at its centre, Hitler wrote, 'Red represented the social idea . . . it was the most exciting; we knew it would infuriate and provoke our adversaries the most and thus bring us to their attention and memory whether they liked it or not. White,' he continued, 'represented nationalism and the swastika Aryan race and by default anti-Semitic.[34] An effective insignia can in hundreds of thousands of cases,' Hitler concluded, 'give the first impetus towards the interest in a movement.'[35]

A year later, the swastika was adopted as the official emblem of the Nazi Party, and in 1935, two years after Hitler became chancellor of Germany, it replaced the tricolour as the national flag of the German Reich. Described as 'a holy symbol' by Hermann Göring, the President of the Reichstag claimed the swastika as 'the anti-Jewish symbol for the world'. Under the aegis of National Socialism, Jews were systematically excluded from German society: prohibited from flying the German flag, stripped of citizenship, forbidden from marrying outside of their race and, whether married or not, from having sexual relations across the race line. In 1941, Hitler implemented the so-called 'Final Solution of the Jewish problem', leading to the slaughter of over six million innocent lives.

So, three decades later, in peacetime Britain, imagine the horror of a Jewish community confronted by a celebrated rock star dressed as Adolf Hitler driving through a north London suburb waving a swastika. This is exactly what Keith Moon did.

A Lousy Publicist

KEITH MOON. VIVIAN STANSHALL. LED ZEPPELIN

Humour was an unlikely survival technique employed by inmates in Nazi concentration camps to cope with the despair and minute-by-minute possibility of death. Robert Clary, best known for his role in the CBS sitcom *Hogan's Heroes*, set in a Nazi prisoner-of-war camp, survived Auschwitz by working in various forced-labour satellite factories, where he added rubber heel taps to wooden shoes and made synthetic fuel from coal. He also performed song-and-dance routines for the camp commanders, using his voice, charisma and comedic portrayals of women to win them over, often singing subversive Yiddish tunes. 'You entertain, but you're going to starve and you're going to die,' he said. 'They can kill you in a second.'[1] For Clary, his protest through the medium of entertainment was a way to retain his dignity in the most desperate of circumstances.

Victor E. Frankl, author of *Man's Search for Meaning*, says that 'There were songs, poems, jokes, some with underlying satire regarding the camp. All were meant to help us forget,' adding that 'of course, any pursuit of art in camp was somewhat grotesque . . . The real impression made by anything connected with art arose only from the ghostlike contrast between the performance and the background of desolate camp life. Humour was another of the soul's weapons in the fight for self-preservation.'[2] This use of comedy has continued in rock music, television, film, radio and literature, where many artists have engaged with the legacy of Nazism by wearing uniforms, imitating the grandiosity of Third Reich rallies and satirising the regime's obsession with detail, all as a way to confront the past and denigrate the perpetrators of mass murder.

The Führer was an obvious target for ridicule. As early as 1940, – a year before the bombing of Pearl Harbor and America entering the war – Ashkenazi Jewish trio the Three Stooges parodied Hitler and other leading figures in the anti-Nazi comedy *You Nazty Spy!* Simultaneously, Charlie Chaplin satirised Hitler in the celebrated film *The Great Dictator*. Born within four days of each other in April 1889, Chaplin observed his resemblance to Hitler, particularly the thin moustache. Both were born into poverty, occasionally homeless, had difficult relationships with their fathers, were ambitious and passionate performers, and used gesture and heightened emotions in their presentations. 'Just think,' Chaplin told his son, 'He's the madman, I'm the comic. But it could have been the other way round.'

British comedian Tommy Handley also saw the similarity and composed the spoken-word ditty, 'Who Is This Man . . . (Who Looks Like Charlie Chaplin)?' 'If it wasn't for the boots and cane and trousers,' Handley recalled in 1939, 'you couldn't tell the two of them apart'. The morale-boosting verse asked what makes this man (Hitler) think he can win the war. 'It can't be the moustache,' Handle jests, 'that only makes us laugh.' Then ridiculing the idea of Hitler playing 'a silent part', the Liverpudlian comedian cautioned against being 'too hard on poor old Adolf'. It ends with the pun, 'He's a godsend to the comics, he's sublime, cartoonists love his make-up, but one morning we shall wake up and find it's Charlie Chaplin all the time!'

Filming of *The Great Dictator* started the same week that Britain declared war on Germany. Chaplin once remarked, 'To me, the funniest thing in the world is to ridicule impostors, and it would be hard to find a bigger impostor than Hitler.' In the early 1930s, British-born Chaplin visited Germany and observed the rise of Nazism, as well as the use of suppression and intimidation to gain electoral power. Although not Jewish, a propaganda newsreel welcomed 'the Jew Chaplin during his visit to Berlin', and excused 'many Germans' who 'unsuspectingly applauded the foreign Jew'. On the eve of war, Nazi propaganda renounced Chaplin, again incorrectly, as one of 'the foreign Jews who come to Germany'. In America, Chaplin was urged to abandon *The Great Dictator*. 'I was determined to go ahead,' he defiantly wrote, 'for Hitler must be laughed at.'

As Adenoid Hynkel, the tyrannical ruler of Tomainia, Chaplin broke his cinematic silence to mock Hitler and his associates, Herring (Hermann Göring) and Garbage (Josef Goebbels). Simultaneously, Chaplin played a Jewish barber who, sent to a concentration camp during the destruction of his hometown ghetto, escapes only to be mistaken for Hynkel. In the film's climax, Chaplin delivers a dramatic monologue, an impassioned plea for unity and humanity. 'To those who can hear me, I say, do not despair. The misery that is now upon us is but the passing of greed, the bitterness of men who fear the way of human progress. The hate of men will pass, and dictators die, and the power they took from the people will return to the people.'

Further defending liberty against the onslaught of men of machine-like minds and hearts, Chaplin addressed the audience directly. 'You, the people, have the power to make this life free and beautiful; to make this life a wonderful adventure . . . let us use that power! Let us all unite!'

Banned across Europe and in several US cities including Chicago for fear it would antagonise the local German population, *The Great Dictator* was nonetheless a box office success. Over time, Chaplin's powerful oration has served both as a warning from history and a potent reminder of Hitler's ruthless dictatorship. In 1941, Franklin D. Roosevelt invited Chaplin to make the speech at his third inaugural gala. Introduced by the American actor Douglas Fairbanks Jr, Chaplin walked onstage to a rousing reception. He began, 'I would like to help everyone, if possible, Jew, gentile, black man, white . . .' The six-minute appeal received rapturous applause, demanding Chaplin return to the stage to take several bows.

The impact of Chaplin's address continues to resonate six decades later. In 2004, American rapper Mos Def included an excerpt from the speech in his song 'War'. Scottish songwriter Paolo Nutini ended 'Iron Sky' with an extract from Chaplin's plea to humanity. In 2016–17, Coldplay's A Head Full of Dreams tour featured a combination of electronic sounds with Chaplin's speech. While in 2019, U2 released 'Love Is All We Have Left', overlaid with the actor's oration, which was also used to introduce their eXPERIENCE + iNNOCENCE world tour. Yet, had Chaplin known about the horrors of German concentration camps, *The Great Dictator* would never have made it to the big screen. 'I could not have made fun of the homicidal insanity of the Nazis,'[3] he wrote in his 1964 autobiography.

Chaplin's awareness underscores the utilisation of historical events as a means of entertainment, particularly when addressing sensitive subjects. The Nazi regime was responsible for the extermination of millions, yet in the years following the war, the Third Reich became the subject of relentless parody in British and American culture. Television programmes such as *Dad's Army, Secret Army, The Kenny Everett Television Show, Hogan's Heroes, The Phil Silvers Show* (with Sergeant Bilko) and the BBC's long-running sitcom *'Allo! 'Allo!* glossed over wartime atrocities in a thick varnish of fast humour and comic sketches. Tales of individual heroism also found their place in everything from Spike Milligan's* 1971 memoir *Adolf Hitler: My Part in His Downfall* to the children's comics that romanticised missions to hunt down and kill Nazis, such as *Eagle, Victor, Warlord, Commando, Hotspur, Battle, Captain America, All-American Men of War, Frontline Combat,* or *Sgt. Fury and His Howling Commandos.* As activist and journalist Caroline Coon notes, 'The post-war generation grew up with fathers who fought

---

* Milligan served in the Royal Artillery, first in Africa and later in Italy during the Battle of Monte Casino. In his unpublished memoir, *Adolph Hitler, Dictator and Clown*, written in the 1950s and narrated in the first person, Milligan imagines Hitler renaming concentration camps after British holiday resorts, such as *Butlin's* and *Pontin's*. Back at home, Milligan would often dress up as Hitler to amuse his family.

in the war. *The Goon Show* was an absolute staple in my parents' household. It was the idea of comedians satirising Hitler storming around just taking the piss out of him and singing songs about he's only got one ball. You can smell satire a mile away.' Coon insists that post-war comedy was not about glamorising the Third Reich.

As early as 1946, Spike Jones & His City Slickers were mocking Adolf Hitler with their hit song, 'Der Fuehrer's Face'. Written by Oliver Wallace, the song's playful chorus, 'Ja, we is the supermen', propelled the tune to number 3 on the US singles chart.* A year later, the song featured in the Walt Disney anti-Nazi film of the same name, accompanied by a poster featuring Donald Duck squashing a tomato into Hitler's left eye. So it was no surprise when, in 1970, Vivian Stanshall, co-founder of the Bonzo Dog Doo-Dah Band teamed up with the Gargantuan Chums – Keith Moon and John Entwistle of the Who – to record 'Suspicion', a song originally written by the American Jewish songwriting duo Doc Pomus and Mort Shuman, and released by Elvis Presley in 1962.

To promote the single, Stanshall and Moon dressed as Nazis – Moon as Hitler and Stanshall as Reinhard Heydrich, Chief of Reich Security and architect of the so-called Final Solution. Seasoned *Melody Maker* photographer Barrie Wentzell snapped the promotional images. In one shot, Moon is precariously perched on Stanshall's knee, a German cap tilted over his forehead, a fake moustache, and his left hand hovering suggestively over Stanshall's groin. In another, Stanshall grins as he leans towards a glass of champagne while pointing at a wide-eyed Moon. The images radiate slapstick. The next shot features the clowning duo pointing to a map of occupied Europe, their eyes raised in mock seriousness, surrounded by papers and plans. Here are two infamous Nazis – Hitler and Heydrich – reduced to mere caricatures, their power and authority undermined by the antics of a comic and a musician.

---

*   One verse foreshadowed the formation of one of the UK's most successful synth-guitar groups of the 1980s: 'We bring to the world New Order. Heil Hitler's world New Order.'

Years earlier, Stanshall had ventured into similar territory by lampooning the banned music of the Third Reich: jazz. At the start of 'The Intro And The Outro', Stanshall introduced the Bonzo Dog Doo-Dah Band as famous historical figures. From 'big John Wayne, xylophone, and Billy Butlin, spoons' to Princess Anne on sousaphone . . .', he then added, in a smooth nightclub voice, 'And looking very relaxed, Adolf Hitler on vibes . . . niceeee!'*

Back in central London, Moon and Stanshall decided to take their joke further. Their first stop was a speakeasy on Margaret Street, where they entered in full Nazi regalia – medals, armbands and all – and ordered brandies. The landlady, visibly shaken, nearly fainted, and it was later discovered that her husband had died in a concentration camp. Not stopping there, the duo made their way to a German *Bierkeller* near Bond Street. Upon entering, Moon loudly declared, 'Sieg Heil!' As reported by *NME* journalist Roy Carr, they then sang 'Donner Und Blitzen' and 'Englisch Schweinhund', goose-stepping through the room filled with stunned patrons, before being swiftly ejected by an angry landlord. Stanshall marvelled at the fury their stunt provoked. 'It's amazing!' he exclaimed 'People get furious – their veins stick out of their necks. It's the "we fought for your freedom, but you can't dress like that" reaction. It's good to get people furious though – people need to involve themselves in something.' The *NME*, worried about the wind-up, questioned whether it was a 'sick joke or a harmless send-up', noting that the prank had 'provoked strong reactions' and that 'one old lady fainted at the sight of our incorrigible looners'.[4]

Not to be deterred, Moon and Stanshall hired an open-top Mercedes and drove to an enclave of north London populated by a large Jewish community, many of whom had escaped Nazi-occupied Europe. 'Hours later,' Roy Carr reported, 'this deadly duo was espied being chased around Golders Green by an angry shopkeeper wielding a razor-sharp meat axe.' Keith Moon's personal assistant

---

* John Thomson adopted the catchphrase 'niceeee' in the successful 1990s comedy sketch series *The Fast Show*.

Dougal Butler recounted in his memoir *Moon the Loon* that passers-by were 'horrified and appalled when two high-ranking Nazi
officers appear in their shops and demand goods in heavy German
accents'. But they crossed the line when they entered a small bakery
and demanded 'German bread'. The Jewish proprietor, scurrying
from behind her counter, chased them up the street, 'screaming at
them' and throwing various 'heavy duty baker's products' at them.
Butler, reflecting on their 'tasteless performance', admits that joke
was in poor taste but clarifies that Moon was not motivated by
malice. 'I do not think that he considers even for a second that
Jewish ladies will be deeply offended by his appearance in Nazi
uniform. It is just another way of sending up the straight, and he
is reckless as to the implications.'[5]

From an early age, Moon harboured a peculiar fascination with
Nazism. Gerry Evans, a long-time schoolfriend, recounted one
instance at Finchley Road Underground station when Moon discovered an unattended announcement booth and, unnoticed, made
a chilling announcement over the Tannoy system: 'All Jews line
up here, ready to be gassed', in a mock German accent. Laughing
hysterically, Moon then ran onto an open train carriage to escape
before anyone could catch him. Evans noted that these bizarre,
Gestapo-style impersonations would become a recurring theme in
Moon's life. 'He was not anti-Semitic,' Evans insisted. 'He was not.
He had nothing against Jews. It was just that for some reason he
thought that was funny.'[6]

When Moon was asked about the consequences of his actions,
he offered a brief perspective on post-war comedy. 'That kind of
thing couldn't backfire,' he said.

It backfired in 1945 when they lost the war, and they were
doing it for real. This is why I like the *Monty Python* brand of
humour. It's part of today's culture; it's today's universal humour.
Nothing's sacred anymore. Everything is there to be used. You
can do virtually anything. Just as long as it's done correctly, and
you add to it. Okay, Hitler started out with some ideas . . . knew
how to sell them . . . sold them and very nearly succeeded. But

because they were the wrong ideas, they failed. That's what I mean when I say nothing is sacred . . . and anyway, he had a lousy publicist![7]

Moon made a valid point, noting that television comedy is contextualised by its broadcaster providing a framework, of sorts, for the humour. Conversely, wearing a Nazi uniform and engaging in harassment is limited to those directly involved, and devoid of any context, can be perceived as offensive and inappropriate. A similar criticism could be directed at Jimmy Page.

In 1968, Page formed a new group out of the recently defunct Yardbirds. Prophesying that the venture would go down 'like a lead balloon', Keith Moon inadvertently supplied the guitarist with the idea to call the new group Led Zeppelin. Unknowingly, both Moon and Page shared a sartorial interest in Nazi uniforms. According to the celebrated rock groupie Pamela Des Barres, Page would regularly wear SS regalia. 'We saw a lot of Zeppelin and they were not aging gracefully,' Des Barres wrote in her titillating memoir, *I'm With the Band*. 'Jimmy wore a Third Reich costume . . . and made the "Heil Hitler" gesture.'[8]

As a member of the Yardbirds, Page was photographed wearing a German army tropical pith helmet shield on his lapel featuring an eagle clutching a swastika. A decade later, on 6 April 1977 in Chicago, he performed onstage wearing an all-black outfit that included matching leather jackboots, a cravat and a peaked cap resembling that of an SS officer, adorned with the death's head insignia (*Totenkopf*). This attire was historically worn by SS guards in concentration camps to intimidate their enemies and remind the wearer of their allegiance to Adolf Hitler and their commitment to the Third Reich. Audience reaction to Page's apparel is undocumented but Led Zeppelin's entourage was shocked. 'Jimmy was prancing around in his Stormtrooper uniform backstage,' recalled Jack Calmes (co-founder of PA company Showco), 'goose-stepping and stuff. It didn't go down too well with [the group's Jewish lawyer] Steve Weiss.'[9] Page donned a similar outfit after attending a show by English rock supergroup Bad Company in Fort Worth. 'What the fuck is that!' exclaimed record company employee Sam Aizer.

Perhaps pandering to a Third Reich fixation, Led Zeppelin's 1976 documentary film *The Song Remains the Same* features an introductory scene in which manager Peter Grant and tour manager Richard Cole arrive at a castle dressed as gangsters and open fire on a group playing a board game filled with swastika-branded Chester Gould-like grotesques. When Led Zeppelin returned to England a year later, to a country now in the throes of the punk rock explosion, Page paraded the streets of Camden in Nazi regalia. 'Jimmy and Robert [Plant] came to see the Damned,' recalled the band's manager Jake Rivera. 'I was at the door when they arrived. I remember it because Jimmy was wearing his fucking Luftwaffe outfit.'

At the age of thirty-four, Page stood for the established rock music scene, which was being challenged by the punk movement's call to break away from the past both culturally and politically. For those who preferred to overlook Nazi dress as perhaps the misjudged behaviour of a self-absorbed rock star, a post on Jimmy Page's official Instagram page dated 10 April 2019 raised fresh concerns. '#OnThisDay in 1977', the Led Zeppelin guitarist informed his millions of followers, 'I debuted the Stormtrooper Outfit in Chicago. This show was on an Easter Sunday, it was the first time I wore the Storm Trooper outfit, but not the last.'

Accompanied by a Neal Preston photograph from the show, Page's online despatch received tens of thousands of likes and comments. Tellingly, none condemning or questioning Page's motive. Rather, reaction ranged from the innocent ('Love it', 'Does it get any cooler than this?!') to the puerile ('Fantastic Nazi chic outfit') to the infantile ('Oh yesssssssss!', courtesy of fashion stylist, Katy England).

Then there was outright anger: 'The Nazis did have cool uniforms! Now poor Germany is invaded by Muslim men who rape young German girls, and the world lets it happen.'

Amateur historians questioned the authenticity of Page's uniform and which war it belonged to. The answer was both. In the First

World War, a storm trooper represented a specialist soldier of the German army while during the Third Reich they belonged to a private army notorious for aggressiveness, violence and brutality.

Another post attempted to defend Page's honour – and by association Led Zeppelin's – by pre-empting accusations of prejudice: 'People today think any nazi perophonilia anyone were is anti semetic,' the anonymous contributor wrote, clearly untroubled by punctuation or grammatical accuracy, adding, 'They dont understand the idea of the trophies of war. We conquered the nazis and took their uniforms, weapons,and more and presented them as a sign of victor.'

The collection of messages, shared by fans, historians and right-wing zealots, highlights the significance that a Nazi uniform holds in contemporary times. Of more concern is that Page chose not to contextualise the choice of outfit. Was it the behaviour of someone caught up in a world of rock 'n' roll excess and the distorted reality of global success? Page does not comment. The post simply encourages us to admire the accoutrements of Nazism. In doing so, it glorifies a barbarous regime responsible for murder on an unprecedented scale.

Colour Me Pop

IGGY & THE STOOGES. BLUE ÖYSTER CULT.
SWEET

The era of sixties stars like John Lennon, Mick Jagger and Keith Moon mocking Adolf Hitler shifted in the 1970s to more extreme behaviours and a noticeable increase in the use of the swastika. It appeared that the further in time artists were from the Second World War, the less tangible and real it became.

It is now eighty years since the liberation of the majority of the Nazi extermination camps. These places of horror, discovered by Allied forces in the final months of the war, revealed atrocities almost beyond imagination in a modern functioning society.

The Holocaust is often expressed in numbers. But how do we picture six million murdered human beings? At capacity, Wembley Stadium holds 90,000 people. When multiplied by sixty-six to calculate six million, traditional number-crunching suddenly appears inadequate. Instead, we focus on the palatable, the everyday, that which is comprehensible. Survivors of the Auschwitz death camp often recollect Dr Josef Mengele, who conducted inhumane medical experiments on children and adult prisoners, wearing immaculate tailored uniforms and polished boots. The clean-cut image contrasts sharply with the monstrous process of greeting new arrivals at the camp entrance and thereafter selecting those believed fit for work and those directed to the gas chamber. However, it was often the allure of shiny buttons and polished medals that captivated musicians who were drawn to the Third Reich, thereby leaving a lasting impact on popular music.

At the Monterey International Pop Festival in June 1967, Brian Jones was described as wearing 'a mind shattering gold lame coat festooned with beads, crystal swastika and lace'.[1] * In 1969, guitar player Jorma Kaukonen wore a Native-American silver necklace, mistaken by some as a Nazi swastika, when Jefferson Airplane supported the Rolling Stones at Altamont. 'I wore it for a number of years,' Kaukonen told *Rolling Stone*. 'Obviously, many people saw the Hakenkreuz, not the spiritual item I saw.' In the same year, Trevor Burton wore an Iron Cross when the Move performed their second single 'I Can Hear The Grass Grow' on the BBC series *Colour Me Pop*.

In two of these examples, the swastika is celebrated as an ancient spiritual symbol. But in the latter instance, the wearing of an Iron Cross, blurs the boundary between German military history and an artefact of Nazism. This ambiguity has dogged rock 'n' roll ever since. Moreover, some musicians readily embrace paraphernalia of the Third Reich but do so, they claim, merely from appreciation of the design and not for its associated ideological connotations. A prime example is the former guitar player of Iggy & the Stooges, Ron Asheton.

Like many musicians from the sixties and seventies, Asheton's father fought against the Axis powers during the Second World War. A US pilot, Asheton Snr collected Nazi memorabilia and shared them with his son. Ron developed a fascination for world history. 'I didn't have a lot of friends,' he told journalist Legs McNeil. 'I was mostly into Nazi stuff. I took German class and did Hitler speeches. I'd wear SS pins to school, draw swastikas all over my books, and draw little SS bolts on my arm.'[2]

In 1968, Asheton attended the wedding of his bandmate Iggy Pop to the Jewish-born Wendy Weisberg and daughter of the group's manager. He was dressed in a Luftwaffe fighter pilot's jacket, a white shirt with a Knight's Cross with Oak Leaves and Swords, a jacket with an Iron Cross, leather riding boots and jodhpurs. For reasons that have since been forgotten or occluded, a dispute occurred during the reception party, prompting the arrival of law

---

* Jones bought the outfit from Hung On You, 430 King's Road: shop premises later owned by Malcolm McLaren and Vivienne Westwood.

enforcement officers. When the police objected to an unlawful Sears, Roebuck flag (not specified) waving above them, Asheton countered, 'Okay, if you're gonna bust me, it's gonna be big time,' and proceeded to hoist a swastika on the flagpole.[3]

Asheton's fixation with Nazism ran riot. His collection of memorabilia grew to include flags, medals, clothing and army paraphernalia. Onstage, he sometimes wore a Nazi outfit with a swastika armband. He introduced the band in German before tearing into 'Search And Destroy'. 'It's not that I was a Nazi,' Asheton insisted. 'Maybe that was my shock thing, to wear that stuff.' It had the desired effect. Audiences were not just shocked but insulted. 'I had things thrown at me,' Asheton recounted with little sympathy. 'Or Jewish bands crying, "We love the Stooges man, why are you always . . ." – it's for shock value, man! It's a costume!' Asheton says the worst incident occurred when the Stooges opened for Blue Öyster Cult on New Year's Eve in New York. 'A Jewish friend calls up, goes, "I just saved your ass. I found out the Jewish Defence League was coming down there, they were gonna drag you offstage somehow and beat the shit out of you tonight. I donated a couple of hundred bucks in your name, you owe it to me." I went, "Ohhh fuck!"'

The threat did little to dampen Asheton's obsession. He began wearing a black leather trench coat marked with the letters 'SS'. When Asheton's younger brother, and Stooges' drummer, Scott pinned a swastika on his lapel, *Rolling Stone*'s Charlie Burton sarcastically reported, 'How killer . . . how terribly, terribly killer.'

It's all the more bizarre that Ron and Scott Asheton embraced Nazi memorabilia, especially considering their manager was Jewish. Daniel Feinberg, born in 1939 in Richmond Hills, Queens, later known as Danny Fields, attended Harvard Law School and worked to pacify potential antagonists. 'Please all be assured that Ron's fascination with Nazi memorabilia made him a Nazi about as much as seeing yet another version of "Dracula" will make you into a vampire.' Fields then undermined his convincing defence of Asheton. 'I wish y'all could have seen some of those leather trench coats he had, you'd be eating your hearts out, whatever your religion or politics – with which Ron's great taste had nothing, as far as I could tell, to do.'[4]

Asheton recorded three albums with Iggy Pop – *The Stooges* (1969), *Fun House* (1970) and *Raw Power* (1973) – before leaving and forming The New Order. The phrase belonged to Germany's ambition to reshape Europe under the Greater Reich and impose racial, social and political command (*Neuordnung*). In 1941, Hitler stated at a Nazi rally at the Berlin Sportpalast, marking his eighth anniversary as chancellor, that he believed it would be a significant year for establishing 'a new European order'.

Formed in Los Angeles in 1975, Asheton's New Order recorded the album *Declaration of War*, a collection of demo recordings released two years after the group's early break-up. 'We'd play gigs in front of my big swastika flag,' Asheton proclaimed, simultaneously disassociating himself from Nazi ideology. '[It] was just part of my collection. I had Jewish girlfriends and black buddies. It had nothing to do with promoting Nazism or condoning it. I just enjoyed flash uniforms. But other people freaked – they were like, "It's fascist." New Order didn't mean to put out a Nazi vibe at all. I knew it was probably a bad idea . . . how not to get a record deal in an industry run by Jewish people. "New Order? Let's sign 'em up right now."'[5]

Asheton's flaunting of Third Reich memorabilia, coupled with his minimal explanation, left much to be desired. Whether his actions were a form of rebellion or an attempt to challenge an older generation's obsession with war, he never clarified. The music press matched the guitar player's indifference with silence, ignoring any potential outrage and never questioning his actions. Neither then nor when the posthumous Cleopatra Records Stooges compilation, *I Wanna Be Your Dog*, featured Asheton on the cover artwork in full uniform, including a swastika brassard. What this says about fans of the Stooges is in many ways articulated by the group's straight-talking lead singer, Iggy Pop. 'The ugliest chicks . . . the most illiterate guys . . . people with skin problems, sexual problems, weight problems, employment problems, mental problems . . . it was like what Hitler said, "Go for the lowest common denominator."'[6]

✳

In March 1971, Charles Manson appeared in court with a swastika etched between his eyebrows. 'The mark on my head,' the musician and leader of the California-based cult the Manson Family told the judge, 'simulates the dead head black stamp of rejection, anti-church, falling cross, devil sign, death, terror, fear.' Manson's world view, in part, grew from a very individualistic interpretation of and identification with a batch of songs on the Beatles' 1968 'White Album' – 'Blackbird', 'Helter Skelter', and 'Piggies' – and a foreseeing of a 'race war' between the police and Black America; a sign of an impending 'revolution'. Over three nights in August 1969, Manson's 'Family' brutally and senselessly murdered seven people, including the Hollywood actor Sharon Tate, and smeared the titles of the Beatles' songs on the walls with the blood of the murdered victims.

'Charles Manson interpreted that "Helter Skelter" was something to do with the four horsemen of the Apocalypse,' Paul McCartney reflected in the 1990s. 'I still don't know what all that stuff is; it's from the Bible, "Revelations" – I haven't read it so I wouldn't know. But he interpreted the whole thing . . . and arrived at having to go out and kill everyone . . . It was frightening because you don't write songs for those reasons.'

The juxtaposition of the swastika and Manson's warped inter-pretation of Beatles' lyrics was further complicated when it was revealed that both the maternal grandparents of 'Family' member Catherine Share, known as 'Gypsy', died in concentration camps. The disturbing episode defies rational explanation. But the swastika and, more broadly, Nazi insignia was increasingly becoming a musi-cian's mark of rebellion, detached from its origin, and regardless of the artist's heritage or religion. Moreover, in the aftermath of the Manson Family murders, a band was poised to emerge, character-ised by the controversial use of the term 'cult'.

'I had to tell my relatives I was in a cult now,' says Joe Bouchard, bassist of Blue Öyster Cult.[7] Best known for their international hit '(Don't Fear) The Reaper', which achieved immense commercial success and sales in the millions, the song's appeal lies in its themes of transcending death and eternal love. Formed in the late 1960s, the band became known for incorporating Third Reich imagery into their artwork, album covers, band logo, stage design and lyrics. Given that both lead singer Eric Bloom and producer-cum-lyricist Sandy Pearlman were Jewish makes their story even more perplexing, raising as many questions as answers.

In 1975 the band informed *Melody Maker*, 'We're pain, we're steel, we're a plot of knives, we're obsessed with the technology of matter . . . our symbol is a swastika substitute.'[8] Blue Öyster Cult's logo, a crooked cross on a red background, was inspired by the ancient Greek symbol for chaos. 'Nazism is a style of art that just happened to flower in Germany after the Weimar Republic,' explained Eric Bloom.

> Of course, we're appealing to that as a source of imagery, but it existed before. People see what they want to see. We mine the vein created by Nazi artists. The Doors did that, the Velvet Underground certainly did and it'll be done again. We're more obsessed with the technology of the matter. We utilise the symbols in alchemy like lead, the most debased metal. Saturn and the Greek symbol also have the same chaotic associations. [Our logo has] become a swastika substitute, not as old but old enough to have a venerable history.

At live shows, the band displayed banners with their logo on either side of the stage, with the distinctive umlaut above 'Öyster' prominently positioned behind the musicians. The staging resembled a Third Reich rally. 'It seems significant, then,' wrote *Melody Maker* journalist Chris Charlesworth, 'that on meeting their manager the other day he was carrying under his arm an album of Nazi war hymns which contained several tracks of hysterical cheering as crowds listened to the oration of Adolf. Stuff, explained the manager, to be used on the group's third album, which will be released in May.'[9]

Following the release of the non-charting single 'Hot Rails To Hell' in 1973, which featured a German military figure on the cover sleeve, *Secret Treaties* was introduced as an album centred around the concept of a child prodigy. 'There's no gap between his imagination and his ability to realise it,' Sandy Pearlman explained. 'He can accomplish what he imagines and imagine what he's going to accomplish.'

The album sleeve presented a graphic illustration of the band next to the wing of a Messerschmitt fighter plane. On the inside sleeve, a puzzling (and as it transpired fictional) text read: 'Rossignol's curious, albeit simply titled book, the *Origins of a World War*, spoke in terms of *secret treaties*, drawn up between the Ambassadors from Plutonia and Desdinova the foreign minister. These treaties founded a secret science from the stars. Astronomy. The career of evil.'

The listed songs resembled chapter headings from a Third Reich history text: 'Career Of Evil', 'Subhuman', 'Dominance/Submission'. A fourth track, 'ME 262', referenced Willy Messerschmitt, the inventor of the first operational turbojet-powered fighter plane used by the Luftwaffe in 1944. Written from the perspective of a German pilot attacking a British squadron, Pearlman's lyrics presented a scenario in which 'Göring's on the phone from Freiburg say's you've really done quite a job. Hitler's on the phone from Berlin says 'I'm gonna make you a star'. As a result, Columbia Records was picketed by protesters who believed the label was promoting a Nazi band. 'Sandy wasn't only our manager, he was our visionary,' tells Joe Bouchard. 'He loved history and mythology, he'd read all these books, deep stuff. Things could be dark. People thought we were Nazis, which was almost humorous, but we were sometimes treading in deep water.'[10] Outtakes from the album sessions revealed another song indebted to Nazi hierarchy and Hitler's trusted secretary, 'Boorman [*sic*] the Chauffeur'.

To promote *Secret Treaties*, the quintet from Long Island, New York posed in military uniforms surrounded by maps, canes, a Luftwaffe poster, and Adolf Hitler pictured with a dart through the centre of his decapitated head. A subtitle instructed, 'Aggression unchallenged is aggression unleashed'. The record was banned in shops across Germany; the Jewish Defence League picketed and threatened to sabotage Blue Öyster Cult concerts. As media interest mounted around the group's fascistic interests, so too did a new type of fan, as founding member and drummer Albert Bouchard explained. 'After a gig in Portland, Oregon, this blond, blue-eyed guy came up in full [Nazi Secret Service] uniform, saluting us . . . he freaked us all out.'

The incident prompted an image rethink, as keyboard player and sometime guitarist in the group, Allen Lanier, explained. 'Rock 'n' roll lives off of false imagery. We've dropped all that simply because it wasn't amusing anymore. It was just an in-joke that had run its course.' However, rock critic Richard Metzler claimed in the biography *Blue Öyster Cult: Secrets Revealed!*, that Lanier was 'very anti-Semitic without any irony whatsoever. You know, fuck the Jews, all that kind of stuff . . . I lived with this woman Ronnie, and we would hang out with Allen and Patti [Smith, former partner] a lot, through the mid '70s,' Metzler continued, 'and essentially what made the relationship viable was that we didn't mind their anti-Semitism [in later editions the allegation was amended to 'we didn't mind *his* anti-Semitism' and Smith has maintained a public stance of not being an anti-Semite] But the point is that Allen thought the faux-Nazi stuff was a joke. I mean, everybody took it as a joke. Except, as I remember, Eric [Bloom] thought there was something cool about it, that the Third Reich had its shit together. You know, the Jew in the woodpile was the one that took it the most seriously.'

Chicago-born poet Patti Smith, like many of her contemporaries, was captivated by Adolf Hitler's power to mesmerise large crowds through his commanding 'physical presentation'. Drawing comparison with the evangelist Billy Graham – 'even though he is a hunk of shit' – Smith considered Hitler 'a fantastic performer', and 'black magician'. 'I learned from that,' she revealed in 1972. 'You can seduce people into mass consciousness.'[11] Smith was an avid reader of the Bible and freely took poetic inspiration from texts such as the Song of Solomon, the Psalms and the Book of Isaiah. As a thirteen-year-old she read *The Diary of Anne Frank* and, consequently, broke away from a Jehovah's Witnesses upbringing and embraced Judaism. 'I had great sympathy,' Smith told NPR. 'I mean when I grew up, in the late fifties and early sixties . . . a lot of information came out about the Holocaust and there were trials, and things, and I felt devastated about that as a young girl, and I got very interested in the Jewish faith.' Smith even contemplated conversion. However when confronted with the need for rigorous study of Jewish culture and history, she commented, 'I didn't realise that you just can't be . . . you don't turn Jewish.'[12]

The apparent contradiction of Smith's interest in both Judaism and Hitler is difficult to unravel. It appears to bridge the gap between faith and mass murder, reflecting someone in search of identity. However, this internal exploration, tied to her ambition to be a poet, placed what should have been personal into the public sphere.

Similarly, private indulgence lay behind the inner gatefold sleeve of Van der Graaf Generator's 1971 album *Pawn Hearts*. Pictured in an English garden, the art-rock group formed at Manchester University by songwriter Chris Judge Smith and vocalist Peter Hammill, face one another dressed in black shirts and yellow ties while raising their arms in a salute. 'We took lots of shots (all of which are equally weird),' Hammill wrote the following year, 'and then had a few frames left, so got into the psychedelic Nazis trip!'[13]

In 1998, Hammill passed off the band's humour as Monty Python-inspired while suggesting that the album pose 'was in ironic reference to a statue in Kaiserslautern which had given us chills.'[14] Hammill's terse explanation and an oblique reference to a city in south-west Germany did little to appease record buyers unimpressed with his former group simulating Nazi salutes. And yet, five years earlier, in 1993, Hammill wrote the song 'Primo On The Parapet' as a tribute to Holocaust survivor and author Primo Levi. Regularly performed at concerts, Hammill's eulogy to Levi's courage in the face of Nazi extermination offered the closing stanza, 'There's pain in remembrance but we must learn not to forget'.

The vogue for provocation, as if pop stardom licensed musicians to flaunt societal rules, continued with abandon in the early seventies.

On 5 September 1972, eleven Israeli athletes, including Ameri-can-born weightlifter David Berger, were murdered at the Munich Olympic Games by the Palestinian terrorist group Black September. The Olympics were marketed as Germany's chance to move beyond its past, but the massacre, watched by an estimated nine hundred million people, sent shockwaves throughout the world. Six weeks later, as Mott the Hoople kicked off their American tour at the Hollywood Palladium, the slaughter of Jewish lives 6,000 miles across the Atlantic did not deter singer Ian Hunter strutting across the stage playing a Stratocaster shaped like an Iron Cross, seemingly oblivious to repurposing Nazi ephemera and post-war anti-Semitism.

Meanwhile, the flamboyantly dressed glam rock band Sweet challenged audiences with each new release, from the garden-fresh Native American image for 'Wig-Wam Bam' to a camp portrayal of the Hitler Youth on 'Ballroom Blitz'. In February 1974, Sweet performed on the West German music programme *Musikladen* – filmed in Bremen, a city heavily bombed during the Second World War – wearing glitter jackets adorned with various slogans: 'Bollox!', 'Fuck You' and, on drummer Mick Tucker's back, a large hand-sewn black swastika.

Five weeks earlier, the London-based band, formerly known as Sweetshop, performed their smash hit 'Block Buster!' on the Christmas Day edition of *Top of the Pops*. A prime-time slot in front of an anticipated television audience of ten million was an opportunity for high drama. Marching onstage, bassist Steve Priest flaunted an eye-catching military uniform featuring a *Pickelhaube* spiked leather helmet, an SS tunic, a swastika armband and silver stack heels. The assorted soldierly apparel was rounded off with a full face of make-up and a thin black moustache above Priest's upper lip painted by the BBC costume department. 'I remember being on the floor creasing with laughter,' bellowed guitarist Andy Scott, '"Are we going to get away with this?"'

The supposedly light-hearted get-up was in stark contrast to the heavyweight title of the song. Named after the RAF's weighty aerial bomb, which had enough explosive power to destroy an entire street, 'Block Buster!' introduced itself with an ear-piercing air raid siren. The song rocketed to number 1. In the Sweet's first *Top of the Pops* performance, lead singer Brian Connolly hung an oversized Iron Cross around his neck. Ten months later and Priest was flaunting a swastika wrapped around his left arm. 'It's amazing how everyone still talks about the Nazi uniform,' the bass player reflected in 2010. 'Good old BBC wardrobe department. People always want to know if I was serious. I mean, a gay Hitler. Hello?!'[15]

Seventies Britain was progressively becoming a playground of Nazi mimicry, rarely provoking recrimination. Families had just three television channels to choose from, providing a routine of endless evenings spent in front of the screen, indulging in comedy shows that often featured thinly veiled xenophobia and parodies of the Second World War. One notable figure was Freddie Starr, a German-Jewish comedian, who performed in a pantomime-style Hitler costume, shouting random German phrases. *Monty Python's Flying Circus* took the absurdity even further, featuring sketches like 'Mr Hilter and the North Mine-head By-election' which featured Nazi characters such as Mr Bimmler (Michael Palin), Ron Vibbentrop (Graham Chapman) and Mr Hilter (John Cleese) plotting a National Bocialist take-over of middle-England. Pushing boundaries still more, John Cleese broke rank with a six-part comedy series set in a Torquay guesthouse called *Fawlty Towers*. One of its most famous episodes, 'The Germans', saw Basil Fawlty (Cleese) getting into a heated exchange with German guests and goose-stepping across the dining room. When he mistakenly mixes up the dinner order – 'So that's two eggs mayonnaise, a prawn Goebbels, a Hermann Göring and four Colditz salads' – the guests lose their patience, in the unforgettable exchange:

> *'Will you stop talking about the war?'*
> *'Me? You started it.'*
> *'No we did not!'*
> *'Yes, you did, you invaded Poland!'*

This comedy reflected a country fixated on its past. The images of Nazis in uniform and sets decorated with brightly coloured swastikas not only trivialised the perpetrators' crimes but also influenced a young generation. Indeed, the appearance of a pop star caricaturing the Führer in 1974 left one BBC viewer incredulous:

'You won't believe what's on television!' exclaimed John Lennon during a fabled telephone call with Ringo Starr. 'Marc Bolan is playing a song with Adolf Hitler!'

Bolan it was not. This was the American pop duo Sparks performing their breakthrough single, 'This Town Ain't Big Enough For Both Of Us.' Seated behind his keyboard, Ron Mael observed the surroundings with a judicious eye. Black hair swept to the side. Pencil-thin moustache. To Mael, a nod to Charlie Chaplin. To John Lennon, a tribute to Adolf Hitler.

The eccentric presentation captivated another former Beatle. Alongside fifteen million other viewers tuned in to *Top of the Pops*, Paul McCartney watched Sparks, enthralled. Six years later, McCartney promoted his latest single, 'Coming Up', by impersonating a roll-call of musical heroes from Hank Marvin of the Shadows and himself as a 1963 Beatle to a faultless imitation of Ron Mael. The portrayal of a pop star resembling Hitler, however, was considered inappropriate by one French television station, leading to the banning of Sparks. 'That's when I realised it wasn't something I needed to stand up and defend. In fact, the "look" was more Ronald Colman than Adolf Hitler,' Mael insisted, 'which is funny because that's who I was named after. He was my mum's favourite actor.'[16] Colman, the English-born silent screen star and later Academy Award winner, had a distinctive moustache spread thinly across the width of his upper lip. 'Yes, it did have some unfortunate by-products along the way,' Mael conceded in 2017, 'so I re-thought my facial hair direction. I changed the moustache a bit, it morphed into different things.'[17]

Rock Around the Bunker

SERGE GAINSBOURG. ROXY MUSIC

The Third Reich, when viewed as a theatrical spectacle, created a space where rock stars could divorce themselves from the brutal realities of an extremist regime without censure. Throughout the seventies, this disturbing fetishism coincided with a rising tide of nationalism, as fascism spread throughout mainland Europe. In the UK, the National Front made significant gains at the ballot box, presenting themselves as a legitimate political party. Meanwhile, in France, anti-immigrant sentiment and high unemployment rates fuelled an upsurge in anti-Semitism. In 1972, Jean-Marie Le Pen established the Front National and, two years later, ran for president. Legally recognised as a denier of the Holocaust – that is, the systematic murder of six million Jews, of whom two-thirds were women and children – Le Pen questioned the extent of the extermination programme. In 1987, he famously remarked, 'I'm not saying the gas chambers didn't exist. I haven't seen them myself. I haven't particularly studied the question. But I believe it's just a detail in the history of World War Two.'

Initially, the Front National struggled to gain significant support, securing 190,921 votes (0.7 per cent) in 1974. However, Le Pen's popularity surged in the late 1980s, with the party's electoral vote climbing above four million (14 per cent). In a rare instance of an artist addressing a commercially unpopular subject, Serge Gainsbourg, one of France's most renowned figures in popular music – songwriter, musician, composer, actor, author and filmmaker – used his prominent status to speak out against the growing threat of neo-Nazism.

Born to Russian Jewish immigrants in 1928, Gainsbourg –
originally named Lucien Ginsburg – was twelve years old when
Germany invaded France in May 1940. As upward of 76,000 French
Jews were deported to the east for resettlement – a byword for
extermination – or simply disappeared, with only around 2,500
returning after the war, the Gainsbourg family fled Paris seeking
refuge in the southern so-called 'free zone' administered by the
Vichy government. Though unoccupied by German troops until 10
November 1942, the French police under Marshal Pétain's authority
still conducted clampdowns on Jewish nationals and carried out
mass round-ups. Gainsbourg lived under the falsified name of
Guimbard. 'I have never forgotten that I ought to have died in
1941, '42, '43, '44,' he reflected later in life.

Drawing on his childhood experiences, Gainsbourg released
Rock Around the Bunker in 1975. It became his most provocative
and controversial album, shunned by both the press and the public,
who struggled to accept a playful album mocking the Third Reich.
'The album was poorly received,' Gainsbourg admitted, 'but in fact, I
wanted to exorcise this period that I lived in when I was a kid, where
I was marked with a yellow star. The star of my race . . . the Star of
David. So, to exorcise the matter, I wrote *Rock Around the Bunker*.'[1]

Rather than simply focusing on the story of a Jewish boy living
under German occupation, Gainsbourg channelled his anger into
ridiculing Adolf Hitler. The album depicts him locked in his bunker,
Allied bombs dropping overhead, surrounded by gay SS officers and
Eva Braun listening to American music, much to his annoyance.
'If people find this album in bad taste, or if it really rubs them
the wrong way, then let them,' Gainsbourg shrugged, ahead of its
release. 'Just look at the percentage of collaborators in France back
then . . . they're the ones who'll take it badly.'

Recorded over seven days in London with English musicians,
Gainsbourg, the enigmatic star, embraced a vaudevillian rock 'n' roll
style dripping with musical parody to express his disdain for the
Third Reich. The opening track 'Nazi Rock' referenced the violent
purge orchestrated by Heinrich Himmler's SS on 30 June 1934.
Sanctioned by Hitler, the bloody event – known as the 'Night of

the Long Knives'* – saw the cold-blooded murder of problematic factions within the Nazi elite. Ernst Röhm, head of Hitler's storm troopers (*Sturmabteilung*), was openly gay and frequently visited nightclubs like Berlin's Eldorado, where sexual freedom thrived in defiance of state repression. Outed in 1932 and accused of sexual deviancy by the SS, Röhm was arrested and allegedly handed a pistol at Hitler's behest. Refusing to take his own life, Röhm was shot by the commandant of the newly established concentration camp in Dachau. In this era where sexual choice met the full force of authoritarianism, Gainsbourg invited listeners to join the 'guys', put on black stockings, garter belts and corsets, and dance the 'Nazi Rock'.

The song 'Yellow Star' references the Nazi edict of 29 May 1942, which forced French Jews to wear an identifying symbol across their left breast. For fourteen-year-old Gainsbourg, this act of humiliation was a transformative moment. Rather than surrendering to Nazi oppression, he imagined the star as a symbol of status, like earning a sherriff's badge or a marshal's insignia (*'J'ai gagné la yellow star . . . Y'a peut-être marqué shérif.'*). 'It was like you were a bull,' Gainsbourg seethed, in private, 'branded with a red-hot iron.'[2] The louche musical style of *Rock Around the Bunker* was saturated with sarcasm, oozing from Gainsbourg's every sinew with disdain for Nazi Germany. With hammering piano riffs and shrill female backing vocals, Gainsbourg charted Hitler's gradual descent into drug dependency and psychosis, subtly adding a layer of indignity by casting the German dictator as a French speaker. *'J'entends des voix off . . . tout ça c'est du bluff'* ('I hear voices telling me, "Adolf, you are heading for disaster!" It's all a bluff.'

The barbarity of the regime is further amplified by the ironic brutalism of two songs, 'Smoke Gets In Your Eyes' and 'Eva', which evoke gas chambers installed in extermination camps across occupied Europe and the burning of Jewish bodies in purpose-built ovens. Originally written for the 1933 musical *Roberta* by the Jew-

---

* In 1981, the Australian rock band AC/DC recorded their own 'Night Of The Long Knives' for the album *For Those About to Rock*.

ish-American composer Jerome Kern and lyricist Otto Harbach (the son of Danish immigrants), 'Smoke Gets In Your Eyes' was a favourite of Hitler's mistress, Eva Braun. Imagining her blinded by love and ignorant of genocide raging across Europe, Gainsbourg croons, '*Eva aime . . . smoke gets in your eyes*'.

In 1945, many perpetrators of the Holocaust – Adolf Eichmann, Josef Mengele, Walter Rauff, Franz Stangl, Josef Schwammberger, Erich Priebke, Gerhard Bohne – fled Europe and found sanctuary in South America. With the support of corrupt regimes, the fleeing Nazis established an underground network, securing employment and settling with their families. Gainsbourg wrote of the 'SS In Uruguay' free from extradition ('*Qui parlent d'extraditionne*') and reminiscing about past battles and the tokens of war ('*Croix gammée et médailles*'), enjoying life under a straw hat and drinking papaya juice ('*Sous un chapeau de paille. Je siffle un jus de papaye*'). 'The Pope's silence is missing,' Gainsbourg commented in 1975, 'but I chickened out. I wrote it, but I didn't want to record it. I thought, "Why stir up all that trouble?" The song was supposed to touch on Pope Pius XII's ambiguous stance on Nazism.'

In his original concept for the album cover – unpublished until 2009 – Gainsbourg posed in front of an enlarged black and white photograph of the German army, wearing an SS jacket unbuttoned to show a gold chain. However, the final release featured a self-portrait by Gainsbourg instead. Nevertheless, *Rock Around the Bunker* neither sold in great quantity nor made a significant impact beyond a small enclave of Gainsbourg supporters. French radio refused to play it, and few journalists reviewed it. Some shops even refused to stock it. The unapologetic artist simply said, 'It was clearly an exorcism,'[3] adding, 'I think I missed an opportunity. I should have played it fake, like, *really* over the top. The audience would have caught the second-degree humour – could've been like Hitlerian ovations. That would've been wild. I didn't have that idea at the time, though.'

Rock Around the Bunker challenged a country still coming to terms with its collaboration during the Second World War. Gainsbourg stood as a bold, unflinching voice, willing to face his nation's complicity, while other Western musicians continued to casually exploit Third Reich tropes, as if they were mere theatrical props. In fact, while Gainsbourg recorded what may be considered the first Third Reich resistance record, cinema was celebrating the release of *The Night Porter*, a film exploring a sadomasochistic relationship between an SS officer and a female concentration camp inmate. The art-house picture would resonate deeply with young musicians waiting spellbound in the wings of the coming punk explosion. But in 1973, British experimental storytelling offered little more than innuendo and libidinous wordplay. Enter a collaboration between former Roxy Music synthesiser player Brian Eno and guitarist Robert Fripp, resulting in the instrumental long-player *No Pussyfooting*.

Side two of the record featured one song, eighteen minutes in length, called 'Swastika Girls'. Inspiration for the title came from the ripped page of a bondage publication which Eno stumbled upon outside Air Studios in central London when mixing the track. The loose leaf promised 'swastika girls' on one side and on the reverse a picture of a naked girl giving a Nazi salute. 'I stuck it on the console, and we were just kind of vaguely looking and talking about this as we were recording that piece,' Eno explained, 'and so that became the title.'

The arbitrary tag – 'Swastika Girls' – did little to unwrap the instrumental soundtrack: an electronic loop created by Eno on a VCS3 portable analogue synthesiser. Greater insight into Eno's connection to Nazism comes from his father, William, who served in the British army during the Second World War. Billeted with a family in Belgium, Eno Snr became enamoured by a photograph of the host's daughter, who worked in a forced-labour camp in Germany building Heinkel medium bombers. Eno fell in love. At the end of the war, the young woman returned to her family home. She weighed five stone, had a one-year-old daughter and was dealing with the loss of the child's father, who did not return from the labour camp. Eno waited and, two years later, they married.

The romantic saga, played out in desperate times, offers a fitting backstory to 'Swastika Girls' but it did little to convince record buyers to purchase the album. Instead, it reflects a generation of war children whose family histories provided an intriguing connection to Nazism simultaneously acting as a possible source of creative expression. While there's no indication that Eno harboured right-wing views, 'Swastika Girls' exposed an underground sexual fetishism of Nazism that had informed his previous group, Roxy Music, and would increasingly permeate rock culture throughout the decade.

Roxy Music's self-titled debut album released in 1972 featured 'The Bob (Medley)', a track named after the Battle of Britain, with a soundtrack of bombs and gunfire created by Brian Eno's VCS3 synthesiser. 'Most of my songs have a visual impulse behind them,' singer Bryan Ferry explained, 'except "The Bob (Medley)", which is about the Second World War.' The song's romantic lyrics were shrouded in ambiguity but nevertheless marked the beginning of Ferry's obsession with German culture. In 1973, when Eno casually suggested to a journalist that he might dress as a Nazi onstage because of the Nuremberg Rally-like atmosphere at certain shows, Ferry remarked, 'Yes, we once had something like that at Stoke-on-Trent. I thought it was going to be Munich all over again.'[4] This theme carried over to the 1974 *Country Life* album, where 'Bitter-Sweet' was performed in dramatic, high-camp tones, evoking a *Cabaret*-esque world of 'high-stepping chorus lines' and German wordplay, such as '*Mein lullaby-Liebchen*'.* Ferry described this as capturing 'that kind of real German, Berlin feeling'. In the third verse, he switched to German (the words translated by Eveline Grunwald and Constanze Karoli, who modelled on the album cover), singing, '*Nein – das ist nicht, Das ende der welt, Gestrandet an leben und kunst, Unde das spiel geht weiter, Wie man Weiss, Noch viele schönste . . . wiedersehen*'. ('No – that is not the end of the world, stranded

---

* In 2017, Ferry made a cameo appearance in the German noir television series *Babylon Berlin* and performed 'Bitter-Sweet' in a scene set in a Weimar cabaret club.

between life and art. And the game continues, how to know, many more beautiful . . . see you again').

'That was for a bit of fun,' reflected a non-committal Ferry, 'just to make things more interesting.'

On tour, the influence of Weimar cabaret was unmistakable. Simon Reynolds observed Ferry's Nazi-inspired aesthetic, noting his attire of 'jackboots, padded shoulders and riding breeches', with a 'hint of a Hitler parting in the hair'. The stage decor was equally striking, featuring a gold eagle with a thirty-foot wingspan.[5] Ferry discussed the presentation with *Creem*'s Richard Cromelin while flicking through a tour programme. 'That was a very classic look I thought, like a cruise ship kind of look,' Ferry offered, pausing to admire a particular outfit. 'That silly look, which I alternated on certain nights with that one, which looks a bit Third Reich, Hitler Youth . . . I think people look good in uniforms.'[6]

For Those About to Rock

KISS. MOTÖRHEAD. ALEX HARVEY

In 1973, the rock band KISS courted controversy when their band logo incorporated the distinctive double 'SS' flashes of Heinrich Himmler's *Schutzstaffel* motif. According to the group's songwriter, Sean Delaney, the provocative logo was intentional. Ace Frehley, the guitar player of KISS, was not only of German descent – his grandmother came from the island of Rügen in the Baltic Sea – but also collected Nazi memorabilia. Sketching the character letters K-I, Frehley then placed an SS pin badge on the page to complete the word KISS. 'The K-I stands for you two kikes [derogatory and offensive slang for Jew],' Frehley allegedly sneered at the group's two Jewish members, Gene Simmons (born Chaim Witz, 1949, Haifa, Israel) and Paul Stanley (born Stanley Eisen, 1952, New York), 'and the S-S stands for my heritage.' Incensed, Simmons readied to punch Frehley. Then, as quickly, he pulled back and reflected that if he (Simmons) felt that way, the world would have a similar reaction to the logo.

In the 1950s, Germany banned 'symbols of anti-constitutional organisations', under Section 86a of the *Strafgesetzbuch* penal code and, although not explicitly, included the swastika, SS insignia and the Nazi salute. In 1980, the Bremen Prosecutor's Office stated that the double 'S' in the KISS logo resembled the SS *Siegrune*, the displaying of which in Germany was an offence punishable by imprisonment. Sean Delaney claimed that the two symbols were 'lightning flashes' and 'stood for [electrical] power'. Nonetheless, to comply with legal requirements, the band changed the lettering on their logo and all German-issued records and promotional material to a Gothic font featuring two inverted 'Z' characters.

'There were so many crazy rumours about us in the early days,' Frehley said, clearly exasperated by what he considered to be fabricated stories concerning this attitude towards the Third Reich. 'Like that KISS stood for Knights In Satan's Service, or that we were Satan worshippers or Nazis. And it all turns out to be completely false. Paul and Gene were Jewish, I was brought up a Lutheran, and Peter Criss [drummer] was a Roman Catholic.'[1] Defending the logo, Frehley claimed it was simply 'iconic' and 'cool'. Then it emerged that Frehley had once rushed into Simmons' hotel room wearing a Nazi uniform, shouting 'Sieg Heil'.

'Paul and Peter were there too,' Frehley elaborated.

> We had gone to a toy store in Japan and there was all these old Nazi uniforms. We ended up buying a bunch of them as a joke. We had a few drinks, and we dressed up in the uniforms, and we were taking a few pictures, admiring them, and somebody said, 'Hey, let's knock on Gene's room and surprise him.' In retrospect, it was really not a cool thing to do. I think he was caught off-guard.'

Dressed as Nazi officers, both Stanley and Criss posed with their right arms raised in salute – a prank photographed by Criss' wife, Lydia. However, the stunt backfired when Simmons revealed that his mother was a Holocaust survivor.* In his 2002 autobiography *Kiss and Make-Up*, he recalled that Frehley had a fascination with Nazi memorabilia and, 'in his drunken stupors he and his best friend would make videotapes of themselves dressed up as Nazis'. Despite this, Frehley denied any Nazi sympathies, stating, 'I don't believe in Hitler or his ideology or anything he stood for.' Yet, contradicting himself somewhat, he admitted, 'Yeah, [the Nazis] did have the

---

* 'My mother's parents were Hungarian Jews,' Simmons wrote in his memoir. 'When my mother was fourteen, she was sent to the concentration camps, where she saw most of her family wiped out in the gas chambers. While in the camps, she ended up doing the hair of the commandant's wife, so she was shielded from many of the horrors that befell the other Jews.'

coolest clothes. Regardless of whether or not you agree with Hitler's ideology, there was still something fascinating about his costumes. They had the coolest costumes. It was very fashionable.'

Surprisingly, Simmons likewise differentiates ideology from artifice. 'One word from Hitler and the masses would move in unison,' he commented. 'It was the same with KISS. An amazing feeling of power. A KISS show was a holy experience, like an electric church, and I was all my childhood heroes rolled into one. To say I felt like God up there is not an overstatement. Each show was like a two-hour orgasm.'

The most concerning aspect of this incident is not just the choice to wear Nazi uniforms or even compare KISS performances to Hitler's oratory – it is the decision to share those images and thoughts publicly. Publishing such offensive photographs, as Lydia Criss did in *Sealed with a Kiss*, has far-reaching consequences. Regardless of intent, when rock stars wear Nazi uniforms or mimic salutes, they risk downplaying the monstrousness of the Third Reich. It can turn historical atrocities into mere spectacle, airbrushing the unpalatable with comic veneer and making Nazis seem like a harmless trope rather than a symbol of genocide. Paul Stanley later addressed the issue in his memoir, arguing that Ace Frehley and Peter Criss 'felt powerless and impotent when faced with the tireless focus, drive and ambition of me and Gene. As a result, the two of them tried to sabotage the band, which, as they saw it, was unfairly manipulated by [us] money-grubbing Jews.' [2]

In August 1975, just months before he joined the Eagles, American guitarist Joe Walsh sat down for an interview with journalist Colin Irwin. Suddenly, Walsh brandished a weapon under the nose of the *Melody Maker* writer with a Nazi swastika emblazoned on the handle. 'Do you like this knife I've got?' Walsh taunted Irwin, affectionately stroking the silver blade. 'I like to collect Nazi things. I'm not concerned with the ethics of the war, but the era of Nazi Germany is fascinating. I was gonna go to Germany to collect some stuff, but I understand that people don't really like to talk about it.' [3]

Irwin describes the incident as a 'headline grabber', enlightening readers that having a knife waved in front of him was 'a bit disconcerting when you're having a perfectly innocent conversation'. Drama over, Irwin makes no further comment about the weapon nor indeed why Walsh owned such an item. Here again is an illustration of the unofficial license musicians indulge to act outside of the mainstream and beyond moral or traditional social boundaries. The media and fans alike endow rock stars with reverence, lovingly referring to them as 'outsiders', 'bad boys', or 'renegades' and judging their antics 'cool'. It is a bestowed status primed for abuse, encouraging immoderation, and rewarding excess. It allows for unrestrained actions and tolerates, or overlooks, behaviour that would be considered insulting or offensive elsewhere. Yet, to call out such conduct as wrong, inappropriate or, in some instances, criminal, often provokes the retort: 'Don't be boring' or 'It's rock 'n' roll'.

At the heart of rock 'n' roll lies a sense of absurdity – a freedom to ridicule itself and find humour in the most uncomfortable situations. The record industry grants musicians the liberty to step outside societal norms, both onstage and off, viewing it as an essential part of rock's rebellious spirit. Many artists are drawn to music precisely because it doesn't demand qualifications or obedience to rules. However, this can lead to the misconception that rock stars are unintelligent, neglecting the fact that many are well educated – whether through formal schooling or self-study. While some might regard the use of Nazi imagery as a mindless act of 'stupidity', others may see in it a calculated statement, possibly even one with anti-Semitic undertones. In many cases, such behaviour is brushed off or excused, but when there's no clear explanation, it leaves room for interpretation. The assumption that it's just mindless or playful serves as a shield against guilt.

Today, rock stars are increasingly more accountable to their audience, operating in an environment where inappropriate comments or actions can lead to banning, exclusion or backlash on social media. Yet, in the case of Motörhead and its legendary leader, Lemmy, we see a perfect example of rock 'n' roll's untamed, rebellious spirit, immune to criticism and disturbingly cavalier in the glorification of Nazi iconography, despite the unconvincing attempts to rationalise it.

Legs parted, head rocked back, neck straining to the microphone, Lemmy is a rock star with an irrepressible persona. Singing 'Ace Of Spades' with venom and dressed foot to toe in worn leather, he exudes an imperturbable 'fuck you' attitude. The sartorial coding is rock. And, if not for his age, Lemmy would be the prototype punk rocker.

Throughout his five-decade career, Ian 'Lemmy' Kilmister openly flaunted a Third Reich collection. During the early seventies, as the 'Silver Machine' singer in the rock band Hawkwind, Lemmy wore an SS division *Das Reich* armband. Three years later, in 1975, after his arrest at the US–Canadian border on a drugs possession charge, the group sacked Lemmy. The same year, he formed Motörhead. At their debut appearance at London's Roundhouse on 20 July 1975, the group walked onstage to the pre-recorded soundtrack of jackboot stomps. 'That was fast, considering I'd left Hawkwind in May,' Lemmy wrote in his autobiography *White Line Fever*. 'We opened for Greenslade . . . all the bands those days had intro tapes, and since I've always been a World War Two fanatic, we used a recording from Germany of marching feet and people yelling "Sieg Heil".' Writing in *Sounds*, Geoff Barton concluded, 'The hour-long set that followed could well be described as a rather untogether blitzkrieg.'

When Motörhead's eponymously titled album arrived in August 1977 – stalling just outside the top 40 – the front cover revealed a barely disguised swastika. Designed by artist Joe Petagno, the Nazi symbol appeared on the middle spike of the head of the band mascot, Snaggletooth. Subsequently painted out, Chiswick Records claimed fewer than 150 copies reached record stores. Nevertheless, the embarrassing revelation did little to deter Lemmy, who freely continued to show off Nazi ephemera in public, be it a swastika pendant, an SS *Totenkopf* badge, a War Merit Cross with Swords, Panzer division and *Obergruppenführer* collar tabs or an Iron Cross.

After a 1995 Motörhead concert in Austin, Ministry's lead singer, Al Jourgensen recounted seeing Lemmy dressed in a full Gestapo uniform and spanking a naked woman with a riding crop. While Keith Emerson of the Nice had received unexpected advice from the group's former road manager. 'If you're going to use knives,' Lemmy advised after watching Emerson stab his Hammond L-100 with blades during a performance, 'at least use real ones,' handing over two Hitler Youth daggers.

In 2005, Lemmy invited a documentary crew into his apartment on the Sunset Strip in Los Angeles. They filmed an extensive collection of Nazi artefacts. Titles such as *Auschwitz* and *The Battle of Britain* lined Lemmy's bookshelves. Toy tanks, Nazi pendants and a German war helmet filled a wooden table. A swastika flag decorated the living room wall. Glowing with pride, Lemmy admired the quality workmanship and stitching of a 'beautiful' prized Damascus Luftwaffe sword. 'A work of art,' he gushed, ceremonially easing the blade from the scabbard.

The next scene featured Lemmy dressed in an SS uniform driving a Jagdpanzer 38(t) Hetzer tank. In the film, which aired on Channel 4 as *Motörhead: Live Fast Die Old*, Lemmy flippantly responds to viewers who may consider him a Nazi. 'Well, I've had six black girlfriends so far. So, I'm one of the worst Nazis you've ever met, right? . . . Imagine going to Nuremberg and introducing my girlfriend to the Führer. I don't think so. I just dress how I like to dress. I don't ask anybody else to do it. It's a free country, supposedly. If the Israeli army had the best uniforms, I'd collect them, but they don't. So, there you go. I can't help it. It's ridiculous to think that I could be a Nazi. I'm about as far from it as you could get. Uneducated people who point and go "Swastika! Swastika?" They don't know anything,' Lemmy scoffed, pointing to an Iron Cross from the First World War he wore onstage which predated the rise of the Nazi Party.

Lemmy's deep interest in Third Reich memorabilia and his Nazi-inspired clothing, combined with a naive refusal to recognise the fundamental link between ideology and image, came across as the misguided rationalisations of an overindulged child. 'From the beginning of time, the bad guys always had the best uniforms. Napoleon, the Confederates, the Nazis. They all had killer uniforms. I mean, the SS uniform is fucking brilliant! They were the rock stars of that time. What you gonna do? They just look good.'[4]

Such proclamations were far from isolated. Lemmy repeatedly drew a link between rock 'n' roll and the seductive visual pageantry of Nazi rallies. He vividly described the spectacle of the twin bronze eagles and Albert Speer's awe-inspiring Cathedral of Lights, soaring into the sky 'like pillars of white fire'. He delighted at the brilliance of the beams crossing above Hitler and shining into his face as he stepped onto the podium at a Nuremburg Party Rally of Unity and Strength. 'That's fucking amazing shit!' Lemmy cried. 'If you were twenty in 1933 you would go for him like a knife!' To his biographer, Mick Wall, he added, 'Hitler's rallies were almost like rock concerts . . . he was the first rock star.'[5]

The unquestioning admiration was worthy of a party-political broadcast. In his autobiography, Lemmy listed Hitler's successes: in turning round the economy, defeating inflation, freezing foreign assets, uniting Germany, giving the people purpose. It was commendation worthy of a propaganda show reel, never mind a rock memoir. He then added one more startling achievement. 'He said he'd kill the Jews,' Lemmy writes, 'he killed the Jews.' The words are ugly and shocking and jump out from the page. No balance or commentary. Yes, Lemmy's assessment has truth. Hitler did kill Jews (in collusion with his party and anti-Semitic collaborators across Europe). Nazi Germany did transform itself socially and politically. But much of its wealth came from the state seizing Jewish property and possessions. These counter-arguments are not expressed in the memoir. Nor either disgust or a sense of injustice. Instead, Lemmy marvels at a dictator who delivered on promises regardless of the human cost to Jewish women, children and men, a single-minded viewpoint devoid of human compassion and sensitivity for the victims of Nazism.

Rock stars have a propensity to function like an island, adrift from ordinary expectations. Yet humanity is bound together by a shared responsibility to one another. Not so, says Lemmy. 'I only collect the stuff. I didn't collect the ideas. The more you get into it the more interesting it gets.'[6] 'It was the biggest event that ever happened in history,' he insisted. 'They killed a whole fucking lot of people. And it changed the world. I collect [Nazi paraphernalia] as a safety valve to stop that form of government ever existing again. Europe ignored Hitler for twenty years; and if the French had driven them out of the Rhineland, the German Army, and Hitler, could have been beaten in 1936, his people would have been toppled from power.'[7]

Shifting the argument to modern-day North America, Lemmy criticised the model airplane industry for banning a Nazi symbol on the Messerschmitt 109. 'Are any Jews less dead because they won't allow a swastika on a plastic model?' Lemmy rages, rhetorically. 'No! It's about people not liking the truth.'

In 2008, German authorities investigated Lemmy after he was photographed wearing a Nazi cap to promote an upcoming Motör-head concert in Aurich. 'It's not a nationalistic kind of thing,' he retorted, defending his blatant contravention of the German penal code. 'Don't tell me I'm a Nazi cause I have uniforms! I just don't understand racism; I never thought it was an option.'[8] Then, in 2015, Motörhead's twenty-second studio album *Bad Magic* reproduced an image of a Knight's Cross of the War Merit Cross with Swords on the front cover artwork. The same year, Reuters UK reported the singer saying that Hermann Göring was 'the only one I admire for establishing the Gestapo and accepting blame at the Nuremburg Trials. His suicide,* hours before he was due to be hung,' said Lemmy, was 'fantastic.'

Lemmy's infatuation with Nazism remained unwavering for more than five decades. He saw his collection of Third Reich mem-orabilia as a means to prevent the rise of neo-Nazism, believing it served as a 'reminder of what happened'. And, although an SS uniform represented tyranny and mass murder, he still argued that

---

* On 15 October 1946, Göring died after swallowing a Nazi-issued cyanide capsule while awaiting hanging.

if it looked cool, it was worth flaunting. Yet nowhere does Lemmy acknowledge responsibility towards his audience. His argument always stemmed from a personal point of view, indifferent to how his words or image might be interpreted. By embracing Nazi symbols, he allowed them to shape his identity, revealing rock 'n' roll's reluctance to challenge ideas that, in any other context, would be considered unacceptable

The mid-seventies onwards also saw rock bands experimenting with typography to craft a bold, rebellious identity. Motörhead, Blue Öyster Cult, Queensrÿche, and Mötley Crüe all incorporated umlauts or black-letter script styles, known as Fraktur, first used in sixteenth-century German printing, that echoed the iconography of the Third Reich.

Where Queensrÿche adapted their song 'Queen Of The Reich' to the Middle English cognate 'ryche' to detract Nazi sympathisers, before adding the umlaut, Nikki Sixx of Californian rock band Mötley Crüe had a far simpler explanation. 'We didn't think about its proper use,' he said before seemingly contradicting himself. 'We just wanted to do something to be weird, and the umlaut is very visual. It's German and strong, and that Nazi Germany mentality – "the future belongs to the youth" – intrigued me.'[9] British musician Ian Anderson recalled Lemmy referring to the diacritical sign in Motörhead as the 'Nazi dots', observing that 'in his simple way, [Lemmy] was a bit of a historian about aspects of militaria and warfare, but it might have bordered on the unhealthy side of normal'.[10]

This trend of borrowing Third Reich imagery under the guise of pure aesthetics became increasingly common. Naturally, artists distanced themselves from any ideological association, yet the meticulous visual branding of the regime remained undeniably appealing. For audiences, it raised an uncomfortable question: was it just theatrics, or did it hint at something deeper?

*

The Alex Harvey Band are supporting the Who at Charlton Athletic Football Club on Bank Holiday Monday, 31 May 1976. In front of 100,000 people, Harvey makes a dramatic entrance. First demolishing a brick wall, then goose-stepping onto the stage wearing a leather jacket with a swastika patch sewn over the breast pocket. Harvey's long black hair is swept to the side and a strip of black tape is stuck above his upper lip. 'I was marching down the *Straße* minding my own affairs,' Harvey sings in comically exaggerated German overtones, 'when two Stormtroopers grabbed me. Zey said, "Is your name Adolf,"' and I said, 'Why . . . sure.'

This is the infamous 'Adolf Hitler' version of 'I Was Framed', a song originally written by the Jewish composers Jerry Leiber and Mike Stoller, and recorded by the Robins in 1954, which refers to 'the legal brutality that impacted the Black community'[11] in Los Angeles. In this updated version, Harvey conjures Hermann Göring and Josef Goebbels and the SS taking the 'framed' Hitler to the gas chambers accused of inventing 'some kind of master plan'. In the final verse, Harvey invokes the Allied bombing of Berlin and Hitler's 'little sweetheart' Eva Braun. 'When they burned my balls in petrol, criticised my name', he sings, 'But just be careful baby, because he might come back again'. Harvey then screams to the audience: 'I was framed . . . do you believe me?'

A cry of support rings around the south-east London football stadium. Except, according to journalist Mick Brown, reviewing the 'friendly Führer' for *Sounds*, 'the audience flash *zig-heils* back like *Hitlerjugend* zombies, which makes you think this is a trifle *too* much and not a little tasteless'.

'That was fun,' asserts Harvey to the contrary, taking a step forward to address the crowd. 'But don't any one of you think for one minute that bastard was a good man.'[12]

In Belgium, the song is performed again. This time, Harvey adds an extended declamation against Hitler, beseeching the audience, 'We dinnae wan' fascism, do we?' To his surprise, the 2,000-strong audience scream, 'Yeahh!' 'Harvey tries a second time, but again the audience shriek, "Yeahh!" He raises his eyes heavenward in exasperation. "Don't you understand? You're supposed to say "No!" "Yeahh . . .""[13]

During the tour, Ted McKenna, the band's drummer, recalled performing 'Tomorrow Belongs To Me' from the 1966 Broadway musical *Cabaret*, written by Jewish composer John Kander and lyricist Fred Ebb, in Germany. 'Alex was fearless,' he said.[14] Similarly, Charles Kennedy, the former leader of the Liberal Democrats, said that he had the 'pleasure of seeing them at Parkhead', adding, 'But walking on stage dressed as Hitler, he would probably be run out of town for that these days.'

On occasion, Harvey would perform 'Framed' as a gangster or Jesus Christ, rewriting the words each time to suit the different character. Unsurprisingly, however, Nazi Party members presented the greatest opportunity to blend parody with a sinister dark edge. Fittingly, Harvey introduced 'Tomorrow Belongs To Me' to his repertoire. In the 1972 film adaptation of *Cabaret*, a member of the Hitler Youth, exquisitely dressed in Nazi uniform with combed blond hair and deep blue eyes, performs a rousing rendition of the song. An audience of Nazi sympathisers rise to their feet and bellow the chorus. It made for memorable, if not chilling, viewing. In 1975, Harvey recorded an album of the same name which included references to 'Action Strasse' and 'teaching me to do the goose step'. As a professed pacifist, the Nazi-related theatrics were confusing, but not for guitarist Zal Cleminson, who insisted that Harvey 'despised Hitler and all he stood for'.[15]

In April 1979, Harvey shared the headline billing at an Easter Extravaganza held at north London's Alexandra Palace. The event marked the culmination of Rock Against Racism's Militant Entertainment nationwide tour. Whether Harvey performed 'Framed' or 'Tomorrow Belongs To Me' is not recorded. But at an event organised to celebrate racial unity Harvey's anti-fascist message resonated. The same could not be said of the openly prejudiced frontman Ian Stewart Donaldson, whose notorious right-wing band Skrewdriver performed 'Tomorrow Belongs to Me' as part of a hardcore punk set that injected new meaning into the titles of rock standards including 'Behind Blue Eyes' (the Who), 'Sweet Home

Alabama' (Lynyrd Skynyrd) and 'Back In Black' (AC/DC). Such was Donaldson's detestable commitment to National Socialism he later formed the group Blood & Honour (and thereafter the Klansmen), a name taken from the motto inscribed on Hitler Youth-issued daggers, '*Blut und Ehre*'.

Visions of Swastikas

DAVID BOWIE. QUEEN

It is August 1975. David Bowie is riding on a high wave of commercial success. Having achieved national acclaim as the Weimar-influenced Ziggy Stardust – complete with his iconic feather boa and dramatic, sweeping hand gestures – Bowie reinvents himself. He speaks of 'dictatorship . . . a political figure in the not-too-distant future who'll sweep this part of the world like early rock 'n' roll did.' He calls for an 'extreme right front' to 'come up and sweep everything off its feet and tidy everything up', and cheerily informs the *NME* that his song, 'Somebody Up There Likes Me' is a 'Watch out mate! Hitler's on his way back . . . I could see how easy it was to get a whole rally thing going,' he continued, 'There were times . . . when I could have told the audience to do anything.'[1]

This is the Thin White Duke. Emaciated. Cocaine-fuelled. And as Bowie would later describe him, 'A very Aryan, fascist type. A would-be romantic with absolutely no emotion at all but who spouted a lot of neo-romance – an emotionless Aryan superman.' The character had been waiting patiently in the wings.

In 1969, Bowie had made a chilling prophecy: 'This country is crying out for a leader,' he told *Music Now!* 'God knows what it is looking for, but if it's not careful it's going to end up with a Hitler.' There followed a succession of songs exploring the idea of fascism: 'The Supermen' from *The Man Who Sold the World*, the call to 'make way for the homo superior' in 'Oh! You Pretty Things'; and in 'Quicksand', 'portraying Himmler's sacred realm of dream reality'. Then came thinly veiled references to Nietzsche's *Übermensch*, the biologically superior man, and Edward Bulwer-Lytton's 1971 novel

The Coming Race. The lyrics painted a vision of a masterful Nordic Aryan, steeped in Nazi philosophy and the eugenics practices that were central to Heinrich Himmler's philosophy.*

Defined by the *Oxford English Dictionary (OED)*, eugenics, derived from the Greek meaning 'good race', 'is the science dealing with factors that influence the hereditary qualities of a race and with ways of improving these qualities, especially by modifying the fertility of different categories of people.' Originally a British concept, eugenics led to the sterilisation of more than 60,000 Americans who were judged 'inferior' to the supposed 'superior race'. This practice was banned in 1914. Under Himmler's leadership, the Nazi eugenics programme – rooted in the hierarchical principles of the Jesuit order and the Catholic Church, as outlined by Ignatius of Loyola – sought to prevent those considered weaker or 'feeble-minded' from reproducing. Over time, these 'discarded human beings' were sterilised and, from 1939, as many as 250,000 women, children and men were gassed at six secret clinics in Bernburg, Brandenburg, Grafeneck, Hadamar, Hartheim and Sonnenstein. In August 1941, the facilities were shut down following public outcry led by the Catholic Archbishop of Münster, Clemens von Galen, although the killing continued in a more carefully concealed manner.

Bowie's veiled references to eugenics and his fascination with the connection between Nazism and the occult – particularly through reading Trevor Ravenscroft's *The Spear of Destiny* and J.H. Brennan's *Occult Reich*, coincided with the staged death of Ziggy Stardust at London's Hammersmith Odeon in July 1973. Reinventing himself as Aladdin Sane, Bowie painted a single red and blue 'lightning flash' across his face. This idiosyncratic character, the 'S', was drawn from the pre-Roman runic alphabet and closely resembled the Sig-Rune of the Hitler Youth – a variant of the distinctive double 'SS' insignia used by Himmler's security force, the *Schutzstaffel*. In the 1930s,

---

* It is noteworthy that Himmler expected higher SS, *Einsatzgruppen* (death squads) and police leaders, to be not only 'superhuman' but to be 'superhumanly inhuman' in the extermination of Europe's Jewish population.

Oswald Mosley's British Union of Fascists (BUF) had adopted a similar logo, the Flash and Circle, featuring a white lightning bolt within a blue circle on a red background. Many saw a deliberate connection between the BUF's logo, the Nazi insignia and Bowie's own 'lightning bolt'.

In an early version of 'Candidate' from the 1974 *Diamond Dogs* album – with a sleeve painted by artist Guy Peellaert and influenced by German Expressionism – Bowie boldly declared, 'I'm the Führer-ling'. The album opens with the chilling cry, 'THIS AIN'T ROCK 'N' ROLL! THIS IS GENOCIDE!'* The *OED* defines genocide as the deliberate and systematic extermination of an ethnic or national group. The term combines the Greek *genos* (race or tribe) and the Latin *cide* (killing). The term was coined by Polish lawyer Raphäel Lemkin in preparation for the Nuremburg Trials at the end of the Second World War. Up to this point, no commonly used word existed to describe crimes perpetrated by the Nazis against Europe's Jews. Yet, to Lemkin's dismay, the accused at Nuremburg were indicted for 'crimes against humanity' (i.e. as individuals) not specifically or with emphasis to the mass murder (i.e., those belonging to a group). 'In brief,' Lemkin concluded, 'the Allies decided a case in Nuremberg against a past Hitler but refused to envisage future Hitlers.'

And so emerged the Thin White Duke, infatuated with the Third Reich. For the 1974 Diamond Dogs tour, Bowie briefed set designer Mark Ravitz with three guiding words, 'Power, Nuremburg, and Fritz Lang's *Metropolis*,' adding, 'I want tanks, turbines, smokestacks, fluorescent lightning, alleyways, cages, watchtowers, girders, beams, Albert Speer.'[2] 'Everybody was convincing me that I was a messiah, especially on that first American tour,' Bowie said. 'I got hopelessly lost in the fantasy. I could have been Hitler in England. Wouldn't have been hard. Concerts alone got so enormously frightening that even the papers were saying, "This ain't rock music, this is

---

* In 1996, easy-listening sensation the Mike Flowers Pops incorporated the phrase 'This ain't rock 'n' roll, this is genocide' into the UK Top 40-charting single 'Light My Fire', which included a David Bowie medley.

bloody Hitler! Something must be done!" And they were right. It was awesome. Actually, I wonder,' Bowie contemplated, 'I think I might have been a bloody good Hitler. I'd be an excellent dictator. Very eccentric and quite mad.'

Rock stars are treated like demigods – revered in altar-like arenas and worshipped by frenzied fans. This idolisation often borders on the messianic, making it easy for performers to blur the line between admiration and something darker. 'Rock stars are fascists,' Bowie told journalist Cameron Crowe. 'Adolf Hitler was one of the first rock stars. Look at some of his films and see how he moved. I think he was quite as good as Jagger. It's astounding. And boy, when he hit that stage, he worked an audience. Good God!'

Bowie's unfiltered adoration continued: 'He was no politician. He was a media artist. He used politics and theatrics and created this thing that governed and controlled the show for twelve years. The world will never see his like again. He staged a country. People aren't very bright, you know,' Bowie hypothesised.

> They say they want freedom, but when they get the chance, they pass up Nietzsche and choose Hitler because he would march into a room to speak, and music and lights would come on at strategic moments. It was rather like a rock 'n' roll concert. The kids would get very excited – girls got hot and sweaty and guys wished it was them up there. That, for me, is the rock 'n' roll experience.

A significant influence on Bowie's views was Leni Riefenstahl's 1935 film *Triumph of the Will*, which captured the sixth annual National Socialist Party conference in Nuremberg. The film depicts a mass of people surrendering their individuality to Hitler, with his powerful rhetoric stirring them into a frenzy of exultation and submission.* The opening sequence projected Hitler as a God-like figure, gazing

---

* 'Can't you feel the terrific strength of his personality,' Foreign Minister von Ribbentrop observed at the Nuremburg Trials when screened film footage of Hitler filled a great white screen in the courtroom, 'how he swept people off their feet? A force of personality, it was *erschütternd* [staggering].'

down from his aircraft at the vast swathes of German troops and admirers below, waving swastikas where Albert Speer had arranged for 'veritable orgies of flags in the narrow streets with banners stretched from house to house, so that the sky was almost blotted out'.[3] Set to Herbert Windt's rousing, Wagnerian-inspired score, Hitler salutes the crowd from an open-top Mercedes, a mortal among a sea of enraptured faces staring in electrified awe, shouting and screaming between every giddy intake of breath.

In preparation for the week-long Nazi Party rally, architect Albert Speer (later Minister of Armaments and War Production) created 'a gigantic eagle, over a hundred feet in wingspread' spiked to a timber framework to crown the newly constructed Zeppelin Field. 'Like a butterfly in a collection,' Speer noted in his memoir *Inside the Third Reich*.[4] The grand design included a 'mighty flight of stairs' crowned by a colonnade and flanked at either end by stone abutments. Granite plinths, gloriously invoking ancient architecture, were built to withstand the wind, standing as an eternal monument to Hitler's power. At the lectern, where the leader addressed the 250,000-strong *Volk*, a copper gold-plated swastika within a laurel wreath. In the black night, 130 anti-aircraft searchlights, placed around the field at intervals of forty feet, sent individual rays soaring into the sky that merged into a general glow. Speer rejoiced at the spectacle, calling it 'the feeling of a vast room with the beams acting as mighty pillars of infinitely higher outer walls', simultaneously adding that it had the 'advantage of dramatizing the spectacle, while effectively drawing a veil over the not-so-attractive marching figures of paunchy party bureaucrats'.[5]

Born in Austria to Hungarian parents, Gitta Sereny, Speer's biographer, was travelling to boarding school in England in 1934 when her train broke down in Nuremberg. To her amazement, the eleven-year-old girl was taken to the Nazi Party Congress. She later recalled being 'overwhelmed by the symmetry of the marchers, the joyful faces all around, the rhythm of the sounds, the solemnity of the silences, the colours of the flags, the magic of the lights'. Enraptured, she found herself glued to her seat, only to suddenly be 'standing up, shouting with joy along with thousands of others.

But I understood nothing: it was drama; the theatre of it all that overwhelmed me.' Swept up by a 'seething emotional crowd', she experienced 'pleasure not derived from any person or words but from the theatrical spectacle'.[6]

Across the Grosser Dutzenteich lake, nestled between the former Zeppelin Field and the unfinished Congress Hall, stood Luitpold Hall, its facade adorned with slabs of shell limestone, in keeping with the architectural style of other Nazi monumental buildings. Inside this vast space, Speer created a large platform, flanked by two great banners with the swastika prominently displayed between them and illuminated by bright spotlights. 'I was completely under Hitler's spell unreservedly and unthinkingly held by him,' the twenty-eight-year-old architect later wrote.[7] The effect was both solemn and beautiful. Swastika flags lined endless rows of grey pillars, often adorned with gold ribbon. 'A way of introducing a play of colour into sombre architecture,' Speer explained, 'to intensify the effect of the red' of the flag and create 'scenic drama'. Here, Hitler, surrounded by hundreds of party officials, proclaimed his vision of a 'thousand-year Reich'.

The monumental architecture, the inspired flashes of colour, the cathedral of lights, the adoring crowds encapsulate rock 'n' roll's fascination with the grand, mesmerising spectacle of the Third Reich and exhibits the blueprint of a modern-day rock concert – in fact, since 2004, the former Zeppelin Field in Nuremberg has hosted the celebrated Rock im Park music festival, attracting bands such as Metallica, Red Hot Chili Peppers, Linkin Park and Depeche Mode. It is the screaming girls wetting their seats at the height of Beatlemania. Teenage fans falling at David Bowie's feet in the early seventies.* And it will be Queen's conquering performance at Live Aid in 1985, where holding the crowd in the

---

* Lucy Toothpaste saw David Bowie perform at the Empire Pool (now Wembley Arena) in May 1976. 'I hated it,' says the Rock Against Racism committee member. 'It felt like a fascist rally. Everybody had these "Bowie lights" and this mass of people all worshipping him.'

palm of his hand, Freddie Mercury commanded the stage and ignited a mass cultural celebration that felt like a modern-day bacchanalia. Standing at the lip of the stage, inciting the tightly packed crowd to chant the chorus line, 'We will, we will rock you', Mercury orchestrated 80,000 fans to clap their hands in unison and salute the stage with raised arms. It is spine-tingling spectacle and a reminder of how easily individual will is vulnerable to the collective spirit – awe-inspiring, joyous surrender in a stadium of shared communion. Indeed, in 1977, *Rolling Stone* described 'We Will Rock You' as having 'the atmosphere of a political rally in a Leni Riefenstahl movie'.

In 1984, Queen promoted their single 'Radio Ga Ga' with intercut video footage from the 1927 science-fiction film *Metropolis* (directed by Fritz Lang, a German Jew who refused to co-operate with the Nazi regime). The video showed Queen dressed in red and black leading a mass audience clapping in unison, arms outstretched between beats. 'For all the world like a Hitler rally in Munich or Berlin in the thirties,' observed *Breakfast Time* television presenter Frank Bough, extending his arm in salute for emphasis. 'It was meant to be more Orwellian,' responded Queen's drummer Roger Taylor. 'More mind control and certainly not Hitlerian, but I can see how it could be taken that way.'*[8]

Roger Taylor wrote 'Radio Ga Ga' in an era, as he saw it, where 'the visual side seems to be almost more important, than the aural'. He would probably have been astounded to learn that by 2025 'Radio Ga Ga' would register an incredible 329 million views on YouTube. However, in 1984, as the song slipped from its second spot on the national chart, Queen's new single gatecrashed the top 10. 'It's another bloody Nuremberg rally,' blasted *NME* in a review of 'I Want To Break Free'. Accusing Queen of blending '*Triumph of the Will* chic with British domesticity', David Quantick reminded readers of the earlier 'Radio Ga Ga', 'which gave us wartime

---

* Working as a burlesque dancer, Lady Gaga, previously known as Stefani Joanne Angelina Germanotta, was given her adopted name by her co-workers after the song 'Radio Ga Ga'.

Britain, gasmasks and parlours, Bakelite radios and a fireplace,' followed by outrage. 'And there's that rally again! What's vile about these two videos in particular isn't just the pseudo-fascist imagery,' Quantick continued.

> They do seem rather *proud* of audience manipulation. Like Pink Floyd's live version of *The Wall*, these videos present a vision of reality where life is grim, claustrophobic, virtually pre-television, and the alternative is . . . rock 'n' roll domination! And standing on the great granite monolith while the crowd do the silly hand-claps, Weatherfield [setting of television soap opera *Coronation Street*] or Nuremberg; it's a funny way of looking at things.[9]

The devotion displayed by rock audiences such as these mimics the way the German people surrendered to Hitler, and Nazism, and was so powerfully captured in Riefenstahl's films. It is evident in *Sieg des Glaubens* (*Victory of the Faith*, 1933), which celebrates the first National Socialist Party Congress after Hitler took power, and in the eighteen-minute short *Tag der Freiheit: Unsere Wehrmacht* (*Day of Freedom: Our Army*, 1935) which presents an idealised vision of soldiers, emphasising their physical beauty and their solemn oath of allegiance to the Führer.

Cinema played a vital role in spreading Nazi ideology; initially it served to indoctrinate audiences, and later, under Josef Goebbels's direction, it was used as entertainment laced with subtle Third Reich values. Describing his control of information as 'matchless', David Bowie said of Hitler's Minister of Propaganda, 'Goebbels intrigued me more than any of the other Nazis because of the way he used the media. He was an extraordinary guy. He used the media the way nobody used it. I can remember taking the Trans-Siberian express [in 1976], reading about Goebbels. I wanted to make that book into a movie.'

A passionate anti-Semite, Josef Goebbels spoke openly about 'extermination' and gratitude to Hitler for finding a Final Solution to the so-called Jewish problem.[10] 'This war is a racial war,' Goebbels wrote in his weekly leader for *Das Reich*, warning the German people of an impending battle to save Western culture and civilisation. 'The Jews started it, and they direct it. Their goal to destroy and exterminate our people. We are the only force standing between Jewry and world domination. None of the Führer's prophetic words had come so inevitably true as his prediction that if Jewry succeeded in provoking a second world war, the result would be not the annihilation of the Aryan race, rather the end of the Jewish race.'

Yet, remarkably, despite 'detesting' the Jew 'from the depth of his soul', Goebbels' one-time girlfriend, Else Janke, was a Jewish schoolteacher. Describing her in his diaries as a 'good child . . . loyal, hardworking', the Reich Minister of Propaganda added, 'one can rely on her, and she'll do you every possible favour'. Goebbels nevertheless pronounced Jews 'the poison that is killing the body of Europe'. His subsequent marriage to Magda Ritschel in 1931 prompted Hitler, and Germany at large, to view the couple as the model Aryan family. Such was their commitment to National Socialism that on 1 May 1945 – following the marriage of Hitler and Eva Braun at midnight on 28–29 April and suicide pact a day later – the Goebbels' poisoned their six children with cyanide capsules and committed suicide in the Führer's Berlin bunker.

Historian Laurence Rees argues that it was possible to hate Jews in the abstract 'and yet care for an individual Jew in the flesh'. There are several examples of committed Nazis who lived this contradiction. 'I had relatives who were Jews, and we would meet at family gatherings,' storm trooper Bruno Hahnel told Rees. 'I had a very warm relationship with two cousins who were Jewish.'[11] More startling was the discovery, revealed by author Oliver Hilmes in his book *Berlin 1936*, that the biological father of Magda Goebbels was Jewish. An entry in Josef Goebbels' diary from 1934 suggests that his wife had discovered something 'shocking' about her past. When Magda was seven years old, her mother had an affair with Richard Friedlander, a Jewish merchant who she would later marry. Although not named on the birth certificate, Hilmes revealed that Friedlander was not only Magda's natural father but was also arrested in 1938 and sent to Buchenwald concentration camp, where he died a year later.

David Bowie never made the film about Goebbels. Nevertheless, his unrelenting infatuation with Nazism followed him across Europe. Incidents in London, Berlin and at the Russia–Poland border border provoked national headlines and, subsequently, blighted the reputation of one of rock 'n' roll's most venerated stars. Visiting Moscow on a transit visa in April 1976 with friend and musician Iggy Pop, Bowie saw similarities between modern-day communism and fascism in thirties Germany. 'They marched like them. They saluted like them. Both had centralised governments.' Stopping the pair on the return journey, KGB officers stumbled upon a collection of Nazi ephemera belonging to Bowie. Confiscating the items, he was strip-searched.

Released without charge, Bowie journeyed to West Berlin dressed in a long black trench coat. Crossing Checkpoint Charlie in a chauffeur-driven Mercedes, he posed behind an East German soldier for the benefit of photographer Andrew Kent. Next, Bowie visited Hitler's wartime bunker where he saluted with a stiffened right arm. Allegedly, he made Kent promise never to make the image public. He honoured the agreement. 'I don't remember David ever talking about fascism,' Kent says, quizzed about Bowie's Third Reich fascination. 'I'm Jewish. I never felt uncomfortable with him in any way.'

If at this point Bowie's attraction to Nazism appears shocking, it represents only a fraction of what lay ahead. In interviews, Bowie advanced newly developed theories. One day he was telling reporters he thought the swastika was the most powerful symbol in political history and marvelling how an 'Eastern symbol of the sun' had been appropriated to 'became a symbol of the dark'. The next he was telling a press conference in Stockholm that he was 'the only alternative for the premier in England. I believe Britain could benefit from a fascist leader,' he speculated. 'After all, fascism is really nationalism.' Next Bowie cast himself as a 'future Hitler' and staged his live shows with a bank of white lights dramatically set against a black backdrop. The spectacle conjured a Nuremburg rally. At its centre, Bowie bathed in the afterglow of Albert Speer's Cathedral of Lights.

On 2 May 1976, Bowie again hit the headlines. Returning to England for the first time in two years, the singer arrived at Victoria Station and greeted a horde of expectant fans in an open-top Mercedes-Benz 600, formerly owned by a recently assassinated South American dictator. Standing tall in the back of the limousine, with slicked-back hair and fascistic black attire, Bowie waved to a jubilant crowd. The mode of transport, the clothing and his physical demeanour suggested Bowie play-acting a version of Adolf Hitler. The media pounced. The *Daily Mail* reported Bowie saluting the crowd. The *NME* ran an image of Bowie with an extended right arm and the unforgiving strapline, 'Heil and Farewell'.

'That photograph caused an awful lot of trouble,' says photographer Chalkie Davies.

> The whole thing lasted about thirty seconds. I managed to grab two frames, but, sadly, when I saw the negatives, I realised my image was a little blurry and Bowie's hand had been reduced to a mere sliver. The *NME* needed the picture first thing Monday morning but after I'd sent it, the re-touchers drew a hand onto his arm. When the image appeared in that week's edition, he appeared to have raised his hand in salute. Given the headline – 'Heil and Farewell' – and the copy used a quote about fascism it inflamed the situation. And then the whole thing was blown out of all proportion.

> 'Stormtrooper vibe' – *Sounds*
> 'More Nazi than futuristic' – *Guardian*
> 'Echoes of his recent controversial comments about fascist rule in Britain' – *Melody Maker*

Seventeen-year-old Gary Numan (on the cusp of pop stardom and, in no small measure, indebted to the style of his idol) was in the crowd and adamant Bowie innocently gestured. 'If a photographer takes a whole motor-driven film of someone doing a wave you will get a Nazi salute at the end. I'd be amazed if he did a Nazi salute. I didn't see anyone walking around saying, "What a wanker, he did a Nazi salute." No one. People just thought he was waving at them, and I'm sure he was.'[12]

In Britain to perform a sold-out six-night residency at the Wembley Empire Pool, Bowie told *Daily Express* correspondent Jean Rook, 'I'm astounded anyone could believe it. I have to keep reading it to believe it myself. I don't stand up in cars waving to people because I think I'm Hitler. I stand up in cars waving to fans – I don't write the captions under the picture. It upsets me. Strong I may be. Arrogant I may be. Sinister I'm not. What I am doing is theatre.'

So, Bowie marched on.

Five months later, he reiterated the idea that Britain was 'ready for a new Hitler'.[13] Outraged, the Musicians Union (MU) called for Bowie's expulsion. 'This branch deplores the publicity recently given to the activities and Nazi style gimmickry of a certain artiste and his idea that this country needs a right-wing dictatorship,' blasted Cornelius Cardew, branch executive member of the MU. 'Such ideas prepare the way for political situations in which the Trade Union movement can be destroyed, as it was in Nazi Germany.'

A vote resulted in a 12–12 tie. Cardew made a second impassioned speech, arguing that 'when a musician declares that he is "very interested in fascism" and that "Britain could benefit from a fascist leader" he or she is influencing public opinion through the massive audiences of young people that such pop stars have access to.'

The motion passed: 15 to 2.[14]

To curb a swelling backlash, Bowie attempted to set the record straight. 'What I said was Britain was ready for another Hitler, which is quite a different thing to saying it needs another Hitler.' Then, claiming he was closer to communism than fascism, Bowie made a startling revelation. 'Besides,' he informed *Record Mirror*, 'I'm half-Jewish.' It transpired that Bowie's older half-brother, Terry Burns, was the child of a relationship between his mother and the son of a Jewish furrier, Jack Rosenberg. 'But I stand by that opinion,' Bowie continued. 'In fact, I was ahead of my time in voicing it. There are in Britain right now parallels with the rise of the Nazi Party in pre-war Germany. A demoralised nation whose empire had disintegrated. The trouble lies with the fact that now they're beginning to realise it's disintegrated. They're losing their dignity, which is dangerous. All the National Front needs right now is a leader. One will come along . . .'[15]

Incendiary comments such as this came as anti-fascists took to the streets to defend Britain from a growing rise in nationalism. Bowie relocated to Berlin, to record new material in a former ball-room used by the *Reichsmusikkammer* (Reich Music Chamber) for propaganda concerts and SS dance evenings (until partly destroyed by Allied bombing in 1943). This was Hansa Studios, overlooking the Wall. Where his name was graffitied on the brickwork, the last two letters of Bowie twisted into the shape of a swastika.

Settling into Berlin, Bowie submerged himself in an unsettling world of past and present. He championed the novels of Christopher Isherwood – *Mr Norris Changes Trains* and *Goodbye to Berlin*, the inspiration for *Cabaret* – and rented an apartment in Schöneberg, once home to the author. Writing 'China Girl' with Iggy Pop, Bowie spoke of 'visions of swastikas' and 'plans for everyone'. He recorded 'V2 Schneider' as a tribute to Kraftwerk's Florian Schneider and the prefix taken from the German long-range rockets used to attack London in 1944–5. 'I think there are two bands who now come close to a neo-Nazi kind of thing: Roxy Music and Kraftwerk,' Bowie opined to *Circus* magazine in April 1976. 'It's not Nazism so much as nationalism. I think it may be too clichéd to use the Nazi thing; it's more nationalistic.' [16]

In England, vilification of Bowie reached breaking point. Did he salute at Victoria Station or not? Bowie protested.

That didn't happen. THAT DID NOT HAPPEN. I waved. I just WAVED. Believe me. On the life of my child, I waved. And the bastard caught me. In MID-WAVE, man. And, God, did that

photo get some coverage . . . As if I'd be foolish enough to pull a
stunt like that. I died when I saw the photo. And even the people
who were with me said, 'David! How could you?' The bastards.
I didn't . . . GOD, I just don't believe in all that.

Impassioned explanation: yes. Satisfactory defence: no. Moreover it
came an incredible sixteen months after the event. As speculation
festered, Bowie was cast in the West German-produced film *Just
a Gigolo*. He played a young aristocratic Prussian officer who, on
returning to Weimar Germany after the Great War, finds work
in a brothel. Co-starring Marlene Dietrich in her last film role,
Bowie's character becomes embroiled in Berlin's underworld until
he's murdered in street-battle crossfire between Nazis and Communists. Punk fanzine *Ripped & Torn* published a photograph of
Bowie handsomely attired in tuxedo and bow tie and the cutting
comment, 'You could have been so CLASSY . . . why did you have
to be so NAZI?'

In 1981, the National Front claimed Bowie as one of their own. 'It
was Bowie who horrified the music establishment in the mid-seventies with his favourable comments about the NF,' Joe Pearce,
editor of *Bulldog*, the party's youth magazine, gloated. 'Bowie, who,
on the album *Hunky Dory*, started the anti-Communist musical
tradition which we now see flourishing amidst the new wave of
Futurist bands.' In fact, Bowie told an American interviewer in
1978 that the National Front was not Britain's remedy, rather, 'it's
an answer to an idiot's dream' and that the Thin White Duke had
been a theatrical device 'to show what could happen . . . which
unfortunately backfired'.

A fuller explanation came in 1993 when Bowie finally addressed
his past fascination with Nazism in an interview with *Arena*. 'It
was this Arthurian need. This search for a mythological link with
God,' he said, referring to a pre-war Nazi delegation that travelled
to Glastonbury Tor in search of the Holy Grail. 'But somewhere
along the line, it was perverted by what I was reading and what
I was drawn to. And it was nobody's fault but my own. I was just

looking for some answers. Some secret. Some life force. I had this religious fervour. I didn't even think about what they had done.'

In the same year, Bowie elaborated on his explanation during an interview with Brett Anderson of Suede for a feature in *NME*. 'I wasn't actually flirting with fascism per se,' Bowie said.

> I was up to the neck in magic which was a really horrendous period. All my reading in that particular time were people like Ishmael Regarde, Waite and Mavers and Manley [*sic*] and all these sort of warlocks. It was all the secrets of the cabbalistic practices, an intense period of trying to relate myself to this search for some true spirit. The irony is that I really didn't see any political implications in my interest in Nazis. My interest in them was the fact that they supposedly came to England before the war to find the Holy Grail at Glastonbury and this whole Arthurian thought was running through my mind. The idea that it was about putting Jews in concentration camps and the complete oppression of different races completely evaded my extraordinarily fucked up nature at that particular time. But, of course, it came home to me very clearly and crystalline when I came back to England.[17]

By then a father to Duncan (born in 1971, formerly known as Zowie and then Joe), Bowie expressed his past folly from the point of view of a concerned parent.

> I didn't feel the rise of the neo-Nazis until just before I moved out [of Germany in 1979], and then it started to get quite nasty. They were very vocal, very visible. They used to wear these long green coats, crew cuts and march along the streets in Dr Martens. You just crossed the street when you saw them coming. Just before I left, the coffee bar below my apartment was smashed up by Nazis and the people were pulled out and beaten up. I went down there, and they were quite distressed. I think I gave them something for their window. And I thought – this is not a place for Joe to be growing up. This could get worse.[18]

Bowie's prediction was alarmingly accurate. His analysis that the social and political problems facing Britain in the mid-seventies paralleled Nazi Germany – a dictatorship where freedom of speech and individual right to expression was brutally suppressed and banned; and Jews stripped of their citizenship, ghettoised, starved and, from 1942, physically liquidated – may have been exaggerated. But what lay ahead was an incredible era in British history which would drive a deep wedge between those advocating to 'Keep Britain White' and a resistance movement unprecedented in cultural scale.

Rivers of Blood

ERIC CLAPTON. ROCK AGAINST RACISM. ANTI-NAZI LEAGUE

In 1976, the newly established Rock Against Racism and, a year later, the Anti-Nazi League garnered huge nationwide support opposing fascist activity and challenging racist rhetoric. Both organisations achieved extraordinary levels of success, promoting hundreds of gigs up and down the country and creating a political newspaper to progress multiculturalism. Tens of thousands of supporters attended celebratory Carnivals Against Nazism in London, Manchester, Leeds and Edinburgh dedicated to rejecting far-right politics. Yet, for all its good intentions and immense achievements, Rock Against Racism did little to address anti-Semitism. Significantly, the movement, which united behind slogans such as 'The National Front is a Nazi Front' and 'Love Music Hate Racism', viewed nationalism, and the use of the swastika, as a threat to Britain's Black population, not minority Jewish communities. Hereafter, the swastika's representation in pop music transitioned from symbolising Nazi Germany to embodying broader political ideologies such as fascism, white supremacy and anti-immigrant sentiments.

In April 1968, opposition minister Enoch Powell delivered a fervent speech at a Conservative Association meeting in Birmingham in favour of voluntary repatriation of 'Commonwealth immigrants'. In front of an ATV television feed – later shown on national news bulletins coupled with advance copies of the speech provided to newspapers, ensuring maximum media coverage – Powell quoted a local constituent and predicted 'in fifteen or twenty years' time the black man will have the whip hand over the white man'. The explosive rhetoric cost Powell his place in Ted Heath's shadow cabinet. But in pop music's world of privilege and excess, the overt racism suddenly made him a cause célèbre. 'I think Enoch is the man,' Rod Stewart told the *International Times* in 1970. 'I'm all for him. This country is overcrowded. The immigrants should be sent home. That's it.'[1]

Stewart's comments came amid escalating racial tensions, as clashes between Black youths and police erupted across the country, particularly in Notting Hill and later in Liverpool's Toxteth district. At the same time, the BBC comedy *Till Death Us Do Part* fuelled controversy, with the character Alf Garnett openly expressing prejudiced views on immigrants. This sentiment contributed to a growing backlash against Commonwealth citizens arriving from Uganda, following their expulsion by President Idi Amin in August 1972. Then, on 5 August 1976, at a concert at the Birmingham Odeon, just metres from the Midland Hotel where Powell had made his incendiary observations eight years earlier, Eric Clapton delivered inflammatory comments aimed at non-white people in the auditorium.

'Do we have any foreigners in the audience tonight?' the exalted rock star enquired. 'If so, please put up your hands. Wogs, I mean, I'm looking at you. Where are you?' Target identified, Clapton unleashed a stream of racist bile at 'fucking foreigners' and told them to leave. 'Not just the hall,' he clarified, 'leave our country. I don't want you here, in the room or in my country.' Inebriated, and warming to the intoxicating theme, Clapton persisted, 'Vote for Enoch Powell' and 'stop Britain from becoming a black colony. Get the foreigners out! Get the wogs out! Get the coons out! Keep Britain white! I used to be into dope. Now I'm into racism.'

Eric Clapton's status as one of his generation's finest blues guitarists was firmly established by 1966 when he founded Cream. Not long after, in an *NME* interview, he casually revealed an Iron Cross tucked discreetly inside his shirt. When asked about the renewed fascination with Nazi symbols, the twenty-one-year-old musician commented, 'I don't know why there is a sudden interest in the Nazi uniforms or decorations. I wear this simply because I think the design is great.' Interjecting, Ginger Baker, the band's drummer, added, 'I've got an SS officer's cap. I think it's a good thing to wear these things. It makes a few people remember there was a war – it's not a thing to forget or let happen again.'* Perhaps recognising the unlikelihood of people forgetting a world war, bass player Jack Bruce pondered the possibility of 'the more fanatically interested' having 'the kind of fascination for Nazi items in the same way people have a fascination for horror comics!'[2]

The music archives are full of rock stars pontificating on the themes of Nazism, with such remarks often overlooked or downplayed by the press. Just months before Cream's guileless comments, journalist Keith Altham had reported on the Lovin' Spoonful's trip to the UK to celebrate their hit single 'Daydream'. During the visit, bassist Steve Boone, described as the band's 'long, slender' member, casually revealed his proclivity for wearing a German Iron Cross around his neck, explaining, 'I won it for being the first one up the Navarone pass –" killed three of 'em" and also bragged about being descended from Daniel Boone, the Wild West scout.'[3]

Time and again, journalists would either laugh off or overlook such comments, seemingly in an effort to gain favour or access to the inner circle of fame. At the height of the Clapton controversy, music writer Barbara Charone took a sympathetic approach, attributing the racist outburst to an emotional reaction to something 'someone said, something that triggered off an unexpected part of Clapton's rowdier personality'. 'Maybe it was the drink,' Charone mused in Sounds in October 1976, 'maybe it was just a bad day. But it was so human and typically Eric. How many times have you gotten a bit drunk and spouted out great truths and philosophies only to later blush the next morning?' Similarly, Harry Shapiro, author of Clapton's 1992 biography, Lost in the Blues, passed off the notorious 'Birmingham speech' as a mere 'faux pas' coinciding with 'statements by rock's other chameleon, David Bowie, during his

---

* In his memoir, Hellraiser: The Autobiography of The World's Greatest Drummer, Baker wrote: 'One day I wore a T-shirt with a swastika on it. This did cause some offence, but I explained: "Look, we won the war and so we're entitled to wear the flag of the enemy".'

Berlin days, to the effect that what Britain needed was a good dose of fascism.' He continues, 'Alarmed at such rantings from influential public figures, a left-wing group called Rock Against Racism was formed which held concerts and rallies throughout the Seventies.'[4]

In the years since, Clapton has never apologised. Immediately after the incident, he protested that the 'publicity surrounding the controversy tended to overshadow what was a fine tour. I thought it was quite funny actually,' said the musician who would be inducted into the Rock and Roll Hall of Fame and honoured as Commander of the Order of the British Empire (CBE) for services to music. Confessing to little knowledge of politics or whether Enoch Powell would be 'good or bad' in power, Clapton continued,

> I just don't know what came over me that night. It must have been something that happened in the day, but it came out in this garbled thing. I thought the whole thing was like Monty Python. There's this rock group playing onstage, and the singer starts talking about politics. It's so stupid. Those people who paid their money sitting listening to this madman dribbling on and the band meanwhile getting fidgety thinking 'oh dear'.

Two years later, in 1978, Clapton hit the front pages again when he declared Enoch Powell a prophet. In 2004, he said that the former minister was 'outrageously brave', and his 'feeling about this has not changed'. Yet, in the same year, Clapton told *Scotland on Sunday*, 'There's no way I could be a racist. It would make no sense.' Is it possible that a person – Clapton – can enjoy the company of Black people, listen to music made by Black musicians, and still be racist? Perhaps a racist can readily embrace culture created by non-white musicians but not welcome Black people, for example, living on their street as neighbours. 'I had never really understood or been directly affected by racial conflict,' Clapton wrote in his autobiography, '. . . when I listened to music, I was disinterested in where the players came from or what colour their skin was. Interesting, then, that ten years later, I would be labelled a racist . . . Since then, I have learnt to keep my opinions to myself. Of course, it might also have had something to do with the fact that Pattie [Clapton's former wife]* had just been leered at by a member of the Saudi royal family.'

Keeping 'opinions' to himself hardly reflects someone genuinely trying to apologise or distancing themselves from accusations of racism. During an interview for the high-profile documentary series the *South Bank Show*, Clapton even denied that Enoch Powell's views could be considered racist. A year later, in 2018, speaking on BBC Radio 4, Clapton acknowledged that he had used derogatory terms like 'wogs' and 'coons' onstage. And, while he described the outburst as despicable, he still insisted it was 'funny'.

In the absence of a clear apology, Clapton's subdued remorse reflects a broader culture within the music industry and the media. While rock star misbehaviour is sometimes challenged, it is rarely held truly accountable. On one hand, take Morrissey, former frontman of the Smiths, whose public comments are considered by many as racist, and is now a pariah in quarters of the industry. Conversely, despite allegations of paedophilia dating back to the 1990s, Michael Jackson kept the support of the music industry, his label and the media until his death in 2009. When society fails to call out abuse, whether it's committed by high-profile figures or the public, or when it divorces an artist's actions from their artistry, abuse will persist.

In August 1976, left-wing activist Red Saunders read about Eric Clapton's Birmingham outburst and wrote a letter of condemnation circulated to the music press and *Socialist Worker*. 'Come on Eric,' Saunders' despatch began,

> you've been taking too much of that *Daily Express* stuff, and you know you can't handle it. Own up. Half your music is black. You're rock music's biggest colonist. You're a good musician but

---

* In an interview with the *Sunday Times* in 1999, Clapton confessed to raping and abusing Pattie Boyd while they were married and that he was a 'full-blown' alcoholic who felt entitled to sex.

where would you be without the blues and R&B? You've got to fight the racist poison otherwise you degenerate into the sewer with the rats and all the money men who ripped off rock culture with their cheque books and plastic crap. We want to organise a rank-and-file movement against the racist poison in music. We urge support for Rock Against Racism. PS: Who shot the Sheriff, Eric? It sure as hell wasn't you!

Printed in *Sounds*, Saunders' letter – and pointed reference to Clapton's recent transatlantic success with Bob Marley's 'I Shot The Sheriff' – provoked an incredible response. Messages of support for the formation of Rock Against Racism arrived in droves from all quarters of the country. Acting quickly, Saunders formed an ad-hoc committee and soon established a national campaign focused on live concerts featuring punk (white musicians) and reggae (Black musicians). At the end of each event, members of both bands came together onstage to jam. The message was a visual statement: 'Black and white unite!'

In Rock Against Racism's accompanying agitprop newspaper, *Temporary Hoarding*, the communication was didactic: 'LOVE MUSIC HATE RACISM'. Unfolding the broadsheet revealed a monochrome poster of David Bowie in profile alongside Adolf Hitler and Enoch Powell. 'Only one thing could have stopped our movement,' the accompanying text quoted, 'if our adversaries had understood its principles and from the first day had smashed with the utmost brutality, the nucleus of our movement. Adolf Hitler, 1933.' Overleaf, the copy continued, 'So Bowie discovers Hitler and Clapton urges support for Powell. "Superstars" open their mouths and out comes fascist and racist garbage. Pathetic cover-ups do not alter the fact that they give credence to the ideas of the sewer and make heroes of rats.'

Under the Nazi regime, many minorities including the roughly 230,000 African Germans endured immense suffering. Hitler firmly believed that these 'Rhineland bastards' were of no value. He demonised 'African Negroes' as 'bestial' and 'born half-apes', accusing them of raping 'our women and children' in a vision of an Aryan world 'of human beauty and nobility. Systematically these Negroid parasites in our national body,' he wrote, 'corrupt our innocent fair-haired girls and thus destroy something which can no longer be replaced in this world . . . a world with Negroids and all hopes of an idealised future for our humanity would be lost forever.' From this distorted viewpoint of genealogical purity, Hitler claimed that the mixing of Germans with 'Jews and Negroids' would 'infect' the white race, polluting it with 'the blood of an inferior stock', ultimately destroying the very foundation of the Third Reich's existence.

In contrast, Hitler blamed the Jews alone for Germany's downfall. In both volumes of *Mein Kampf* – 'Reckoning' and 'National Socialist Movement' – he accused world Jewry, along with its illusory ties to Marxism, of ruining the country by controlling education, economics, politics, culture, the media, and contaminating German blood. Interestingly, this distorted world view did not extend to Black people; in fact, Hitler barely mentioned them. But let it be clear: bigotry is not a competition of hatred, judged on word count or lives lost. The loss of any human life in a 'race war' is equally abhorrent. However, despite the swastika representing 'a war against European Jewry', Rock Against Racism identified neo-Nazi activity not by rising anti-Semitism, but by its discrimination against Black people.

'Our job was to peel away the Union Jack,' Red Saunders declared, 'to reveal the swastika.' But beyond a studied exposition of politics and cultural observation in the first issue of *Temporary Hoarding* – tracing a history of immigration to include French Protestants, Irish construction workers, and from the 1880s until 1939, Jews settling in the UK, fleeing brutality in Eastern Europe and becoming victims of racism in London and elsewhere – the history is marginal. Henceforth, the history of Jewish persecution or ongoing anti-Semitism is absent in Rock Against Racism literature, despite repeated historical references to Hitler and Nazism.

In the Carnival edition of *Temporary Hoarding*, a graphic feature titled 'How Did Race-Hate Happen?' invited readers to reflect on a twenty-five-page chronology of prejudice towards threatened minority groups spanning from 1950 to 1978 ranging from Commonwealth citizens arriving in Britain, through race riots, the emergence of the National Front, the battle for independence in Zimbabwe, to Apartheid in South Africa. Moreover, Rock Against Racism campaigned against SUS laws (empowering the police to arrest any reputed offender or suspected person found loitering with intent to commit an arrestable offence), repression in Ireland, and pushed for the registration of bouncers to curb violence at concerts. It launched Rock Against Sexism. It held benefit gigs deploring police oppression against Asians. It held marches against anti-abortion Acts of Parliament and offered solidarity with the Campaign for Nuclear Disarmament. But it did not condemn violence against Jews in modern Britain.

Lucy Whitman, previously known by her punk pseudonym Lucy Toothpaste and an original member of the Rock Against Racism committee, expresses concern over the lack of literature addressing anti-Semitism despite the significant contribution of the movement.

> It is surprising that we did not write about the Holocaust or anti-Semitism. It had not occurred to me before. Many Jewish anti-fascists involved themselves with RAR but none of the founding or core members of the committee was Jewish. We did try to alert *Temporary Hoarding* readers to the dangers of fascism but the connection with anti-Semitism was never spelled out. We did some great stuff, but we weren't perfect. It's interesting to reflect on our weaknesses as well as our strengths. Maybe we took it for granted that the National Front was anti-Semitic, and it did not need spelling out or explained historically as we did with race-hate. But nothing satisfactorily explains it.

Whitman's admirable admission of Rock Against Racism's failings extends to not recognising anti-Semitism as racism and that anti-Jewish prejudice was not a topic of popular song. Moreover, she contemplates the notion that the fight against anti-Semitism did not seem as 'cool' as the fight against anti-Black racism. 'RAR deliberately set out to educate young people about racism and fascism through the medium of popular culture,' Whitman adds, 'and yet we did not feel the need to teach them about the Holocaust or the longer history of anti-Semitism. Nowadays, schoolchildren in Britain learn about the Holocaust but that wasn't the case in the seventies. We read the *Diary of Anne Frank* but that was it. We had to educate ourselves and each other about the horrors of concentration camps and the battles on the streets of Britain between Mosley's Blackshirts and the anti-fascist campaigners of the 1930s.'

Whitman's acute observations and the emphasis she places on context is critical in reaching an understanding of the period. On 22 August 1979, the *Guardian* reported that young kids in Liverpool, incited by the British Movement, daubed Nazi swastikas on a gravestone and left the head of a pig in a Jewish cemetery. In October, *Leveller* magazine spoke out against fascist gangs infiltrating gigs and called for venues to refuse entry to people wearing NF or British Movement badges* and called for a bar on those inciting 'racist or anti-Semitic violence' and 'the banning of obnoxious literature and those who intimidate the audience with fascist saluting'. In issue number 4 of *Temporary Hoarding*, one correspondent, Gary Glickman from Cheshire, called for immediate action.

'Dear Sir,' he wrote, 'being a Jew I was very glad to hear about the movement "Rock Against Racism". I went to the Clash gig in Manchester and was very disturbed by the number of people wearing swastikas and talking about fascism. Please could you send me a news sheet/badge/poster/sticker and info about the movement. Yours, a Jewish punk. Keep on Rockin.' The next edition of *Temporary Hoarding* (spring '78) featured an interview with the fast-talking 'Bard of Salford', John Cooper Clarke, who recalled a gig at the Vortex, London. 'They hated me,' he said. 'I had to get a member of the audience into a headlock! They must all be "People"

---

* The leader of the British Movement, Colin Jordan, envisaged a new flag combing Nazi insignia and the Union Jack. 'I said let it be a red, white and blue swastika not a black one.'

readers. One lad had swastikas tattooed on his cheek! The place was full of bums. It upset me for at least TEN MINUTES!' Asked whether the 'NF types' and 'anti-Nazi ideas' referenced in his poetry are the main enemy, Cooper responded, 'No, but they're the most immediate. But I try to reach people through their humour – not purely politics. Racism never owed anyone a living. They are set stereotypes which rely on existing prejudices. But I think people have a built-in laughter mechanism. If you touch that you're away.'

The dramatic rise of the National Front in the late seventies encouraged a renewed wave of aggressive and violent confrontation aimed at racial minorities. Established in 1967 as an overtly racist organisation, the National Front called for an 'all-white Britain' and the repatriation of 'foreigners'. Its leaders aligned themselves with Nazi ideology. 'Hitler put Germany on its feet,' Martin Webster (a former member of the National Socialist Movement) told the *People* in 1962. 'We and fellow Nazis will do the same for England. We are building a well-oiled Nazi machine in this country.' Three years later, Webster added, 'Adolf Hitler showed the way to a proper, fair and final solution to the Jewish question.'

Dedicated to building a British neo-Nazi organisation, John Tyndall participated in paramilitary activities. When arrested and brought to court, the chairman of the National Front refused to swear an oath on the Bible, instead declaring, '*Mein Kampf* is my doctrine.'

The National Front was committed to fielding a candidate in every constituency during the next general election. They saw a rise in electoral support and secured notable gains in both local and by-elections, at times outperforming both Labour and the Liberal Party.

Writing in the punk magazine *ZigZag*, in September 1977 – to kids 'looking for a riot, a riot of your own' – Tony Parsons foresaw the National Front banning 'all music with black origins from the airwaves and replacing the "jungle music", as they put it, with Great British military marching music . . . They honestly believe blacks, Jews, browns, name it, to be on the level of animals,'

Parsons raged. 'They carry Union Jacks and Klu Klux Clutz [*sic*] banners and, their favourite of all, swastikas.' Parsons then quoted John Tyndall from a recently published interview in the *Sunday Telegraph;* 'The main idea of wearing the uniform is that some of us felt we needed to capture the imagination of youth. We wanted glamour and excitement.'

When the Anti-Nazi League (ANL) formed in late 1977, its founding statement read, 'For the first time since Mosley in the thirties there is the worrying prospect of a Nazi party gaining significant support in Britain. Like Hitler with the Jews, the British Nazis seek to make scapegoats of black people.' The ANL promised a campaign on a 'national and massive scale', distributing leaflets and posters in the millions. Notably, once again, little of the literature addressed anti-Semitism.

So why the title Anti-Nazi League?

'There was a tradition in British Labour history of anti-leagues, and we wanted to make it straightforward and use the pejorative title "Nazi" to pin the description on them from the beginning,' explains founding member Paul Holborow. 'The National Front was a Nazi party. Within their ranks, they had people who denied the Holocaust, who followed *Mein Kampf,* and their leaders were photographed in Nazi uniform. The essential point is that there was an umbilical connection between Martin Webster, John Tyndall and their forbearing Nazi predecessors. Webster was a highly effective organiser and dragged the National Front from their openly Nazi origins to making a serious electoral challenge.'

Members of the Anti-Nazi League received a yellow card that featured a poem written by Lutheran pastor Martin Niemöller. Having embraced the anti-Semitic doctrines of the Nazi Party in the 1920s, Niemöller became an outspoken critic of the Third Reich after Hitler rose to power in 1933. Arrested four years later – after what Albert Speer described as 'a rebellious sermon in Dahlem' and provoking Hitler into 'a fit of rage'[5] – Niemöller was charged with conducting activities against the state. Released seven months later, he was immediately rearrested by the Gestapo and interned at Sachsenhausen and then Dachau concentration camps. Liberated in 1945, Niemöller's post-war poem, 'First They Came' encouraged German citizens to take responsibility for their complicity in the Holocaust.

> First they came for the Jews
> and I did not speak out –
> because I was not a Jew
> Then they came for the Communists
> and I did not speak out –
> because I was not a Communist
> Next they came for the trade unionists
> and I did not speak out –
> because I was not a trade unionist
> Then they came for me –
> and there was no one left
> to speak out for me

Despite support from MPs, actors, writers, musicians, sports personalities and trade unionists, the Anti-Nazi League – formed by members of the Socialist Workers Party – upheld an aggressive anti-Zionist stance. 'We are as likely to support the National Front as the Anti-Nazi League,' the chair of the Board of Deputies of British Jews told ANL research director Nigel Harris.[6] 'Yes, I'm an anti-Zionist,' concurs Paul Holborow, 'but what unites us is opposition to the Nazis.' According to founding member Peter Hain, after heated deliberation Jewish communities 'came on-board . . . but there was a certain reserve.'

Forming a cultural alliance with Rock Against Racism, the Anti-Nazi League offered political and financial support. At the Carnival Against Racism on 30 April 1978, an estimated 80,000 people marched seven miles from Trafalgar Square to Victoria Park in east London to enjoy a day of reggae and punk from the likes of X-Ray Spex, Steel Pulse, the Clash and the Tom Robinson Band. Blowing whistles and waving banners, marchers held aloft giant papier-mâché casts of Adolf Hitler and John Tyndall. The carnival celebrated a year of successful counter-demonstrations, outnumbering the National Front with anti-fascist support.

Protest marches habitually descended into ugly, violent battles, for example in Wood Green and Lewisham (1977), and Birmingham and Manchester (1978). Protected by uniformed police, often out-numbering the protesters, the National Front nevertheless increased their vote at the ballot box It prompted the leader of the opposition Margaret Thatcher to speak out on national television. 'People are really rather afraid that this country might be rather swamped by people with a different culture,' she said during a *World in Action* interview intended to woo right-wing sympathisers to the Conservative Party. 'The British character has done so much for democracy, for law and done so much throughout the world that if there is any fear that it might be swamped, people are going to react and be rather hostile to those coming in.'

Here was the dividing line of British politics: the fear of immigrants versus a new Britain embracing multiculturalism. The argument raged in Parliament, the media and on the streets, where neo-Nazis fought against anti-racist forces. The cultural mood of the country shifted. The playful use of comedy to satirise the Third Reich that defined the 1960s and early-to-mid 1970s abruptly halted, replaced by a nihilistic, anarchic brigade of agitators and musicians intent on destroying the old order. Reclaiming England for a new generation. This was the end of respect: for the country's forebears, for the old ways, for the past, for everything antiquated. A New Order emerged, unscripted and unrehearsed, violently wrenching at the chains of the establishment.

This was punk rock.

2.

ROCK AND ROLL GAS CHAMBER

Adolf Hitler addressing a crowd of 15,000 party faithful at the Berlin Sportpalast, 26 September 1938.

Too Fast to Live Too Young to Die

MALCOLM McLAREN. SEX PISTOLS

The story of punk and the swastika begins with Malcolm McLaren. A Jewish trader who tried to reshape British culture to a twisted view and, for a brief bright brilliant moment, succeeded. Born 22 January 1946 to Martin Levi (later Edwards) and Emily Isaacs, the daughter of a tailor, Malcolm was raised into religion. Music writer Peter Simmons, better known as Penny Reel, described McLaren's early stomping ground, north London's Stoke Newington and Stamford Hill, as a 'Jewish playground' populated by 'working-class rough Jews; sporting men, gamblers, card-players, kalouki-players, boxing men, football men, the Schmuter-trade people, the rag-trade people. They were kind of comedy Jews really, the parents' generation spoke Yiddish, and the grandparents' generation spoke Polish and token Yiddish.'[1]

At thirteen McLaren was bar mitzvah-attired in a 'sharp double-breasted suit especially cut for him by his grandfather'.[2] Around the same time, his family moved to Hendon, a leafy, predominantly Jewish suburb in north-west London. He attended Avigdor, a private Jewish school, but felt increasingly disconnected and alienated – adrift in an unstable home life and searching for his own identity. His rebellion led him through a revolving door of art schools – Saint Martins, Harrow, Chelsea, Walthamstow and Croydon. 'I had a different cause in life,' McLaren later mused. 'Not a career, but an adventure.'[3]

In 1972, aged twenty-six, he married Jocelyn Hakim, a French-Turkish Jew, to secure her British citizenship in exchange for £50.[4] A year later, in partnership with a former schoolteacher,

Vivienne Westwood, McLaren opened Too Fast To Live, Too Young
To Die (formerly known as Let It Rock),* a designer clothes shop
on the outer edge of Chelsea's fashionable King's Road. It housed
Nazi memorabilia. 'Malcolm was in awe of the symbolism,' says
shop assistant and punk icon Jordan (born Pamela Rooke).

> Not just the swastika, but a lot of artefacts from the era that were
> extremely beautifully made. The Nazi Youth badges. They were
> extremely rare – I had one, an original enamelled Nazi Youth
> badge. A triangle split up with the swastika in the middle – a
> lot of rings, including gold SS wedding rings, which weren't
> for sale because they were originals. There were a few things
> for sale: mock-ups from the regalia shops,† the straight wing
> badges, swastika hankies.[5]

In 1974, McLaren and Westwood gained international exposure by
designing swastika-branded clothing for Ken Russell's film *Mahler*.
Based on the life of Gustav Mahler, actor Antonia Ellis (as Cosima
Wagner) displayed a studded glittery swastika across the back of
her Valkyrie dominatrix leather suit, a detail McLaren's biographer described as 'eye-popping'. 'We worked on this huge German
Catholic creature with a Nazi helmet,' McLaren said of the film's
climactic dream sequence when the Jewish composer confronts his
Aryan inner self. 'We used a "Dominator" bike-tyre T-shirt, and
the skirt was very short, in leather, and had a zip right down the
front of it. Either side of that we had this huge Jesus cross in brass
studs. This was right down the centre of the crotch and then on the
back was this huge swastika in brass studs.'[6] Matched with a Nazi

---

* On 2 May 1974, McLaren wrote to Roberta Bayley sharing news of a song he
had written called 'Too Fast To Live Too Young To Die'. 'I have the idea of the
singer looking like Hitler using those gestures, arm shapes etc and talking about
his Mum in incestuous phrases.'
† McLaren bought a Nazi eagle badge from a Portobello Road market stall
selling military regalia and original and imitation Nazi memorabilia run by Tony
Walker, author of *Snides* (2004) and *How to Win a Gunfight* (2007).

helmet, whip and leather boots, costume designer Shirley Russell boasted it gave her husband's film 'the perfect anti-Semitic feeling'.[7]

In 1976, now aged thirty and thirty-five respectively, McLaren and Westwood sold their array of Nazi ephemera to impressionable punks. On the cusp of launching the Sex Pistols and drawing mainstream attention to his newly renamed King's Road shop, SEX, McLaren informed adult magazine *Gallery International*, 'If I take my fantasies to the extreme, it is because extremity is where it's at.'[8]

Here: a Jewish shopkeeper-cum-music impresario dealing in the language and artefacts of Nazism. 'Maybe McLaren thought it was amusing to reduce a symbol of unspeakable evil to a badge worn by silly teenagers,' contemplates Lucy Whitman, 'thus reducing its power to a sort of comic book level.' According to his secretary Sophie Richmond, McLaren viewed the swastika as 'mysteriously subversive rather than explicitly anything'. He was trying to make 'a more general point about leaders which was too subtle for the average National Front-er,' she says, 'or even the average punk.'[9] However, in a diary entry dated November 1976 – within days of the release of the Sex Pistols' debut single 'Anarchy In The UK' – Richmond expressed concern about McLaren's (and artist Jamie Reid's) modus operandi. 'What worries me is fascism,' Richmond wrote of the political limitations of running a rock 'n' roll band. 'That rebellious stance (making kids question) could equally lead rightwards as leftwards.'[10]

One-time manager of the Clash Caroline Coon says, 'I'm terribly suspicious of Jews being anti-Semitic.' Disgusted when the swastika was introduced to punk, Coon damns McLaren for perverting the course of rock 'n' roll and argues that fascism is about sexuality, power and male strength. 'People tried to defuse the horror of the swastika by using it, but that's not how it was worn,' Coon explains.

He was fifteen years older than the kids he was manipulating and managing. He was bringing his perversity, his hateful ways, his destruction, and taking the Pistols in a direction that I don't think innately they wanted to go. When Jews get excited about dead bodies and the trauma of their past as a sexual turn on, that's very suspect. And that was going on, at the King's Road shop in plain view.[11] McLaren had his gimp masks and the whole panoply of sadomasochism. He enjoyed shocking people, crashing sexual boundaries. But when it slips over into the welfare of children . . . it was corruption. Those who admire Malcolm ignore it. It's a perverse sick element that is part of the narrative of punk. He was using young people to express his money-making schemes, his pseudo politics, and his cynical view of life. It was deeply immoral. Malcolm was a monster. He was fulfilling his own desires at the expense of everybody else.

Paul Gorman's *The Life & Times of Malcolm McLaren* (2020) spans 800 pages but barely addresses one of McLaren's most controversial obsessions: the swastika. Beyond fleeting references to a particular T-shirt design or a Nazi armband, Gorman offers no insight into McLaren's fixation. Yet, elsewhere, the book examines his alleged predilection for child pornography. Equally perplexing – perhaps even more disturbing – is the silence from the British media. Not a single review questioned the contradiction between McLaren's Jewish heritage and his appropriation of Nazi imagery.

In a 1996 interview, McLaren discussed 'demystifying' and 'reclaiming' the swastika, asserting that the military understands fashion better than designers like John Galliano. He also argued that style is not just about a uniform – 'looking better than the guy or girl next door' – but embodies fascism, elitism, and serves as a signifier of class. Then pronouncing that the 'Nazis had the best clothes sense', McLaren further contended that their impeccably designed uniforms showed they 'understood more about fashion than any other regime or military' and 'did it better than anyone else', adding pointedly, 'and their icon was the swastika'.

McLaren believed that by beautifying the swastika and pairing it with a range of new colours, they could 'destroy' its negative associations. Moreover, presenting the swastika alongside other iconic images, such as Christ on the cross and the Queen of England, made an anti-fashion statement.

Demystifying, reclaiming and destroying may appear incongruous ambitions. But the resulting 'Destroy' shirt* was McLaren and Westwood's most successful creation. Journalist-cum-author Jon Savage described it as 'an explosion of contradictory, highly charged signs'.[12] Jordan hailed it a 'masterpiece', adding that by incorporating the swastika – 'the most potent symbol of the Second World War', Westwood was 'trying to demystify the icons used by tyrants'.[13] If challenged, Westwood instructed the staff of SEX to counter criticism by saying, 'We're here to positively confront people with the past.'[14]Asked, in 2009, if she regretted the swastika on the shirt, Westwood screamed in response. 'No, I don't! We were just saying to the older generation, "We don't accept your values or your taboos, and you're all fascists."'[15]

When Westwood published her memoir in 2014, there was little explanation about her or McLaren's use of the swastika. Instead, a rather disturbing picture began to appear. First it was revealed that her Paris showrooms on rue du Mail had once been the headquarters of the Gestapo. Then her new collection bore the suggestive label 'VW GOLD LABEL SS' [spring/summer]. Furthermore, as her co-writer Ian Kelly put it, 'the Second World War is the Book of Genesis for modern British culture', with films and stories from that time shaping 'the way Britain thinks about itself'.[16] According to Kelly, 'because no one had quite done leather, danger, death and shock like the Nazis, elements of their iconography crept into Vivienne and Malcolm's designs'.

'Ironically,' Kelly continues, 'it was America and the [New York] Dolls that gave Vivienne and Malcolm their most controversial

---

* White cheesecloth muslin with extended sleeves, strait-jacket clasps and D rings at the end and on the shoulders, which semi-opened and fastened by Velcro tabs. Screen-printed in red and black or yellow and pink, the design showed an inverted crucifixion, a large swastika, an enlarged postage stamp with the decapitated head of the Queen, and the word 'DESTROY' in thick black letters. The bottom corner of the shirt reproduced lyrics from the Sex Pistols' 'Anarchy In The UK': 'I am an anarchist don't know what I want but I know how to get it. I wanna destroy the passer-by. I wanna be anarchy.'

motif: the swastika.' Why? Because according to the band's singer, David Johansen, they had 'doodled the Nazi badge since high school: historically neutered of its power to terrify. It was part of the semiotics of shock for a generation distanced from the realities of the Holocaust.' While Kelly acknowledges that 'for many, the swastika was an emblem too far, still specifically allied to the politics not of freedom but of repression', Westwood offers a different perspective: 'Malcolm wanted to shock – I was worried . . . about the swastika, but Malcolm being Jewish, had his reasons for wanting to do that kind of thing. We weren't only rejecting the values of the older generation; we were rejecting their taboos as well.'[17] Finally, Kelly points out that having 'flirted with the death-cult imagery of the Third Reich,' Westwood looked for 'inspiration in the language of violence as well as its imagery'.[18]

Selling Nazi memorabilia from a small shop in Chelsea was unlikely to attract nationwide controversy. However, that all changed with the arrival of the Sex Pistols. Making their television debut on 4 September 1976, appearing on the north-west network programme *So It Goes*, the show's presenter Tony Wilson warned the audience that the Sex Pistols were 'one of the most reviewed and reviled rock phenomena of recent weeks'. Following a chaotic burst of noise, the group launched into a furious rendition of 'Anarchy In The UK', with singer Johnny Rotten yelling, 'Get off your arse.' Having introduced the performance, at Wilson's request – 'the Sex Pistols are, if possible, even better than the lovely Joni Mitchell' – Jordan now stood at the side of the stage dressed in black trousers, white boots and a pale green shirt adorned with the printed slogan 'DANGEROUSLY CLOSE TO LOVE' and an upturned German eagle clutching a swastika. The addition on her upper sleeve of a red armband communicated militaristic fetishism. The head of Granada Television was incensed. Sidney Bernstein was not only Jewish and the producer of *Night Will Fall*, the Allies' filmed liberation of Nazi concentration camps, but was responsible for banning German-manufactured microphones on the studio floor. During rehearsal, a stand-off between Bernstein and Jordan, who had initially insisted on wearing a swastika armband, threatened the Sex Pistols' live broadcast. Wilson intervened and Jordan agreed to cover the offending symbol with a piece of white paper tape.

It would be the first of many such confrontations.

One night, Jordan ventured into London's West End wearing a swastika armband. Arriving at Club Louise, Caroline, a Jewish DJ confronted her. 'She came up to me looking to punch my lights out talking about the war and Belsen and tattoos on people's arms.' It came 'out of the blue', says Jordan who, unprepared for the degree of hostility, let rip. 'Well, you're making a mystery out of this all over again and another drama, and this is to make people remember it.' 'It made me really mad,' Jordan reflected, 'because I understand if an old man who'd been in a concentration camp or who'd been one of the rare people to survive had come up, but there's this on-going generation after generation of horror at it. It's obvious that I wasn't a Nazi.'[19]

Or was it? In 1976, Jordan presented a fearsome image. Bold make-up, eyes blacked out, blonde beehive, tight leather skirt, heels and a swastika armband. The curated look was confrontational and calculated to shock. For a young Jewish girl – Caroline the DJ – raised with stories of the Holocaust and living through a period of resurgent right-wing activism, the swastika represented an obvious threat. Jordan thought otherwise. 'I couldn't believe at the time that people could be so touchy, all that time ago,' she told Jon Savage. 'We all know what happened, this was my attitude, and we all know it was wrong, and to all intents and purposes, there was no Nazi Party now. There was this genius who was also a loony, Hitler, and it's all out of taboo, I thought, by that time.'[20]

On another occasion, Jordan visited the all-night club, the Candy Box, accompanied by Johnny Rotten and soon-to-be Sex Pistol Sid Vicious, where once again, her shirt sparked a reaction. 'My grandmother and grandfather were killed by the Nazis,' a young woman complained. 'But what do you know?' Jordan retorted aggressively, annoyed at the stranger 'being so touchy'. 'It was history,' Jordan scoffed, retrospectively, 'handed down twice by then.'[21]

The three above incidents present the swastika as a symbol deliberately worn to shock. At the same time, Jordan praises Hitler's 'genius' and insists on framing the swastika as an artistic symbol, denying its association with ongoing persecution while claiming to demystify its significance. The confused messaging permeated the nascent punk scene. Then, suddenly, the swastika was at the centre of a media storm.

On 1 December 1976, the Sex Pistols agreed to a short interview on the Thames Television regional magazine programme *Today* after the rock group Queen unexpectedly cancelled late in the day. Broadcast live at 6.15 p.m., footage of the Sex Pistols performing 'Anarchy In The UK' was followed by two and a half minutes of uninhibited, alcohol-fuelled chaos in the studio. In a moment that betrayed both decorum and professionalism, seasoned television presenter Bill Grundy goaded the band to 'say something outrageous'. Guitarist Steve Jones responded with a stream of expletives: 'You dirty bastard', 'You dirty fucker' and finally, 'What a fuckin' rotter!' It was sensational viewing and unlike anything ever seen on national television. Media outrage followed:

'The Foul-Mouthed Yobs' – *Evening Standard*
'The Filth and the Fury' – *Daily Mirror*
'Rock Group Start a 4-Letter TV Storm' – *the Sun*
'Fury at filthy TV chat' – *Daily Express*

But for all the front-page headlines – indeed, an unceasing stream of analysis that now spans over fifty years – a small, but hugely significant detail of the interview is largely overlooked.

Behind the group, a small coterie of fans commonly known as 'the Bromley Contingent' – Siouxsie Sioux, Steven Severin, Simon Barker, Simone Thomas – stand dressed in de rigueur punk outfits sneering at Grundy. On several occasions the camera cuts to a close-up of bass player Glen Matlock. Behind him, a swastika armband worn by Barker is clearly visible in the top left-hand corner on the screen. The fashion provocation passes without comment.

Two months earlier, *New Society* reported on a Sex Pistols concert at the 100 Club where 'throughout the entire performance, one girl wearing a swastika armband maintains a Nazi salute'.[22] The following May, *Evening News* journalist John Blake coined the phrase 'Rock's Swastika Revolution', drawing unsubstantiated connections between the Sex Pistols' shows and National Front support. Despite this, both the Grundy incident and the media coverage that followed only resulted in passing mentions of the swastika. Again, the failure of media journalism to hold musicians and a burgeoning scene to account raised ongoing concern. While profanity seemed to shock the British public, the potent symbol of the Third Reich provoked little reaction. If this suggested a country largely unshaken by punk's use of Nazi imagery, the Sex Pistols' next move would test the limits of public tolerance.

Nothing in rock 'n' roll history could have prepared listeners for 'Belsen Was A Gas'. The very idea of a rock group making light of the Holocaust was inconceivable – until punk's Year Zero. Yet, the Sex Pistols did just that, presenting a chilling, unapologetic and simultaneously ironically humorous portrayal of life in a concentration camp – an act that remains truly shocking. Johnny Rotten cleverly exploited the double meaning of 'gas' – referring both to a vapour used to kill by poisoning and/or asphyxiation and to the slang term for something enjoyable. The song opens with the haunting lines: 'Belsen was a gas, I heard the other day, in the open graves where the Jews all lay'.

Established in 1940 as a *Wehrmacht* POW camp (otherwise known as a *Stalag*), Bergen-Belsen came under the authority of Himmler's SS in April 1943 as an 'exchange camp' to house and trade Jewish hostages for Germans prisoners interned abroad. During Belsen's existence, tens of thousands of inmates lived in appalling conditions, deprived of food, clean water and sanitation. Disease and starvation were widespread. An estimated 70,000 people were murdered. Among them, sixteen-year-old Anne Frank. But contrary to what is suggested in 'Belsen Was A Gas', the camp was not a site of extermination, nor did it have a gas chamber.

Initially camp life offered prisoners a quasi-cultural existence. Unlike most concentration camps across Europe – more than 44,000 between 1933 and 1945 – inmates organised lectures and musical recitals, wore their own clothes and were permitted to be with their families. Blankets were issued and there was a minimal amount of food. Nonetheless, when British forces liberated Bergen-Belsen on 15 April 1945, they were confronted by a scene of unimaginable horror. In a short period, Bergen-Belsen had lost all trace of humanity. Food and water were scarce, a typhus epidemic raged, and everywhere dead bodies were piled into mounds. Those who survived were little more than skeletal frames, barely able to walk. It was a picture of hell

The Sex Pistols' introduced 'Belsen Was A Gas' to their live set in late 1977. Following the shocking opening lines, Johnny Rotten delivered a second uncompromising verse. 'Life is fun, and I wish you were here they wrote on postcards to those held dear, oh dear'. Remarkably, postcards played a critical role at Belsen and many other camps, serving to reassure Jews awaiting news of family members who had been 'resettled in the East'.* Historian Laurence Rees notes that, 'They [Jews] were instructed to write postcards home explaining how well they were being treated, in an attempt to dispel rumours that Auschwitz was a place of extermination.'[23] Similarly, Jews who were transported fifty miles north-west from the Łódź ghetto to the Chelmno extermination camp in northern Poland – if they survived the journey – were instructed to send postcards to their families. On 25 July 1944, thirty-one letters arrived, which according to the *Chronicle of the Łódź Ghetto* were all postmarked 19 July. 'Fortunately, it is apparent from these cards that people are faring well and, what is more, that families have stayed together,' the copy read. 'The ghetto is elated and hopes that similar reports will soon be arriving from all the other settled

---

* Postcards from Auschwitz arrived at Theresienstadt, a unique show camp where the Nazis actively encouraged cultural activities. As a result the Red Cross believed Auschwitz-Birkenau was a labour camp. After writing their well-wishes, the Jews were murdered in gas chambers.

workers.'[24] In fact, having completed the writing task, the Jews at Chelmno were systematically murdered in mobile gas vans.*

In another dreadful episode, Anita Lasker-Wallfisch, a former cello player in the woman's orchestra at Auschwitz, and later liberated from Bergen-Belsen on 15 April 1945, wrote to her sister, Marianne in London. On 29 August, she asked, 'Do you read the papers?' before mentioning that she had written an article that might be published in the *Jewish Chronicle, New Statesman* or *Daily Mirror*, in response to a piece in the *Daily Express* 'about Germany's "Gayest Holiday Town" . . . its name, Belsen.'[25] Photographs of the camp, taken by the British Army and Photographic Film Unit, had already shocked the world. Yet, four months later, a British newspaper had reduced a place of death and despair into a 'gay' holiday resort.

On 22 August, Roy Beamont of the *Daily Express* reported, 'I have just spent two days in Germany's gayest and happiest towns,' describing a place where

> laughing men and girls parade the streets, swim, fish, boat, ride, dance, go to the theatre or cinema, hold sparkling wedding feasts, open air concerts and play every imaginable sort of game. Its inhabitants are of every nationality under the sun, from Chinese to German Jews. It is Europe's greatest holiday town. It is the home of 15,000 men and women convalescing their way back to normal life. They are plump and healthy; their eyes sparkle and their brains are alert. They get good food, levied from the local German towns, and every possible entertainment.[26]

This shockingly disingenuous post-Holocaust portrayal was followed by an article on 2 October, again in the *Daily Express*, headlined, 'The Death Music of Auschwitz', which described Lasker-Wallfisch, the niece of the chess master Edward Lasker, playing cello in an orchestra for SS guards as they selected victims for the gas chamber. That same day, the *Daily Mirror* reported that a

---

* Of the 400,000 Jews transported to Chelmno only two survived.

search had been announced for undiscovered mass graves at Belsen following the disclosure that 40,000 internees were still missing. If the contradictory reports left British readers confused, it marked the beginning of a blasé, distorted understanding of the horrors faced by those who survived Nazi concentration camps.

'Be a man, kill someone, kill yourself,' Johnny Rotten sneered as the Sex Pistols played 'Belsen Was A Gas' at their last live performance in San Francisco on 14 January 1978. Backed by a ferocious rhythm section, Rotten's sarcastic delivery challenged the listener to laugh at the dark humour or squirm at the depravity of human behaviour. 'It's one of the most frightening things I've ever heard,' wrote American music critic Lester Bangs. 'You wonder exactly what you might be affirming by listening to this repeatedly. On one level Johnny Rotten [. . .] is an insect buzzing atop the massed ruins of a civilization levelled by itself [. . .] on another level he's just another trafficker in cheap nihilism with all that it includes.'[27]

Months earlier, Rock Against Racism interviewed Rotten concerning growing support for fascism on the streets of England. Never mind that in 1976, Ray Stevenson photographed Rotten wearing a badge of the German imperial eagle with a swastika in its claws pinned upside down on a McLaren/Westwood-designed black bondage suit. In March 1977, when the Sex Pistols signed to A&M Records, Rotten sprayed 'swastikas on the photos of the record company's various artists'.[28] And, in July, he wore a 'Destroy' T-shirt with a swastika at its centre when the group performed 'Pretty Vacant' for *Top of the Pops*. Now he informed Rock Against Racism, 'I despise [the National Front]. No-one should have the right to tell anyone they can't live here because of the colour of their skin or their religion or whatever, the size of their nose. How could anyone vote for something so ridiculously inhumane?'

Yet when stories of the Pistols new song ('Belsen Was A Gas') filtered through the punk community, Rock Against Racism ignored it. 'It's incredible that we didn't say anything,' admits Lucy Whitman who, describing her appearance in 1977 as very thin, with hair cut noticeably short with a razorblade, adds: 'At a gig, a boy said to me, "You look like you've just come out of Belsen."' In the same year, Whitman created a fanzine called *JOLT* and expressed her feelings about a growing trend towards fascism. 'I was alarmed and indignant from the very beginning about the idiotic fascination with swastikas in punk,' she says.'

> In the early days, some punks flirted with Nazi regalia in a naive attempt to be 'provocative'; they were soon slapped down by those who had a better grasp of what the Nazis stood for; people like Bernie Rhodes [Clash manager]. We were the generation whose parents had been through the war. So, the Nazis were the enemy. Most people had sacrificed a lot to defeat the Nazis. So, borrowing a Nazi symbol was a like a slap in the face because it would get up our parents' noses. The enemy who had brought so much suffering to the British people. Most punks who wore swastikas had not a fucking clue what it stood for. It was just a symbol of up yours to authority.

Tony Drayton, the editor of the punk fanzine *Ripped & Torn*, recalls people reacting with shock, saying, 'What's this?' and 'All these rumours about this terrible song.' To satisfy his readers' curiosity, he reprinted the lyrics of 'Belsen Was A Gas' in the next edition. 'I didn't like the words,' Drayton explains. 'By this point, I was anti-Nazi. I thought it was in bad taste, but not as bad as everyone was making out.' At the same time, a recording of the last Sex Pistols concert in San Francisco featuring 'Belsen Was A Gas' began circulating as a bootleg single. Initially issued in a plain white sleeve, record dealers designed their own cover artwork. One popular sleeve showed monochrome images of gas chambers, ovens, mass graves and typed references to Nazi extermination camps.

Departing the stage in San Francisco with the immortal words, 'Ha, ha! Ever get the feeling you've been cheated?', Rotten walked out on the Sex Pistols. Returning to England, he formed a new group, PiL, and revived 'Belsen Was A Gas'. Meanwhile, guitarist

Steve Jones and drummer Paul Cook ventured to Rio de Janeiro to cut a record with the infamous 'Great Train Robber' Ronnie Biggs. The unlikely collaboration with a man who had previously only sung in pubs produced two new songs. The first was a re-recording of 'Belsen Was a Gas' retitled, 'Einmal Belsen war wirklich vortrefflich' ('Once Belsen was brilliant'). Biggs, who claimed to have read *The Diary of Anne Frank*, focused on a particularly gruesome aspect of the treatment of Jews when they arrived at death camps. He wrote, 'Dentists searched their teeth for gold, frisk the Jews for banknotes fold. When they found out what they'd got line them up and shoot the lot'.

Arriving at camps, Jewish prisoners hid valuables out of fear. Despite this, camp guards inspected every orifice of their bodies. Any items found were processed and added to a growing heap of riches meant for transport to the Reich. Prisoners were then 'selected' for work or, if deemed unfit, channelled to the gas chamber – or as Biggs coldly described, simply shot. Even in death, a body still had value: gold teeth were extracted and melted down.

Writing in his memoir, Biggs said, 'We recorded "Belsen Was a Gas" which I must say I wasn't too happy about. I did find these words a little disgusting.' Challenged by *Record Mirror*, Biggs claimed that he was not 'cashing in on a very sick episode in history' and pointed to the fact that the song was already recorded by the Sex Pistols before he got involved with them. 'Anyway,' he insisted, incorrectly, 'Belsen was a gas. People got gassed. It was an attack on the people who perpetrated those outrages. It isn't defending them in any way.'

Not content to scrape the barrel of inspiration – let alone attempt to resuscitate the dying breath of the Sex Pistols – a second new song materialised. 'No One Is Innocent (A Punk Prayer)' called on God to save criminals and sinners, including the Sex Pistols, Bill Grundy and the Moors Murderers' Myra Hindley and Ian Brady. Next, Biggs pleaded clemency for Martin Bormann and Nazis on the run. 'They wasn't being wicked, God', Biggs hissed, 'That was their idea of fun'.

Martin Bormann retrieved the bodies of Hitler and his bride, Eva Braun, after their joint suicide at 3.30 p.m. on 30 April 1945.

Standing beside Josef Goebbels above the Führer's Berlin bunker, Bormann watched as 180 litres of petrol ignited the two bodies. Then, attempting to escape the encircling Red Army, Bormann swallowed a cyanide tablet. This was confirmed in 1972 when his remains were discovered in West Berlin, ending years of speculation that he had escaped to South America via Rome. At Nuremberg, Hitler's trusted aide was condemned to death *in absentia*.

'We were rather drunk by the time we came to make the recording,' Ronnie Biggs said of 'No One Is Innocent', 'which explains why it may have appeared a little out of tune.' In the 1980 documentary-fiction *The Great Rock 'n' Roll Swindle*, Biggs wore a psychedelic swastika T-shirt, given to him by Malcolm McLaren. He performs 'No One Is Innocent' on Copacabana Beach alongside Steve Jones and Paul Cook and a lookalike (American actor Jim Jeter) dressed as Martin Bormann in full Nazi regalia. If the absurdity of the film destroyed any last vestiges of the Sex Pistols' remaining credibility, the cheap evocation of a Nazi criminal plunged the group into a deep well of ridicule.

Despite being banned on the radio and not stocked by most high street chain stores, 'No One Is Innocent' still sold well. 'It is inarguable that a massive number of these sales come from the fact that the Pistols have reached the frontiers of irreverence and toppled over into rather questionable taste,' Tim Lott posited in *Record Mirror*. 'There appears to be an exoneration of some peculiarly nasty activities, like torturing children. Like gassing Jews. Like slaughtering unfortunate Europeans.'

In an attempt to defend himself, Biggs insisted, 'The punk prayer isn't just a joke. I put a lot of my sentiments into it. Whether it's in bad taste or not depends how you look at it. The message of the song is simply this: if God is going to save the Queen, then he should save Myra Hindley, and Martin Bormann, and Ian Brady. He has to save everybody or nobody. Because no one, absolutely no one, is innocent.'[29]

The Sex Pistols' indulgence of the Third Reich raises questions of intent and awareness – questions that may be linked to Steve Jones' troubled past. Molested as a child by both a stranger and

his stepfather, Jones, writing in his memoir *Silly Boy*, also admitted
he wasn't particularly 'bothered' when Malcolm McLaren would
'fuck about with kiddie porn shit'. Given this detachment, it's little
surprise that he 'never thought twice' about wearing a swastika. 'It
felt more important to shake things up a bit than to worry about
hurting other people's feelings,' he wrote. 'I hadn't really got my
head around the concept of the concentration camps by the time
the Sex Pistols were happening, so to me Vivienne's "Destroy"
T-shirts with swastikas on were just about being shocking.'[30]

On a trip to Islington, Jones bought two swastika flags from
Call To Arms, a military shop specialising in German war souvenirs, run by 1960s pop crooner Chris Farlowe. Best known
for his 1966 hit 'Out Of Time', Farlowe insisted, 'It's nothing
political. [But] selling German stuff was really strange for my
father. I remember I had a big oil painting of Heinrich Himmler
in my bedroom. My father walked in one day and went, "Take
that off the wall!" I said, "I'm selling it, Dad. It's not political.
"Take the fucking thing off the wall!" So, I took it off the wall.'[31]
In August 1975, Farlowe welcomed *Melody Maker* journalist Allan
Jones into his shop and presented the journalist with an SS bugle
engraved with a Third Reich eagle for inspection. 'Bloody lovely,
innit,' Farlowe marvelled, 'Travelled a hundred miles last night
just to get it. Bloke I got it off got it in Hamburg at the end of
the war. The SS cleared out this building and left all their bleedin'
musical instruments.'[32] Surrounded by medals in glass cases, an
assortment of weapons and a swastika flag, Jones has the good
grace to describe the coveted bugle as 'the odious symbol of the
fallen Reich'.

Meanwhile, Steve Jones hung the swastika flags on his living
room wall, believing the Nazi regalia 'in sync' with his dark mood
of the time. Now a former Sex Pistol – young, uneducated, and, by
his own admission, indifferent to hurting others – he saw it as an
extension of his inner turmoil. Over time, a photo of Jones wearing
a swastika T-shirt beside Sham 69's Jimmy Pursey circulated online.
'Every time I see that, it makes me cringe,' Jones wrote in *Lonely
Boy*. 'It was weird really because I'm not racist and never have been.

I suppose it was just a way of summing up the darkness I felt . . . the Nazi phase was the next logical step.'

Yet nothing about that phase was 'logical'. As his drug addiction deepened, Jones began selling off his home's furniture, piece by piece. 'I'd sold it all to buy dope, even the Nazi flags had gone,' he recalled. Then, unable to resist a facetious remark, he added, 'that place just didn't feel like home without them'.[33]

When the Sex Pistols reformed in the mid-1990s, Johnny Rotten (now known as John Lydon) described 'Belsen Was A Gas' as a 'very nasty, silly little thing that should've ended up on the cutting room floor'.[34] Still, the song featured in the group's reunion set. Expanding the wordplay of the original lyrics, Lydon rhymed 'Oh dear' with 'Hitler was queer', while Jones, Cook and Matlock answered with the Yiddish expression, 'Oy vey!' Asked how much he wrote of the original song, Lydon exclaimed, 'All of it! I credited Sid [Vicious] for a laugh because I wanted him in the Pistols. Originally Sid came up with the title, something like 'Belsen Was A Gag'. Gas came in because of a T. Rex song, "Life's A Gas". It's one of my favourite pop singles. Although it sounds nothing like it, it is how I connect things. It was an absurd song. It's over the top. It's ironical. It's so completely, clearly not pro- that at all. Yet again . . .' Lydon tailed off, implying the song had been misunderstood by journalists and critics, 'There we go . . .'*

The writing of 'Belsen Was A Gas' was popularly attributed to Sid Vicious, a year before he replaced Glen Matlock as the Sex Pistols' bassist.† The original lyrics included the rhyming couplet:

---

*   The quote is from a conversation I had with Lydon in 2012. We were in a recording studio in rural England where PiL had just returned from touring. Asked whether they performed 'Belsen Was A Gas' in Israel. Lydon replied, 'No, never thought of it.'

†   In May 2025, the phrase 'BELSEN WAS A GAS' BY SID VICIOUS accompanied by three love hearts, was graffitied beneath a mosaic of the musician by the French street artist Invader, on an exterior wall on Hanley Steet, just off Oxford Street in London.

'Belsen was divine if you survived the train. Then when you got inside it's auf wiedersehen'. The rhyme may have been witty, but it showed no empathy towards the persecution of innocent Jews. Vicious performed the song with the short-lived 'bedroom band', the Flowers of Romance. Viv Albertine, a one-time member of the group (later of the Slits), admits the song was 'horrifying', but insists 'not in some namby-pamby, isn't it naughty, isn't it wrong, but accentuating the vileness of it, rather than saying, oh its wrong in a social-worker type of way'. She also acknowledges that people like Sid Vicious, herself and Siouxsie Sioux were 'slightly naive' for wearing swastikas, adding that if people misunderstood, 'we didn't give a shit'. Albertine claims Vicious was the first to wear the Nazi emblem in the punk scene, pinning it to his back, saying, '[He] did it like Lenny Bruce would use the word "nigger" to devalue it, to bring it into context where it's not important.'[35]

Albertine's view seems to absolve Vicious, implying that by wearing the swastika, he rendered it meaningless. Yet when he wore a T-shirt featuring the Cambridge rapist mask, Albertine was 'pissed off', explaining 'how frightening it was for women on the streets, and how hard it was to laugh at it'. The Cambridge rapist mask-T-shirt, designed by Malcolm McLaren and Vivienne Westwood, glorified a man guilty of sexually assaulting as many as ten women. Albertine's comments highlight indifference towards the swastika but indignation at male sexual violence. Both repugnant.

In April 1978, Sid Vicious (born Simon John Ritchie) strolled through the Jewish quarter of Paris exposing a swastika T-shirt worn beneath a hardened leather jacket. Sneering and gesticulating, he flashed a flick knife at scandalised onlookers. He jeered at a gendarme, eyeballed an old lady and smeared a cream cake across the face of a glamorous woman he encountered in a street doorway. Now a solo artist, Vicious took advantage of the trip to France to buy presents valued at over £2,000 for his American girlfriend, Nancy Spungen. The expensive shopping haul included clothes, underwear, leather trousers, jewellery, make-up and a Nazi belt. It was an unusual gift for a twenty-one-year-old raised in Philadelphia to middle-class Jewish parents. Diagnosed schizophrenic aged seventeen, Spungen moved to London via New York in December 1976. At first befriending the Sex Pistols, the one-time stripper-cum-call girl attached herself to Vicious. 'Sid is so sweet and kind,' she swooned to *Record Mirror*.[36]

Film footage captured Vicious and Spungen lying on a Paris hotel bed. They discuss the premature demise of the Sex Pistols. Dressed in a rubber outfit, Spungen gently cajoles the semi-comatose Vicious out of his drug-induced stupor. He wears a sleeveless red T-shirt emblazoned with a large black swastika. The scene is compelling: a former Jewish sex worker and a drug-addled punk rocker. On 8 April 1978, the young couple featured on the front cover of *Record Mirror* Vicious with clenched fists eyeballing the lens, Spungen a step behind starring insouciantly at the camera and clutching her boyfriend's arm. 'All I know is that Sid looks pretty frightening in his red T-shirt with the black and white swastika on the front, his chain and padlock and his black leather bikers' boots,' gushes awed journalist Rosalind Russell. It is the only mention of the Nazi symbol in the feature published in an edition of the weekly music paper devoted to the promotion of the forthcoming Rock Against Racism/Anti-Nazi League Carnival.

On 12 October 1978, New York Police Department officers discovered the dead body of Nancy Spungen in the Chelsea Hotel. Seven days later, her cremated ashes were scattered over the family grave at King David Memorial Park, a Jewish cemetery in Bensalem, Bucks County, Pennsylvania. Accused of Spungen's murder and released on bail, twenty-one-year-old Vicious died from a heroin overdose on 2 February 1979. Three weeks later, a cover of Eddie Cochran's fifties rockabilly classic 'Somethin' Else', performed by Vicious, was posthumously released and credited to the Sex Pistols. On the sleeve was a comic graphic of Vicious clad in black leathers and ubiquitous swastika T-shirt. Despite the inflammatory image, the record peaked at number 3 on the national chart and could be found racked on the shelves of mainstream outlets such as WHSmith and Woolworths.

In the intervening years, the swastika had become a symbol inextricably linked to the Sex Pistols and, particularly, Sid Vicious. He wore the provocative T-shirt while lounging in a deckchair in London's Hyde Park, basking in the summer sun. In an archive interview with director Julien Temple for the *Great Rock 'n' Roll Swindle* film, the acne-ridden, cigarette-smoking youth gestures aggressively at passers-by, raising his arm and fist in a gesture of defiance, to signal 'Fuck off'. The footage, now on YouTube, has been viewed by more than a million people. Yet, of the thousands of comments posted, not one acknowledges the Nazi symbol filling half the screen. One might imagine that if this were an image of a lynching during America's segregation or a woman being sexually assaulted, the video would be swiftly removed after a public outcry. The absence of such a reaction to the swastika suggests either the symbol's weakened impact as a sign of anti-Semitism, or equally disturbingly, that people simply don't care.

Deutschland Über Alles

SIOUXSIE & THE BANSHEES. LONDON SS.
THE CLASH

Three controversial incidents link the swastika, punk culture, and one of its central figures, Siouxsie Sioux. In each case – two in London and one in Paris – Sioux (born Susan Ballion, 1957) displayed the Nazi emblem as a provocative modern weapon. Here was the anger of a nineteen-year-old upstart railing against the old order and a country that offered little hope. Sioux was punk. She rejected the past. Embraced the 'No Future' cry. And set out to antagonise.

On 29 August 1976, the Sex Pistols played at the Screen on the Green in Islington. Although still unsigned, their live shows were building a reputation for riotous behaviour. A Pistols gig was a forum to express yourself, to dress in defiance of the status quo and to be outrageous. Arriving in north London to watch Rotten, Cook, Jones and Matlock, Siouxsie Sioux, eye-catchingly gussied up, was wearing little more than a corset and a single thigh-length vinyl boot. Balancing on an ankle-strapped heel on her left foot and posing in front of Ray Stevenson's camera, Sioux insolently exposed a swastika brassard wrapped around her right upper arm. Viewed today, as indeed then, the image was scandalous. Incredibly, *NME* ignored the Nazi emblem and instead reported on Sioux's 'tits out' pose. It was hardly surprising. Three weeks earlier, Scottish rock singer Alex Harvey stood in front of a Third Reich flag draped in full Nazi regalia and drew no comment. Indeed, in May, David Bowie supposedly gave a Nazi salute at Victoria Station and initially caused little more than a ripple in the music papers. Images of

Bowie, Harvey and Sioux shocked. But editorial condemnation was perversely mild.

A week after the Screen on the Green show, Sioux travelled with the Sex Pistols to Paris on a three-day jaunt. Dressing for an evening rendezvous, Sioux slipped a swastika armband over an outfit more notable for bare flesh than fabric. 'We were walking to this club,' recalled Bromley Contingent escort Simon Barker, 'and suddenly these guys jumped out with knives, really hassling us. When we got in to the club, Siouxsie got punched by this guy who tried to grab her tits, and then it got so bad we were moved to another part of the club for our own protection. We just waited in the dressing rooms until the promoter said it was safe for us to leave.'[1]

Defeated in just six weeks, in May 1940, France surrendered sovereignty to Nazi rule. Then, having established the Vichy government – in the unoccupied free zone in the south – the puppet government collaborated with round-ups of non-French Jews and facilitated the deportation of women, men and children to concentration camps in the east. For a modern Western democracy, humiliating defeat and post-war condemnation of anti-Semitic co-operation was cause for ongoing national shame. Now, here was the swastika on the arm of a young punk flagrantly disregarding the disgrace of a humbled nation. 'Silly girl,' John Lydon wrote with a satisfied surge of *Schadenfreude*, 'she wore practically nothing except swastikas and a see-through titless bra in a former Nazi-occupied country.'[2]

Unfazed and perhaps unaware of Lydon's unsympathetic attitude, Sioux returned to England and pushed the boundaries of social acceptability to their extremes. Booked to open the Punk Rock Festival – for the Sex Pistols, Clash and Subway Sect – at London's 100 Club on 20 September 1976, Sioux formed an impromptu group. In need of equipment for the stand-in drummer (soon-to-be Sex Pistol Sid Vicious), Sioux appealed to the manager of the Clash. Eyeballing Sioux's swastika armband, Bernie Rhodes refused.

'Fucking old Jew!' Vicious lashed out.

Today, Rhodes says, 'She could have found something else to shock. What about literature, what about some other imagery, something creative. It's easy to pick up a swastika and wave it around.'

Arriving at the 100 Club, Sioux was not wearing the Nazi emblem. 'Then suddenly she's got one on her arm,' says Caroline Coon.

Malcolm McLaren was doling them out from a box. Siouxsie wanted to be in with McLaren because he is the power with the money. She's doing it to please Malcolm. She was nineteen. The idea of shocking was very central to what kids were doing then. The whole point of the punk movement and the way that young people were expressing their anomie was to be noticed. That's what was so interesting about Bernie's argument: if you want to be noticed you must shock in a more intelligent, more thoughtful way.

According to Rhodes, McLaren returned from an unspecified 'trip north' armed with swastika-branded ephemera. 'Siouxsie wore one of the shirts,' Coon wrote in 1977, 'more because it was there than anything else. She said that as a symbol of shock, the swastika was the only thing around. I don't think she thought very much about it. As a symbol or an emblem it was a random choice. A bad accident. A bit of a red herring. But the Clash are into specifics, not red herrings. If we're going to use emblems, then they should be nearer the mark. People can do what they want. But we don't think the swastika means anything relevant to us.'[3]

Bernie Rhodes agrees: 'It's very easy to disrupt and divide,' he says.

I've always been about trying to construct something. The swastika was nothing to do with me. I had fights with Vivienne because of all of that. Why do you think I broke away from Malcolm and did the Clash? I had their amps painted luminous pink. If Siouxsie used it, we would have been associated with the swastika. I felt she was mucking about with a loaded gun. We didn't want anything to do with it.

Rhodes' ideological stance, which led to a fall-out with McLaren over the swastika, was embraced by the Clash's frontman Joe Strummer. 'Bernie was a Jewish refugee from the oppression in Europe, or rather his mother was, so it was close enough for him to take that seriously, whereas I don't know where Malcolm came from . . . it was messing with things they didn't understand.'[4]

According to Rhodes, his maternal grandparents were 'shot in Russia against the wall,' though no one ever spoke of whether it occurred before or after the revolution. His mother, who spoke little English and mainly Yiddish 'had a tiny little shithouse one room shed in Stepney with a curtain between us'. During the ages of eight and fifteen, Rhodes lived in a Jewish orphanage. 'I've always suppressed my identity,' he says of his religious upbringing. 'It was only when it was my family, which was my group, my people. You had all these others, the *NME* crowd: Tony Parsons, Julie Burchill and all the other half-wits that were around. They wanted to be middle-class book writers. It's all bollocks. I was ridiculed non-stop because I was a threat.' Singling out Siouxsie Sioux for alleged 'fascistic interests', Rhodes says he was the only one 'that called it out. Everyone was saying, "Oh Motörhead. Lemmy! Lemmy!" You've got so many people . . . I could tell you hundreds of them.'

Performing as Suzi [*sic*] & the Banshees, the group – featuring Sioux (vocals), Steven Severin (bass), Marco Pirroni (guitar) and Sid Vicious (drums) – plugged into the Sex Pistols' amplifiers and for twenty-four minutes, they delivered an atonal, cacophonous noise, fired by an incessant guitar drone and high-pitched vocal wailing. Impressing an awed audience with mangled versions of rock classics like 'Knocking On Heaven's Door', 'Twist And Shout', '(I Can't Get No) Satisfaction', and 'Smoke On The Water', it was more of a punk statement than a show of virtuosity. At the peak of the assault, Sioux recited 'The Lord's Prayer' and the Nazi anthem, 'Deutschland, Deutschland über Alles' – 'Germany above all!'

Reflecting the mood, Vicious wore a yellow 'Belsen Babies' T-shirt, ripped open at the front and defaced with swastikas and felt-tip ramblings about Dr. Mengele's experiments scrawled across the back.[5] Handwritten in black ink down the front was the chilling message, 'I hate Jews.'

As the band stumbled offstage, Palmolive of the Slits confronted Pirroni, accusing the group of supporting Nazis. Raised under Franco's fascist regime, the drummer, born Paloma Romero, would soon return to Spain to fight political oppression. Her objection, however, was largely unsupported. Punk dissent was more about posturing than substance. And so, the swastika became acceptable. Not as a symbol of Nazi tyranny, but as part of the emerging punk movement.

In October 1976, Siouxsie Sioux arrived at Louise's nightclub in Soho dressed in a jaw-dropping combination of fetish wear and Nazi trimming. *Sounds* journalist John Ingram detailed the particulars after Sioux removed her mac. 'A simple black dress with a plunging V neckline, black net loosely covering her pert breasts. A home-made swastika flash was safety-pinned to a red armband. Black strap stilettos, studs gleaming, bound her feet, fishnet tights and black vinyl stockings her legs. Her short black hair was flecked with red flames.'[6]

'It was always very much an anti-mums-and-dads thing,' explained Sioux. 'We hated older people. Not across the board, but generally the suburban thing, always harping on about Hitler, and "We showed him", and that smug pride; and it was a way of saying, "Well, I think Hitler was very good, actually." A way of watching someone like that go completely red-faced.'

'To us these weren't badges of intolerance,' Steven Severin of the Banshees added, 'but symbols of provocation to an older generation that had to get out of the way to make room for younger voices. When it was a small movement, you could use symbols like that.'[7]

One might ask, who exactly is being shocked? Or how many of the older generation were even aware of punk – passengers on the Bromley to London train, or those walking past Sioux on their way to Soho – likely a small number. Fewer still if an overcoat covered the swastika. It would take several train rides or strolls through busy streets to truly attract attention. Certainly, no one at a punk gig would be outraged. The real question is whether the intended provocation fell flat – or whether history has simply amplified its meaning.

Fed up with looking backwards but equally attracted to well-groomed outfits, colourful emblems and leather finishing, Sioux says, 'The culture around then was *Monty Python*, Basil Fawlty, Freddie Starr, *The Producers* – "Springtime For Hitler". It was very much *Salon Kitty*. It was used as a glamour thing. And you know what? I have to be honest, but I do like the Nazi uniform. I shouldn't say it, but I think it's a very good-looking uniform.'

Here, once again, a musician was deliberately separating the symbols of a totalitarian state from the crimes it committed. When a journalist advised against such comments 'for fear of upsetting the PC mob', Sioux conflated personal grievance with indifference for those persecuted under the Third Reich.

> Yeah. It's almost like you feel like saying, 'Aw, come on. Nazis – they're brilliant.' Political correctness becomes imprisoning. It's very – what's the word . . . it's being very Nazi! It's ironic but this PC-ness is so fucking fascist. In America, they're especially touchy about Nazis and it's so Nazi! You go to LA and it's so segregated. It's very Nazi and the irony is they don't get it. They don't realise how Nazi they are about taking offence to mentioning the word Nazi.[8]

Incensed by the outburst, Julie Burchill accused Sioux of making a fashion statement out of the death of millions of people. 'Siouxsie is well into her twenties,' Burchill wrote in the *NME*, 'so ignorant youth is no excuse. Therefore, she must be either evil or retarded.' The pair never met. But nonetheless, Sioux dismissed Burchill's attack as envy. 'It was an excuse,' Sioux reflected in 2005, 'she didn't want to like us . . . fat old cow.'[9]

Amid rising opposition to their use of Third Reich imagery, the Banshees struggled to attract record company interest. 'One year on it's the Nazi vibe that is holding back the potential hordes,' Jane Suck observed in *NME*. 'Siouxsie & the Banshees reckon Belsen was a gas! It's more akin to Visconti's *The Damned* than the Third Reich but feed the flames and you'll get a blaze.' Concern intensified when the band refused to play for Rock Against Racism. 'I love getting people's backs up,' Sioux taunted. 'It's like laughing at spastics. The main thing is that you don't know where the money's going. I'd rather do something like Rock Against Rabbit-Breeding. Men planting their sperm and watching women's bellies grow, when they don't have the means to support children, is very frightening . . . I hate the extreme left and the extreme right because they're both wrong.'[10]

'If you don't object to Jews or blacks or pink men or whatever, why should we play a RAR gig?' guitarist John McKay offered, overlooking the participation of many Black and Jewish musicians. 'There's an inverted snobbery there. If I was black, I'd be very insulted by RAR.'[11]

Year on year, Sioux steadfastly defended her actions, rejecting accusations of anti-Semitism. Despite wearing hand-made swastikas and agreeing with most of her peers who saw The Damned that it looked great, Sioux says, 'There was nothing coming out about what went on in the concentration camps and probably we would have been the first people to be persecuted if that was to happen again, but it was a way of getting back at the older generation that we hated.' The swastika, she says 'was purely out of high camp, nothing else'[12] and 'certainly not meant to be a political statement. At the time, I was very much into mixing up various symbols: the crucifix, the swastika and, later on, the Star of David. I think everyone generally was pretty much ignorant of what the Holocaust and the war meant. It was really just a thing of the older generation, and the young people were always getting beaten up about the war. It was just a way to piss off the older generation. It was very much more high camp than death camp.'[13]

Tellingly, where the Banshees floundered, the posthumous Sex Pistols flourished. Dead from a heroin overdose at the age of twenty-one, Sid Vicious left behind a Third Reich-influenced legacy that continues to be heavily exploited. In 1979, Virgin Records released Sid Sings, a live album primarily recorded over

three nights in September 1978 at Max's Kansas City, New York.*
A swastika adorned the label artwork styled from the neck and
headstock of four Fender Jazzmaster guitars. Jamie Reid originally
created the design as 'Music Keeps You Under Control' and later
reworked the distinctive pattern to promote the Dead Kennedys'
single 'California Über Alles'. The image, coupled with marijuana
potted plants also decorated with swastikas, represented, Reid said,
'how hippies sold out'.† When NME's Adrian Thrills accused him of
peddling tedious images, Reid responded that he wouldn't expect
'radical chic journalists to understand its stunning condemnation
of the music business. I find the whole hysteria that surrounds the
swastika quite amusing.' Reid countered, 'It's just a bunch of old
Leftists getting tied up with dialectics rather than facing up to the
real issues.'

Concerned about the negative response to Reid's artwork, Richard Branson wrote to NME to clarify that Virgin Records does not
support right-wing beliefs. 'Being liberals to the point of oafishness
we have always made a point of printing all the artwork given to
us by the Pistols' camp, including full-page attacks on ourselves.
We also presumed, wrongly as it turned out,' Branson's missive
continued, 'that by demystifying and trivialising the swastika, much
as Sid himself did by wearing it on his increasingly grubby T-shirts,
it would be seen as an object of ridicule.' Expressing 'distaste' for the
National Front, Branson accepted that 'even one Jew or immigrant
offended' justified the NME's position. 'The public don't have to buy
it. Unless they want to,' the record company mogul signed off. 'Roll
on Flogging A Dead Horse. Yours, Richard Branson.'[14]

Meanwhile in Germany, a new pressing of Sid Sings forced the
record label to substitute the swastika with a blank spot to comply

---

* Earlier in the month, Mick Jones played guitar with Vicious at Max's in a set
that included 'Belsen Was A Gas'.
† Reid would use a similar design for the artwork of Bow Wow Wow's 1981
single release 'W.O.R.K. (N.O. Nah No! No! My Daddy Don't)' which featured
a swastika created from the word 'Work'.

with federal law.* In the UK, wearing a swastika has never been illegal – except between the years 1939 and 1945. Similarly, there was no law against distributing or publishing material that promotes racial hatred until the Public Order Act 1986. This legal definition was flouted during a sale at Omega auction house on 31 October 2023, which featured a collection of original 1970s King's Road McLaren-Westwood-Reid artefacts,† including two celluloid sheets with the phrase, 'Take a deep breath and dance – this is the Rock 'n' Roll GAS CHAMBER'. They sold for the £500 hammer price.‡

One day, – sometime in 1976 – manager Bernie Rhodes organised a meeting at The Bush pub on Shepherd's Bush Green. Opening a bag, he took out a huge swastika and slapped it down on the table. 'If you're going to be called London SS,' he apprised the two young punks (Tony James and Mick Jones), 'you're going to have to live with that! . . . I didn't want to be involved in that nonsense,' reflects Rhodes, adding. 'I was a figure of fun; Tony James always put me down.'

The man behind the mythologised punk band London SS was a musician of Jewish-Russian descent, raised by a religious grandmother and three 'really Jewish old ladies'. When the women confiscated a T-shirt adorned with a German Iron Cross, Mick Jones was relieved that his prized Nazi memorabilia collection had gone undiscovered. The band's choice to name themselves London SS – a nod to Heinrich Himmler's infamous *Schutzstaffel* – raised questions about punk rock's inherent conflict, as it sought

---

* Six months earlier, the compilation album *Some Product: Carri on Sex Pistols* forced the German record label to cover an image of Sid Vicious in a swastika T-shirt with a price sticker.

† Formerly known as SEX, in December 1976, the renamed shop Seditionaries featured large photographs supposedly of Dresden after an Allied bombing attack during the war.

‡ The clothing store BOY, co-founded in 1976 by Israel-based businessman John Krivine who later managed the punk group Chelsea, obtained the printing rights to all Jamie Reid designs as a result of a licensing deal with Vivienne Westwood, worth a paltry £200 in the late seventies.

to create outrage against the backdrop of growing neo-Nazi activity. According to founding member Tony James (later of Generation X and Sigue Sigue Sputnik), London SS was a name Jones had 'kicking around'. 'There's nothing simpler for shock value than Nazism, drugs, or dodgy sexuality,' James opined. 'It was naive . . . we hadn't thought at all about the Nazi implications. It just seemed like a very anarchic, stylish thing to do.'[15]

In his former group, the glam rock band Hollywood Brats, keyboard player Stein Groven, popularly known as Casino Steel, proudly wore a swastika.[16] One of the group's songs, 'Vampire Nazi', described a boy with 'teeth like daggers' who goose-stepped in Camden Town wearing an Iron Cross and a Hugo Boss-'designed' cape. It is claimed by some that Steel proposed the name London SS. For his part, Jones claimed 'SS' stood for Social Security while admitting to concealing the band's name from his Jewish grandmother. In later years, he confessed to feeling ashamed of the moniker. 'We really wanted to be shocking like the New York Dolls,' Jones recalled in 2008. 'We were young and stupid. It's funny now, Tony and me are working together, and every day we have to deal with that. It's our punishment for being so stupid. It makes us both cringe.'

London SS never formally recorded or played live, often viewed more as a side project than a serious venture. That all changed in June 1976, when Jones, along with bassist Paul Simonon and vocalist Joe Strummer, formed the Clash. Over the course of their eight-year career, the band became commercially successful, politically charged and fiercely anti-fascist. On the eve of headlining the Carnival Against the Nazis in April 1978, Jones told *Temporary Hoarding*, 'I'm half-Jewish.' He then smiled and added, 'So I suppose the NF will try and send half of me back to Lithuania.' His flippant comment referred to the far-right National Front's determination to cleanse the pop charts of 'ethnic' undesirables.

'Is this the future of Rock 'n' Roll?' *Sounds* asked on its front cover ahead of the spring carnival beneath portraits of twelve other singled-out stars, the word 'DEPORTED' stamped across their faces in bold red block capitals: Paul Simonon (the Clash), Phil Lynott (Thin Lizzy), Poly Styrene (X-Ray Spex), Charlie Tumahai (Be Bop Deluxe), George Csapo (Bethnal), Carl Levy (Cimarons), Errol Brown (Hot Chocolate), Ari Up (the Slits), Freddie Mercury (Queen), Ray Lake (the Real Thing), Jean-Jacques Burnel (the Stranglers), and Rita Ray (Darts). This, editor Phil Sutcliffe informed readers, would be the repercussion of a National Front government. Deportations would deprive music of new wave, soul, punk, reggae, power pop, heavy metal, blues and rock musicians. 'Women's Liberation is men's Liberation. Black Liberation is White Liberation. My liberation is yours and yours is mine,' read Sutcliffe's rousing rhetoric. 'That is the superb fabric of freedom.'

While the words were noble, the gallery overlooked British-based Jewish musicians. No Mick Jones. Nor Danny Kustow, the guitarist from the Tom Robinson Band. Instead, *Sounds* framed the issue around 'immigration' and 'overcrowding' and, yet, under the feature heading 'Don't Follow Leaders', an image of a swastika and the rubric, 'And never wear this.'

The feature, written by *Sounds* editorial staff – Phil Sutcliffe, Caroline Coon, Vivien Goldman, Jon Savage and Pete Silverton – argued that 'Swastika chic' which was popular at the beginning of punk, and adopted by thousands as part of punk's strategy to 'shock indiscriminately by whatever means', had been 'thoroughly underestimated' and contributed to a 'brutalizing effect'. Referring to 'Belsen Was A Gas' and the Vibrators' 'Nazi Baby', *Sounds* argued that 'irony and satire' are 'notoriously hard concepts to communicate'. While recognising that neither the Sex Pistols nor the Vibrators made explicit statements against Nazism and more pointedly that such statements were absent in their lyrics, the article concluded, 'This uncertainty in the case of such an emotive and associative title ['Belsen Was A Gas'] is surely irresponsible.'

In an interview with Martin Webster, Caroline Coon challenged the National Front's 'national activities organiser' over his historic anti-Semitic beliefs and suggested that the party had shifted its focus to Black people. 'No,' said Webster refuting the accusation. 'We've never been an anti-black or an anti-Jewish movement.' Today, Coon says Webster was trying to make himself more popular. 'Being anti-Semitic had run its course,' she says. 'Jewish immigrants had been integrated. The new influx was black. Webster was using the same language, but instead of Jew he put black.'

During a time of heightened racial tension, ambiguity was a blunt weapon. The fear that the Clash's debut single 'White Riot' was a covert anthem for racist supremacy chimed with the suspicion that 'Belsen Was A Gas' promoted the extermination of Jews. 'You have to decide which side you are on,' John Lydon opined when asked about the threat of the National Front in March 1978. 'You can't stand back apathetically. I'm never, never, going to have anything to do with a military organisation based on hatred and ignorance.'

The genuine fear of a far-right uprising in late-seventies Britain inspired the Clash to imagine a modern-day 'English Civil War'. 'It's just around the corner,' Strummer told *Record Mirror* quoting from the song's agitated chorus: 'Johnny hasn't got far to march. That's why he's coming by bus or Underground.' Asked if the Clash was exaggerating the threat of the National Front, Mick Jones pointed to facts. 'In 1928, Adolf Hitler got 2.8 per cent of the vote. In 1939 there was no one voting for anyone else.'

The rise of totalitarianism and the ease with which the Nazi Party democratically seized power echoed across the Clash's next record. 'We will teach our twisted speech to the young believers,' Joe Strummer sang on '(Working For The) Clampdown'. 'We will train our blue-eyed men to be young believers'. It was produced by Guy Stevens, the former DJ and manager of Mott the Hoople, who listed Bob Dylan, the Rolling Stones and Jerry Lee Lewis among his formative influences. 'They have one thing in common,' he told *Sounds* in March 1974, 'the gift of compelling attention, of drawing the mass together, of making them think and feel as one' – a quality Stevens also admired in Hitler, whom he considered 'the best showbiz operator ever'.[17]

The swastika's presence in punk is seldom addressed by the media, suggesting a widespread cultural acceptance. In the absence of criticism, musicians are presumed innocent of right-wing views or exonerated by idolising fans. The idea that an artist might be perpetuating the traumas of the Nazi regime or even endorsing Third Reich ideology is typically dismissed. Instead, there is a void where neither debate nor censure exist. So it is ironic that John Lydon, of all people, characterised punk's ambiguous embrace of the swastika when, speaking in the late eighties, he revealed, 'I thought Siouxsie and Sid were quite foolish. Although I know the idea behind it was to debunk all this crap from the past, wipe history clean and have a fresh approach, it doesn't really work that way.'[18] It was an observation that neatly summed up UK punk and, albeit unintentionally, the shocking embrace of the swastika that had simultaneously permeated the North American new wave scene.

Blitzkrieg Bop

NEW YORK DOLLS. RAMONES. ELECTRIC EELS. DEAD BOYS. RESIDENTS

On 6 October 1973, Egypt and Syria attacked Israel, sparking the three-week Yom Kippur War. A month later, the New York Dolls flew to Britain to promote a European tour with an indefatigable urge to shock and offend. Posing for *Melody Maker*'s Jewish photographer Bob Gruen, a subsequent cover image featured the five Dolls in a bundle of back-combed hair, gauche poses and guitarist Johnny Thunders openly displaying a swastika armband. Yet the accompanying interview by journalist Roy Hollingworth made no mention of the sartorial accoutrement. Then, fresh from an appearance on the BBC's *Old Grey Whistle Test*, the Dolls hotfooted across the English Channel to France. Arriving at Orly airport, Thunders threw up in front of Europe's rock press while singer David Johansen pulled out 'his best German officer impression' – 'Vee did not co-operate viv the Naz-ees'[1] – which was greeted with nervous amusement, *NME*'s Nick Kent noted.

In Hamburg, the German media asked the group if they were enjoying the country, Thunders – again exhibiting a Nazi armband – responded with spectacular insensitivity. 'We wanna play a benefit gig at Belsen,' he said, reeling in the press corps like an angler casting bait, 'or someplace like that, y'know?' Falling into the trap, a journalist innocently pipes up, 'For all the Jews that died in the camp on the site?' 'Narrrwww . . .' Thunders drawled, winding in his catch, 'for all the Nazis who gotta hang out in trees in fuckin' South America.' Feeding the frenzy, Thunders then informed the tightly packed press of journalists that German beer tasted 'like junkie's piss'. Next, Jewish bandmate Sylvain Sylvain (born Sylvain Mizrahi) asked, 'Why are all Krauts so fucking fat?' 'It's all them Jew-meat sausages,' countered Thunders.

Onstage, the New York Dolls brazenly displayed Third Reich *objets d'art*: a death's head insignia on black tunics, a swastika etched onto the head of Johnny Thunders' Gibson guitar. 'At some of the Dolls' shows it became hip to wear swastika armbands,' recalled singer Jayne (later Wayne) County. 'Not because they were anti-Semitic – they didn't even know what that was – but because it was decadent and fashionable.'[2]

Just as Mick Jagger imitated Adolf Hitler in Berlin in 1965, so David Johansen goose-stepped onstage during 'Private World' using his finger to mimic the Führer's moustache. The music press thrived on the unrestrained debauchery and expressed no qualms about potential offence. Nick Kent included the New York Dolls in his top 10 *Let It Rock* 'Critic's Choice' for 1973, placing 'Boredom' in a category of its own with the enigmatic phrase: 'Viva Rock 'n' Roll Fascism.' Looking over his shoulder, punk chronicler Jon Savage noted, 'An occasional swastika band on Thunders' arm was just a good metaphor for obnoxious intent.'

In punk's rock 'n' roll high school of crass unpleasantness there was to be no room for taboo. Copying the swastika was regarded as an act of mindless provocation. 'In grammar school you get a loose-leaf book and the first thing you draw in it is a swastika and a skull and crossbones. You carve a swastika in a desk,' twenty-four-year-old David Johansen explained. 'You don't know what fascism is, it's not anti-Jewish at all. Kids don't care anything about that shit. When you want to make a statement about how bad you are, that's how you do it.' In a similar fashion, Mexican landlord and designer Arturo Vega decorated his loft apartment in the East Village, New York with painted Day-Glo swastikas, which he rented out to the Ramones. Vega said, 'The colours represented this man-made madness. I always thought that to conquer evil, you have to make love to it. You have to understand it.'[3]

Vega judged the responses to his fluorescent swastikas, claiming, 'The people that act so defensively are always the people who are closet fascists,' adding that, 'the paintings find you out.' The attraction to such imagery speaks to a broader issue: artists drawn to the darkest corners of human nature often fixate on Nazism, history's ultimate expression of evil. The leaders of the Third Reich, many of them middle-class and well educated, manipulated the German public through masterful propaganda, introducing authoritarian policies step by step. Yet, their brutality – rape, torture and mass extermination – found eager accomplices across occupied Europe, particularly among men. These collaborators not only rounded up Jews but also carried out mass executions – leading to as many as two million deaths in what became known as the 'Holocaust by bullets' – and helped administer concentration camps. It is the sheer horror of these acts that has fuelled a perverse fascination with the Third Reich for generations, helping to explain rock 'n' roll's enduring obsession with its imagery.

Breaking out of Forest Hills, Queens, the Ramones descended on Manhattan armed with 'Blitzkrieg Bop'* and lightning Nazi verse. 'I'm a shock trooper in a stupor, yes I am,' bass player Dee Dee Ramone declared in 'Today Your Love, Tomorrow The World', and 'I'm a Nazi Schätze you know I fight for fatherland'. In German, *Schätz* means 'gem' or 'treasure' used as a term of endearment in the way English uses 'sweetheart' or 'honey'. 'I thought the lyrics were funny,' says Ramones manager Danny Fields. 'Dee Dee wasn't talking about the extermination of a race, it was more a one-on-one thing, you know, "When the bedroom door closes, I'm a Nazi." He was like a kid saying a dirty word to see if he got his mouth washed out with soap.'[4]

Behind the Ramones lies a surprising connection to Jewish and German heritage. Singer Jeffrey Ross Hyman, better known as Joey Ramone, was born to Jewish parents in 1951. Drummer Tommy

---

* From the German – *Blitz* meaning lightning and *Krieg* meaning war – a violent campaign intended to achieve early, decisive victories in Poland, France and the Soviet Union through speed and surprise.

Ramone was born Tamás Erdélyi in Budapest in 1949. His Jewish parents survived the Holocaust with the assistance of neighbours, but his extended family tragically perished in the death camps. Bassist Dee Dee Ramone (born Douglas Glenn Colvin, 1952) grew up in post-war Germany near Hitler's Berchtesgaden retreat in Bad Tölz, Bavaria. The son of an American soldier and a German mother, his family moved to Pirmasens, in the newly established German state Rhineland-Palatinate, where he scavenged the countryside for war relics like steel helmets, gas masks and bayonets. 'I was fascinated by Nazi symbols,' said Dee Dee, who would trade these objects at school. 'They were just so pretty.'[5]

Jewish. German. European. And enthralled with Third Reich emblems. 'It wasn't, "Oh, I'm a Nazi and all you Jews better watch out!"' says Danny Fields. 'It wasn't anything like that. It wasn't political. It was sexual . . . I don't blame people or condemn them for being fascinated. But if there was the remotest hint of them [the Ramones] embracing what the Nazis advocated, I would have severed my relationship instantly with them.'[6]

Legs McNeil, co-founder of the influential *Punk* magazine, believed the new wave movement was a white experience – 'fuck the black experience' – and argued that the Ramones' Nazi references were more about rebelling against seventies norms than embracing extremism. But Lester Bangs saw something darker. In a September 1978 interview, Johnny Ramone recalled a charged encounter with British journalist Tony Parsons. 'The guy had a hammer and sickle button on,' he spat, still seething. 'He was a commie, and I knew it as soon as I saw him. I had him pegged.' When Bangs suggested that wearing a logo didn't make someone a Communist, Ramone fired back:

'Well, then why's he wearin' it? For effect?'

'You think everybody that wears a swastika is a Nazi?' Bangs countered.

'Umm . . . maybe,' Ramone faltered, 'Probably. Or at least they want to be a Nazi.'

Admission hanging in the air, Bangs pressed the point.

'Don't you think kids put stuff like that on just to make people mad?'

'I dunno,' Ramone replied, 'I don't like it when I see it. I know a lot of people are offended when they see swastikas, but swastikas are a little more camp than hammer-and-sickle buttons. I mean, the Nazis lost the war, and there's no threat right now of any Nazi thing, but there is a communist threat.'

Drawing his attention to the rise of the National Front in the UK, Bangs informs Ramone that 'English kids have the threat of a right-wing takeover'.

'Yeah,' Ramone reacts, 'but do they want the communists just to come and take over?'[7]

The following year, Bangs submitted to the *Village Voice* an essay titled 'The White Noise Supremacists', identifying punk as both a scene and a stance riddled with self-hate. 'Anytime you conclude that life stinks and the human race mostly amounts to a pile of shit,' Bangs postulated, 'you've got the perfect breeding ground for fascism.' Dismissing the likes of Ron Asheton and his Nazi fetishism, Bangs reasoned that the Stooges never accompanied their music with right-wing rants nor did Asheton in his later band, 'which many people were not exactly thrilled to hear was called the New Order. Swastikas in punk are basically another way for kids to get a rise out of their parents and maybe the press, both of whom deserve the irritation,' Bangs concluded.[8]

Formed in Cleveland, Ohio, in 1973, the Electric Eels' short-lived career traded on deliberate provocation and violent audience confrontation. The use of the swastika in their imagery was something original member John D. Morton purposed 'to confront those [Nazi] issues'. Following in a tradition of provocateurs like author William Burroughs and comedian Lenny Bruce, Morton added, 'I greatly admire Charlie Manson's forehead swastika tattoo.'

Designing the Electric Eels' infamous Special Extermination Music Night, Morton designed a poster that drew on a conceptual art, Dadaist sensibility. 'I had been drawing swastikas since the second grade,' he explained. 'My Dad was a World War Two vet of Battle of the Bulge, and all my fifth-grade peers did likewise. We played Army and the swastika looked – and still does look – REALLY COOL! We Eels were certainly aware of the shock value of what we were doing.'

Performing 'Spin Age Blasters' – 'Pull the triggers on the niggers' – the Electric Eels ad-libbed provocative lyrics sourced from American Nazi Party literature. One such example was the quarterly *Stormtrooper* (1964–8), described by its editor, John Patler, as 'the official news magazine of the American Nazi Party' which typically featured anti-Semitic propaganda and demands for the release of Rudolf Hess. Its back pages offered 'Nazi Literature and Other Items For Sale', that included photographs of George Lincoln Rockwell (leader of the ANP) and Adolf Hitler, booklets, leaflets, armbands, lapel pins, recordings, stickers and copies of the anti-Semitic forgery *The Protocols of the Learned Elders of Zion*.

Since 1936 and the formation of the German American Bund under the leadership of Fritz Kuhn and sanctioned by Rudolf Hess, American support for Nazi ideology had attracted members in the tens of thousands. Modelled on the Hitler Youth and the SS, the Bund established several training camps and, on 20 February 1939, held a sold-out rally at Madison Square Garden, attended by 20,000 members dressed in Nazi uniforms and carrying swastika flags and banners. Although there is no public documentation to support this view, it is reasonable to assume that many musicians had parents who supported the movement and were indoctrinated by German-American National Socialist beliefs. Nevertheless, Eels' guitar/keyboard player Paul Marotta insists that the group's engagement with Third Reich imagery was simply, 'Shock tactics . . . confrontational art' and 'meant to be satire'.

Quartered in the Chelsea Hotel, Midtown Manhattan, the Dead Boys arrived from Cleveland, Ohio enthralled by the Electric Eels. As a thank-you gift to their hosts, the punk newcomers presented the Ramones with Nazi Mothers' Crosses (*Ehrenkreuz der Deutschen Mutter* – The Cross of Honour of the German Mother). Meanwhile lead singer Stiv Bators busied himself shaving a swastika into the pubic hair of the photographer Eileen Polk. Then, with guitarist Jimmy Zero, he rampaged through the corridors of the Chelsea naked beneath a Nazi flag. Knocking on doors and singing 'Springtime For Hitler' [from 1967 film *The Producers*), Bators beat members of the crew with a whip. On another occasion, Dead Boys drummer Johnny Blitz was hospitalised where, according to Legs McNeil, a Jewish surgeon refused to operate after discovering a swastika tattooed on his torso.

In preparation for a studio recording session, producer Genya Ravan fearlessly objected to the group's hostile conduct. Arriving at Electric Lady Studios to record what would become the 1977 debut album *Young, Loud and Snotty*, the producer noticed that instrument cases belonging to the Dead Boys were emblazoned with swastikas. 'I got really mad,' Ravan wrote in her memoir *Lollipop Lounge*, 'and read them the riot act.' Threatening to cancel the session unless the group removed the offending symbols, Ravan then proceeded to berate the band. 'Do you realise your manager (Hilly) is Jewish, your producer – me – is Jewish, and the owner of this studio, who's doing us all a favour by letting us record at these prices, is Jewish?'

Ravan's indignation met with an astonishing admission. 'I don't even know what the swastika thing stands for,' one Dead Boy replied. Next, Ravan informed the group that the owner of the studio had a number tattooed on his arm. 'I had to explain to them what Auschwitz was,' she exclaimed, 'and that I'd lost both my brothers and my relative in Poland to those Nazi fuckers. "So, get those fucking things off your equipment."' The following week the swastikas had been removed. Hearing of the episode, John Morton of the Electric Eels commented, 'We would not have removed our Nazi regalia if the record producer made a big stink about her parents being in Dachau or something.'[10]

Demonstrating a similarly obstinate spirit, though with a more humorous twist, the Residents followed up in 1976 with their second album, *The Third Reich 'n Roll*. The front cover depicted the clean-cut, smiling face of *American Bandstand* television host

Dick Clark as a Nazi clutching a carrot, surrounded by cartoons of miniature Hitlers cavorting and dancing with people on clouds. Alongside a back sleeve displaying swastikas, the Residents drew a parallel between the brainwashing of American teenagers and the seduction of the Nazi Youth forty years earlier. They called it 'the fascism of rock 'n' roll'.

Unsurprisingly, the record generated a mixed reaction. In the UK, *Sounds* praised *Third Reich 'n Roll* as, 'Funny – and frightening' calling it 'one unqualified masterpiece'. In Germany, it was swiftly banned, due in equal parts to its unsettling cover art and controversial content. The album consisted of two sprawling musical suites – 'Swastikas On Parade' and 'Hitler Was A Vegetarian' – mixed with popular songs of the 1960s, from Chubby Checker's 'Der Twist Beginnt', to the Beatles' 'Hey Jude' and the Rolling Stones' 'Sympathy For The Devil'. Designed by Homer Flynn, the promotional images were just as incendiary, showing the Residents wearing giant swastika-shaped neck collars, oversized swastika glasses and Hitler moustaches. Today, the record continues to divide opinion, attracting both fans and critics, while the group remains silent, offering no explanation for their work.

On both sides of the Atlantic, fascination for the Third Reich, in particular the swastika, increasingly fed the creative output of musicians coupled with an insouciant responsibility to its founding ideology. The bridge between first and second generation survivors of the war, and indeed the Holocaust, continued to widen. As a result, Nazism increasingly became a tool of exploitation, devoid of responsibility and, as concerningly, sensitivity towards its victims. Indeed, titillation and sexual deviancy now became a primary influence in Third Reich cultural expression.

Fascist in the Bedroom

THE DAMNED. *SALON KITTY. THE NIGHT PORTER.* MADONNA. LADY GAGA

In 1970s Britain, knowledge of Nazi extermination camps was minimal. Documents discovered by the Russian army at the end of the Second World War remained unreleased, and explicit imagery of the Holocaust was largely confined to specialist books and films. Many schools barely covered the subject. In this cultural vacuum, ignorance replaced knowledge and sensitivity. For punks, the swastika – once a Nazi symbol of genocide and oppression – became something else: a mark of rebellion. It was as much a part of the movement's aesthetic as dyed hair, leather jackets and bondage trousers, wielded as a weapon of provocation and a rejection of traditional values. Auschwitz survivor Renate Lasker later reflected on this generational detachment: 'Now, half a century has gone by, and a new generation has grown up, a generation which is probably as bored of hearing about concentration camps as we were with the stories of the front line in the Great War.'[1]

Looking back from the twenty-first century, the swastika shocks in an age that increasingly values racial tolerance. But in the 1970s, punk rock marched like a battalion without a commanding officer – amorphous, undefined, fighting against forces that were neither clear nor articulated. The angry mob shouted 'Anarchy' and 'White Riot', wore swastikas and spat at strangers. Mick Farren wrote in *NME* that 'Nazi badges and armbands are turning up at clubs and at rock concerts as an essential part of street couture.' Concerned that the vogue for fascist imagery was fuelling right-wing support, Farren confronted Dave Vanian, the lead singer of the Damned. 'It's just part of the show,' Vanian countered, an SS badge pinned to his tuxedo lapel. 'Anything you use to jolt people, to get them going, has got to be worth it.'[2]

Backstage at the Manchester Apollo, where the Damned were opening for seventies glam rock icons T. Rex, Farren expressed his concerns about the dangerous impact Nazi posturing was having on their audience. 'Are you asking if the band should be responsible for what the audience does?' Vanian retorted defiantly. 'No,' he spat, 'that's their responsibility.'[3]

Vanian was not the first member of the Damned to wear a Nazi symbol. In November 1977, bass player Captain Sensible flaunted a swastika armband during a concert at London's Roundhouse. Then, at a photo shoot for the group's second single, 'Neat Neat Neat', he fastened a Nazi badge onto the lapel of his white cloth jacket. Neither Vanian nor Sensible drew attention to their swastikas. Nor did they offer any explanation, reflecting a growing trend where repurposed Third Reich artefacts received minimal condemnation and created a critical void for Nazi imagery to seep into the cultural mainstream. For many, the primary influence came from film.

The Damned took their name from Luchino Visconti's film of the same name starring Dirk Bogarde, Ingrid Thulin, Helmut Berger and Charlotte Rampling.* Set in 1930s Germany, the film is a stylised melodrama depicting the dramatic and self-destructive fall of a wealthy industrialist family during the early years of the Third Reich; a garish world of moral decay, where incest, rape and paedophilia thrive in 'an elite society where everything is permissible', as the tagline proclaimed. Loosely based on the murder of Ernst Röhm (head of Hitler's storm troopers) and other similarly compromised members of the Nazi Party, *The Damned* offered audiences dazzling

---

* Some members of the band have cited Wolf Rilla's 1960 horror film *Village of the Damned* as a key influence. Steve Strange credited Visconti's film as the inspiration behind Visage's 1982 single 'The Damned Don't Cry', while also admitting that Dirk Bogarde was the person he most hoped to impress with his music. Meanwhile, John Foxx, before founding Ultravox, revealed that they had once considered naming the band the Damned.

uniforms, cross-dressing and backdrops of swastikas draped in rich fabric. Dave Vanian's 1978 stage appearance – white-faced and with slicked-back hair – was described by Mick Farren as resembling a look-a-like Helmut Berger in the movie of the same name.

By the 1970s, British cinema was increasingly dominated by the dark allure of the Third Reich, as sexually explicit films birthed the genre of 'Nazisploitation'. Films with titles like *SS Experiment Camp, Deported Women of the SS Special Section, The Beast in Heat* and *Last Orgy of the Third Reich* flooded the market. Among them, two films – *Ilsa: She Wolf of the SS* and *Love Camp 7* – struck a particular chord with the musicians who would later form the punk movement. These films appealed not just for their titillating content, but for their almost seductive portrayal of Nazi imagery – uniforms, flags and symbols – that would later become an unsettling part of punk's visual language.

Directed by Lee Frost, *Love Camp 7* follows the story of a Jewish scientist rescued by two American officers, who infiltrate a concentration camp as sex slaves and uncover the abuse of female prisoners. 'All the youthful beauties of Europe enslaved for the pleasure of the Third Reich,' read the titillating poster copy depicting a bound woman, hands tied above her head, stripped and whipped by two German officers. 'We guarantee you that you will not live long enough to forget the things you will witness and experience inside . . .'

The British Board of Film Classification rejected the film for violating its strict guidelines, 'where a central concept of the work is unacceptable such as a sustained focus on sexual rape, other non-consensual sexually violent behaviour or sadistic violence'. While the ban prevented this and similar films from general release, it did little to stop a growing demand for eroticised Nazi imagery. From under the counter, sex shops sold men's adventure magazines filled with daring quests and explicit sexual stories featuring graphic depictions of women in lingerie, stockings and suspenders, bound and gagged by muscle men or Nazi officers glorifying flagellation and torture, with sensationalist titles such as, 'Nazi Love Slaves

Revenge', 'Yvonne's Ordeal Under the SS Lash' and 'The Nazi She-Devil Who Killed for Kicks'.

A publishing genre emerged, known as *Stalag* fiction, sexualising sadistic female SS guards abusing and torturing American pilots and Jewish prisoners. During the 1960s, hundreds of thousands of copies were sold in Israel, reflecting a furtive fascination with the intersection of pornography and Holocaust trauma. Assuming the pen name Sven Hassel, Børge Willy Redsted Pedersen published fourteen novels – translated into eighteen languages – including *The Legion of the Damned* (1953), *SS-General* (1960), *Reign of Hell* (1971) and *Blitzfreeze* (1973). When the authors were accused of distributing anti-Semitic pornography, sales declined.

Tinto Brass' 1976 carnal sex romp, *Salon Kitty*, portrayed women as sexual objects to stimulate erotic desire. Set in 1930s Germany and based on a true story, the film depicts Berlin's infamous wartime brothel, which was not only an epicentre for sexual adventure but a hub of espionage. The brainchild of Reinhard Heydrich,* and aided by Walter Schellenberg, a member of the Reichsführer-SS's Security Service, the brothel was rigged with hidden microphones installed behind bedroom walls. These devices relayed conversations through thick cables to a secret monitoring room concealed in the building's basement where wax discs recorded the dialogue exchanged between trained operatives and unsuspecting customers.

---

*   Popularly known as 'the Hangman' and by Hitler as 'the man with the iron heart', Heydrich rose swiftly through Nazi ranks to become chief of the Reich Security Main Office and in 1941 acting Reich Protector of the Protectorate of Bohemia and Moravia. Believed to be part Jewish, Heydrich was nevertheless a vehement anti-Semite responsible for establishing the network of industrialised killing centres in Eastern Europe. On 27 May 1942, a team of Czech assassins and members of Winston Churchill's Special Operations Executive (Churchill's secret army) shot Heydrich. He died eight days later. In his honour, Himmler named the organisation administering the extermination camps – Chelmno, Bełżec, Sobibór, Treblinka and later to include Majdanek and Auschwitz – *Aktion Reinhard*. These first four purpose-built facilities would murder a combined 1.7 million people.

Sixteen-woman auxiliaries were recruited from within the ranks of the Waffen-SS, chosen for their intelligence, multilingual skills, commitment to National Socialism, attractiveness and 'a liking for male company'. Posing as sex workers, the women seduced high-ranking party officials and foreign diplomats including the German foreign minister Von Ribbentrop, Reichsführer SS Heinrich Himmler and the Italian foreign minister Galeazzo Ciano, son-in-law of fascist leader Benito Mussolini. At the end of each day, the women submitted a written report and, if necessary, an aural account of their sexual encounters. Yet, incredibly, neither the owner of the premises at Giesebrechtstrasse 11, Kitty Schmidt,* nor the staff knew of the hidden recording devices concealed within the fabric of the building.†

The astonishing story inspired the 1974 novel *Madam Kitty* written by Peter Norden, a pseudonym for Josef Gustav Walter Fritz, a former pilot in the Luftwaffe. It sold over five million copies worldwide. Tinto Brass' exploitative adaptation of the book emphasised explicit nudity and incorporated cruel and sadomasochistic sexual acts. One scene follows another of women being humiliated or degraded to excite men. In one example, a semi-naked woman, dressed in little more than stockings and a swastika garter belt, is mutilated for the pleasure of SS officers against a screen projecting a speech by Adolf Hitler.

Screened in London in 1977, *Salon Kitty* found a receptive audience among punk rock's extended fraternity, which was already enamoured with another key film of the period, *The Night Porter*. Directed and co-written by Liliana Cavani in 1974, *The Night Porter* was a psychological thriller, both erotic and disturbing in equal

---

* Arrested attempting to flee Germany in 1938, Schmidt spent several weeks in solitary confinement. Threatened with deportation to a concentration camp, Schellenberg proposed Salon Kitty as a bordello for spying.

† The state-of-the-art recording equipment was developed in collaboration between AEG and IG Farben, the company responsible for the manufacture of Zyklon B used in Auschwitz-Birkenau and Majdanek extermination camps from 1942.

measure. Set in Vienna in 1957, a former SS officer (Dirk Bogarde) re-enacts a pseudo-masochistic relationship with a concentration camp survivor (Charlotte Rampling). Having endured beatings and rape during the war, Rampling's character now identifies with her perpetrator and willingly indulges in sexual and psychological role-play.

Acknowledging the emerging trend of 'Nazi chic', *Chicago Sun-Times* critic Roger Ebert condemned the film, calling it a 'shallow exploitation of that theme, containing no real insight or understanding', and labelled *The Night Porter* as a 'nasty' and 'despicable' attempt to titillate audiences by 'exploiting memories of persecution and suffering'. Marketed as 'a controversial audience-grabber', one theatre marquee prominently displayed the phrase 'A kinky turn-on!' attributed to a supposedly enamoured *New York Times* critic. However, those who read the full review found it began with the blunt statement: 'Let us now consider a piece of junk.' This harsh criticism resonated with Holocaust survivor and renowned author Primo Levi, who described *The Night Porter* as 'beautiful and false', arguing that the film was based on Cavani's idea of sex and one that had 'nothing to do with the camps'.

Cavani's previous works included the four-part television series *Storia del III Reich*, which documented the rise of the Third Reich and *La donna nella Resistenza*, detailing Italy's struggle against fascism and women's role in the resistance. Nonetheless, *The Night Porter* created a world where sexual exploration masked a murderous regime and, in doing so, blurred a line between historical accuracy and sadomasochistic voyeurism. Bogarde's chilling portrayal of an SS officer gained added resonance when he revealed in a prime-time television interview that he had witnessed the liberation of Bergen-Belsen while serving as a soldier in the British army. 'The gates were opened and then I realised I was looking at Dante's Inferno,' the actor told chat show host Russell Harty. 'I still haven't seen anything as dreadful. And never will. There were mountains of dead people. I went through some of the huts and there were tiers and tiers of rotting people, but some of them who were alive underneath the rot and were lifting their heads and trying to do the victory thing – that was the worst. After the war,' Bogarde determined, 'I always knew that nothing, nothing, could ever be as bad.'*

To witness the depths of human suffering and then portray a perpetrator of Nazi brutality neatly ties together the relationship central to *The Night Porter*. However, one scene more than any other is responsible for the film's enduring cultural appeal. Dressed only in an SS peaked cap, black boots, underwear, suspenders, black opera gloves, and braces covering her nipples, Charlotte Rampling (as Lucia) delivers the haunting song, 'Wenn Ich Mir Was Wünschen Dürfte' ('If I Could Have A Wish'). Gaunt and pale-faced, she captivates the audience, including an onlooking Bogarde and members of the SS, while performing the 1930 song by German-Jewish composer Friedrich Hollaender, which was famously recorded by Marlene Dietrich in 1960.

The sexual dimension of *The Night Porter* has an enduring influence on pop music more than half a century after its release. Leaving aside its deeper meaning, the film's visual iconography has influenced a generation of performers. Adam Ant started 'doing the Charlotte Rampling look' in 1978, telling *Ripped & Torn* that he 'ripped the crotch out of a pair of girl's tights and put them on a T-shirt'. A decade later, Madonna appeared topless in her 1990 video for 'Justify My Love' wearing only suspenders and a peaked leather cap. Shot in black and white in a sultry hotel room, Jean-Baptiste Mondino's promotional film self-consciously simulated Rampling's provocative sexual foreplay in *The Night Porter*, creating a sensual atmosphere that matched the singer's seductive vocal delivery. The video portrayed Madonna as both dominatrix and object of

---

* In 2008, *The Times* critic John Carey made a dramatic assertion while reviewing Bogarde's published diaries, suggesting that, 'It is virtually impossible that he [Bogarde] saw Belsen or any other camp.' By cross-referencing the liberation date of Bergen-Belsen (15 April 1945) and Bogarde's wartime record, Carey concluded, 'things [Bogarde] overheard or read seem to have entered his imagination and been mistaken for lived experience'.

male desire, turning it into a celebration of sex where she holds control, laughing while orchestrating sexual fantasy, voyeurism and indulgent pleasure.

A year later, after declining an invitation to appear in the pop promo and with Madonna preparing to publish *Sex*, her book of erotic photography, Dirk Bogarde received a fax at his agent's office in New York. It read: 'Madonna is currently working on a book of photographs with Steven Meisel. The book is a collection of their interpretation of erotica. Both Steven and Madonna have expressed interest in using Dirk Bogard [*sic*] in these photographs [. . .] Unfortunately I cannot give you more details about the content of these photographs but, if Mr Bogard is interested, Madonna or Steven would be happy to call him to discuss the project in depth.'[4]

Bogarde declined the request.*

'Justify My Love' topped domestic charts around the world. Yet the promotional film deliberately overlooked *The Night Porter*'s disturbing context in which a Jewish concentration camp prisoner is forced to comply with her captor's sexual desires. During the Nazi regime, women – defenceless and at the mercy of 'state-legitimised' male violence – suffered unspeakable horrors. The scene portrayed in *The Night Porter* may have been fictionalised, and, understandably, few survivors have shared the sexual encounters they endured as prison inmates. Yet one testimony by Hubert Pfoch, a member of the illegal Austrian Socialist Youth Organization, recalls the Commandant of Treblinka, Dr Irmfried Eberl, ordering female Jewish prisoners to dance naked for him on tables. Pfoch's account is corroborated by SS Sergeant Franz Suchomel who, noting the

---

* In the early nineties, Madonna's request to play Leni Riefenstahl in a mini-series based on her memoir was rejected by the film-maker. A similar request by actor Jodie Foster was also turned down.

In 2011, Riefenstahl's name appeared in the credits of Madonna's second film *W.E.*, which attracted criticism for its 'soft' portrayal of the Duke and Duchess of Windsor's 1973 visit to Hitler's Bavaria retreat. The film downplayed their possible negotiations for an alliance with Germany and notably omitted their sympathetic view towards the Nazi regime.

incident happened in a kitchen and not on a table, further added that hearing about it later, Christian Wirth, the inspector of *Aktion Reinhard* – the plan to systematically murder the Jews of Nazi-occupied eastern territories – 'had the poor girl shot'.[5]

Madonna drew on the imagery of *The Night Porter* and other films from the era as a cultural indulgence, detaching Nazi aesthetics from its ideological roots and effectively overlooking their connection to the Holocaust. 'I *do* like things to be a bit sick,' she told *Record Mirror* in 1984. 'That film *The Night Porter* with Dirk Bogarde and Charlotte Rampling . . . Oh my God! . . . what an incredible movie. And *Salon Kitty* . . . absolutely sick! Not sleaze! But I do like *realness*. *The Night Porter* touches on a subject people don't like to talk about – that people are drawn to things that cause them pain – they *want* it. I'm drawn to those kinds of things.'[6]

When an updated recording of 'Justify My Love (The Beast Within Mix)' included an adapted passage from the Book of Revelation – 'They say that they are Jews, but they are not, they are a synagogue of Satan'– Madonna found herself at the centre of renewed controversy. The Simon Wiesenthal Center accused the singer of being 'incredibly insensitive and potentially dangerous'. Madonna was incensed. 'People can say I am an exhibitionist, but no one can ever accuse me of being a racist. I am not even going to try to defend myself against such ridiculous accusations,' she responded, further adding, 'I certainly did not have any anti-Semitic intent when I included a passage from the Bible on my record. It was a commentary on evil in general. My message, if any, is pro-tolerance and anti-hate. The song is, after all, about love.'[7]

While the dispute surrounding Madonna highlighted the sensitivity of Jewish communities to anti-Semitism in pop culture, the influence of *The Night Porter* raises questions about the boundary between Holocaust remembrance and divorcing Nazi symbolism from its doctrine. This issue resurfaced in later films like *La vita è bella* (*Life Is Beautiful*, 1997) and *The Boy in the Striped Pyjamas* (2008), both of which have been criticised for using comedy and exaggerated narratives to manipulate audience's emotions at the expense of historical accuracy. However, while both of these films attempted to bring the Holocaust to mainstream audiences, *The Night Porter* veered in a different direction, using sexual fantasy rather than historical insight. As a result, the film continued to appeal to artists who were either drawn to its provocative content or were willing to strip away its historical context and focus solely on its imagery.

In 2001, Marilyn Manson released 'The Fight Song' with an accompanying promotional video that drew heavily from the imagery of *The Night Porter*. Wearing braces over a bare torso, elbow-length black leather gloves and an SS-style visor cap, Manson aped Charlotte Rampling's character. The performance showed people scaling wire fences, the symbol of an SS death's head on the bass drum and, in the closing frames, a burning goalpost evocative of a Ku Klux Klan fiery cross. The modern-day enemy suggested America, but the symbolism belonged to Nazi Germany.

And so, the influence of *The Night Porter* persisted.

In 2009, Lady Gaga's debut album *The Fame* sold over five million copies in the US (eighteen million worldwide), becoming the fifth-bestselling album of the year. The promotional film of the record's third single, 'LoveGame', saw the twenty-three-year-old Italian-American singer in the familiar outfit worn by Charlotte Ramping in *The Night Porter*: elbow-length leather gloves, a pair of braces over a bare chest and a peaked cap perched on her head. 'We did this set-up that looked like *The Night Porter* where she is naked under the Nazi uniform,' Gaga explained. 'Fashion is everything to me. It's just as important as the music. I don't want to exist to the British people as just one song. I want to be a true artist who affects their culture in the same way that I've affected American culture.'[8]

Another song, 'Alejandro', resonates to the sound of jackboots marching and the deafening roar of a massed crowd played over emotive strings evoking 1930s Germany. Dancers in black leather military uniform, designed by Emporio Armani, goose-step alongside an image of the Star of David, and a man wearing a long leather jacket, a black kepi and a red armband. Then, from a throng of male performers with beautifully toned bodies wearing only black underwear and boots, Lady Gaga appears in a leather conical bra. Midway through the dance routine she pulls at the cups and the nipples extend to form the barrels of a machine gun. When the nine-minute spectacle was posted online, the artist's website crashed. Critics cooed over the futuristic, fascistic imagery while fans linked the black leather, religious iconography and sexual fetishism to commentary ranging from a tribute to Weimar Germany to a statement on Franco's dictatorship in 1930s Spain.

'The religious symbolism is not meant to denote anything negative,' assured director and fashion photographer Steven Klein, 'but represents the character's battle between the dark forces of this world and the spiritual salvation of the Soul.' While Lady Gaga described 'Alejandro' as 'a celebration of my love and appreciation for the gay community,' adding, 'I admire their bravery and the love they have for one another.'

The apparent flirtation with the theatricality of fascism escalated when Lady Gaga appeared at a rally to support the democratic nominee Hillary Clinton during the 2016 US election. Dressed, according to many anonymous observers, as a 'futuristic Nazi', Gaga addressed the crowd in a high-collar, black-buttoned military jacket with a silver pendant, a red armlet on her right sleeve, and blond swept-back hair. Bought from a collection previously owned by Michael Jackson and worn during his visit to the White House in 1990, the outfit provoked an online media storm for its similarity to Third Reich couture.

'Lady Gaga is dressed literally like a Nazi,' read one tweet.

'Is that Lady Gaga with the Nazi armband hanging out with Hillary on stage?' read another.

'She's sick, sick, sick,' read a third, summing up the views of hundreds of shocked fans.

Picking up the story, CBS News – and the *Express* in the UK – published a selection of critical comments. 'Prominent alt-right activist and author Mike Cernovich joked, "Lady Gaga comes out as alt-right." He also took a poll asking his followers, 'At tonight's Hillary rally, does Gaga look more like a Nazi or a Satanist?'[9]

In response, Gaga tweeted a thinly veiled attack at the Republican nominee, Donald Trump. 'You divided us with hateful language & fear. I love everyone in this country, and I vote for @HillaryClinton to unite us.'

So why the red and black costume and Nazi Germany imagery?

As a sartorial statement, paired with video imagery clearly influenced by *The Night Porter*, a pattern begins to form: another global star connecting pop success with fascism and dictatorship. Yes, Lady Gaga may have avoided direct political rhetoric, but what is the audience to think? Without any clarification from the artist, the public is left to draw their own conclusions. Thus, we see symbolism evoking the Third Reich, an artist who neither affirms nor rejects it, and an audience free to interpret the imagery according to their own political leanings.

Rock 'n' roll thrives on such ambiguity, sparking debate and, in doing so, raising an artist's profile. But we must ask: where does cultural expression end, and social responsibility begin? There is a growing tendency to examine the Holocaust's impact on survivors, their children and grandchildren. In *The German Trauma: Experiences and Reflections 1938–2001*, Gitta Sereny gives voice to individuals whose lives are still shaped by the horrors their parents or grandparents endured. These stories reach beyond the camps, revealing often-overlooked experiences such as rape by liberators and the post-war silence maintained by many survivors. For these individuals, the Holocaust – along with the swastika and other symbols of the Third Reich – remains a vivid, unshakable presence, not something to be dismissed or forgotten. We must also acknowledge the role of women under Nazi rule, who were largely repressed and often marginalised in historical narratives. Hitler believed women were 'equal but different from men' and their lives should centre around the three 'Ks': *Kinder, Küche, Kirche* (children, kitchen, church). Despite this subjugation, a small group of women in rock music have openly embraced the swastika.

Fascinating Fascism

FETISH CLOTHING. SIOUXSIE SIOUX

In 1975, American intellectual Susan Sontag wrote an influential review of *SS Regalia* by Jack Pia for the *New York Review of Books*. Promoted as an illustrated history of a violent century, the book jacket described the haunting symbolism of the SS's iconic initials. 'They stand for naked power, secret violence, for the knock on the door in the night.' Sontag regarded the paperback as one 'to be purchased at airport magazine stands and in "adult" bookstores', and argued its appeal was 'sexual'. This argument was based on the book's front cover which was emblazoned with a large black swastika on an SS armband over which a diagonal yellow stripe read, 'Over 100 Brilliant Four-Colour Photographs. Only $2.95'. 'Exactly,' Sontag highlighted, 'as a sticker with the price on it used to be affixed – part tease, part deference to censorship – on the cover of pornographic magazines, over the model's genitalia.'

Sontag, like her boyfriend, musician Richard Hell (born Richard Meyers of German descent), was Jewish. Her journalistic insight identified the link between uniforms and sexual fantasy, highlighting the association of power with completeness. As she noted, 'The SS was designed as an elite military community that would be not only supremely violent but also supremely beautiful.'

The stylish black uniforms of the *Schutzstaffel* are often attributed to Hugo Boss, but they were actually designed by Karl Diebitsch, with input from graphic designer Walter Heck. In 1929, Heck created the distinctive double Sig-Rune, which would later become emblematic of Himmler's elite guard. As Hauptmann A.D. Freiherr von Getting noted in 1934, 'The civilian insigne of the

SS consists of two runic characters, both of which stand for the S-rune of the Nordic runic alphabets. As the runic alphabet knows no vertical or horizontal strokes – for these were more difficult to carve – it is to be made sure that the runic characters are always slanting.'¹ Heck, working for the badge manufacturing company Ferdinand Hoffstätter, was paid just 2.50 Reichsmarks for the rights to his design. It wasn't until 1944 that Himmler discovered this arrangement and, as a token of appreciation, offered to buy Heck a family home and garden – on the condition that he was married and had two children.

Hugo Boss, a member of the Nazi Party since 1931, supplied the uniforms and also outfitted the Hitler Youth, relying on forced labour and later prisoners of war for production. Historian Lucy Adlington explains that 'Aside from elite Nazi males, who'd have personal tailors – sometimes "Aryan", sometimes even co-opted Jewish tailors – the majority of men received uniforms made in these factories.' Moreover, as Susan Sontag noted, 'For fantasy to have depth, it must have detail.' SS uniforms embodied this principle with precision: tricot jackets, silver screw buttons, medals and badges, along with the infamous death's head symbol on the collar adorned with silver cord. The black visor cap featured a tricot top, velvet band, silver piping and a wire chin strap with pebbled buttons, and metal reinforcement to keep its shape, while leather belts and black riding boots with iron heels completed the look. 'The appearance was both dramatic and menacing,' noted *SS Regalia*.

Amid the economic turmoil following the 1929 Wall Street Crash and the Great Depression, the Nazi Party presented itself as a beacon of strength and stability. Its striking uniforms, which emphasised discipline and order, played a crucial role in elevating Hitler to power. The very meticulousness of the Nazi outfit, a reflection of the totalitarian regime to come, spoke to a deeper subconscious eroticism, stirred by tight-fitting boots, gloves and the fetishist appeal of gleaming leather. Lucy Adlington notes that while the Brownshirts' uniforms were 'more ad-hoc and didn't feature great tailoring', the SS uniforms 'were not only more impressive from a construction and embellishment point of view – the rank badges and flashes etc. – but also associated with immense power and status. Humans can't help responding to that,' she continues, 'even if they despise the regime. Fear and admiration can be so entwined, particularly if you're from a sub-group or culture that is at risk of persecution. For young people in agreement with National Socialist ideology, or even adjacent to it, uniforms were part of the appeal.'

Adlington further notes that one appeal for female factory workers encouraged to become concentration camp guards was not only the pay but also the allure of the uniform. 'This followed very neatly, and deliberately, from the National Socialist emphasis on youth and uniforms via the Hitler Youth and the German Girls League.' She also observes that much of the post-war fetishisation of SS uniforms, particularly in mainstream media – 'such as the uber-evil Nazi officers in *Indiana Jones* or the sexualised portrayal of "harmless" female SS in *'Allo 'Allo*' – has contributed to the continued fascination, including in BDSM (sexual practices that include bondage, discipline, dominance, submission and sadism) contexts. 'This fetishization continues to some extent in collections of Nazi garments and textiles. Some garments were clandestinely kept by their owners and revered by them, and, in turn, by their children. Right-wing sympathisers now seek out Third Reich "memorabilia" as an act of homage, connection, and reverence.'

Such was the uniform's power that concentration camp inmates often noted the attractive appearance of their captors. Despite the unrelenting brutality, the ever-present threat of beatings, executions or the gas chamber, survivors remembered the aesthetic allure of the SS guards. In her memoir *Playing for Time*, the musician Fania Fénelon recounts her deportation to Auschwitz and her encounter with the camp guard Maria Mandl.* 'As SS, she's a

---

* In 2014, *Pechmarie*, an Austrian-made documentary, explored the life of Maria Mandl, drawing on her last written testament. She was executed after the Kraków Trial for complicity in the deaths of over 500,000 female prisoners.

bitch,' Felon remarked. Mandl, a fan of opera, ordered Felon to perform *Madame Butterfly*, her favourite aria. Yet, Felon also found herself acknowledging Mandl's striking beauty: 'As a woman, she's exceedingly beautiful,' she observed. 'The long leather topcoat of the lovely Frau Mandl opened elegantly to reveal her silk-clad legs.'[2]

Holocaust survivor Anita Lasker-Wallfisch writes about Josef Kramer, the Commandant of Auschwitz-Birkenau, who was known for brutal acts like smashing a woman's skull with a club yet could also be moved to tears by the music of the camp orchestra. Lasker-Wallfisch recalls playing the violin for Heinrich Himmler while dogs savagely ripped apart two women. Even amid such brutality, she showed generosity in describing Irma Grese, the sadistic twenty-year-old SS *Oberaufseherin*, as 'good-looking'.* [3] Similarly, Lydia Gradzilowa, a Russian prisoner at Ravensbrück, the women's extermination camp in northern Germany, wrote a poem about the cold-hearted guard Dorothea Binz, who regularly whipped, tortured or set her dog on prisoners. 'A beautiful blonde. With shinning blue eyes and locks of hair.'[4]

These surprising observations reveal the humanity of Holocaust survivors, who despite being surrounded by evil, appreciated pulchritude. Fania Felon lived because she could sing, and Anita Lasker-Wallfisch because she played the violin – both under a regime that understood the power of music. In the evening and regularly on Sunday mornings, SS guards would visit the music block for concerts or variety shows, seeking light relief after a day of 'selections' at the ramp. Day and night, one of nine camp orchestras played marches and popular songs as prisoners filed five abreast through the gates of Auschwitz. 'Marching like automatons,' Primo Levi wrote in *If This Is a Man*, 'their souls are dead, and the music drives them, like the wind drives dead leaves and takes the place of their wills.'[5] On their return, their numbers had significantly

---

*   In November 1945, Grese, known as the 'Hyena of Auschwitz' for her sadistic behaviour, stood trial before a British military tribunal in Lüneburg, Germany, was sentenced to death, and hanged.

diminished, weakened by starvation and the unrelenting demands of forced labour.

The elegant appearance of an SS soldier was intentional. It was the reason that Dr Mengele appeared on the 'selection' ramp at Auschwitz-Birkenau immaculately dressed in uniform, his boots shining like mirrors. 'Just as the Germans wanted to create a self-fulfilling prophecy that those whom they fought were inferior,' noted historian Laurence Rees, 'so by dressing and acting as if they were members of a master-race they wanted to force their enemies to subscribe to the belief that the Nazis were indeed their superiors.'[6]

The step from uniforms *in situ*, as it were, to theatrical use by rock musicians is small. Consider this definition of fascism: 'Total power over others; sexual or otherwise, the exotic, the unknown, domination and enslavement.' That is not to imply that artists drawn to Nazi uniforms necessarily embraced its ideology. However, as the narrative unfolds, a connection emerges between Nazi uniforms, sexual desire and titillation, and rock music, especially in the punk aesthetic. Writing in *The Mass Psychology of Fascism*, psychologist Wilhelm Reich argued that not only does sexual repression strengthen 'political reaction', but it also encourages man to find 'substitute gratifications. Thus, for instance,' Reich contends, 'natural aggression is distorted into brutal sadism. From the point of view of mass psychology, the effect of militarism is based essentially on a libidinous mechanism. The sexual effect of a uniform, the erotically provocative effect of rhythmically executed goose-stepping, the exhibitionistic nature of militaristic procedures.'[7]

Reich further examined the role of the swastika and its capability of 'stirring the deepest reaches of one's emotions'. Tracing its roots to Semites in Spain, Jordania and Greece and in Indo-Germanic culture, Reich uncovers its origin as a 'sexual symbol' representative of 'two interlocked human figures' and as a contributing factor to unconscious emotional reaction.[8] Put simply: a subconscious association between sex and the swastika may be the secret of its enduring power and fascination.

This understanding connects to Alexander Mitscherlich, one of Germany's foremost psychologists, who suggested 'a homo-erotic relationship', between the young, handsome Albert Speer and the charismatic Adolf Hitler, whom Speer saw as a heroic, powerful protector. The opinion 'was not entirely wrong', Speer told his biographer Gitta Sereny.[9] In 1936, during a visit to Hitler's Berghof mountain retreat, Speer recalled that the Führer fixed his eyes on him and played the child's game of daring not to look away. 'I don't know how long it lasted,' recalled an amused Speer. 'It felt like a long time, many minutes. I could hear the buzz of voices around us while I felt this charged silence between him and me. It was he who looked away first. I had won,' Speer laughed. 'One of my closest associates summed up the character of this remarkable relationship: "Do you know what you are? You are Hitler's unrequited love!"'[10]

In the 1970s, Tom of Finland (born Touko Valio Laaksonen) was accused of being a Third Reich sympathiser. The Finnish artist responded by expressing disgust for 'the Nazi philosophy, the racism, and all the rest', but added: 'Of course I still drew them. They had the sexiest uniforms!' It was no coincidence that an admirer of Tom of Finland, Adam Ant, would serve his punk apprenticeship advertising homoerotic fetishism and flaunting the link between sex and violence. So too Siouxsie Sioux.

Bearing a swastika armband in 1976 had marked Sioux as a provocateur on the nascent punk scene. 'Looking like a bunch of reject SS officers,' observed fanzine writer Tony Drayton of the Banshees in a live review. Now, three years later, Siouxsie & the Banshees released the double A-side single 'Love In A Void' coupled with 'Mittageisen (Metal Postcard)' from their debut album. On the lead track, Sioux sang 'too many Jews for my liking'.

'Too many Jews . . . fat businessmen,' Julie Burchill screamed in astonishment, 'I do not see the connection.'[11] 'I, self-righteous square that I am, consider "too many Jews for my liking" to be the most disgusting and unforgivable lyric-line ever written, though God knows there has been more appalling filth written within rock and roll than in every other branch of the entertainment business taken together.'

The band responded with bassist Steven Severin telling *Sounds* journalist Vivien Goldman, who was Jewish. 'That's gonna be changed when we think of something to put in. It was never meant to be anti-Semitic.' Sioux further clarified, '"Too many Jews" means, like, too many fat businessmen,' but she conceded, 'It was stupid anyway. We knew what we meant.'

What Sioux meant was an ill-judged stereotypical representation of Jewish people as, in her words, 'skinflints'. 'Obviously a lot of people didn't get it that way, so it was changed,' she said.[12]

The insulting verse and its weak justification led the far right to claim Siouxsie & the Banshees as their own. Suddenly, the National Front became a threatening presence at the group's shows. As rumours circulated of stiff-armed salutes and the provocative imagery onstage, drummer Kenny Morris told *ZigZag*, 'People who think we're fascists are stupid for believing the press. Nazi salutes and swastikas are just gestures – very emotive symbols – but they're not intended to be fascist.' Then, revealing more than he intended, Morris confirmed the group's use of Third Reich ephemera. 'It's important that the kids realise that a swastika is just a device used in our case to shock. In the case of the Nazis, it was used for political ends. The danger lies in people not understanding the reasons why we're doing these things.'

'We just like to get people's backs up,' Sioux corroborated. 'We've got a morbid sense of humour. I think that everyone finds sick things funny if they're honest about it.'[13] Soon after, the band released the single 'Israel', issued in a die-cut gold sleeve with a Star of David on a black background. Asked to explain the song's meaning, Sioux told *Sounds*, 'It's not about religion as such, it's more general. A disillusioned person, or a whole race who've ceased to understand or believe in what they held to be the truth. It tries to put across, you shouldn't cover what you feel inside by teaching or attitudes imposed on you. It emphasises the strength of the individual.'[14]

Onstage, Sioux changed from swastikas to crucifixes and the Star of David. 'I think I've always been very attracted to very strong imagery whether it's religious or cinematic or pop cultural,' she told American fashion magazine *V* in 2002. 'I remember seeing an exhibition of John Heartfield's photomontages. The way he used the Nazis' own propaganda to attack them was so incredibly powerful. I think at that time there was also still a certain naiveté. I remember in films like *Salon Kitty* and *The Night Porter*, you were more aware of the imagery than the political and social implications.'[15]

Indeed, the song 'Mittageisen' (Metal Postcard) – a portmanteau combing the German *Mittagessen* ('midday meal') and *Eisen* ('iron') – was dedicated to the German propaganda artist, John Heartfield. In 1929, Heartfield worked for the left-wing periodical *Arbeiter-Illustrierte-Zeitung* (*AIZ*: 'Workers' Illustrated Magazine'). Three years later, after Adolf Hitler became chancellor, Heartfield and the *AIZ* editorial staff fled to Czechoslovakia. As war loomed, he produced a luminous collection of anti-Nazi art and magazine covers, so effective that when the Nazis invaded the Sudetenland in 1938, he was fifth on the Gestapo's most-wanted list.

'Mittageisen' drew from two sources. The first, Reichsmarschall Hermann Göring's infamous 1936 'guns versus butter' propaganda speech in which he denounced food luxuries in favour of weapons and industrial output. 'We have no butter, comrades, but I ask you: would you rather have butter or guns? Shall we bring in lard or iron ores? I tell you, being prepared makes us powerful. Butter only makes us fat!' The second was John Heartfield's celebrated art piece *Hurrah, die Butter ist Alle!* (Hurray, There's No Butter Left!), a complex photomontage that critiques the senselessness of war and its toll on innocent civilians. It shows a family at a dining table gorging on metallic objects surrounded by swastika-decorated wallpaper and a framed image of Hitler. A baby in a pram bites down on an axe branded with a Nazi symbol. The caption reads: '*Erz hat stets ein Reich stark gemacht, Butter und Schmalz haben hochstens ein Volk fett gemacht*' – 'Ore (iron) has always made an empire strong; butter and lard have made a people fat at most.'*

The cover sleeve of the Banshees' record featured Heartfield's image and on the reverse the song's lyrics printed in German gothic font. To minimise controversy, Polydor reduced the frame of Heartfield's original artwork to remove the appearance of swastikas and placed a record company logo over the framed image of Adolf Hitler.

'Metal is tough, metal is clean, metal won't rust when oiled and clean', Sioux squawked in German over pounding drums and abrasive guitars, 'Metal will rule in my master scheme'. If the first-person incantation suggested a Nazi sympathiser, Sioux told *Melody Maker* in 1979, 'What lies around the swastika I hate, but I also don't identify with blind patriotism either. I couldn't write a song based around Heartfield if I had that attitude.' Addressing her appropriation of Third Reich symbolism, she added, 'I used certain make-up and a swastika for people to stand back and be repelled. I did it to cause a reaction – not because I supported Nazism. Maybe we could say we had misjudged the reaction, especially from those people who were very sensitive to it.'[16]

As punk moved into the mainstream, Sioux's combative use of Third Reich rhetoric softened and with it came a more thoughtful

---

* In 1997, the Prodigy used an extract from the quote in a booklet to accompany the release of their album *The Fat of The Land*. Although unattributed, Liam Howlett, a founding member of the Prodigy, acknowledged its source in a forthright interview with *Addicted to Noise*. 'This is like a Nazi quote. It's like Hermann Göring, Hitler's right-hand man. This is the quote he made during the war. Now a lot of people have picked up on this in England. You can imagine what the press have been like, "Oh the Prodigy are Nazis . . ." All this crap, you know. To simply answer that question: yes, the quote is a Nazi quote and no, we're not Nazis.' Then, as many have before, Howlett used skin colour in his defence. 'We've got two black guys in the band. So, to even suggest that is totally brainless anyway. I look upon that quote as like a sample. I take it out of its original context, put it in my own context and it means something completely different. It has power and it has the right message for what we want. It has nothing to do with what it's originally about.'

consideration of its social impact, sparked only when skinheads latched on to it to promote racist views. 'I thought, "Whaat?" Hang about. I'm completely opposite in my views on race. I liked the look of it, the colours, red, white, and black. Then it became an issue, and I thought fuck off. No way.'[17]

'It took a long time to live down the Nazi thing, from us having worn swastikas and that line in "Love In A Void",' Steven Severin told Jon Savage.[18] But still the Banshees resisted making a clean break. In an interview with *ZigZag*, the band spoke of their fears for the modern world ruled by a powerful leader instituting a 'master scheme', and an England of 'daily orders over totalitarian loudspeakers'.

'Everyone needs someone to guide them,' suggested Sioux.

'At the moment England is like a gaping wound,' agreed Kenny Morris. 'It's just waiting for someone to jump in.'

'Heartfield put down the establishment,' interjected John McKay. 'He was older and wiser than us and knew how to use photomontage. All we had to use were Nazi armbands.'

'Now it's something you're made to be very *unaware* of,' continued Sioux. 'It's on the TV all the time. It's such unconscious manipulation. It's as subtle as turning on a light bulb. You're often not aware of supporting things.'[19]

Deutscher Girls

ADAM & THE ANTS. *RIPPED & TORN*

'Decadent . . . imperfect . . . and to piss people off,' says Marco Pirroni, guitarist for punk band the Models, explaining his decision to wear a swastika armband in 1977. During their short-lived existence, the group released one single but are perhaps mostly remembered for the provocatively titled 'I Wanna Form My Own Nazi Party'. Pirroni describes the song as a

> cynical look at all the silly punks who wear Nazi armbands. We wore swastikas because we thought they looked cool. We weren't Nazis. I had no political views. We had no problem with Jews, Pakistanis, gays, or anyone else. We just hated everyone who lived in the straight world. None of us fitted in anywhere and that's the way I liked it. I always thought that if gays had adopted the pink swastika instead of the pink triangle that would have said it all.[1]

Vivien Goldman was unimpressed. In 1977, warning that audiences were more likely to miss the point 'while cheerfully marching out of the gig singing that they want to form their own Nazi party, and . . .' she cautioned *Sniffin' Glue* readers 'that ain't no joke'.[2]

Of German Jewish descent, Goldman grew up seeing concentration camp numbers tattooed on the arms of her parents' friends.*

---

* Another music journalist from the era, Charles Shaar Murray of *NME*, recalled how his grandmother was forced to scrub anti-Nazi slogans from the streets of Vienna when the German army invaded Austria in 1938.

'Swastikas made me feel sick,' she wrote, 'even though I told myself they were an ancient Aryan symbol and that punks just wore them to piss off their parents.'[3] As a child of immigrants, for her the arrival of Rock Against Racism was a huge relief. 'Before they met in London, both my parents had escaped Nazi Germany unlike most of my family. The failure of the safer world to believe what was happening helped kill them and shred my past.'[4]

In 1976–7, Goldman hosted a New Year's Eve party in her Ladbroke Grove basement flat. Sid Vicious arrived (with Viv Albertine from the Slits) wearing an open black leather jacket and a large swastika emblazoned across his T-shirt. Sensing the tension, the couple swiftly departed, much to Goldman's relief and sparing her the prospect of a 'ghastly confrontation'. However, in another incident, Caroline Coon recalls visiting a club with Goldman and as they descended the stairs, they encountered Vicious. Holding a broken bottle, Coon says, "He shoved it into Vivian's face. It was horrifying.'

Shortly after, Goldman wrote about the swastika in *Sounds*, singling out 'the disturbing trend towards fascism' and 'the idolatry of Nazi symbols that the young-punks-about-town delight in.' Quoting from Jon Savage's fanzine *London's Outrage*, she pointed out: 'Their stock response is that it's a demystification device, taking the evil out of the swastika the way Lenny Bruce removed the taboo from swear words. Realistically, swastikas and other fascistic paraphernalia are worn to *shock*, to separate the punx from the boys.'

Sceptical of 'high-flown theorising' that went over most people's heads while inadvertently giving free publicity to the National Front, Goldman predicted how punk fans would react to the growing trend of Third Reich-themed songs.

Instead of listening to the Vibrators' lyrics when they sing 'I'm Gonna Be Your Nazi Baby', they're bound to just check it thus: Nazi = desirable item = let's go out and buy some camp Nazi gear, and maybe they weren't such bad lads after all, and I never did like those blacks/gypsies/Jews anyway . . . . Every time the Models sing 'Nazy [*sic*] Party', they should consign themselves to the ovens for irresponsibility.[5]

Suddenly songs about Nazism were all the rage. Following the Sex Pistols 'Belsen Was A Gas', the Vibrators' 'Nazi Baby' and the Models' 'Nazi Party' came the Valves and the two-minute-busting invitation 'For Adolfs' Only'. Signed to Zoom Records, which operated out of Bruce's Record Shop in Edinburgh, the group were awarded Single of the Week in *Record Mirror*. 'Half mickey takes half drilled energy,' wrote Tim Lott under the modish sub-heading 'Nazi punk'. '"EIN ZWEI DREI FIER FUNF" counts Dee Robot in screaming monotone and "I got my uniform I'm OK, I can do the goose-step any day." Bizarre. Over the obnoxious sub-Stooges guitar hack. Robot spells – "A-D-O-L-F- P.A., ADOLF WAS A PISS ARTIST, OK" Sounds ridiculous, and of course it is, but love it just the same.'[6]

Marco Pirroni, a self-declared misfit, was disillusioned with nationalists who wanted to keep England white as well as the legions of ignorant punks who wore or painted a swastika on their faces and leather jacket. 'Just admit it, we were thick. Let the fucking shithole sink into the sea,' he lamented despondently. To escape the drowning masses, Pirroni formed an alliance with Adam Ant, playing a pivotal role in transforming Adam & the Ants from an undervalued punk quartet in the late seventies into an unstoppable force in the burgeoning eighties pop mainstream. Rejecting songs about Nazi fetishism, Ant's evolution into the 'dandy highwayman' stands as one of the most dramatic makeovers in the pages of pop history.

On 6 November 1975, Ant (born Stuart Leslie Goddard) watched the first live performance of the Sex Pistols at Saint Martin's School of Art and, mesmerised by the 'don't give a fuck' attitude, immediately left his group, the support act Bazooka Joe, to form the Ants. Within weeks, the twenty-one-year-old singer faced accusations of closet Nazism. One popular live song, 'Dirk Wears White Sox', referenced Heinrich Himmler in impish wordplay. 'You gotta concentrate on camp in a concentration camp'. Mocking 'men of action' who get rid of foolish people and seduce followers with free uniforms, shiny boots and soft leather, the song ends with the advice to 'leave your wardrobe', 'forget your social bent' and bring 'decadence . . . out in the open'.

Elsewhere, 'Il Duce' spoke of Italian dictator Benito Mussolini – 'Fatty fascist, hanging from your fat feet' – and the execution of Hitler's ally by Italian partisans on 28 April 1945.* 'Nietzsche Baby' mentioned black leather, a swastika, the chosen few, and Fräuleins in uniform who 'break the heart of any Stormtrooper', ending with the warning: 'Don't turn your back cos she might shoot ya'. While another song, 'Deutscher Girls', Ant introduced in German, *'Erinner die Locken der Deutschen Mädel'* ('remember the curls of the German girls'). Enthralled by their 'blonde hair' and 'pigtails' in 'Camp 49, way down on the Rhine', the refrain asked, 'Why did you have to be so Nazi?'

Accusations flew.

'We've had more dirt thrown at us than a corporation dust-cart,' Ant complained in November 1978. Accepting that 'certain imagery marked' his writing, he avowed an abhorrence of Nazism. 'Deutscher Girls' caused all the problems, he told *Melody Maker* in 1980.

I saw a film once by Leni Riefenstahl, about the 1932 [*sic*] Olympics,† I saw those wonderful German girls, hundreds of them all in a row. Now I'm a great one for history, and there was a war in 1939, and atrocities were committed. But this was very much along the lines of Mel Brooks' *The Producers*, and I just imagined a love story between a member of the Hitler Youth and one of those girls – because every kid in Germany at that

---

* First recorded in 1978, Cabaret Voltaire's 'Do the Mussolini (Headkick)' was, as the band explained, inspired by a 'newsreel where Mussolini had just been killed off, and there's all the peasants standing around, and the corpses on the ground, and some geezer kicking the corpse about'.

† In November 1938, Leni Riefenstahl promoted her film *Olympia* (about the 1936 Berlin Games) in North America. However, in the wake of the recent Jewish pogrom across Germany known as Kristallnacht, she faced widespread criticism and film boycotts in both the US and Great Britain.

time, whether they liked it or not, just had to do it, they had
no choice in the matter.

Ant understood correctly: state pressure made it difficult not to join
the Hitler Youth or the League of German Girls (Bund Deutscher
Mädel). A student at Hornsey College of Art, he meticulously studied subjects before writing songs. The Ants' debut album *Dirk Wears
White Sox* brimmed with historical references ranging from Italian
futurism and the shooting of John F. Kennedy to Hitler's infamous
'Tabletalk' lectures. The title of the latter song referenced recordings
Hitler's private secretary Martin Bormann edited of the Führer at
his mountainside retreat in Bavaria,* between July 1941 and March
1942, and other monologues of the period. Delivered to an inner
circle of selected guests, the subject matter traversed foreign affairs,
religion and culture to personal reflections on friends, enemies,
ambitions and secret dreams. Albert Speer, contradicting his once
professed love for the Führer, regarded the 'endless monologues' as
'rambling nonsense', noting in his prison memoir that, '[Hitler] was
that classic German type known as *Besserwisser*, the know-it-all. His
mind was cluttered with minor information and misinformation,
about everything. I believe that one of the reasons he gathered
so many flunkies around him was that his instinct told him that
first-rate people couldn't possibly stomach the outpourings.'†
    In 'Tabletalk', Adam Ant explored the rumoured love affair
between Hitler and his niece Geli Raubal, the daughter of his
half-sister, Angela. He sings, 'Don't like your stare, don't like the
arm in the air, your style is so brash and that silly moustache'. Journalist William L. Shirer described Raubal – 'flowing blonde hair,

---

* In 1936, David Lloyd George visited Hitler at Berghof, Obersalzberg. Writing
in the *Daily Express*, the British prime minister described him as 'a born leader of
men. A magnetic dynamic personality with a single-minded purpose, a resolute
will, and a dauntless heart.'
† The 'Tabletalk' ('Tischgespräche') recordings serve as evidence of Hitler's
knowledge of the Holocaust. In October 1941 he stated, 'It is good if the fear that
we are exterminating the Jews goes before us.'

handsome features, a pleasant voice and a sunny disposition which made her attractive to men' – as the woman Hitler was deeply in love with and, according to party comrades, intended to marry. He was thirty-six. She was seventeen. It is unclear whether Raubal's feelings for Hitler were reciprocated. They both suspected the other of having affairs. Hitler, believed to have masochistic tendencies, forbade her to return to Vienna to study as an operatic singer. In 1932, following an intense five-year relationship, Raubal allegedly committed suicide in the luxurious nine-room apartment they shared in Munich. Hitler's Walther pistol was found on the floor, along with an unfinished letter on the table. A coroner's report indicated the gunshot had pierced Raubal's chest below the left shoulder and reached her heart, but no inquest was conducted into her death.

'Hitler's political enemies had a field day,' wrote his biographer Ian Kershaw, 'Stories of violent rows and physical mistreatment mingled with sexual innuendo and even the allegation that Hitler had either killed Geli himself or had had her murdered to prevent scandal.' Though Hitler was not in Munich when Raubal died, Kershaw argues that 'it is not easy to see the reasoning for a commissioned murder to prevent a scandal being carried out in his own flat. As it was, the scandal was enormous.'[7]

In October 1979, Adam Ant made a video for 'Tabletalk', directed by Stephanie Gluck, dressed in leather trousers and a Vivienne Westwood 'Anarchy' shirt. The design featured bleached-out stripes reminiscent of a concentration camp uniform, along with the stencilled situationist slogans 'ONLY ANARCHISTS ARE PRETTY' and 'DANGEROUSLY CLOSE TO LOVE'. A small rectangular portrait of Karl Marx, and an optional upturned *Parteiadler* (eagle and swastika) stitched on the pocket or collar – not visible in the film – adorned the shirt. An armband marked with the word 'CHAOS' completed the outfit.

Two years later, a reinvigorated band embraced Burundi drumming and Native American culture, complete with a warrior's white stripe across Adam's face. Amid the mania surrounding *Ant Music*

– with hits like 'Dog Eat Dog', 'Stand And Deliver' and 'Prince Charming' – 'Deutscher Girls' unexpectedly shot into the UK top 20 singles chart. Released by the group's former record label, EG, the controversial reference to being 'so Nazi' became the sanitised 'so nasty' and 'Camp 49 way down on the Rhine' the softened 'lover of mine'. Despite the edits, Ant refused to perform the song on *Top of the Pops*, and in his absence, the BBC invited the in-house dance troupe Zoo, who pouted in heavy make-up and delivered thigh-slapping kicks while dressed in traditional German attire.*

The absurd interpretation of the song in many ways mirrored Ant's reference to the 1967 comedy film *The Producers* written and directed by Mel Brooks. The story centres on a theatrical agent (Zero Mostel) and his accountant (Gene Wilder) who hatch a plan to make a fortune by producing a Broadway musical guaranteed to fail. Their plan is simple: raise millions in non-returnable investments, stage a surefire flop, and pocket the leftover money once the show closes. When they stumble upon *Springtime for Hitler* – a production they deem 'the worst musical ever written' – they're convinced they've found the perfect disaster and successfully raise the funding. On opening night swastikas drape the stage. The audience watches, mouths agape as high-kicking chorus members in shiny boots and black stockings parade across the stage in a sumptuous spectacle of Nazi pageantry and theatrical camp. Stunned, people begin to walk out. But then, something shifts. Laughter breaks out in the auditorium as Hitler appears as a hippy, stoned and making drug references. The play becomes an enormous success and 'the producers' are ruined.†

---

* When Ant started performing live again in 2010, after a fourteen-year absence, 'Deutscher Girls' was performed with the original 'so Nazi' chorus.

† In 1983, Mel Brooks revived the wartime comedy *To Be or Not to Be*, starring in the film adaptation alongside his wife, Anne Bancroft. A recording of the title song, subtitled 'The Hitler Rap' and performed by Brooks, charted across Europe, including the UK (number 12) and Germany (number 11). In an accompanying video – and in television appearances – Brooks dressed as Hitler, surrounded by swastikas and bare-chested, leather-clad dancers singing the chorus line 'Don't be stupid, be a smarty, come and join the Nazi Party.'

Satirising Hitler brought Mel Brooks widespread acclaim, but in the world of pop, exploiting the tropes of Nazism drew more concern than applause. Despite the musical appeal of 'Deutscher Girls' – and much there is to appreciate – Adam Ant's lyrics seemed to echo Hitler's vision of the perfect German woman; one whose role was to reproduce Aryan children and ensure the Third Reich's survival for a thousand years. Ant has always stood by every song and word he has written, citing comedian Lenny Bruce as an influence. He said, quoting Bruce in 1978, 'Do not sweep it under the carpet. Bring it out because there's nothing there.'[8]

Still, in an era of street violence between neo-Nazis and anti-fascists, drawing attention to taboo subjects invited misinterpretation. Ant protested. 'Deutscher Girls' was not about concentration camps. '[It was] about a guy who falls in love with a girl – albeit a member of the Nazi Youth. A few people have come up to me and said, "Oh, you're really into swastikas," and I say well do you read the words? When they come back after reading it, they say, we can see its anti- now.'[9]

To drive the point home, Ant created a collage for *Ripped & Torn* with the sardonic title, 'OH! HOW I LOVE THE PRESS' and signed, 'ADAM (nasty Nazi puerile toilet-boy) ANT'. The design featured a backdrop of swastikas and Adolf Hitler in various semi-naked sadomasochistic poses, with Ant's head emerging from an upturned toilet in the bottom corner of the image. 'I've a right to like German girls a lot,' he barfs.

Tony Drayton was ecstatic: 'A page of swastikas and fetish and Hitler,' says the editor of *Ripped & Torn*, who gleefully printed Ant's rhetorical tagline, 'TABOO OR NOT TABOO . . . THAT IS THE QUESTION.' 'All this sex going on. It was powerful, a brilliant comment against Nazism: "Here: this is what you think I am."'

The copy was dismissed as 'pathetic garbage' by *NME* journalist Julie Burchill, who added the biting comment, 'back to sixth-form college, Tony'. A self-proclaimed philo-Semite (a person who favours or supports the Jews), Burchill had discovered her father's *World at War* magazine collection at the age of fourteen, which introduced her to the 'complex horror' of the Holocaust. Unimpressed by

Nazi posturing, Burchill was disgusted when Adam Ant shared his fetish for Nazi women in an interview. Alongside celebrities such as Dirk Bogarde, Shirley Bassey, Tommy Steele, Perry Como, Anthony Newley and Brian Inglis, Ant proudly added the name of the sadistic SS officer Ilse Koch to his roll-call of heroes. 'She's a new one,' he remarked in *ZigZag* in November 1977, boasting that he had written a new song about her.

Ilse Koch, née Köhle, was a former stenotypist before joining her husband, Commandant Karl-Otto Koch, at Buchenwald concentration camp as a guard. Koch soon acquired a reputation for her brutal treatment of prisoners, beating them with a riding crop and forcing them into physically exhausting tasks for her own amusement. After the war, Koch faced criminal charges including physical abuse and ordering the execution of prisoners with 'interesting' tattoos. In 1947, the International Military Tribunal at Nuremburg viewed film footage of twelve hundred civilians being marched from the nearby city of Weimar, by order of Chief of Staff of the Army, Dwight D. Eisenhower, to witness the atrocities at Buchenwald. 'There are many smiling faces,' the commentary relayed in a sombre tone, 'and, according to observers, at first the Germans act as though this were something being staged for their benefit. One of the first things that the German civilians see as they reach the interior of the camp is the parchment display. On a table for all to gaze upon is a lampshade made of human skin, made at the request of an SS officer's wife. Large pieces of skin have been used for painting pictures, many of an obscene nature.'

In his substantial work, *The Rise and Fall of the Third Reich*, William L. Shirer documented the disturbing practice of recycling human flesh belonging to healthy and young victims, shot in the neck, and skin free from defects, to manufacture ornamental objects such as lampshades, book covers and gloves.[10] One such artefact even bore the words 'Haensel & Gretel'. The press was quick to condemn Koch, with *Time* magazine reporting that 'Justice had caught up with the red-headed, forty-year-old Witch of Buchenwald', adding that she was 'sexually psychotic'.[11] Other sources described her as a 'sadistic pervert', 'sex-hungry' and accused her of indulging in orgies.

In 1947, Ilse Koch and thirty other defendants stood trial at an American military court in Dachau charged with 'participating in a common design to commit war crimes'. She was sentenced to life in prison but released in 1949. When news reached a twenty-one-year-old Woody Guthrie that US Commander General Lucius Clay had reduced Koch's sentence from life to just four years – on the grounds that 'there was no convincing evidence that she had selected inmates for extermination in order to secure tattooed skins, or that she possessed any articles made of human skin' – Guthrie penned a song in her name. The ballad, written from the perspective of an inmate in Buchenwald with a number tattooed on their skin, included a litany of brutal atrocities: a girl mauled to death by hounds, a man shot by guards, people starved to death, the systematic murder of new arrivals, gold extracted from teeth, and cracked heads and bodies turned to chimney smoke in the furnace. 'Old Ilse Koch was jailed,' sighed Guthrie, 'Old Ilse Koch went free.'*

After her release in October 1949 from Landsberg prison – where Adolf Hitler had written *Mein Kampf* in 1924 – Koch was immediately rearrested. Under strong pressure from the US Senate, she was re-tried before a West German court in January 1951. Despite testimony from former prisoners who had been forced to make macabre objects in Buchenwald, and a witness, Walter Retterpam, who recalled seeing Koch strike a prisoner across the face with a riding crop while shouting, 'I dare say you are looking at my legs!' the prosecution failed to conclusively prove Koch's involvement in the alleged crimes. Nevertheless, Chief Prosecutor Johann Ilkow described her actions as part of a 'common design' to abuse prisoners, noting her complete surrender to her 'sexual instincts

---

* On the original typed lyric sheet, Guthrie noted that the words should be sung to the tune of the bluesy African-American prison song, 'Another Man Done Gone'. In 2006, the Klezmatics recorded a version of 'Old Ilse Koch' crediting words to Woody Guthrie and music by Lorin Sklamberg.

without shame'. As a result, Koch received a second life sentence. The press revelled in her alleged sexual misdeeds, often blurring the line between fact and sensationalism. The *Washington Post* reported that she would sexually excite inmates by 'striding through the camp in tight riding breeches' and 'removing her blouse'. Yet, as historian Sir Richard Evans concluded in 2024, much of the evidence surrounding Koch's actions was based on rumours and unreliable sources – such as stories about lampshades made from human skin and tattooed skin collected from living prisoners – and was of 'doubtful veracity'.[12]

In 1967, Koch hanged herself using bed sheets in her cell at the women's prison in Aichach, Germany. Her time in Buchenwald remains a deeply disturbing chapter in history. Yet, by the late seventies, her sadism formed the basis of anti-Semitic baiting, as Rock Against Racism's Lucy Whitman recounts. 'One day when I changed trains on the tube a stranger and I stood together scratching out the words scrawled on a poster: "Jews make good lampshades".' For those who casually flirted with Third Reich iconography for shock or amusement, this was an alarming reminder that they were doing so despite the suffering of innocent victims. Like Adam Ant's public flirtation with Nazi imagery, it signified a troubling and expanding shift in popular culture, where Nazism was being used as a vehicle for sexual fantasy.

In April 1978, Julie Burchill interviewed punk acolyte Jordan, who having received a stream of letters from an infatuated unknown suitor, later identified as Adam Ant, joined his group as a vocalist and then interim manager. 'All politicians are boring,' Jordan groaned to Burchill. 'Everyone hates the NF except the NF, that's all there is to it.' When Burchill pointed out that 'Your boy Adam sings Nazi songs,' Jordan exclaimed. 'Oh God! He's the last person who'd put on a swastika. He's just an incredibly *sexual* person who's mad about German girls.' 'Like Ilse Koch, you mean,' Burchill probed.[13]

Shortly afterwards, *NME* journalist Nick Kent reviewed an Adam & the Ants performance at London's Marquee Club. He not only backed Burchill's accusation that Ant sang perverted Nazi songs but used the opportunity to impress on readers that the singer's hero, Ilse Koch, was better known as Ilsa the She-Wolf, the commandant of a Nazi concentration camp responsible for the deaths of innumerable prisoners through the most gut-churning slow torture imaginable.

Directed in 1975 by American film-maker Don Edmonds, *Ilsa, She-Wolf of the SS* featured a sadistic camp commandant – loosely based on Ilse Koch, the so-called Bitch of Buchenwald – who attempts to prove that women can endure more physical pain than men and therefore are entitled to serve in the German army. In the name of 'medical research', Ilsa leads an SS team sterilising and conducting gratuitous and sadistic acts of violence on women. However, by projecting images of swastikas and SS uniforms, the film links sexual dominance and desire to Third Reich atrocity – gang rape, castration, flogging, human scientific experimentation, torture – creating a spectacle designed to provoke voyeuristic pleasure. Here, Ilsa takes off her trousers, pulls up her leather boots and, straddled above a visiting high-ranking Nazi dignitary lying prostrate on the floor, urinates on him.

The narrative was loosely based on fact. But as with all Third Reich-related pornography the purpose was to penetrate the viewer's mind with images of sexual fantasy over historical truth. 'The film you are about to see is based on documented fact,' forewarned the film's opening credits.

> The atrocities shown were conducted as "medical experiments" in special concentration camps throughout Hitler's Third Reich. Although these crimes against humanity are historically accurate, the characters depicted are composites of notorious Nazi personalities; and the events portrayed have been condensed into one locality for dramatic purposes. Because of its shocking subject matter, this film is restricted to adult audiences only. We dedicate this film with the hope that these heinous crimes will never happen again.

Banned in both Germany and by the British Board of Film Censors in the UK, *Ilsa, She-Wolf of the SS* still managed to be a financial success, spawning three sequels and attracting a devoted cult following. In 1986, the American rock band Murphy's Law recorded the song 'Ilsa', celebrating the notorious commandant and reducing the film to its most lurid aspects. 'Aryan bitch, goddess in black, hard just like a rock. If you fail to satisfy, she'll cut off your cock'.

To counter the escalating narrative, Adam & the Ants offered to perform for Rock Against Racism. 'We want to do a RAR gig because we want to straighten out certain people without having to write stupid letters to music papers saying how nice I am really,' Adam Ant explained to *Temporary Hoarding*'s Lucy Whitman. 'I am not really a wardrobe Nazi. And the only way to do that is with actions.'[14]

Dumbfounded by the rumours surrounding the band, drummer Dave Barbe (also known as Barbarossa, the code name for Nazi Germany's invasion of the Soviet Union in June 1941) stepped in to clarify the facts.

> How can they call us a Nazi band when we've got a coloured drummer? I've got a Jewish mother, and the other side of my family is black; I mean, surely, I must be the most anti-Nazi bloke around! If the National Front ever get in power, I'll be kicked out of the country right away. I wouldn't go around supporting people who wrote songs in favour of Nazism. I've got a lot to worry about if they get in. That's why doing these gigs are good for the band because it's important to do this just to clear the air.

When the media labelled 'Deutscher Girls' as a 'Nazi number', Ant defended the song, emphasising that its true inspiration came from the film *The Night Porter*. While admitting that blonde German girls 'running around in gymslips' appealed to him, he clarified that the lyrics – describing filling 'your bath with the finest champagne' and licking 'your skin dry' – imagery drawn from *Salon Kitty* – were a form of performance, not personal belief. 'If I want to write fantasy numbers about Dirk Bogarde films then I'm entitled to. If people call me a Nazi on stage – that's fine because I accept that they can call me whatever they want – as an artist. But offstage, if they infer that I'm that privately, then they're in big trouble because I'm not a fucking Nazi. I hate Nazis.'

Ant, of Romany heritage,* argued that his background gave him 'more reasons to hate them [Nazis] than anybody else'. His stepfather, a tank driver in the British army who was part of the first wave of soldiers to have liberated Bergen-Belsen, later suffered a breakdown. 'He'd seen six years of war, but he'd never seen nothing like that,' Ant explained. When Whitman suggested that Nazism in songs treated with 'sordid glamour . . . might appeal to people who are fed up and frustrated and think it sounds more exciting than boring everyday life', Dave Barbe retorted, 'Fucking hell! If I thought I was playing in a group that was furthering – bringing out their fantasies and making them a reality – or sort of helping the National Front, I'd leave. They're just humorous songs, they're really funny, you can laugh at Nazism in those songs, instead of being frightened.'

And so, on 17 June 1978, Rock Against Racism presented Adam & the Ants at Southbank Polytechnic with the disclaimer, 'Some people say Adam Ant should be seen and not heard. The music press call them Nazis, we think they've just seen too many Dirk Bogarde movies. See them live on the night the posing has to stop.'

Rock Against Racism's prominence in the late seventies helped to distinguish anti-fascist bands from neo-Nazis, though many of the aligned acts had ambiguous political backgrounds. In 1977, Mark Stewart (later of the Pop Group) arrived at punk's first dedicated club, the Roxy, dressed in black Nazi regalia. When questioned on camera by student film-maker Simon Holland, he nonchalantly replied, 'I like it. I wear what I like,' as the screen

* An estimated quarter to half a million Sinti/Roma lost their lives during the Holocaust.

filled with fluorescent green, hand-drawn swastikas, adding, 'My girlfriend made it for me.[15]' Yet, by the release of the Pop Group's second album, 1980's *For How Much Longer Do We Tolerate Mass Murder?*, Stewart was more concerned about discussing current affairs, the threat of nuclear war, famine in East Timor and Pol Pot's reign in Cambodia.

Then there was Gaye Advert of the Adverts , who in March 1977, while supporting the Jam, performed with 'Fuck Off' scrawled onto her T-shirt and a swastika painted on the headstock of her bass guitar. A year later, a woman attacked the singer of the Angelic Upstarts, outraged to see him wearing a swastika armband. 'She set about me with her umbrella,' singer Thomas 'Mensi' Mensforth explained. 'I tried to tell her it doesn't mean anything, we only do it to annoy people, but she wouldn't listen. So, I ran away. Never moved so fast.'

When news reached the National Front that Mensi wore a T-shirt with 'Fascism Kills' scrawled across the front and his group performed in front of a backdrop that read 'Smash the Front', they contacted the police to complain that Angelic Upstarts were abusing their party.

Punk thrived on such contradictions. The Prefects, formerly known as Church of England and then the Gestapo, regularly performed the song 'Bristol Road Leads To Dachau', in which singer Robert Lloyd compared the 1974 IRA pub bombings and the arterial road leading out of Birmingham city centre to Nazi concentration camps. 'From Birmingham via Belfast to Belsen you're gonna get burned to death', Lloyd wrote. 'Don't think Auschwitz couldn't happen now and to think somebody could stop that train. Those are not bakeries, those are crematories'. Interviewed by the *NME*, Lloyd explained, 'In Birmingham we had some really heavy pub bombings. There was this pub where I used to meet this girl regularly, and once I didn't turn up. The pub got bombed and she was fucked up . . . so I wrote this song.'[16]

Then, in August 1977, Tony Drayton made a dramatic plea for an end to punk's obsession with Third Reich imagery, beseeching readers of *Ripped & Torn* with the headline 'WHEN DID YOU STOP WEARING THAT NAZI PARAPHERNALIA?'

Like many teenagers outside London, Drayton was drawn to Third Reich memorabilia through adverts in the back pages of the music press. The infatuation abruptly stopped with a candid admission of guilt. 'I first started wearing the swastika in the form of my iron cross around my neck back in July '76 because it looked so good and also it caused outrage and shocked people really well. Not because I hated Jews or anything like that. The only thing I liked about the Nazi regime was their organisation and determination.'

Today, Drayton is embarrassed by his teenage infatuation. 'At the time, it seemed perfectly logical. It came from seeing a photo of Siouxsie Sioux at a Pistols gig at the Screen on the Green. She was wearing fishnet clothing, tits out, and a swastika armband. I was in Scotland. I thought, "That's what punks do: they wear swastikas." They were for sale in the *NME* small ads. I bought a ring, an armband and a necklace for about 75p. It was pantomime shock. It was the same reason I wore a plastic Union Jack flag to a Saturday night disco; ripped it up, safety-pinned it through a black T-shirt and then put a swastika armband on the side. It got a reaction, and I thought, "Oh, wow!"'

Never actually hearing Siouxsie & the Banshees, Drayton says, 'It was just the power of the image and the live review. It should have died away but then Malcolm and Vivienne did the Destroy T-shirt with the swastika in the middle. So, it became a prominent part, an iconic image. Then there was Sid Vicious and the swastika shirt. I thought it was totally wrong.'

Before his punk epiphany, Drayton, when accused of being a 'fucking Jew hater', argued in favour of 'Jew killing'. 'I was trying to be indignant and ignorant,' he says with refreshing candour, 'to not be proved wrong. It's like the more you paint yourself into a corner, the more ridiculous things you say. It's about not admitting you're wrong.' Then he abruptly stopped and, for the first time, considered the implications of Nazi terror. 'I realised the disgusting side of the regime,' he wrote in *Ripped & Torn*, 'the mass extermination of anybody who spoke against them, and the enforcement of a dictatorship that meant no freedom to the individual. And also, the stupid idea of creating a master race of blonde youths by killing anybody who didn't conform to their standards.' While urging readers to stop wearing Nazi regalia, Drayton admitted that the swastika was 'the best symbol anyone's ever come up with' and yet signed off with the brave entreaty, 'but I'll never wear one again, will you?'

An immediate response came from Mark Perry, the former editor of *Sniffin' Glue*. After forming Alternative TV, the band released their second single 'How Much Longer?' 'How much longer will people wear Nazi armbands,' Perry demanded. 'Talk about anarchy, fascism, and boredom. You don't know nothing and you don't really care.'

If punk was ready to shake off the shackles of its Nazi posturing, the time was now. With right-wing extremism on the rise, suddenly, seemingly out of nowhere, a new youth movement surfaced championing multiculturalism over racism.

Born in Coventry, they called it 2 Tone.

3.

LOVE IN A VOID

'*Mit Gewalt aus Bunkern hervorgeholt*' (Forcibly pulled out of bunkers).
A Nazi propaganda press image taken during the 1943 Warsaw Ghetto
uprising of a group of Jewish women, children and men forced out of
a bunker by armed German soldiers (SS-Rottenführer Josef Blösche
holding a sub-machine gun) and later deported to Majdanek or
Treblinka extermination camps.

Master-Racial Masturbation

2 TONE

At the dawn of the eighties, 2 Tone emerged as the dominant British street culture, promoting integration between Black and white musicians. Though not entirely unprecedented – think of Sly & the Family Stone or the Equals – rock history had typically seen musicians stick to their own ethnicities. Suddenly, here were the Specials with five white and two Black members; the Selecter with six Black and one white; and the Beat neatly harmonised with three white and three Black musicians. From 1979 to 1981, these bands, along with Madness, UB40, Bad Manners and the Bodysnatchers, dominated the British charts, contributing to the Coventry-based 2 Tone label achieving more commercial success than punk.

However, a right-wing minority soon infiltrated 2 Tone concerts, subjecting the groups to Nazi salutes and racist insults: the Specials targeted in Newcastle, Leeds and Uxbridge; the Beat at Brighton's Top Rank; and Bad Manners and the Bodysnatchers at Camden's Electric Ballroom and in Guildford. The *London Evening News* ran a headline 'Don't Rock with the Sieg-Heilers' above a photo of the multi-ethnic Selecter. 'The media ran with the idea that in some way or another we were on the side of these racist skinheads', recalls lead singer Pauline Black, herself of mixed Jewish-Nigerian heritage.

While swastikas were rarely seen, agitators – often skinheads – would direct Sieg Heil salutes at the bands and disrupt performances between songs. To the bafflement of most, they would then dance when the Caribbean-inspired rhythms took over, adding to the confusion. In an attempt to make sense of this contradiction, Madness frontman Suggs joked, albeit uncomfortably, 'There was a period where you thought, "Jesus! It's happened. We've been taken over by the Nazis.'" He later expressed his abhorrence of racism in an interview with the BBC, stating, 'It started off like a fashion for a lot of kids. It was like football teams and then it was Nazis.' As a teenager, Suggs had been part of a gang that targeted Asian youths. 'When I was fourteen/fifteen I was in a gang that went Paki-bashing, at sixteen not so much.' But by seventeen, he told anti-racist fanzine *Guttersnipe*, he 'was finished with all that', particularly after seeing 'a mate's dad strutting about in a Nazi uniform. Now my old mates come up to me and tell me they like the band but why do we play nigger music?' [1]

Onstage, agitators were called out and shamed, with spotlights often directed at them. In some instances, bands would walk off-stage in protest. At Brunel University, the Specials even jumped into the crowd to chase the ringleaders out of the building. But it is Suggs' personal reflection that offers the clearest insight into the escalating problem. Many young people, searching for an identity, turned to neo-Nazi groups because they offered a sense of belonging and camaraderie, not out of political belief but for the thrill of violence and the adrenaline rush. Before joining the Specials, Terry Hall, much like Suggs, had fought in violent clashes between white gangs and local Black youth, including future band members Lynval Golding and Neville Staple. But as they grew older, more self-aware, and more socially conscious, many of these young men abandoned their specious pretensions.

At the time, though, in the midst of the 2 Tone movement, it made little sense. As Jerry Dammers of the Specials put it in 'Do The Dog': 'Master-racial masturbation causes National Front frustration'. While Dave Wakeling of the Beat echoed the sentiment in 'Two Swords': 'I've never been one for the punch-ups but look I really hate those Nazis'.

Madness, the only all-white band on the 2 Tone label, incurred the wrath of the press as racist incidents marred their concerts. At the Electric Ballroom on 18 November 1979, a crowd of right-wing skinheads and National Front members hurled racist abuse at the support act, Red Beans & Rice. Suggs and co-frontman Chas

Smash stepped in to confront the extremists. 'I had to come out and say, "Stop fucking around. We wanted this band on the bill,"' says Smash, who then jumped into the audience and was punched in the face and 'kicked in the bollocks', while Suggs reacted by kicking over a microphone stand and storming off the stage.

Over a two-year period, right-wing fanatics used Madness concerts to recruit new members, intimidate the audience and taunt the band with Nazi gestures. In 1981, the Centre for Contemporary Studies published a report on neo-fascist recruitment at rock concerts. The BBC's *Newsnight* singled out Madness in a feature called 'The Rock and the Right'. In response, the band issued a statement, read by presenter Joan Bakewell, categorically denying support for 'any political group which has racial politics'. They highlighted that their first hit, 'The Prince', was 'dedicated to a Jamaican, Prince Buster, who is the godfather of ska and reggae' and emphasised that 'the record was released on a label belonging to the Specials, who have both black and white members'. The statement concluded with the band's strong condemnation of racism and a call for 'fans of all ages and all nationalities do likewise'.

Such was their frustration that Madness threatened to split up if the fighting did not stop. 'We're only in this game for a laugh and if we are forced to drop out then none of us would have any regrets at all,' threatened saxophonist Lee Thompson. 'We don't want anything to do with the National Front. As far as I'm concerned, if they start venting their political feelings at our gigs, then we can call it a day.'

In October 1981, Madness faced more criticism when the inner sleeve of their new album, 7, appeared to feature three swastikas. Nigel Dick, the group's press officer, wrote to *Record Mirror* to explain that the symbol, printed on a scarf worn by drummer Daniel Woodgate which was a gift from a friend who had recently visited India, was an ancient emblem of peace, harmony and unity. Dick pointed out that the scarf also featured the Indian mantra 'Om Namah Shivah' ('everything is one'), and reiterated, 'Once again, may it be absolutely clear that Madness do not support any racist policies and hope that their fans of all ages and all nationalities do likewise.' Despite this, an editor's note at the end of the letter read: 'But surely if you have to go to such lengths to explain the ambiguous symbols employed by Madness, they're better left alone?'

Neo-Nazi activity at gigs was by no means limited to 2 Tone bands. Many punk groups, from the Ruts in south London to Stiff Little Fingers in Northern Ireland, played for audiences divided by political and religious persuasion. As singer Jake Burns verifies, 'We started to attract a right-wing following and people would Sieg Heil.' Disillusioned by the persistent violence at 2 Tone shows – at times even stabbings – and the ongoing media disputes, Jerry Dammers channelled his anger into a new song, 'Ghost Town'. Vocalist Terry Hall, whose grandfather was German Jewish, sang poignantly over a haunting reggae backbeat: 'Bands won't play no more. Too much fighting on the dance floor.' Another Specials track, written by Jamaican-born guitarist Lynval Golding, also tackled bigotry: 'With a Nazi salute and a steel capped boot you follow like sheep inna wolf clothes'. Golding, who had been the victim of three racist attacks, questioned the senselessness of the violence: 'Why did you try to hurt me? Did you really want to kill me, tell me why, tell me why, tell me why?' The record topped the UK charts. But where 'Why?' confronted neo-Nazi hatred, Dammers' next song, 'War Crimes (The Crime Remains The Same)', addressed the ongoing conflict between Israel and its neighbouring Muslim states.

Founded in 1948, the state of Israel offered a homeland for persecuted Jews and Holocaust survivors, but in the early 1970s the Palestine Liberation Organization (PLO), under the leadership of Yasser Arafat, led a succession of cross-border raids from Lebanon. On 11 April 1974, eighteen Israelis, including eight children, were killed, followed by the deaths of twenty-two children in an attack on a school just a month later. This violence ignited a civil war between the PLO and the Lebanese Christian militia. Then, on 3 September 1982, a Palestinian shot and wounded the Israeli ambassador in London. In retaliation, Israel invaded Lebanon and launched a nine-week bombing campaign on the capital Beirut, driving Arafat and more than 1,000 Palestinians out of the country. However, around 2,000 armed men were believed to have stayed.

On 16 September, Christian Militia entered the Sabra and Shatila camps and slaughtered the remaining residents. 'The bombing of civilian targets in Beirut was way over the top,' Dammers told the *Daily Mirror* on 21 December. '[The Israelis] are stooping to the same level as the Nazis.'

The question of securing Jewish and Palestinian homelands in the Middle East remains a highly divisive issue. Yet, for a secular, middle-class English musician in 1982 to compare the systematic extermination of six million Jews during the Holocaust to the ongoing conflict was naive at best. 'From the graves of Belsen where the innocent will burn to the genocide in Beirut, Israel, was nothing learned?' encapsulated an oversimplified view of the ideological origins of the Third Reich and its pursuit of the so-called Final Solution.

The story of 2 Tone is an acute illustration of the journey many adolescents take when forming their adult identity. Music plays a critical role in the ideological path young people follow and, for that reason alone, engagement with political rhetoric and fascistic imagery must be treated with absolute care and understanding of its emotional power. Sadly, in the dying embers of punk, and despite the positivity of the 2 Tone movement, Nazi intonations remained largely unchallenged, benefitting a new crop of groups in a coming era of unrestrained confrontation.

Indeed, in some instances, the defiant stance of their predecessors seemingly inspired, not curbed, a new wave of musicians drawn to the imagery of the Third Reich.

An Ideal for Living

BLONDIE. SHAM 69. JOY DIVISION

Two golden rules when touring Germany: do not mention the Nazis; do not talk about the war. So instructed *Melody Maker* reporter Harry Doherty. So when Debbie Harry gave a 'brisk' Sieg Heil during a performance in West Berlin, Doherty was horrified. It is 1978 and Blondie are on a European tour. This band are smashing it. It is the year of breakthrough hits such as 'Denis', '(I'm Always Touched By Your) Presence, Dear', 'Picture This', 'Hanging On The Telephone' and the multi-platinum chart-topping *Parallel Lines*. But here, in Berlin, Chris Stein thinks vocalist Harry's Nazi gesture was 'a bit rude'. She protests. 'I don't think that's true because if anybody has had to live with that stigma, these people have. I mean, what do they expect? All I see on TV is fucking Nazi films.' Pointing out that it is the English, not the Germans, who are obsessed with the war, Stein adds, 'They're still celebrating the fucking victory. It's funny as hell . . .'

Then comes a startling admission. 'Well,' Harry says, returning to her Nazi greeting, 'it was part of the song, "Contact In Red Square" *Astrovia sweet comrade*. I thought the salute was Russian. I dunno. I'm fucking American. Anyway, lately I've been thinking about being more nasty. I mean, when people spit on you and act like idiots, why shouldn't I Sieg Heil at them?'[1]

The conversation drifts into a tirade against punk rock audiences, leaving *Melody Maker* readers to ponder Harry's ignorance. Meanwhile Stein, Blondie's Jewish guitarist, explains his collection of Nazi memorabilia was a reminder that they 'had won . . . that the Jews had won'. Even more puzzling was the persistent rumour that Blondie were named after a German shepherd dog gifted to

Adolf Hitler by Martin Bormann in 1941. Upon hearing this, Stein threatened to change the group's name to 'Adolf Hitler's Dog'. In a 2017 interview on WBUR, Boston, Stein commented, 'The Hitler's dog thing? I don't know if I knew about that [then],' adding with impressive historical accuracy, 'There's no "e" on Hitler's dog's name; it was B-l-o-n-d-i.'

New wave artists did not confine ill-considered Third Reich references and impudent stage gestures to the stage. Singer-song-writer-cum producer Nick Lowe called his manager a 'Little Hitler', while Elvis Costello categorised a feuding couple as 'Two Little Hitlers'. In a 1978 *Record Mirror* live review from Ulster Hall, Belfast, it was noted that when Costello mentioned '"Mr Oswald with the swastika tattoo", the thicker members of the audience', drawn in by the mention of the leader of the British Union of Fascists, 'saluted the stage with a raised arm ignorant to the anti-fascist sentiment of ["Less Than Zero"]'.

Saluting, it now appeared, was all the rage.

Julie Burchill observed that 'Sham 69 may have come on no end in two years from wearing swastikas'[2] but singer Jimmy Pursey's public anti-fascist stance had not filtered through to the group's increasingly right-wing audience. Attending a concert, the *Guardian*'s Val Hennessy set the scene. As she stood in a queue, jostled by hundreds of fans, 'Ankle-deep in beer cans, an army of thuggish youths, tattooed with swastikas, chanted: "There's only one Hitler." The girls explained: "That's the British Movement mob. They've had it in for Sham ever since Jimmy joined Rock Against Racism."'[3]

In February 1978, at the London School of Economics, the professed 'Sham Army' – fans of Sham 69 – chanted 'Sieg Heil' and scrawled Nazi graffiti on the walls, causing £7,500 worth of damage. It was hardly surprising. In 'Rip Off', Jimmy Pursey wrote about 'foreign feet down Oxford Street' and 'faces from places I've never been'. The music press was filled with images of Sham 69 fans saluting the stage, more reminiscent of a Nuremburg rally than a concert. The band walked onstage to the patriotic 'Land Of Hope And Glory' flanked by an informal entourage including members of the National

Front and the British Movement.⁴ Pursey believed he could steer Sham 69's audience toward supporting Rock Against Racism. But the attempt backfired. Gigs turned violent, with shows erupting into pitch battles. When the band announced they would play RAR's Carnival 2 in London's Brockwell Park, Pursey was met with death threats. Sham withdrew. Undeterred, Pursey appeared unannounced and told the crowd: 'I'm here because I support Rock Against Racism.' Many ignored the clear anti-racist message. In July 1979, police arrived at the group's avowed 'Last Stand' at London's Rainbow Theatre with dogs, and on horseback. In the aftermath, Sham 69 fell apart.

'Nobody can remember the beginning of Sham 69 and the things he said then. Now he tries to disconnect himself from his past.' This is Bernard Sumner speaking to *Sounds* in November 1978 about Jimmy Pursey, whom he accuses of being 'an out-and-out racist'. The irony of the criticism isn't lost on the frontman of Joy Division. 'Everyone calls us Nazis,' Ian Curtis chimes in.⁵

Formed in 1976, initially as Warsaw and later becoming Joy Division (and eventually New Order), the story of Ian Curtis (vocals), Bernard Sumner (guitar), Peter Hook (bass) and Stephen Morris (drums) is one steeped in controversy, confusion, misunderstanding, bitter resentment and a morbid fascination with Nazism. People deliberated: Warsaw as in Ghetto or 'Warszawa' from David Bowie's *Low*. The band would walk onstage to the charged instrumental track by Bowie. The music 'had a cold, austere feeling to it and Warsaw seemed to us to be a cold, austere place,' Sumner explained.⁶ At Manchester's Electric Circus on 2 October 1977, Sumner sauntered up to the microphone and shouted, 'Have you all forgot Rudolf Hess?'

Hess, a fanatical Nazi and trusted confidant of Adolf Hitler, played a pivotal role in Nazi propaganda. In 1926, while Hitler served a nine-month sentence for treason following the failed Munich Beer Hall Putsch, Hess notated and edited *Mein Kampf*. Then, on 10 May 1941, Hess made an extraordinary attempt to alter the course of the war. He flew a Messerschmitt-110 fighter plane over 1,000 miles from the Bavarian city of Augsburg to the west coast of Scotland, where he parachuted into Eaglesham, hoping to meet the Duke of Hamilton. Having met him previously at the 1936 Berlin Olympics, Hess sought to negotiate peace with the Allies. 'We will guarantee England her empire,' Hess confided in Albert Speer, 'in return she will give us a free hand in Europe.'[7] The British arrested Hess and placed him in custody.

The timing of the mission was incredible, with London ablaze from enemy incendiary bombs. When the British government did not respond, Hitler accused Hess of having 'pacifist delusions'. Held as a prisoner of war and tried at Nuremberg in 1946, Hess simulated selective amnesia; dramatically, he regained his senses and made a closing statement from the dock. Despite claiming that Jewish people had access to a hypnotic drug capable of poisoning their enemies, Hess was declared sound of mind and convicted of war crimes. He was sentenced to life imprisonment.*

When Eugene Bird's book *The Loneliest Man in the World: Rudolf Hess in Spandau* was published in 1976, it coincided with mounting media calls for his release.† Both Ian Curtis and Bernard Sumner read it, and it became an influence on Joy Division's song 'Warsaw'. The track features the cryptic refrain 'Three-one-G', referencing Hess' prison number, 31G-350125. Over three verses, Curtis alluded to Hess' role in Hitler's 1923 attempted coup d'état, his later disillusionment with National Socialism and his eventual conviction at Nuremburg. Sumner later remarked, 'It's very sad. It obviously affected me in some way, but fuck knows why I blurted that out,' reflecting on the obscure allusion to Hess made during the performance at the Electric Circus.[8]

Bass player Peter Hook, unsure whether 'Warsaw' had 'even been written' at the time of the Manchester show, says the song

---

*   Incarcerated at Spandau Prison along with Albert Speer, until the latter's release at midnight on 1 October 1966, Hess would serve a further twenty-one years as the sole inmate. Hess proclaimed himself the Führer of the Fourth Reich and became an unlikely icon for neo-Nazis. On 17 August 1987 he was discovered hanging from a strap of wire in the prison exercise yard.
†   In 1980, Angelic Upstarts released 'Lonely Man Of Spandau' containing the chorus appeal, 'Let him go'.

'wasn't *about* Rudolf Hess' nor does he understand why Sumner made the comment.[9] 'Those of us within it had not a moment's doubt that it was anything dicey,' insisted journalist and fan Paul Morley, suggesting that at worst it was clumsiness rather than something 'terrible'.[10] Whether all those 'within it' brushed off Sumner's ambiguous comment is undocumented. Nonetheless, Joy Division would soon have to field renewed accusations of being Third Reich sympathisers. But not before the Yobs – a pseudonym for the English punk group the Boys, featuring former members of London SS and the Hollywood Brats – released their 1977 Christmas single, 'Run Rudolph Run'. In the song – originally recorded by Chuck Berry in 1958 – the London-based Yob fashioned an unlikely relationship between Santa's reindeer and a Nazi war criminal, with a single sleeve showing Rudolf Hess outside Spandau Prison decorated with a superimposed red nose.

On 1 September 1939, the German army invaded Poland, marking the beginning of the Second World War. As depicted in the 2002 film *The Pianist* – based on Władysław Szpilman's bestselling 1946 memoir – and in scenes replicated and in scenes replicated throughout occupied Europe, the Jewish population was ordered to wear an identifying yellow star, stripped of their civil rights, rounded up into ghettoes and ultimately deported to death camps.

On 19 April 1943, the Warsaw Ghetto rose in armed resistance. Although the four-week uprising was ultimately unsuccessful, it showed that Jews would not meekly submit, defying the common portrayal of them as 'lambs to the slaughter'. In truth, revolt occurred throughout Nazi-occupied Europe, but against a highly organised and orchestrated machine, expert in the art of deception, many never realised their fate until it was too late – either receiving a bullet in the back of the head or being tricked into entering a gas chamber disguised as a shower.

The date of the Warsaw Ghetto uprising was significant. It fell on the eve of Pesach, the Jewish festival celebrating the Israelites' biblical escape from slavery in Egypt. The English name, 'Passover', was also the title of a Joy Division song. In his memoir *24 Hour*

Party People, Tony Wilson, founder of Factory Records, recalls the conversation when Warsaw transitioned into Joy Division. The scene takes place in a 1974 maroon Peugeot 506 estate. Wilson is driving. The band and their manager are seated front and back.

BAND	'We've got a new name.'
MANAGER	'Why?'
TONY WILSON	'You can't put Warsaw on a poster. Everyone would think it was a holiday advert.'
IAN CURTIS	'Joy Division. Do you know what that is?'
TONY WILSON	'I think so. When the Germans used to pick out women, they thought were racially pure and make them have sex with them . . . bit Nazi.'
BERNARD SUMNER	'Yeah, but it's also kinda cheery. You know, JOY.'[11]

Foreseeing an outraged headline – 'Granada Man Owns Nazi nightclub' – Wilson was 'easy . . . after all,' he mused, 'it was still punk.' Naming Jordan, Sid Vicious and 'the swastika doll on the sleeve art of the late-period Sex Pistols', Wilson reasoned, 'And since the music industry was an obscene form of prostitution, [I] was quite up for it.'

The action cuts (in the film adaptation) to a stage in Derby where Joy Division play a disastrous gig. Neo-Nazi skinheads salute the group whereupon Wilson (played by Steve Coogan) and Peter Hook (Ralf Little) jump into the audience. The fight that follows is juxtaposed with footage of Wilson (a presenter on the regional television programme *Granada Reports*) commentating on fuel shortages, striking public sector workers and the National Front marching through Manchester city centre. Backstage, a journalist thrusts a microphone underneath his nose:

'Your band, Joy Division, is named after a group of women who were captured by the SS for the purpose of breeding perfect Aryans. Isn't that sick?'

'Have you ever heard of situationism or postmodernism?' Wilson responds in a superior tone. 'Do you know nothing about the free play of signs and signifiers? Yes, we've got a band called Joy Division. We've also got a band called Durutti Column. I'm sure you don't need me to point out the irony there.'*

So why Joy Division?

Peter Hook, in his 2012 memoir *Unknown Pleasures* says (inaccurately), '"Joy Divisions" was the name given to groups of Jewish women kept in concentration camps for the sexual pleasure of Nazi soldiers. The oppressed not the oppressors. Which in a punky, "No Future" sort of way was exactly what we were trying to say with the name.' Asked if Joy Division were Nazis, Hook hissed, 'No. We're not fucking Nazis. We're from Salford.'[12]

Bernard Sumner says that when he read the 'harrowing book [*House of Dolls*] about the Nazi concentration camps', he 'came across a reference to a section where women were housed for the pleasure of Nazi officers on leave. It was known as the *Freuden-Abteilung*, the Joy Division, and that phrase just leapt out at me immediately as the perfect name for the band.' Sharing the book with Ian Curtis, Sumner says that he understood the 'dodgy ground' the name inhabited and that it would 'get up certain people's noses' but at the 'height of punk . . . it was acceptable to be unacceptable' and 'in no way was it used for "shock value".' Rather that Joy Division were 'sticking two fingers up to what we regarded as normal society' – and that included some journalists. 'We did have reservations about it, but in the end, it just felt like it was our name . . . it was simply a great name for a band.'[13]

'For me,' Sumner concluded – after acknowledging that, amid all the hate and dominance of fascism, there was an undeniable beauty in its art, architecture, design, and even the uniforms – 'it seemed to meet all the criteria we were looking for: our sound, our image, even the way the words looked physically on paper . . . it

---

* Led by Buenaventura Durruti, the Columna Durruti was an anarchist military unit formed during the Spanish Civil War (1936–9) in opposition to General Franco's fascist regime.

certainly didn't mean we were Nazis or had any kind of sympathy with them, because we didn't.[14] Now, I probably wouldn't pick it, because I know it would offend and hurt people, but back then, I was very young and, well, selfish.'

The name Joy Division met with a wave of criticism. 'We knew we weren't Nazis,' insisted drummer Stephen Morris, 'but we kept on getting letters in the *NME* slating us for harbouring Eichmann in the coal cellar. [It only] encouraged us to keep doing it, 'cos that's the kind of people we are.'[15]

Camp brothels, or *Lagerbordelle*, were created under a directive from Reichsführer-SS Heinrich Himmler to Oswald Pohl, the SS administrator of concentration camps, to function as an incentive for 'healthy' prisoners to increase productivity in armaments and to combat homosexual activity that was common in camps, where prominent prisoners often exploited adolescent boys (known as 'pipels') for sexual relations. Himmler, who feared that homosexuality was transmittable and could spread within the ranks of the SS, established these state-sanctioned brothels. 'I consider it necessary to provide in the most liberal way hard-working prisoners with women in brothels,' he stated.

Between 300 and 400 women, registered by the SS on index cards and known as 'brothel detail, code: 998' 'volunteered' for forced sexual labour in ten concentration camps – Mauthausen, Gusen, Neuengamme, Sachsenhausen, Ravensbrück, Buchenwald, Dachau, Auschwitz, Flossenbürg and Mittelbau-Dora – housed in what were known as 'special huts' or 'dolls' houses'. In the summer of 1943, construction of a new brothel began in Block 24 adjacent to the main gate at Auschwitz (the fifth across the concentration camp network).* Situated on the first floor, the SS fitted the former barrack rooms with beds and curtains and decorated the walls in elegant colours. Valued prisoners – cooks,

---

*   Inmates nicknamed the brothel 'Puff'. It was organised by SS doctor Siegfried Schwela until his murder by the resistance, and from August 1943 by Oswald Kaduk.

hairdressers, firefighters, those working for the SS – were issued vouchers, worth two marks, to 'cash in' at the brothel. Before entering the block, 'customers' had to undergo a medical examination conducted by an SS doctor to ensure they were 'clean'. Jews and Soviet prisoners were forbidden from using the brothel to uphold Nazi 'blood purity' laws.*

Typically, German women – and later Polish and Russian – from the woman's camp at Ravensbrück were sent to the brothels as sex workers. At Auschwitz, prisoners were trafficked from the nearby sub-camp at Birkenau. But make no mistake: this was legalised rape. The brothels were places of brutality and humiliation. Women volunteering for 'very light labour', in the hope of earning a piece of bread or a promise to be released after six months, soon discovered the deception. Women were examined – for venereal diseases – and sterilised, not only to prevent pregnancy in the short term, but consequently, if a prisoner survived the ordeal, to terminate their potential as birth mothers.

For two hours every evening, six days a week, and afternoons on a Sunday, approximately twenty young women had sex with as many as ten men in one day. Overseen through concealed peepholes in the door, male SS guards ensured each woman spent no longer than fifteen minutes with a 'customer' and used only the missionary position, while taking advantage of the opportunity for voyeurism.

Work in Block 24 provided an opportunity to eat, fend off starvation and cling to the possibility of survival. Women received food and clothes, taken from new arrivals, and were housed in relative comfort in warm rooms with furniture. A rare memorandum from 5 November 1942, written by SS doctor Sigmund Rascher about women used for rewarming in freezing experiments, revealed the following: 'One of the women assigned showed unobjectionably Nordic racial characteristics: blond hair,

---

* Introduced in 1935, the Nuremburg Race Laws which forbade sexual relations between Jews and people 'of German or related blood' were the first overt indication of mass population acceptance of Nazi racial purity policy.

blue eyes, corresponding head and body structure . . . I asked the girl why she had volunteered for brothel service, and she replied, "To get out of the concentration camp." To my objection that it was a great shame to volunteer as a brothel girl, I was told, "Rather half a year in the brothel than half a year in the concentration camp.'"[16]

Research suggests that 34,140 female inmates were forced into sexual slavery, though few survivors have publicly spoken out about their ordeal. 'Sex slavery was not identified as such in the judicial cases dealing with the SS crimes,' says Insa Eschebach, director of the Ravensbrück Memorial Museum.[17]

The discovery of brothels was revealed in a documentary about concentration camps produced by the Psychological Warfare Division at the end of the war. 'Dachau had its own brothel for the use of guards and favoured prisoners,' a laconic voiceover informed viewers over film footage. 'As the women died, they were replaced by a fresh contingent from the woman's camp at Ravensbrück.' Sidney Bernstein, the film's director, enlisted the help of Alfred Hitchcock in a supervisory role. The British director gave critical advice: to film long shots ensuring there would be no doubt about the authenticity of the evidence and the unimaginable atrocities committed in the name of National Socialism. The resulting fifty-minute documentary *German Concentration Camps Factual Survey* remained incomplete due to concerns that its release could negatively impact relations between the Allied victors and the post-war economic development of a denazified Germany. It wasn't until 1985 that the Imperial War Museum painstakingly reconstructed the preserved footage.*

The topic of brothels was rarely addressed in Holocaust literature, but Alain Resnais' 1956 documentary *Nuit et Brouillard* (Night and

---

* Hanuš Burger wrote and directed a twenty-two-minute Anglo-American version of the documentary, *Death Mills* (Die Todesmühlen). The English-language version, directed by Billy Wilder – whose parents and family members perished in Auschwitz – was distributed by the United States Department of War in 1945.

Fog*) stood as a notable, albeit brief, exception. The thirty-minute black-and-white film, narrated by Michel Bouquet, depicted the rise of the Nazi Party, accompanied by a stark, atonal soundtrack scored by Austrian composer Hanns Eisler. The film presented the cold, mechanical brutality of the regime. One unsettling scene featured the kapo, a concentration camp prisoner selected to oversee others in forced labour, as Bouquet's narration described: 'The kapo has his own room . . .' – the camera pans across a neat room equipped with a table, chair, flowers, sink, and bed – 'where he can hoard supplies and receive his favourites in the evening.' As the camera moves to Block 24, Bouquet's narration continues, 'Luckier still, the kapos had a brothel . . . better fed women, but prisoners still, doomed like the others to die.'

The term 'Joy Division' originates from the 1953 novella *House of Dolls*, in which the author, Ka-tzetnik 135633 (his former prison name and number) coined the phrase *Freuden-Abteilung*. This German expression, a translation of the original Hebrew, combines the words *Freuden* (joy) and *Abteilung* (division). The story, which blurs the line between fact and fiction, follows seventeen-year-old Daniella Preleshnik, who is arrested on a school excursion to Kraków and sent to a ghetto, then a concentration camp. There, she is examined and molested and branded with the alphanumeric code 'SN A135633'.

The book's cover depicted an image of a woman with her head thrown back, her shirt ripped open, and the inscription 'FELD-HURE' (field whore) burned into her flesh above her breasts. The accompanying text spared the reader no detail. 'Daniella lay upraised knees fastened to two vertical iron rods mounted to the table to

---

* The title, 'Nacht und Nebel' originated from Hitler's December 1941 directive to make political opponents in conquered territories vanish without trace into the night and fog of the unknown, as well as Generalfeldmarschall Keitel's edict which permitted execution without trial. In 1946, Keitel was found guilty of war crimes and the International Military Tribunal in Nuremburg sentenced him to death by hanging.

which she was strapped.' Ka-tzetnik then details acts of ritual sexual humiliation and surgical experimentation ranging from artificial insemination and miscarriage to premature deliveries and sterilisation. Elas, an ex-prisoner sentenced to life for murder and known to the inmates as 'the Master', is described wearing tight-fitting riding breeches tucked into her boots. On 'Enjoyment Day', she instructs Preleshnik and her fellow inmates to give their guests, German soldiers en route to the Russian Front, 'full satisfaction' and to 'smile and act happy'. Failure will result in a beating and execution.

Upon its publication, *House of Dolls* was denounced by Yad Vashem, the World Holocaust Remembrance Center, as erotic fiction. This did not quash worldwide sales. However, nothing quite matched the extraordinary testimony Ka-tzetnik gave at the Eichmann Trial on 7 June 1961. Called to the witness stand, the Jewish-Polish author, born Yehiel Feiner and now known as Yehiel Dinur, addressed the packed courtroom. Speaking in Hebrew, he said,

> I do not regard myself as a writer writing literature. This [*The Doll's House*] is a chronicle of Auschwitz planet. I was at the Auschwitz camp for two years. The time there is not a concept as it is here, on our planet. Every fraction of a second has a different wheel of time. The inhabitants of that planet had no names. They had no parents and no children. They were not clothed as we are here. They were not born there and did not give birth. They lived and breathed according to different laws of nature. They did not live according to the laws of this world of ours. Their name was a number: Kazetnik so-and-so.

Clearly restless, the witness suddenly darted from the stand. Then fainted. Lying face down on the courtroom floor, Dinur – who was later believed to have suffered a stroke – was promptly lifted by medical staff onto a stretcher and carried out of the hearing, leaving the public gallery in stunned silence.

By 1978, the year Joy Division officially formed, sales of *House of Dolls* had already surpassed one million copies. In his introduction to *So This Is Permanence*, a collection of the late Ian Curtis' writings, Jon Savage suggests that the Holocaust deeply affected the members of the group. Certainly, Curtis' lyrics and Joy Division's austere musical style reflects themes of self-doubt, morbidity and an intense engagement with the history of the Third Reich. In the song 'They Walked In Line', Curtis paints a vivid picture of guards 'all dressed up in uniforms so fine they drank and killed to pass the time', coupled with, 'Wearing the shame of all their crime with measured steps they walked in line'. Similarly in 'Atrocity Exhibition' he describes 'the horrors of a far-away place', 'bodies twisting' and 'mass murder on a scale you've never seen'. The song's refrain, 'This is the way, step inside', evokes the grim imagery of a gas chamber. Curtis' world view is bleak, full of existential questioning and despair. His lyrics praise 'the glory of loved ones now gone' and explore themes of brutality, suffering, the burning of both heart and soul, anaesthesia, the 'doors of hell's darker chambers' and a God who in his wisdom 'took you by the hand'.

On Joy Division's second album, *Closer*, released two months after the death of Ian Curtis, there is more desolate lyricism conjuring images of war, resettlement, shootings and gas chambers. Curtis read broadly. His literary collection included volumes by T.S. Eliot, Antonin Artaud, Dostoyevsky, Nietzsche, Jean-Paul Sartre, Hermann Hesse, J.G. Ballard and the anti-fascist German visual artist John Heartfield, whose photomontages of Adolf the Superman and Göring the Executioner documented resistance to the Third Reich.

The history of Joy Division is marked by contradiction but especially so when it comes to their ambiguous relationship with Nazism. On one hand, Curtis and Sumner, well-read, educated young men in their twenties, channelled their fascination with the Third Reich into their music. On the other hand, their work sometimes seemed to glorify a brutal regime, using shocking imagery that perhaps reflected their own darker obsessions. This ambiguity was clear when Joy Division performed for Rock Against Racism – though many bands took part simply to earn the generous £50 fee – while the artwork for their debut single featured unsettling Nazi imagery.

Released on 3 June 1978, *An Ideal For Living* was a four-track EP presented in a fold-out poster sleeve with a drawing of a Hitler Youth member banging a drum strapped around his neck. 'This really struck me as a powerful image that blended perfectly with our new name, our sound and with the kind of image we had in mind for Joy Division,' explained Bernard Sumner who, having found the image in Manchester Central Library, carefully traced it onto paper with a pencil and inked the design.* 'Fuck it,' thought Sumner, contemplating its capacity to outrage.[18]

Opening the sleeve revealed even more troubling imagery: a German soldier nonchalantly pointing a submachine gun at a young Polish Jewish boy wearing a newspaper carrier's cap and knee-length socks, his hands raised in surrender. The original picture is one of the most iconic from the Holocaust, taken by an anonymous photographer and captioned *Mit Gewalt aus Bunkern hervorgeholt* ('Forcibly Pulled out of Bunkers'). The full image shows a huddled group of women and children emerging from hiding during the 1943 Warsaw Ghetto Uprising. It is believed the boy was deported to either Majdanek or Treblinka extermination camp. The soldier was identified as SS-Rottenführer Josef Blösch, a notorious sadist known within the ghetto as 'Frankenstein' due to his monstrous behaviour, which included beating and raping women and shooting children for looking at him. Blösch was arrested in 1969 in East Germany, tried, and executed.

The credit for each musician featured an umlaut, traditionally placed over vowels in Germanic languages, in the name of each instrument – Bernard Albrecht, 'Güitar', Ian Curtis, 'Vöcals', Stephen Morris, 'Drüms' and Peter Hook, 'Bäss'. Notably, Sumner's name was now Albrecht. The guitarist dismissed rumours that the pseudonym originated from Prinz-Albrecht-Strasse, the Berlin headquarters of

---

* In 2023, Shadowplay, the self-titled 'definitive Joy Division tribute band', reproduced the image to promote upcoming live dates promoted by Flag Promotions.

the SS/Gestapo, and said he adopted it after mishearing a television programme discussing the German playwright Berthold Brecht. 'It sounded a bit like Bernard Albrecht, and I just thought, "That'll do." It was just a bit of fun,' he added.[*]

When Rob Gretton became Joy Division's manager, he insisted the band withdraw the controversial single sleeve, warning, 'Everyone thinks you're Nazis.'[19] The band complied, but the media scrutiny continued. In September 1978, Mick Middles of *Sounds*, in a rare moment of music press distaste, bemoaned a band still locked 'inside Nazi history chic, a subject that has been exploited beyond tolerance'.

Of the music on *An Ideal For Living*, the lyrics of 'No Love Lost' focus on women forced into prostitution in a concentration camp and incorporated a spoken-word excerpt from *House of Dolls*: 'In the hand of one of the assistants, she saw the same instrument which they had that morning inserted deep into her body. She shuddered instinctively. No life at all in the house of dolls. No love lost.' According to Jon Savage, the passage 'fits the relentless yet spacious motorik [*sic*] of the music extremely well. Other [Joy Division] songs like "Leaders Of Men", "Warsaw", "Conditioned" and "Crime Against The Innocents" were barely disguised regurgitations of their source: lumpy screeds of frustration, guilt, shame and anger with militarist and totalitarian overtones.'

The music press was far from enthusiastic. Alan Lewis' appraisal in *Sounds* was typical: 'Another Fascism for Fun and Profit mob judging by the Hitler Youth imagery and Germanic typography on the sleeve.'[20]

Peter Hook distances himself from the cover. 'Looking at it now,' he wrote in 2016, 'I can see the problem. I mean, *An Ideal For Living*? It even sounds Nazi. Not to mention the way we dressed – grey shorts, short hair, thin ties . . . let's face it, there was quite a

---

[*]   In the 1920s, Rudolf Hess studied at Munich University under Professor Karl Haushofer, an exponent of geopolitics and Nazi ideology before he joined the resistance against Nazism. His son, Albrecht Haushofer, was arrested and shot for participation in the 1944 conspiracy to assassinate Hitler.

lot of evidence against us.'[21] However, if an apology seemed forth-coming, Hook passed off the indulgence as youthful folly. 'Nothing more than a bunch of lads obsessed with the war,' he wrote. A band falling in with the 'most unpalatable, shocking side' of punk and more about outrage than ideology. 'We didn't have a political bone in our bodies,' he concluded.

Promoters thought otherwise. On 30 March 1979, a Joy Division concert at Walthamstow Youth Centre was promoted with images of a fighter plane, a North African tank and Russian soldiers marching in surrender. 'We cut some pictures out of a magazine called *Purnell's History of the Second World War* and collaged them together,' says Martin Comey, who co-designed the poster with David Pils, a youth worker and singer from the support band, SX.[22]

'There's fucking Nazis riding on the fucking tank!' exclaimed Peter Hook.

On 23 August 1975, Ian Curtis married Deborah Woodruff, who had a Jewish great-grandfather, at St Thomas' Church in Hen-bury. During the ceremony, the groom sang the 'Kaiserhymne' ('Emperor's Hymn'). Written in 1796 by the Austrian-born com-poser Joseph Haydn, the hymn was updated in 1841 by the poet August Heinrich Hoffmann von Fallersleben to include the German national anthem. In 1922, the newly re-titled 'Deutschlandlied' became a favoured song of the Weimar Republic. Curtis' interest in Third Reich imagery seems to originate from a fascination with its style and history. According to his widow, the appeal was with the uniforms and psychological elements, rather than warfare itself. 'All Ian's spare time was spent reading and thinking about human suffering. I knew he was looking for inspiration for his songs, yet the whole thing was culminating in an unhealthy obsession with mental and physical pain.'

Revealing that she had 'cringed' when her husband told her the origin of the name Joy Division, she wrote. 'It was gruesome and tasteless, and I hoped that the majority of people would not know what it meant. I wondered if the members of the band were intending to glorify the degradation of women.'[23]

On 18 May 1980, Curtis hanged himself. It was the end of Joy Division. But the start of a legacy that endures. Today, Joy Division tote bags and T-shirts are a popular high street fashion. The merchandise sells in stores such as Urban Outfitters and HMV and is worn by celebrities such as Iggy Pop, Kate Moss, Kristen Stewart and former members of One Direction. Moreover, the name Joy Division has long surpassed its original association with the Holocaust. For many teenagers, the term has lost its connection to the band, and more profoundly, to its historical reference as the name for a brothel in a Nazi camp. Furthermore, the term persists in media usage even where other contentious band names and song titles have been prohibited.

In 1981, BBC Radio 1 banned the song 'Celebrate The Bullet' by Coventry seven-piece band the Selecter, following the murder of John Lennon. Similarly, in 1991, Bristol-based Massive Attack abbreviated their name to Massive after the release of 'Unfinished Symphony' coincided with a Coalition bombing campaign during the Gulf War. 'The lyrics might not necessarily be about war,' a BBC spokesperson told the trade journal *Music Week*, 'but if they were played after a bulletin which announced a tragedy, it would be offensive.'[24] Bomb the Bass, in a move reflecting the same sensitivity, changed their name to Tim Simenon, the band's founding member, when the BBC compiled a list of sixty-seven songs deemed 'unsuitable' for daytime radio. Listed were tracks like 'Atomic' by Blondie, 'Love Is A Battlefield by Pat Benatar and 'Walk Like An Egyptian' by the Bangles. Likewise, MTV pulled videos by the B-52s and a further eleven songs including Aerosmith's 'Don't Want To Miss A Thing', Iggy Pop's 'Corruption' and 'Boom!' by System of a Down.

Despite the controversy often surrounding band names and song titles with sensitive themes, Joy Division avoided censorship entirely, references to Nazi death camps and rape not sufficient to stir BBC indignation. Following Ian Curtis' death, the band's transformation into New Order marked not only a new musical chapter but also a shift in how boundaries of acceptability were explored, and, invariably uncontested.

Zyklon B Zombie

NEW ORDER. A CERTAIN RATIO. THROBBING GRISTLE. FINAL SOLUTION

'Then the *new order* came out,' author Ka-tzetnik wrote in *House of Dolls*, 'the Jew-mark will be sewn over the heart.'

The New Order was Adolf Hitler's vision to reshape Europe racially and genetically. It is also the name of one of Britain's most successful pop groups. The phrase even appears opposite a reference to 'Joy Division' in *House of Dolls*. Despite the historical implications, the band maintains that their name came after their manager read an article in the *Guardian* titled 'The People's New Order of Kampuchea' which covered the fall of Pol Pot's Khmer Rouge, and the 'new order' established in Cambodia. According to Bernard Sumner, the epithet was 'completely neutral' and had no 'fascist connotation. We knew we had to dissociate ourselves successfully from Joy Division,' he explained, so 'a new moniker was essential'.

When New Order announced themselves there followed a storm of media suspicion. 'Fuck everyone,' the band responded. 'Fuck the world, we're just going to do what we want to do and get on with it.'[1]

'Never at any point did any of us consider a certain Mr Hitler and his bloody *Mein Kampf*.' 'Honest!' Peter Hook exclaims. 'Shows you how daft we were. We just thought it summed up our new start perfectly.' Then, describing 'a certain physical sensation you get from flirting with something like [the Holocaust],'' Hook adds, 'we thought it was a very, very strong feeling.'[2]

And so, a picture emerged: a group named Warsaw, a shout-out to Rudolf Hess, a name change to Joy Division referencing a Nazi brothel, the adopted cognomen Albrecht, a Hitler Youth cover sleeve, lyrics wrapped up in Third Reich messaging. And then: New Order.

By the early 1980s, the ambiguity surrounding New Order gave way to a colourful onslaught of glossy magazine features and a fresh synth-pop sound consigning lingering fascist sympathies to the shadows. Then, in 1983, when the north-west quartet secured their first top 10 hit, 'Blue Monday', *Viz* magazine presented a parody of the band, with one of the characters presenting *Top of the Pops* introducing a band called Third Reich playing their new single 'Blue Sunday'. We'd landed ourselves in it again,' scoffed Bernard Sumner, 'yet another layer of disaster to add to the litany of disasters.'

For Tony Wilson, the founder of Factory Records, it came at a time of mounting criticism. First, *Private Eye* accused him of being a fascist for signing Joy Division and then again when the band became New Order.[3] Next, he was criticised for releasing records by the post-punk group A Certain Ratio, whose name was seen by some as a reference to the Nazi categorisation of Aryan purity, specifically the idea of 'a certain ratio of non-Jewish blood'.[4]

The 1935 Nuremburg Race Laws defined cultural groups for 'the Protection of German Blood and German Honour'.* The legislation excluded Jews from German society, stripped them of their national identity and divided those considered 'pure Aryan' from those with Jewish family ancestry. However, what characterised a 'Jew' or 'Jewishness' proved difficult to define. According to historian Laurence Rees, 'Nazi law categorised a Jew as anyone descended from at least grandparents who are racially full Jews; that is, grandparents who were observant.' Thus, 'your religious ancestry determined race'. The issue was complicated when certain Jews looked Jewish but were not legally classified as Jews. Or those who were not religiously observant but technically qualified as Jews.[5] Added to which was the question: what did

---

* Signed by Rudolf Hess, the act forbade sexual relations between Jews and Germans.

'Jewish blood' mean? Examining a blood group does not reveal a person's religion, or, in Nazi terminology, race. There is not an exclusive Jewish blood type.

Factory's signing of A Certain Ratio became the focus of a local Manchester newspaper, and to Tony Wilson's annoyance 'transformed into a piece of vicious slander'. As a result, DJ John Peel informed late-night Radio 1 listeners that having 'just read in the *NME* that Factory are fascists' he would not be 'playing anymore ACR records'.[6] The band protested their innocence, claiming the idea came from a 1974 Brian Eno song called 'The True Wheel', which included the line 'looking for a certain ratio'. Yet it is a scene in the drama-documentary *24 Hour Party People* that reveals most about the ongoing controversy. The group are sitting backstage dressed in their new stage outfits: khaki shorts, brown shirts, white socks and sandals.

Tony Wilson enters.

'You look fantastic!' he proclaims.

'You reckon?' the band reply. 'We look like the bloody Hitler Youth, man.'

'I think you look like scouts,' Wilson winces.*

When news broke that the New Order/Tony Wilson-owned Hacienda nightclub was playing a video reel which included footage from the Nuremburg rallies and images of the Holocaust, sourced from a TV history of Western civilisation, the controversy rapidly escalated. 'Somehow, the *Jewish Chronicle* picked up on it and plastered headlines all over the city: "'GRANADA MAN OWNS NAZI NIGHTCLUB",' Wilson explained, echoing his comments made several years earlier when Warsaw became Joy Division. 'God! God! Actually, *Private Eye* was nothing compared to the *Jewish*

---

* In his 2022 memoir, *When Does the Mind-Bending Start?* Gordon King, guitarist with World of Twist, wrote of A Certain Ratio, who rehearsed next door, they 'all looked like members of the Hitler Youth'.

Chronicle. It was incredibly upsetting: I mean, most people say their best friends are Jewish, but mine really are.[7]

When it was discovered that the compiled film footage was the work of VJ Claude Bessy, Peter Hook commented, '[He] got us into all sorts of trouble. The *Jewish Chronicle* did a front-page story about Tony along the lines of "TV presenter shows Nazi propaganda in own club". But it wasn't him, it was Claude – and it was all done in a very punky way, commenting on events of the day.'[8]

And yet, still more allegations followed.

Preparing for an interview on Channel 4's *Loose Talk* on 27 September 1983, Tony Wilson was relaxing backstage. 'Suddenly, this drunken, half-attractive woman, ex-editor of a national women's magazine' asked him how he liked making lightshades out of babies' skins, in reference to Ilse Koch's barbaric practice conducted in Buchenwald concentration camp. Bemused, Wilson ignored the comment and walked onto set. Here, presenter Steve Taylor asked Wilson in front of a live audience, 'Are you a fascist?'

Wilson's reply was blunt. 'No! Neither I or Factory nor any of our musicians are fascist. In fact, quite the opposite.' He pointed to his close Jewish friends within Factory Records – one Black director and another who was an Orthodox Jew – as evidence. He also explained that the name Joy Division referenced those oppressed by fascism and highlighted the nature of pop musicians as 'prostitutes' in the societal sense. When a heckler accused him of flirting with fascism, Wilson gave an impassioned, if rambling, defence, stressing the significance of context and punk's influence.

> The use of the Nazi image in 1976 as part of the nihilistic, anarchistic approach to life, anything that would shock. And although I don't like flirting with fascism, fascism is the black hole of Western civilisation. The suffering that you're talking about in your statement: six million Jews, twenty million Russians . . . is unthinkable. The people flirting with it are people using it, now, as a way of getting at our young bands, at me, and my record company. In 1976 it had a real point. When Sid

Vicious wore swastika armbands no one thought he was a fascist. He wasn't flirting with fascism. He was making a nationalistic, anarchistic statement that made one of the major changes in our culture; the biggest change since 1963. The Pistols were that important. They used it. Joy Division used it.

Did the Sex Pistols or Joy Division use Nazi symbolism as an ideological cultural statement or was it simply a case of a misguided youth being justified by a middle-class intellectual? Sid Vicious wore the swastika to provoke and offend, not to make any political statement. Wilson's cloak of highbrow rhetoric did not impress, and the scent of controversy trailed after him into the next decade. When invited on BBC 2's *Reportage*, the music mogul addressed the issue of complacency within the music press, claiming it had allowed 'Nazi chic' to permeate the mainstream. He reminded presenter Magenta Divine that he had convinced Jordan to cover up her swastika armband during the Sex Pistols' appearance on Granada Television. 'If you're doing it to shock,' Wilson argues, 'you're saying it's a terrible thing, otherwise you wouldn't be doing it.' But Stuart Cosgrove, a fellow guest, interrupted, advising Wilson that rather than trotting out swastika pomposity and tired lines about a generation fixated on the war, he should 'try telling that to a twelve-year-old Asian, who maybe lives in a council housing estate and is having shit shoved through the letterbox'.[9]

Throbbing Gristle came to the attention of the public in a cascade of Holocaust-inspired stage design, logos and record promotion. In 1978, the group established Industrial Records, riffing on the insignia of the crematoria at Auschwitz I. Vocalist Genesis P-Orridge described it as a 'cold, aesthetic image' symbolising unequivocally and with unerring precision the 'malignancy' Throbbing Gristle 'intended to expose'. He added, 'A factory of death literally, just as a factory is symbolically the cause of creative death, death of self-worth to so many in industrialised societies.'

Photographs of death camps flashed behind the group when they performed. 'To explore the darker and obsessive sides of the human condition,' P-Orridge reasoned. 'I'm fascinated with pictures that seem innocuous unless you're given additional information, so the picture has no [inherent] quality of evil or goodness.'[10]

Educated at the independent Solihull School, Genesis P-Orridge (born Neil Andrew Megson, 1950) watched a television documentary which showed rows of naked women forced into orderly queues to enter a gas chamber. 'It really stuck in my head because it seemed so crazy and stupid, like a bus queue,' he told Jon Savage in 1978. Contemplating the image, P-Orridge saw an opportunity for what he called 'satirical humour' likening the use of chemicals in gas chambers to punk's celebrated fanzine, *Sniffin' Glue*. 'We used to introduce it [the song] by saying, 'This is called 'Zyklon B Zombie' – it's a bit like Coca-Cola except worse for your teeth. I had this vision of the ultimate punk sniffing Zyklon.'[11]

Shortly after, P-Orridge posed for a photograph at the gateway of Auschwitz, informing *NME* that the record label logo featuring the camp's gas chamber 'seemed appropriate for our music. It's also one of the ultimate symbols of human stupidity. I like to remind myself how stupid people are and how dangerous they are. Humanity as a whole is stupid to allow anything like that to begin to occur.' Asked to comment on the link between Nazi death camps and industrial music, P-Orridge says that the local Polish population knew Auschwitz during the war as 'the factory of death' and that the name of their album *Music from the Death Factory* was 'a metaphor for society and the way life is ... everybody lives in their own concentration camp.'[12]

Co-founder of Throbbing Gristle, Cosey Fanni Tutti (born Christine Carol Newby) picked up the thread. 'The image of the death camp was a comment on the inhumanity of building an actual killing factory. The TG sound was to be evocative of the subject matter ... we felt it important not to shy away from grim realities and were mindful of [George Santayana in *Life of Reason*, 1905]* saying, 'Those who cannot remember the past are condemned to repeat it.'[13]

---

* Spanish-American philosopher vilified in some quarters for expressing anti-Semitic opinion.

Unsurprisingly, Throbbing Gristle's provocative rhetoric and use of Third Reich imagery aroused complaint, accomplishing exactly what they aimed for. Fascinated by the mechanics of Nazism, their controversial actions were supported, or excused, with pseudo-intellectual argument. Their history is filled with a string of contentious moments that have come to characterise the band.

Writing in her memoir, *Art Sex Music*, Tutti recalls a COUM performance (a precursor to Throbbing Gristle) at the Howff Club, London in April 1974 where principal member Foxtrot Echo sang 'Bormann Of The Jungle' 'dressed as Martin Bormann in an ankle-length Nazi leather coat'.[14] Funded by the British Arts Council, the group described the show as 'art-based work'. The following year, in Amsterdam, Echo wore an SS leather coat and hat and riding boots, and wielded a blowtorch. In a celebration of sadomasochism, Tutti 'strode on stage dominatrix-style, naked save for high heels and a strap costume'. Centre stage, chained, unclothed, and tied to a large wooden X-shaped cross, Genesis P-Orridge whipped and pissed on Tutti's legs as she inserted a lit candle in her vagina.

On a trip to San Francisco, the group participated in what they called a 'Nazi Love' photo session with a member of the Bay Area Dada group. Posing nude in a room with just a 'single bed and black cover and pillows with a Nazi flag laid in the middle'.[15] Tutti described herself 'bent over with the sharp blade of a shiny dagger held delicately but precariously just inside the lips of my pussy'.[16] Photos from the shoot sold as postcards and as a T-shirt at BOY on the King's Road. 'Yes, I think I can claim that I initiated it,' Foxtrot Echo told *Just Glittering 5* of the 'Nazi interest' that defined Throbbing Gristle. 'I know Genesis was interested in a lot, but I was just fascinated by lots of Nazi design and ways of approaching things. It wasn't that I was fascist. None of us were. We couldn't be. We'd all have been exterminated in Nazi Germany. We were all social deviants. But there was some power to it that was interesting to experiment with and of course it had a lot of associations with an audience of that generation. It was quite beguiling and fascinating, but you had to watch you didn't use it in too much of a gratuitous or superficial way.'[17]

Throbbing Gristle identified themselves by their logo; a power flash, designed by band members Chris Carter and Cosey Fanni Tutti, inspired from three seemingly unconnected sources: the insignia of Oswald Mosely's British Union of Fascists, the lightning bolt painted across the face of David Bowie's alter-ego Aladdin Sane, and the universal symbol for electricity. 'The funny thing is,' Carter told *ZigZag*, 'the National Front thinks [the lightning flash] is the Socialist Workers Party, and the [SWP] think it's the National Front.'

Today, on the group's official website, a link titled 'THE THROB-BING GRISTLE FLASH SYMBOL' invites readers to learn more. The brief history explains that the symbol became the group's 'primary logo in 1976' when Chris Carter saw a Greater London Council 'High Voltage: Danger' sign. The text notes that, 'Unbe-known to TG at the time, David Bowie had used the same symbol inside a circle and of near identical shape and proportions to the TG flash for his Ziggy Stardust tour of 1973'.[18] Interestingly, there is no mention of Heinrich Himmler's protection squad, the SS, yet the resemblance to their emblem is hard to ignore.

The website also features a gallery selling Throbbing Gristle merchandise, including a single 'S' flash over a black and red arm-band, which, according to Tutti, was chosen to symbolise anarchy, not its striking resemblance to the Hitler Youth symbol. Another item for sale is a blue and white armband with horizontal stripes, reminiscent of the Israeli flag. An additional link encourages fans to buy a set of three stickers reading, 'THIS SYNTH KILLS FASCISTS'. It is unclear why fascism is mentioned here – beyond reference to the hand-painted message written across the body of Woody Guthrie's guitar, 'THIS MACHINE KILLS FASCISTS' – especially when the group's history suggests that the flash symbol was inspired by the universal sign for electricity. Perhaps it is a subtle message for visitors exploring Throbbing Gristle's obsession with Nazism.

The title of the group's debut single 'Zyklon B Zombie' presented artwork featuring a canister of Zyklon B and the image of Chris Carter taking a shower. The juxtaposition left little to the imag-ination. Zyklon Blausäure, commonly known as Zyklon B, was manufactured by the German company Degesch to kill infestations of lice. In late summer 1941, Karl Fritzsch, Commandant Rudolf Höss' deputy, had the thought that if Zyklon B killed insects, then why not humans? Conducting experiments in the sealed basement of Block 11 at Auschwitz, some 250 selected prisoners from the camp hospital were gassed along with an estimated 600 Soviet POWs. Historian Laurence Rees noted that 3 September 1941 marked the repurposing of Auschwitz from a concentration camp to a death factory, where up to 3,000 Jewish prisoners at a time were crammed into custom-built gas chambers with hermetically sealed doors.[19] 'Herded into a rectangular shaped cavernous space – in the belief they were to be de-loused and showered – a hatch was lifted from the roof above and, instead of warm water flowing through fake fitted shower heads, an SS soldier dropped pellets of Zyklon B through a hatch into a wire column fixed within the chamber. When the substance reacted with oxygen in the room, the helpless victims asphyxiated. It took no more than twenty minutes. The mound of dead bodies were then transferred to purpose-built ovens and burnt. Meanwhile, the gas chamber was cleaned – of blood and detritus – and prepared for the next party of unsuspecting Jews. This was a death machine. It was unrelenting, ideologically driven and the worst display of human behaviour the world has ever witnessed.'*

The vinyl copy of 'Zyklon B Zombie' revealed the coded messaging 'Salon Kitty' scratched into the run-out groove of the disc. The lyrics narrated the journey of a 'little Jewish girl' escorted to a gas

---

* According to the post-war testimony of Rudolf Höss, the supply of cyanide gas, in the form of Zyklon Blausäure, was distributed by Tesch & Stabenow and manufactured by IG Farben, one of the largest chemical and pharmaceutical companies in the world. IG Farben employed slave labourers from Auschwitz and played a role in the medical experiments conducted at both Auschwitz and Mauthausen concentration camp. Thirteen of the company's directors were found guilty of war crimes at the Nuremburg Trials.

Majdanek was the only other camp to use Zyklon B to exterminate prisoners.

chamber and an SS guard administering Zyklon B pellets 'while the people in the chamber . . . form a pyramid'. The language was noticeable for the absence of empathy. 'Like, when you go under gas at the dentists,' P-Orridge described the sound of the music, 'everything gets distorted, and you get this rush in your ears, like Cosey's guitar in the middle – so the actual aural content is like an exact parallel, as well. It's a perfect unit. Most people don't know what Zyklon B. is: they probably will *now*.'[20]

And so Throbbing Gristle's obsession with Nazi Germany went on.

The sleeve of 'Subhuman' displayed a macabre pyramid of human skulls, sourced from *The Apotheosis of War*, a mid-nineteenth-century painting by Russian artist Vasily Vereshchagin, echoing the offensive term associated with Hitler's description of non-Aryans. For the sleeve of 'Discipline', Throbbing Gristle posed outside Berlin's former Ministry of Propaganda. On the back, Val Denham, a visual artist, was pictured holding a Hitler Youth dagger above the caption 'Marching Music for Psychic Youth'. In a similarly provocative vein, the sleeve for 'Distant Dreams (Part Two)' included a monochrome photograph of discarded walking frames from Auschwitz, paired with an image of a tree-lined road running through the camp's barracks.

Throbbing Gristle never achieved mainstream success, yet their records sold in the tens of thousands, with 'Zyklon B Zombie' alone reaching 60,000 copies. Even in today's world of online sharing, the group continue to attract significant attention and, if anything, their myth has grown. They've also had a lasting impact on experimental industrial bands like Whitehouse, Sutcliffe Jugend and Death in June, the latter of which explore disturbing themes such as rape, sadism and Nazi symbolism.[21] In 2018, Dylan Miller from the *Quietus* posed the rhetorical question, 'Why We're Investigating Extreme Politics in Underground Music'. 'The deliberate obfuscation of motive was a standard technique for generating mystique amongst many of these groups – did they really want to bring about a new Holocaust, or did they just like shouting about it? Many of these early noise boys, now older and perhaps wiser put it down to youthful indiscretion; some have chosen to maintain their tired mystique, while others remain defiantly unapologetic.'[22]

Pop culture's fascination with extremes has left behind an unsettling legacy — particularly in the music industry's casual reproduction of Third Reich-era imagery, often stripped of responsible context. When Rough Trade Records opened a new shop on London's Denmark Street in October 2024, its stairwell gallery featured an original framed promotional poster of Throbbing Gristle. The central image was a photograph of the gas chamber at Auschwitz, with the words 'MUSIC FROM A DEATH FACTORY' above and marked by a single 'S' flash below. It suggests the presence of an unspoken boundary – one where the horrors of Nazi Germany are dangerously blurred with their symbolic reappropriation in popular media.

Take, for instance, a concert poster from 1979 which appeared across London advertising an upcoming show at the Electric Ballroom featuring Joy Division, Scritti Politti, the Monochrome Set and A Certain Ratio. In stark bold capitals, the type read, 'FINAL SOLUTION PRESENT JOY DIVISION'. For anyone with even a basic understanding of the Holocaust – 'Final Solution' being the extermination of European Jews, and 'Joy Division' referring to the name of a concentration camp brothel – the phrase is deeply disturbing.*

Kevin Millins and Colin Faver established Final Solution in 1978. As well as signing acts and designing artwork for Small Wonder Records, the company promoted concerts across the country, often featuring quirky, quasi-political, graphic-led posters featuring naked or skeletal bodies. Based on London's Pentonville Road, their roster favoured post-punk groups such as Joy Division, Bauhaus, the Fall, Throbbing Gristle, A Certain Ratio, Cabaret Voltaire and Spear of Destiny. The enmeshment with Holocaust terminology and imagery coupled with the choice of bands they promoted suggested that the name 'Final Solution' had sinister connotations.

---

* Another later poster billing read: 'Final Solution Present New Order'.

The term Final Solution is inextricably linked to the mass murder of Europe's Jews during the Second World War. But again, here is an example of the pop mainstream turning a blind eye to language associated with the Holocaust. Disturbingly, Millins and Faver were not the first to appropriate the phrase. In 1976, Pere Ubu released a self-funded 'Final Solution' as part of a series of provocatively named songs. Hailing from Cleveland, Ohio, the band claimed that title came from a Sherlock Holmes story. Indeed, beyond the line 'it seems I'm the victim of natural selection' there is no direct suggestion in David Thomas' lyrics to the extermination of Europe's Jews. Rather, the song presents a protagonist as someone 'misdirected' and in need of a 'cure' – by who and for what is left unclear. This ambiguity fuelled a wave of rumour and accusation. In response, Thomas explained the song was inspired by a television documentary about a terminally ill cancer patient who chose to end his life. The band ultimately removed the song from their live set, telling *Record Mirror* that they no longer wished to be 'associated with any of that Nazi stuff'. In a similar vein, 'Triumph Of The Will' from Devo's album *Duty Now for the Future* was an overt reference to the Third Reich. In this instance, Leni Riefenstahl's 1935 film of a Nuremburg rally. Although there was no direct reference to Nazism, the song portrayed a male protagonist needing to satisfy his sexual desire before dying – by rape, if necessary.

The worldwide success of 'Whip It' in 1980 catapulted Devo into the pop spotlight, complete with a platinum-selling album and the iconic look of bright-red flowerpots on their heads. The satirical presentation divided critics. 'Regrettably missing from the evening's music was the sense that Devo has anything in the least to say,' opined *Rolling Stone*, adding that their 'show bore all the orgiastic earmarks of a Nuremberg rally for spud boys.' When founding member Gerald 'Jerry' Casale read the review, he responded with dry sarcasm: 'Well, obviously, we're Nazis and clowns.' The comment didn't go unnoticed – it inspired the now-infamous headline: 'Sixties idealists or Nazis and clowns?' Nonplussed, Casale commented, 'They're all right, all those people. They're right on it. We're assholes. Everything they accuse us of is true. We're subhuman idiots who threaten them.'[23] The willingness to brush off media criticism was echoed years later, when *News-Press* revisited the controversy in 2016. 'People called us Nazis,' Casale recalled. 'They called us clowns. So, we ended up making jokes about it. We went, "OK, let's be Nazi clowns!"'[24]

The language of Nazism continued to occupy the post-punk landscape, revealing artists' thoughts beyond music. Whether these references pointed to personal ideological beliefs or were simply creative tools was rarely addressed in interviews. This absence of clarification creates a frustrating gap in our understanding but also reflects an era where musicians used Nazi-related ideas without needing to justify their choices. A prime example is Elvis Costello, who, as noted earlier, flirted with Third Reich associated terminology. In 1979, the inner sleeve of his third album *Armed Forces* featured the phrase 'EMOTIONAL FASCISM' – the record's working title. One track, 'Chemistry Class', alluded to a sexual encounter with the cautionary metaphor: 'Are you ready for the final solution?' The song then transitioned into the closing track, aptly titled 'Two Little Hitlers'. These examples aren't evidence of pro-Nazi sentiment – far from it. But they reflect pop music's tendency to experiment freely with language, sometimes at the cost of downplaying the weight of historical context.

Four years earlier, journalist Lester Bangs invited similar debate, asking whether the German electronic group Kraftwerk had 'The Final Solution to the Music Problem?' Printed first by *Creem*, including the graphic of a German eagle clutching a swastika, and then, in September 1975, by *NME*, the interview with the band was introduced by a set of provocative quotes, presented in italics:

> 'In the beginning there was feedback: the machines speaking on their own, answering their supposed masters with shrieks of misalliance.'
> 'In the music of KRAFTWERK, we see the fitting culmination of this revolution, as the machines not merely play the human beings but ABSORB them . . .'

*'We are very much interested in origin of music, source
of music. The Pure Sound is something we would like very
much to achieve.'*

*'We cannot deny we are German, because the German
mentality, which is more advanced, will always be part of
our behaviour.'*

*'We create out of the mother language and the machines,
from the industry of Germany.'*

'We have power.'

'It is also possible to damage your mind . . .'

The words 'masters', 'machines', 'pure', 'revolution', 'German
mentality', 'advanced', and 'power' stand out in what Bangs calls
'the German Scientific Method', steering readers back towards a
stereotypical Nordic sensibility connected to its Nazi past.

Kraftwerk played with irony, skilfully incorporating language and
imagery associated with the Third Reich.* The band's colours – red
and black – were linked both to the Nazi Party and the work of the
Russian-Jewish artist El Lissitzky. The seminal 1974 album *Autobahn*
was originally packaged in a sleeve designed by Emil Schult. It
showed a black Mercedes, the model famously used by Adolf Hitler,
alongside a VW Beetle, known in Nazi Germany as 'the people's
car' or the 'Kraft-Durch-Freude-Wagen' ('strength-though-joy car').
Rays of sunlight illuminate green-topped mountains and open blue
skies, promising either a brighter future or, perhaps, Hitler's vision
of *lebensraum* ('living space') – a policy of imperialistic expansion
driven by racist ideology. Although the first section of the autobahn
system was completed in 1932, it was under Hitler's regime that the
road network expanded, both as a means of creating employment
and, more significantly, for military transportation.

Kraftwerk revelled in such ambiguous symbolism. The album
cover of *Radioactivity* featured a picture of the Volksemp-

---

* In his 1947 autobiographical work, *If This Is a Man*, Holocaust survivor
Primo Levi describes arriving at 'Kraftwerk' where the cable-laying Kommando
works in an Auschwitz sub-camp.

fänger-VE301 ('the people's receiver') which played a critical role in Nazi propaganda. Promoted by Josef Goebbels as one of Europe's most affordable radios in Europe – limited in range to Germany – its code, VE301, referenced Hitler's ascent to power on 30 January 1933. Despite rumours, Kraftwerk persistently rejected any affinity with the Third Reich, even as provocative language, like that included in Lester Bangs' interview, suggested otherwise. Part of Kraftwerk's appeal lay in their use of pre-Nazi visual motifs and their vision of a Germany reborn – unshackled from its fascist past. Still, the group wasn't immune to complicated historical ties. Florian Schneider-Esleben, one of the founding members, was the son of a Luftwaffe pilot turned architect. In 1968, his father designed the Cologne-Bonn Airport terminal – an iconic brutalist structure with a Star of David-shaped roof visible from above. Rather than being held back by such associations, Kraftwerk looked ahead, declaring: 'Welcome to the electronic world, welcome to change, welcome to the future and progress.'

Provocative language, once considered taboo in Germany, was gaining mainstream acceptance. In 1981, the Düsseldorf-based electronic duo Deutsch Amerikanische Freundschaft (DAF) released *Alles is Gut!* on Virgin Records featuring 'Der Mussolini'. The record's homoerotic cover and the song's chorus 'Tanz den Adolf Hitler' ('dance the Adolf Hitler') poked fun at Nazism's obsession with physical perfection, reducing 'die Führer' to a mere dance-floor novelty. Frontman Gabi Delgado-López explained. 'The singing isn't like rock 'n' roll or pop. It's sometimes like in a Hitler speech, not a Nazi thing, but it's in the German character, that CRACK! CRACK! CRACK! way of speaking.'[25]

Welcome to the Cabaret

HUMAN LEAGUE. LOU REED. SPANDAU BALLET. SPEAR OF DESTINY

New Romantics saturated the early eighties in an explosion of androgyny, luminous colour and devil-may-care dandyism. Anything to escape the dreary lingering aftermath of the Second World War, a drab world of bomb shelters, Formica furniture and endless bleak grey skies. The New Romantics came of age in a country riven by social and political struggle, class division, racism, homophobia, public sector strikes, electricity black-outs, heaps of uncollected rubbish, train strikes, school strikes and a growing sense of alienation increasingly disconnected from the mainstream. Then, as if from another planet – or, as a new generation of entranced fans liked to say, 'from Mars' – David Bowie arrived. Orange hair, tight-fitting clothing, and an arm slung lazily around the shoulder of his male guitar player, Mick Ronson. Bowie was a multicoloured vision of something 'other', his flirtation with fascism buried. His wild space-age vision spoke to kids on the outer fringes of acceptable society as Bowie's influence was reinvented for a new youth movement.

In the early stages of the electronic music revolution in Sheffield, the Human League emerged as one of the pioneering groups. At their early performances, lead singer Phil Oakey enlisted Philip Adrian Wright to enhance the experience with projected visuals. 'He had a real interest in people who manipulated the media to their own advantage,' Oakey explained. 'He was absolutely fascinated by Hitler, to the point where some people thought he was a fascist. But, in fact, he was just interested in the images and propaganda. That used to turn up on stage: we'd turn round and look up and see a big Hitler projected behind us, and go, "Oh no!"[1]

A hundred and fifty miles south of Sheffield, a group of young musicians in London were also fascinated with Germany's past. In studying pre-war Berlin, they uncovered a world of misfits adorned in heavy make-up and extravagant costumes, immersed in sexual adventure. This influence was fuelled by the writings of Christopher Isherwood and the stage play *Cabaret*, which opened in the West End in 1968 staring Judy Dench. The play was later adapted into a film featuring Liza Minnelli as the glamorous Sally Bowles and Joel Grey as the sly emcee. Directed by Bob Fosse, the film won eight Academy Awards in 1972, evoking an era of sexual promiscuity and underground debauchery. In his autobiography *Tainted Life*, Soft Cell's Marc Almond reflected on 'the divine decadence' of Sally Bowles and how he 'inhabited' the pages of Isherwood's Berlin.

The seductive allure of Germany's capital captivated the New Romantics, the backdrop to the pioneering music of their heroes, David Bowie and Lou Reed. Bowie's production of *Transformer*, Reed's breakthrough album, was not only steeped in the gender fluidity of 1970s New York but also paved the way for Reed's next record, *Berlin*. Attracted by the 'idea of a divided city', the album opened with nightclub chatter, setting the stage for a shadowy world of drug use, prostitution, domestic violence and suicide. According to Victor Bockris, Reed's biographer, 'Before going on tour, Lou had gone to see Andy Warhol at the Factory to ask advice on how to do the lights for the shows with a limited budget. Warhol advised Lou to use the stark, raw lighting Albert Speer designed for Adolf Hitler's speeches: intense white spotlights against a black background, setting the whole spectacle in high contrast.'[2] Onstage, Reed born in 1942 to Russian-Jewish parents, memorably proclaimed that he had 'no god apart from rock 'n' roll'. The *New York Times* described his heavily made-up appearance as a 'cultivated "Dachau panda" look', with cropped peroxide hair and black circles painted under his eyes'.[3]

When Reed shaved an Iron Cross* into the temple of his platinum-blond hair, *Newsday*'s Dave Marsh observed, 'It is like *Cabaret* without Liza Minnelli. In fact, maybe what Reed really looked like was an elongated Joel Grey without the makeup.'[4]

Reed never visited Berlin, unlike his acolyte David Bowie who increasingly immersed himself in the overlapping worlds of Nazi fanaticism and cocaine-fuelled pop stardom. The influence of both artists powered the nascent New Romantic scene. Bertie Marshall, a member of the Bromley Contingent and infatuated by all things *Cabaret*, reinvented himself as 'Berlin'. At just fifteen, he dared to provoke: dressed in a white shirt, black tie, cropped black hair, black tights and thigh-length boots. 'I particularly liked the Nazi look,' he gloated, 'so well-tailored, and all black.'[5]

The sartorial choice of Marshall neatly symbolised a new generation's unthinking adoption of Third Reich imagery as fertile material for creative expression. Cultural appropriation merged with ideological investigation. During a weekend trip to Berlin, aspiring writer Robert Elms came across a line of graffiti scrawled on a nightclub toilet wall. It read, 'Rudolf Hess, all alone, dancing the Spandau Ballet'. Inspired by this, Elms returned to London and decided that Spandau Ballet was the perfect name for his friend's new group, which had previously been known as Gentry. The phrase referred to the movements of a body hanging from a gallows, which would writhe and contort, as if dancing.†

Located beneath a brothel in London's Soho, Billy's nightclub opened in a celebration of David Bowie. Established in 1979 by Rusty Egan and Steve Strange, Billy's would soon become an epicentre of flamboyant glamour and peacock styling. Seizing the moment, the newly christened Spandau Ballet presented themselves

---

* Reed would later sing 'I believe in the Iron Cross', passed off in 2003 with the comment, 'I was young. I was having fun.'
† Spandau was also the name of the manufacturing company which produced machine guns for the German Army during the Great War.

as the house band. Guitarist and songwriter Gary Kemp remembers descending the basement stairs of Billy's and hearing music that sounded neither rock nor disco. 'It was a slow, pulsating, Germanic sound,' he recalled in the documentary *Blitzed: The 80s Blitz Kids Story*. 'There was this idea that it was some sort of reproduction of Weimar Germany, that it was very decadent . . . it was the most exciting place I'd ever walked in to.'

Billy's was short-lived. However, relocating to the edge of Covent Garden, the freshly named Blitz (an abbreviation of Blitzkrieg) conjured, in name, one of the darkest periods of London's history. The 1940s decor – simple tables and chairs, red and white gingham tablecloths, melted-down candles and period posters – conjured the era of wartime austerity. The air raids, falling bombs, and Londoners huddled in Underground stations faded quietly into silence. Rusty Egan played a selection of experimental sounds and synthesisers, crossing David Bowie and Kraftwerk with songs from the soundtrack of *Cabaret*.

The unusual blending of wartime nostalgia and modern electronic music gave Spandau Ballet a distinctive sound and look, but it also led the British music press to question the group's credibility. *Record Mirror* criticised the debut album sleeve for its 'classy white-on-white affair, with a cod-classical design of a naked male form looking suitably noble and muscular'. The review also scrutinised Robert Elms' accompanying inner sleeve prose, highlighting phrases such as 'immaculate rhythms', 'music for heroes', 'stirring vision' and 'journeys to glory' and voiced concerns about the glorification of the 'beautiful and clean, heroic young man'. 'The last thing on earth that Spandau need,' warned critic Sunie Fletcher, 'is to link themselves with some sort of Aryan Youth ideal, smacking hideously of Hitlerian master-race notions.'

Although not accusing them of fascism, Fletcher nevertheless described Spandau Ballet as teetering on the edge of the 'tempting blond, muscular noble dream of it all . . . try playing "Muscle Bound",' the copy suggested, 'back-to-back with "Tomorrow Belongs To Me" from the soundtrack of Bob Fosse's *Cabaret* . . . the mood is the same. Tread very carefully for all our sakes.'

Spandau Ballet were incensed. In an indignant letter to *Record Mirror*, they responded,

> Thanks very much indeed for nothing for just stopping short of calling us Nazis in your review of our album last week, that was really wonderful of you. We aren't Nazis, fascists, or Tories. Indeed, we are not stupid either, as you seem to imply with your patronising "little knowledge" comment. We are quite conversant with the political history of the 20th century, and we don't need lectures from you or anyone else. Yours is the ignorance in not realising that heroic and classical imagery has been used in many other contexts too numerous and varied to mention.

To back up the complaint, Robert Elms sent an additional letter, pointing out that he held a BSc in history and politics from the London School of Economics. He added, 'The suggestion that either myself, or the band, are fascists or that we are toying with pseudo-fascist imagery – is so unfounded that it is almost fraudulently laughable.'

Predictably, the spat attracted public attention, but few would have predicted the National Front youth magazine *Bulldog* hailing the group's album sleeve as a fine example of 'musclebound Nordic' art. Fortunately for Spandau Ballet, the controversy eventually faded and with it any lingering doubt about the group's political affiliations. The same could not be said for the broader scene they were part of, where some in their circle of friends continued to flirt with the Third Reich as a form of posturing.

Opening Club for Heroes on Baker Street on 4 June 1981, Steve Strange paraded before an expectant queue in a pair of jodhpurs and an SS-style leather coat. The high-status power play was reminiscent of Franz Stangl, the Commandant of Sobibór and Treblinka extermination camps – and later convicted of the murder of 900,000 people – who welcomed transports of Jewish prisoners also wearing white jodhpurs and SS leathers. In London, four decades later, Strange selected who could enter the club based on appearance, allowing some in while rejecting others.

Long before their association with the New Romantic scene, Japan pursued a Bowie-inflected new wave sound, crafting songs that reflected on 'Suburban Berlin' and depicted the city as one of 'flirting new ambition' and 'indifferent industrial crimes'. In 1980, lead singer David Sylvian acknowledged *The Night Porter* as a key inspiration for the band's track 'Nightporter', commenting that it 'shared a mood, an atmosphere, with [its] namesake'. However, it was Kirk Brandon, the lead singer of Spear of Destiny, who would attract the weight of judgement for the band's Nazi-inspired themes. In the 1980s the group released five albums, scoring their biggest hit in 1987 with 'Never Take Me Alive'. Their name originated from the story of Longinus, the Roman centurion who pierced Christ on the cross with the spear, a weapon that many believed possessed sacred or occult powers. According to Trevor Ravenscroft's 1972 bestselling book *The Spear of Destiny*, the Nazis became obsessed with the spear, convinced that in their hands, it would allow them to control the world.

Before Spear of Destiny, Kirk Brandon fronted the post-punk outfit Theatre of Hate. At early shows, the group arrived onstage to the stirring sounds of Richard Wagner's *Ride of the Valkyries*. The German composer vehemently hated Jews and wrote anti-Semitic papers matching the popularity of his classical scores. For Adolf Hitler, and many leading Nazis, they were an important touchstone. The Wagnerian influence on Theatre of Hate's artwork, and later Spear of Destiny's, coupled with Brandon's Aryan blond looks, sparked accusations of fascist sympathies.

During a heated exchange in May 1984, *NME*'s Amrik Rai accused Brandon of being a Nazi sympathiser. Allegedly, Brandon violently threatened the journalist but later defended himself, calling Rai a 'bogeyman' and claiming that 'he just launched straight into some kind of hypothetical situation about the SS. It was *News of the World*-type journalism – the self-same journalism that that paper was meant to despise'. In 2002, Sean Regan revisited the confrontation, asking Brandon about rumours that he had made anti-Semitic remarks directed at Spear of Destiny's producer. 'I never actually said that,' Brandon insisted, explaining that his solicitor had advised him against suing the *NME* for the trouble it would cause.

The situation escalated when Spear of Destiny appeared on Channel 4's weekly music programme, *The Tube*. In response to a question from host Tony Fletcher about their potential chart success, Brandon suddenly leaned into the microphone and declared, 'I'd just like to say I'm not gay [and] I am not a Nazi.' Taken aback by the unprompted statement, Fletcher feigned innocence, replying. 'I didn't ask any of these questions and I wasn't going to either.' To viewers, the unsolicited statement seemed out of place, yet given Brandon's past, fuelled conjecture.

In 1979, Brandon's former group Pack of Lies released their debut single on the SS Records label, whose initials are associated with Henrich Himmler's *Schutzstaffel*. 'I can tell you about the SS thing as I was the drummer,' Rab Fae Beith explained. '[We] had nothing to do with the mixing or choosing the record label. It was all Terry [Razor, Stiff Records marketing]. The first we knew was when we received a debut 45 rpm single. SS does stand for Secret Service, Terry's office!'[6] According to Brandon, Secret Service Records was 'abbreviated to SS by the pressing plant on the centre of the disc and catalogued as SS1'.[7]

Though SS Records raised eyebrows with its name, it wasn't the first label to carry unfortunate echoes of Nazi terminology. In the 1970s, Swan Song – a label tied to Led Zeppelin, Bad Company and Dave Edmunds – used the 'SS' prefix to catalogue releases without attracting controversy. Still, even seemingly innocent choices can spark speculation. Writing on the punk fanzine website Kill Your Pet Puppy in 2008, Tony Puppy (previously known as Tony Drayton, editor of *Ripped & Torn*) recalled a conversation with Kirk Brandon who told him the 'SS' label was set up by his manager, who also looked after Flock of Seagulls. Known for their 1982 hit 'Wishing (If I Had A Photograph Of You)', the band became the subject of a strange rumour suggesting fascist sympathies – mockingly rebranded in jest as 'Flock of Sieg Heils'. Drayton's closing remark, 'I kid you not,' highlighted the surreal and often satirical nature of such subcultural speculation.

Olympia

THE SKIDS. OI! THE BIRTHDAY PARTY

In 1979, Scottish post-punk band the Skids released their second album, *Days in Europa*, featuring cover art of a male Olympic athlete being crowned with a laurel wreath by an Aryan woman. Richard Jobson, the singer, stumbled upon this image at a flea market in Kreuzberg, Berlin. While displaying the swastika was illegal in Germany, Nazi memorabilia wasn't banned. Consequently, the weekly *Flohmärkte* became a treasure trove for items like copies of *Mein Kampf*, stamped documents and Nazi uniforms. The image itself is from a 1936 edition of the *Berliner Illustrirte Zeitung*, a weekly illustrated magazine that provided a guide to the Berlin Summer Olympics. Physical education was central to Nazi philosophy, praised by Hitler in *Mein Kampf*, where he advocated daily exercise and twice-daily sports in school. His passion for athleticism was tied to his vision of a 'pure blood' race, superior to the chaff (specifically Jews), and framed in Darwinian overtones: the survival of the fittest.

The 1936 Berlin Olympics were seen as a symbol of Aryan perfection, providing Nazi Germany with an opportunity to showcase its physical superiority to the world. During the opening ceremony, a 100,000-strong audience cheered a meticulously rehearsed theatrical spectacle. As athletes entered the stadium, waving their national flags and parading past Hitler seated in the grandstand, attention turned to how each team greeted him. The difference between a Nazi and an Olympic salute lies in the positioning of the raised arm: the Nazi salute thrusts the right arm forward, while the Olympic salute extends the arm to the side. While the French team saluted Hitler, Great Britain did not; a decision partly influenced by a misunderstanding during the 1936 Winter Games in the market village of Garmisch-Partenkirchen, when an announcement had incorrectly claimed that the British team saluted in Nazi style.*

Day two of the summer games brought more hullabaloo when Hitler agreed to *not* congratulate winning athletes from nations other than Germany. Twenty-four hours later, American athlete Jesse Owens won the first of four gold medals. Hitler was not impressed. According to Albert Speer, 'Each of the German victories, and there were a surprising number of these, made [Hitler] happy, but he was highly annoyed by the series of triumphs by the marvellous coloured American runner, Jesse Owens. People whose antecedents came from the jungle were primitive, Hitler said with a shrug; their physiques were stronger than those of civilized whites and hence should be excluded from future games.'[1]

During the Olympic fortnight, signs forbidding Jews from having equal domestic rights were removed, as the regime did not want visitors to Berlin to be alarmed by racial cleansing measures. For Jewish athletes, the clampdown on civil liberties had prohibited them from joining sporting associations, effectively barring them from competing in the games. For Hitler, the Olympics served as a platform to celebrate the Aryan archetype: blond hair, tall, muscular and perfectly proportioned. Some forty years later, these descriptions controversially aligned with the male and female athletes featured on the Skids album cover, *Days in Europa*.

---

* In October 1936, a German newspaper gleefully reported the display of both the swastika and the Union Jack outside the County Hotel to mark a boxing match between a Nottingham team and a visiting Stuttgart police force team. In 2021, BBC News highlighted that the event was used for Nazi propaganda, with an article revealing that the city's sheriff had led a cheer for Hitler, and the hosts had given the Nazi salute when the German national anthem played. During the same visit, the German boxing team gave a straight-armed salute in front of the statue of First World War pilot Albert Ball. A year earlier, in 1935, a swastika was flown over White Hart Lane, home to Tottenham Hotspur, who have a strong Jewish fan base, and three years later, the England national team gave Nazi salutes before a match against Germany in Berlin.

'Nazi undertones,' *Sounds* proclaimed.

'Not so,' protested Richard Jobson. 'I was thinking more of the five rings on it, the symbol of European unity.'[2]

In November 1979, however, when the Skids performed their new single, 'Working For The Yankee Dollar' on the *Old Grey Whistle Test*, Jobson wore a striking black-and-white outfit adorned with a Deutsche Olympia Erinnerungsmedaille (German Olympic Memory Medal) and an Iron Cross. The artwork for the record mirrored the controversial artefacts featuring a Third Reich-era anniversary postage stamp inscribed with 'Deutsches Reich', dated '30 January', and beneath it, the image of a nude male figure holding aloft a torch. Choices such as these only drew attention to the fact that throughout the year, the Skids accentuated the double 'S's in their name on the sleeves of their records, a detail that, intentional or not, replicated the SS logo.

Meanwhile, the National Front once again claimed a victory, sending letters of support. One such letter arrived from Wolverhampton, ahead of the Skids' engagement at the Lafayette Club. 'There were 300 NF skinheads in the crowd giving Nazi salutes,' Jobson explained. 'We did Beethoven's Ninth like we always do before "The Olympian"* and they went wild. It was horrible.' To add to the confusion, while the Skids supported Rock Against Racism and the Anti-Nazi League, Jobson claimed to be 'indifferent to the National Front' and openly wary of 'foreigners', adding that he could hardly be a Nazi when he was about to share a flat with a 'coloured bassist', Barry Adamson [of Magazine], who was of Jamaican and English heritage.[3]

The unsavoury rhetoric and promotion of Nazi-related imagery raised concerns for the group's record label, Virgin, who perhaps wanted to distance themselves from criticism after issuing Sex Pistols' records featuring swastikas. A solution came when *Days in Europa* was remixed. Seizing the opportunity to downplay

---

* "Olympian" was about the undue pressure put on young men to be somebody in the traditional sense of masculinity,' Jobson explained. 'This was something we all rejected.'

the negative publicity, Virgin issued a new cover which, as they explained, offered fans a choice, clearly differentiating the two products. Yet when the album arrived in record shops, the new cover featured an illustration of a man and a woman embracing, with the original artwork of the 1936 Berlin Olympics* framed on a wall behind them. 'People missed the irony of *Days in Europa*,' Jobson contended, 'and misread the lyrics as having some kind of fascist fetish thing going on. I hate fascists and everything they stand for.'

DJ John Peel was far from convinced and informed late-night listeners that he was uncomfortable with promoting tracks that he felt glorified Nazism. Jobson objected, arguing that punk had been notorious for its nihilistic outlook and irreverence towards the Third Reich. 'The cover,' he said, 'was powerful enough to get past the negativity of how other bands had used similar imagery. I was reading about the changing face of Europe in the 1930s,' Jobson continued, 'and felt the album caught some of that mood in the lyrics albeit in a more contemporary sense of what Europe was becoming. I still love the sleeve.† The controversy had no weight; at the same time, for example, nobody questioned Joy Division or their booking agent Final Solution. Now, there's something to get curious about.'4

Rather than deflect attention from Jobson, further suspicion was aroused with the 1981 recording 'Blood And Soil' – a slogan adopted by the Nazi Party (*Blut und Boden*) to evoke the idea of a racially

---

* New Order's post-2015 world tour employed a striking audiovisual prelude to introduce each live performance. A film montage of grainy, black-and-white archival footage – including sequences from Leni Riefenstahl's *Festival of Beauty* (1936) – depicted divers in slow motion, their forms frozen in mid-air synchronised with Wagner's *Das Rheingold: Vorspiel*. The theme was further reinforced by the live album *NOMC15*, whose cover features a diver from the Berlin Olympics.
† In 2024, the Skids announced a *Days of Europa* 45th anniversary tour (featuring special guests Spear of Destiny) to coincide with a reissue of the album. The record and the promotional tour poster, printed in the German-style Fraktur typeface, both featured the original 1936 Berlin Olympics cover.

pure Aryan people and the territory Germany intended to con-
quer – and 'The Night Of Crystal' an imagined dialogue between
Hitler's architect, Albert Speer, and Reich Propaganda Minister
Josef Goebbels. Reviewing Jobson's spoken-word solo album *The
Ballad of Etiquette*, factions within the media labelled Jobson a
Nazi. 'Suddenly I became a sort of Goebbels figure,' he complained.[5]
The accusation gained support when the Skids' released their third
album, *The Absolute Game*.

Initial copies of the top 10-charting record came with a limit-
ed-edition disc, titled *Strength Through Joy*, a phrase that Jobson
claimed he had borrowed from Dirk Bogarde's 1977 memoir.*
The term 'Strength Through Joy' ('Kraft Durch Freude') originally
referred to a programme organised by the Nazi Labour Front in
the 1930s designed to allow 'low-paid workers to enjoy supervised
activities, holidays and leisure time'. Hosted at holiday resorts,
the initiative politicised many young Germans, persuading them
to dedicate their lives to the Fatherland while participating in
quasi-military performances and outdoor gymnastics. By 1936,
'Strength Through Joy' had more than thirty million members, all of
whom received a *Sport und Staat* (Sport and State) handbook with
an introduction by Hitler extolling the virtues of physical prowess.

Similarly inspired by the phrase, journalist Garry Bushell compiled songs by artists such as the 4-Skins, Cock Sparrer and Last
Resort for 1981 album *Strength Thru Oi!*† released in collaboration
with *Sounds* magazine. The record's front cover featured Nicky
Crane, a member of the British Movement Leader Guard who
was serving a four-year prison sentence for racist violence. Crane
posed bare-chested with gritted teeth, his fist clenched, and a visible
swastika tattoo on his arm, which was airbrushed out of subsequent
copies. When *Daily Mail* journalist Simon Kinnersley exposed the
model's right-wing background, Bushell denied knowing about
it, claiming he was unaware of Crane's political affiliations. 'I take

---

* The phrase 'Strength Through Joy' is used by Bogarde in his memoir
A Position Struck, but not in relation to Nazism.
† A sequel to 1980's *Oi! The Album*.

full responsibility for *Strength Thru Oi!*' Bushell asserted, 'I gave the album its title. But it was never knowingly a pun on the Nazi slogan Strength Through Joy. Let's be honest, who knew? How many people my age was that up on Third Reich sloganeering? The Skids had released an EP called *Strength Through Joy* earlier that year, and that's what I based the pun on.'[6]

Oi! had its roots in the punk rock scene and name-checked Sham 69 and the Angelic Upstarts among its key influences. Both bands had attracted neo-Nazi followers, and their shows often descended into fights between British Movement supporters and anti-fascist activists. As leader of the Angelic Upstarts, Mensi supported Rock Against Racism but was not averse to making derogatory remarks about 'niggers' and expressing regret that Enoch Powell, who he said was 'not a racist', had not become prime minister.[7]

Opinions such as these defined Oi! Journalist and broadcaster Stuart Maconie described the movement as 'punk's stunted idiot half-brother, musically primitive and politically unsavoury, with its close links to far-right groups'. A vivid example of this is the Cockney Rejects, whose anthem 'Oi, Oi, Oi' became a rallying cry for working-class disillusionment and the rejection of 'politicians' and 'wankers'. The band's frontman, Stinky Turner (born Jeff Geggus), was no stranger to controversy, having been arrested at age fourteen for harassing an Asian man. By sixteen, he was wearing a Sex Pistols T-shirt emblazoned with a swastika, signalling his provocative stance. Unsurprisingly, the band's radical image attracted far-right followers, particularly from the British Movement, which Turner mockingly referred to as 'the German movement', while advocating an anti-fascist stance. [8]

In July 1981, three Oi!-associated bands – the 4-Skins, Last Resort and the Business – organised a joint performance at the Hambrough Tavern in Southall, a west London area known for its South Asian community, and the site of past racist violence, including murder. As tensions rose, right-wing skinheads began intimidating locals, only to be met by the Southall Youth Movement, a group of mixed-race, anti-racist and anti-fascist protesters.

The situation quickly escalated with petrol bombs thrown and the tavern set ablaze. Joe Pearce, the twenty-one year-old editor of *Bulldog* magazine, declared triumphantly, 'All Oi! bands are NF; the musical wing of the NF.'[9]

Two hundred miles north, in Bradford, the March Violets became part of a growing list of bands with unfortunate Third Reich con-notations. The term 'March Violets' was initially coined to describe those who joined the Nazi Party after Adolf Hitler became Chancel-lor on 30 January 1933 – often referred to as latecomers to the cause.

While a band without commercial success might slip by unno-ticed, the same could not be said for others. The Birthday Party courted controversy in 1983 with the release of their *Mutiny!* EP, recorded at Berlin's Hansa Studios. On a black cover adorned with red roses, the title of the record made a provocative statement, using religious iconography, including a swastika in place of the 'N' in 'Mutiny'. This bold choice led to intense media scrutiny, with many questioning the band's intentions and the message behind the artwork.

'Never have I considered what the inference of having this particular symbol is,' singer Nick Cave told *NME* in 1984.

> Rather it has always constituted part of my sense of humour as regards what is controversial and what isn't. It's still tempting for me to use that particular device. In the case of the swastika, I've always used it in the most deliberately moronic fashion. It's finding those symbols and thoughts that are far more shocking in certain environments than they are in others. As I've said, certain clichés in the right context can still be reasonably effec-tive. The swastika, as I've used it, is effective – I've also used it in contexts that certain people that I find totally intolerable will be repulsed by.[10]

The 'deliberately shocking' and 'irresponsible' humour Cave directed at unnamed individuals of course did not take into con-sideration the deep trauma carried by those directly affected by the swastika. Moreover, guitarist Mick Harvey shrugged it off, telling biographer Ian Johnston: 'It was just a belly laugh for us. Hansa Studios was right near the wall and used to be a Nazi ballroom. The ghost of the Nazi era was so powerful in Berlin in the early eighties. Every week there was this programme on TV called *Forty Years Ago** with Hitler and Nazi propaganda footage. The swastika was an obvious reference to that.'[11] Despite this, the band's German label refused to distribute the record with the symbol visible, forcing staff at Mute Records – founded by Daniel Miller, the son of two Austrian-Jewish refugees – to black out the swastika on every single copy by hand.

---

* First broadcast in 1973, the German-made television documentary reflected on newsreels tracing the rise of the Nazi Party.

Who Makes the Nazis?

THE EXPLOITED. THE FALL

'I think it's safe to say that Wattie Buchan is something of a legend.'[1] So pronounced *Record Mirror's* Ronnie Gurr in 1981. Known for his provocative image, Buchan, the lead singer of punk band the Exploited was photographed wearing a swastika shirt and standing alongside former members of far-right group Skrewdriver. In another notorious image, he posed with a group of skinheads who raised their arms in a Sieg Heil salute in front of SS lightning bolts. When confronted about his controversial choices, Buchan, who has a swastika tattoo on his arm, responded, 'We're called fascists. But I'll wear what I want to wear. It's my life and all the people that tell me not to wear swastikas, well they're fascists.'

Although Buchan had served as a soldier in the British army and openly criticised Israel's treatment of Palestinians, rumours circulated that he was a member of the National Front and had a swastika flag hanging in his home. Nevertheless, he adamantly rejected any association with Nazism. 'To me, it's just a bit of material,' Buchan told Gurr, offering a disclaimer to readers with a nervous disposition. 'I just like the design of the swastika. Look, I hate most Pakis, but I like Jamaicans. I hate a lot of white people. In fact, I hate more whites than Pakis so I'm not really racist.'

Explicit prejudice did little to hinder the Exploited's popularity. In October 1981, the group achieved their highest chart entry (number 31) with 'Hitler's In The Charts Again', a track that openly referenced Nazi death camps; 'You look like a tramp put you in a camp. Join the shower queue in your dancing shoe'. The second verse quoted from the Sex Pistols with the cheap rhyme, 'Keep on movin' fast, remember Belsen was a gas'. Later, the band re-worked the Pistols' 'Holiday In The Sun', describing people 'put into camps and left to rot and die', 'a camp full of horror' and even the 'raping of women'. If swastikas, racist rhetoric and brawling with Asians, as Buchan admitted to doing in the mid-eighties, was meant as an anti-fascist statement, it was largely lost on their expanding far-right fan base. Tragically, in 2017, a fan died of stab wounds after trying to stop neo-Nazis Sieg-Heil-ing outside a concert in St Petersburg. The Exploited expressed their condolences and condemned the attackers as 'fucking scummy cunts'. A further statement on Facebook read: 'There are a lot of people here talking shit as if it is the Exploiteds [sic] fault that this kid got killed outside a gig. Let's get a few points cleared up. If we had seen any cunt sieg heiling at our gig we would have had them kicked the fuck out. Nazis skins or punks are cunts and are NOT welcome to our gigs EVER. We are there to play Music which we love.'

In the fading years of punk, Mark E. Smith founded the Fall. A self-proclaimed non-musician, Smith positioned himself as a master of words – verbose, inventive and singular in his approach. Blessed with a fiercely devoted fan base, the Fall would become the ultimate outsider band, rarely breaching the national charts but consistently topping the independent ones. As the group's spokesperson, Smith was a constant presence in the music press, offering his distinctive and often controversial opinions until his death from cancer in 2018. Known for his fascination with the Third Reich, Smith often drew journalists into deep discussions about modern-day issues and historical events.

Smith's father was too young to serve in the Second World War, but his grandfather, a sergeant who fought in France, took part in the Allied evacuation. 'He took on the Waffen SS with his bare hands in 1940 at Dunkirk because his rifle jammed,' Smith told *NME*. 'All the officers had scarpered, so my grandad and his lot had to stick around to enable those buggers to get away. He was only four foot eleven! Far too small to be taking on the whole of Nazi Germany, but he did alright. He never got any medals or anything, but his house was covered with daggers and iron crosses, which I suppose were all the decorations he needed.'²

In 1997, Smith revealed that his grandfather 'killed four SS men with his bare hands', adding,

> Now I live in an Orthodox Jewish area, and my dentist, he's always got this Holocaust stuff out, and I go in there with fair hair and that, and he's there in his skullcap, got *Schindler's List* posters up in his surgery. And he's poking round my fuckin' teeth. So I'm like, 'Hang on, my grandad killed four SS men, you know,' and suddenly – 'Oh! Well, if he ever wants to come in here for free dental treatment, he's very welcome.' I said: 'Well, he's dead.' And he says: 'Well he's more than welcome then.'³

At sixteen, Smith dropped acid and frequented Manchester clubs, wearing a swastika armband. 'We used to try and cause fights with heavy metal gangs and get bands to play proper music and real heavy stuff like that,' he told *NME* in 1981. 'But it's funny, coz that's all coming back now, like with Oi!'⁴ Smith's political views, however, were harder to decipher. 'I change my politics every day,' he admitted to *Blast!* In a conversation with *Jamming* he added, 'Sometimes I'm a fascist, sometimes I'm a Nazi.'⁵

In 1982, Smith posed the question 'Who Makes The Nazis?' on the Fall's fourth studio album, *Hex Enduction Hour*. The song – its title a play on words (Macht-make, Wehrmacht-German army) – launched into an eclectic list of targets: from the BBC and George Orwell to the Burmese police, from 'balding smug faggots' to 'intellectual half-wits', and even the disconcerting 'Remember when I used to follow you home from school, babe, before I got picked up for paedophilia'. These disparate elements were united by the song's shouted refrain, '"Who makes the Nazis?"

Deciphering Smith's lyrics is an all-consuming passion for the Fall's fans, especially online. Smith often provided illuminating insight. 'I think singing about Nazi Germany and flying monks from Tibet is a lot more interesting than love songs,' he told *Jamming* in 1984, 'some surreal thing that will stimulate people and make them laugh. It's a lot more interesting than "Baby I Love You".'

In 1983, Smith fell in love and married. 'Mark loved Jewish women,' said Brix Smith-Start, his wife and later a much-admired Fall member. 'He thought they were really sexy. He loved Jewish people. Our neighbourhood, Prestwich, was and is a Jewish neighbourhood. He was really tolerant of lots of things.' Granddaughter of a Russian émigré, Smith-Start says of her grandfather, 'He was a real Jewish American success story. We learned so much about history, and the history of Jewish people. There was a real sense of where we came from. And when they didn't want us to understand something, my grandparents would speak Yiddish. Traditional family holidays like Passover were also major events. I even loved Yom Kippur. And Hanukkah was great – I got presents every day.'[6]

On tour one night, the group discovered an old woollen Nazi blanket with a swastika design tucked under a mattress in a *Gasthaus* in a German university town. '[Mark] freaked out and called us all in to have a look. He was completely obsessed with history and wars,' Smith-Start wrote in her memoir, *The Rise, The Fall, and The Rise*. 'Everywhere we went it was all about the war. This happened there, that happened there. He used to watch *The World at War* over and over again – a twenty-two-and-a-half-hour documentary series. By being with me it gave him a direct connection to the war. He always called me a Jewess.'

When the band arrived in Munich, Smith asked a local to show him evidence of Germany's past. To his delight, the amateur historian directed him to two beer halls: one marked the site of Hitler's failed 1923 putsch; and the other was where the Red Rose anti-Nazi student resistance met. Coincidentally, it was also the same street where the Nazi Party had formed. Smith wrapped up his historical tour at the Spear Disco, built on the grounds of the former Nazi Party headquarters. 'It was really hard to get in, but we were with him, so we were OK,' Smith told the *NME*. 'It was fine until they knew we were British. It was very sub-Gothic inside, and all made up in the style of 45 years ago. No flags, but pretty much what the Hacienda wants to look like really. The people who run the disco are very protective; they don't let British rock groups in. I don't blame them either.'[7]

Smith's fascination with Judaism was evident throughout his work. In 1986, Smith-Start brought this to life in his play *Hey! Luciani: The Life and Codex of John Paul I*, where she portrayed an Israeli commando hunting former Nazis. Dressed in army camouflage with submachine guns strapped across her chest, she sang 'Haf Found Bormann'. At the cryptic end of the nonsensical 'Garden', Smith-Start shouted, 'Jew on a motorbike!'*

In 1990, Smith pushed the boundaries further, dressing his band-mates in SS uniforms for the promotional video for 'High Tension Line'. 'I just thought it would be a good crack,' he explained. 'All these bands into shocking people are as tame as fuck.' Addressing would-be sceptics, Smith added, 'I made everybody cover up the SS symbols and swastikas. I'm very anti-Nazi, actually. What they did was criminal. They put German art back about one hundred years.'[8] Five years later, in 1995, Smith named the Fall's live album *The Twenty-Seven Points*, a reference to Adolf Hitler's 1920 National Socialist *25-Punkte-Programm*, albeit numerically incorrect. The programme had called for the nationalisation of all businesses, land and finance reform, and the exclusion of all Jews. 'The 27 points are what the Nazis brought in to take away everybody's freedom in Germany,' Smith enlightened *Q* magazine, adding, 'and they're all contradictory points as well.'[9]

Smith turned history into a subject of intrigue for post-war rock audiences. His conversations were often enlightening and educational. Yet the Third Reich imagery he used was frequently presented without context or clarity. Thus, when an audience saw a swastika that was all they saw, devoid of its historical significance. And by donning an SS uniform, Smith effectively glamorised the

---

* 'The Jew on a motorbike is a gentleman by the name of Sol Seaburg,' Start-Smith revealed to *Forward* (formerly known as *The Jewish Daily Forward*). 'Sol was the singer in a band called FC Domestos but was also our part-time van driver. When not driving the van, he rode a motorbike.'

very people he claimed to despise. In his 2018 obituary, Ted Kessler shared a revealing anecdote from twenty-seven years earlier, when Smith greeted him before a fanzine interview:

"'Kessler?' Smith repeated slowly, rolling my surname around his jowls. "Jew or Nazi?"

'It's an icebreaker [which] served my father (a Jewish refugee from Nazi Austria) well at his weekly poker games.'[10]

4.

NEVER MIND
THE SWASTIKAS

'Selection' of Hungarian Jews from Carpathian Ruthenia at Auschwitz-Birkenau, May or June 1944. Taken by either Ernst Hofmann or Bernhard Walter, both members of the SS.

This Way for the Gas,
Ladies and Gentlemen

WOODY GUTHRIE. RUSH. LEONARD COHEN.
PAUL WELLER. DEAD KENNEDYS

Today we are accustomed to images from concentration camps – of dead bodies and survivors reduced to emaciated, skeletal forms. This has not always been the case. What started in the fifties and sixties as a lampooning portrayal of a defeated enemy evolved in the seventies to wearing the emblems of Nazism to provoke an older generation. As many musicians argued, they had little knowledge of or access to Holocaust imagery or, if they did, they chose not to engage with it. As public understanding of the Holocaust deepened, the media became more discerning, increasingly distinguishing between genuine extremism and artists using such imagery purely for shock value.

Tellingly, it was not until 1991 that the Holocaust became a compulsory topic within the English secondary school history curriculum, although not in Northern Ireland, Scotland or Wales. As a result, children born before 1977–8 would have received little or no formal education about Hitler's extermination programme. Similarly, in the US, the first curriculum designed for public schools was created in New York in 1973, but as of today, only twenty-two states mandate Holocaust education. Identifying how popular culture – through books, film and television – has portrayed the atrocities of the Second World War helps to explain the varying ways musicians have toyed with Nazi symbols and how generational attitudes have shifted over time.

The term 'Holocaust', originally derived from the Greek *holokauston* and the Hebrew *olah* (a burnt sacrifice offered whole to God), first became current during the 1950s, particularly after its use by

Jewish historians, and then its prominence at the trial of Adolf Eichmann. On 11 May 1960, the Israeli secret service daringly captured the former SS officer in Buenos Aires. Smuggled out of Argentina, Eichmann faced trial for his role in the organising, identifying and transportation of Jewish people from across Europe to extermination camps in Poland. He was accused and charged with fifteen counts, including crimes against the Jewish people, crimes against humanity and war crimes. The trial began on 11 April 1961 and was broadcast to fifty-six countries. A global audience watched daily news reports, film of Nazi atrocities and live testimonies from survivors. Pathé News screened excerpts in cinemas, while the BBC hosted panel discussions. For the first time, the world saw irrefutable evidence of the Nazi mass-murder programme.

In a BBC interview, assistant prosecutor Gabriel Bach shared the testimony of a survivor who recalled seeing 200 children singing in a gas chamber to help give themselves courage. At the same moment, a train carrying potatoes arrived at the camp, and an SS officer took twenty children from the chamber to unload the cargo. Once the doors were sealed again, the remaining 180 children were gassed. Stories like this shocked the courtroom and the watching world. Over a hundred survivors provided 'factual background' on conditions in the concentration camps, forced labour and the process of extermination – many of them sharing their experiences with the world for the first time. Still, as *New Yorker* correspondent Hannah Arendt, who had been rescued from Nazi Germany by the American War Board, observed, 'On trial are [Eichmann's] deeds, not the sufferings of the Jews, not the German people or mankind, not even anti-Semitism and racism.'[1] *

---

* After a thirteen-month trial, Eichmann was sentenced to death and executed by hanging on 31 May 1962, despite the lack of documentary evidence submitted to the court. One piece of evidence that was rejected was a transcript, which was marked with Eichmann's handwritten notes containing his admission of his role in the extermination of Jews and his regret that more were not killed. Historians believe that the transcript, based on hours of recorded conversation, was excluded after pressure from the Israeli government, which was concerned about preserving diplomatic and economic relations with post-war Germany. The audio tapes, discovered in the late 1990s, were later sold to Eichmann's family and eventually made public.

The execution of one of the key architects behind the so-called Final Solution intensified the search for other fugitive Nazis. The discovery of Klaus Barbie, the infamous Butcher of Lyon, Ivan Demjanjuk, the Ukrainian SS-trained guard of Treblinka known to inmates as Ivan the Terrible, Josef Mengele and Franz Stangl, the Commandant of Sobibór and Treblinka, made international news. However, they were no match for the public's insatiable appetite for acts of heroism depicted in post-war cinema.

In 1946 *The Stranger*, written, directed by and starring Orson Wells, became the first Hollywood film to feature footage of the Holocaust. Similarly, *Judgment at Nuremburg*, which premiered in West Berlin in December 1961 during the trial of Adolf Eichmann, presented a stark portrayal of Nazi atrocities. Directed by Stanley Kramer, this three-hour Oscar-winning courtroom drama, starring Spencer Tracy and Marlene Dietrich, included real footage from liberated concentration camps – Majdanek (22 July 1944), Auschwitz-Birkenau (27 January 1945), Buchenwald (11 April 1945) and Bergen-Belsen (15 April 1945) – showing starved bodies, lampshades made from human flesh, bulldozers pushing corpses into man-made ditches, and children revealing tattooed numbers beneath their coat sleeves. 'We did not know,' Dietrich's character pleads in the film, surrounded by former German soldiers who sing, drink and smash down beer glasses. 'We have to forget to go on living.'

In contrast, the cinematic phenomenon *The Sound of Music* told the true story of the Von Trapp family's escape from Nazi-occupied Austria in a blaze of sentimentality and song. The soundtrack, featuring music by Rogers & Hammerstein, was the bestselling album of 1965, 1966 and 1968, outselling the Beatles, the Rolling Stones, the Beach Boys, Simon & Garfunkel and Bob Dylan. The film's bright Technicolor gloss and emphasis on wholesomeness reflected post-war attitudes. Similarly, film and television placed emphasis on dramatic escapades – whether at sea, in the air or on land – to focus on conflict rather than the horrific realities of a brutal regime. This all changed in 1973 with a groundbreaking twenty-six-part documentary narrated by Sir Laurence Olivier.

The World at War marked a broadcasting landmark, meticulously examining the rise of a new Germany in the 1930s, the Nazi invasion of Europe, North Africa, conflict in the Atlantic, the Battle of Britain and (in Episode 20) the persecution of Europe's Jews and the events leading to the so-called Final Solution. 'Genocide (1941–1945)'* contained shocking footage and interviews with both Jewish survivors and Nazi perpetrators, revealing horrific details of the extermination programme and killing factories. The episode was introduced by Olivier's only on-screen appearance, in which he forewarned viewers of the film's disturbing content.

'Every person, without exception, is capable of doing the worst things just to live another minute,' says Rudolf Vrba, who in April 1944 escaped from Auschwitz-Birkenau, aged nineteen. 'The idea for a mother, being told by a "gangster" [the false name for Jewish prisoners collecting luggage described by the SS] after this terrible journey that her children are going to be gassed, was an utterly outrageous idea in her mind. Because, after all what she suffered, here comes a 'gangster' who wants to increase her suffering. So, she was tempted to go immediately to the next neat officer and say that "This man says! Sir! That my children are going to be gassed!" And he says, "Madam! Do you think we are barbarians?"'

Vrba's forced labour on the *Judenrampe* (Jewish ramp) where transports from across occupied Europe arrived for 'selection' – either left, to the gas chamber or right, to forced labour – emphasised the significance of individual stories in Auschwitz and other camps. This type of contribution to the *World at War* encouraged viewers to imagine what for many was beyond imagination. It is part of the reason the 1978 NBC drama series *Holocaust: The Story of the Family Weiss*, starring James Woods and an up-and-coming Meryl Streep, achieved success in penetrating the psyche of television audiences to unprecedented effect. Originally aired over four days in the United States, then broadcast on the BBC and throughout Europe, the four-part series captivated an estimated 120

---

* A further two-part documentary examined in finer detail the road to the 'Final Solution' and the fate of Europe's Jewish population.

million viewers. In West Germany, the programme attracted the country's largest-ever audience, with around twenty million people – approximately one-third of the population – tuning in to follow the fate of the Weiss family. The series also played a significant role in popularising the term 'Holocaust'.

'The story is gripping, the acting competent, the message compelling, and yet,' Elie Wiesel, a Nobel laureate and Holocaust survivor, cautioned, 'the calculated brutality of the killers, the silent agony of the victims, the indifference of the outside world – this TV series will show what some survivors have been trying to say for years and years. And yet . . . everything is wrong with it . . . Untrue, offensive, cheap: as a TV production, the film is an insult to those who perished and to those who survived.'[2] Spared scenes of random brutality, starvation and violent humiliation, audiences nevertheless watched helpless as the middle-class Weiss family stoically walked into the gas chamber.

Saving the viewer from explicit visual detail also marked the approach of French film-maker Claude Lanzmann whose acclaimed 1985 documentary *Shoah* (the Hebrew word for the Holocaust, meaning catastrophe, destruction, annihilation, little-known outside of Israel before its release) was, in many ways, a studied reaction to the sanitised portrayal of the Weiss family. Lanzmann and his team visited former Nazi deaths camps and their surrounding neighbourhoods interviewing local witnesses and interspersing vivid colour footage of overgrown rail tracks, empty fields, tall pine trees, desolate graveyards and extant brick foundations. Twelve years in the making, the result was a spellbinding nine-and-half hour film, which won numerous awards and was lauded by critics as a cinematic masterpiece.

In stark contrast, *Playing for Time* (CBS, 1980) drew much criticism. Based on Fania Fénelon's memoir, *The Musicians of Auschwitz*, Arthur Miller's screenplay depicted a world of exhaustion, hunger, dehumanisation, prisoner hierarchy, jealousies, hatred and nation groups vying against one another. Anita Lasker-Wallfisch, a fellow orchestra inmate, insisted that the reality inside Auschwitz was not a 'vindictive mob of unruly girls who stole and betrayed each other at every opportunity'. In October 1979, Fénelon appeared on *60 Minutes* to express strong objection to the casting of Vanessa Redgrave, a vocal supporter of the Palestine Liberation Organization, proposing instead that Jane Fonda or Liza Minnelli should play the role. 'She [Redgrave] is not me,' Fénelon told a press conference at Yeshiva University of Los Angeles. 'She is a fanatic. I do not accept to be played by a woman who is the opposite of what I am.'[3]

Playing for Time coincided with the serialisation of American cartoonist Art Spiegelman's Pulitzer Prize-winning graphic novel *Maus: A Survivor's Tale*. In the same year, William Styron's highly acclaimed novel *Sophie's Choice* was adapted for the screen starring Meryl Streep, now one of Hollywood's most lauded actors. In the devastating end piece, Sophie is arrested and sent to Auschwitz where she is forced to either save the life of her son or daughter. *Premier* magazine voted it the third-greatest movie performance of all time and Streep won the Academy Award for Best Actress.

This period proved pivotal, as Holocaust-related stories gradually began to permeate popular culture. Books such as *The Diary of a Young Girl* (published in English in 1952) became a sensation, later being adapted into a Pulitzer-winning Broadway play in 1955 and an Oscar-winning film in 1959. Other notable literary works included Martin Amis' *Time's Arrow: or The Nature of the Offence* (shortlisted for the Booker Prize in 1991) and *The Zone of Interest* (2014), as well as Bernhard Schlink's *The Reader* (1995). Likewise, films such as *Escape from Sobibor* (1987), *Au revoir les enfants* (1987), *Schindler's List* (1993), *La vita è bella* (1997), *The Boy in the Striped Pyjamas* (2008) and *Son of Saul* (2015) all played key roles in dramatising personal stories of heroism and tragedy, while educating audiences about life under Third Reich occupation.

The gradual shift in storytelling paralleled a change in how rock 'n' roll began processing Nazism. In the eighties, and particularly the nineties, popular culture developed a more empathetic and nuanced understanding of the Holocaust. Although many artists still flirted with Third Reich imagery, an increasing number of songwriters created soundtracks to accompany stories of profound suffering and loss, blending sweet melodies with poetic imagery, and even weaving unexpected tales of romance, compassion and the resilience of humanity's unbreakable spirit to triumph over cruelty. As the swastika flew high over the history of popular music, many artists used their artistry to fight fascism and deliver poetic messages of humanitarian resistance and solidarity with anti-Semitism.

As early as 1941, Pete Seeger adapted lyrics from an old square dance into a protest song for his group, the Almanac Singers. Co-written with Millard Lampell, 'Round And Round Hitler's Grave' spoke of tying 'a rope around his neck' while cautioning: 'Mister Hitler's travelling mighty fast but he's on a one-way [single] track. Started down that Moscow road but now he's coming back'. An additional verse, written by folk singer Woody Guthrie, predicted that Hermann Göring and Benito Mussolini would be hung out to dry. 'I have done a lot of reading and studying about the true nature of the enemy that we are fighting,' Guthrie wrote in 1944, 'and it has been my work to create stories, songs, radio programs to inspire people to do more work and to fight harder to win this war as soon and as thoroughly as we can.'[4]

In addition to writing patriotic anthems with titles like 'Tear The Fascists Down', 'All You Fascists Bound To Lose' and 'Talking Hitler's Head Off Blues', Guthrie stencilled the phrase 'THIS MACHINE KILLS FASCISTS' onto the body of his guitar, wielding the instrument like a shotgun against tyranny.

In the tradition of Seeger and Guthrie, Tom Paxton wrote 'Train For Auschwitz (I See A Long Train Coming)', articulating with plain-spoken verse the human cargo 'jammed into the boxcars . . . condemned to die'. Documenting the brutal process of their extermination – herded into 'a giant shower room' and poisoned by Nazi gas – Paxton ends the song with the chilling realisation that 'hundreds of these murderers' are still walking 'the earth today'. Written in 1961, at the height of the Eichmann Trial, Paxton spoke out about unrepentant war criminals and the world's tolerance of fugitive Nazis hiding in Argentina, acutely observing, 'A lot of cover-ups and excuses made'.

Three years later, Bob Dylan (born Robert Zimmerman to Jewish parents) evoked the Holocaust with characteristic archness. Contributing to the ongoing political debate on retribution versus reconciliation, Dylan sang, 'When the Second World War came to an end we forgave the Germans, and we were friends', before delivering the pointed computation, 'Though they murdered six million, in the ovens they fried, the Germans now too have God on their side'. While allowing Dylan his poetic licence, in the years since he wrote 'With God On Our Side', studies have shown that of the six million Jews slaughtered in the Holocaust, an estimated 2.7 million were murdered at industrialised 'killing centres'. According to the United States Holocaust Memorial Museum, two million Jews were executed in mass-shooting operations and related massacres, and between 800,000 and 1,000,000 were killed in ghettoes, labour camps and concentration camps. An additional 250,000 died in other acts of violence outside camps and ghettoes.

Addressing the bewildering failure of victorious post-war nations to deliver justice, particularly concerning the 3,000 members of the *Einsatzgruppen* (death squads who rounded up Jewish women, men and children for execution) – of which only 200 faced trial, most receiving short prison sentences before being released back into society – historian Gitta Sereny concluded, 'There has been an extraordinary failure for almost fifty years now, both in Germany and the rest of the world, to consider the genocide of European Jewry in its whole context.'[5]

Opened in March 1933, Dachau was Germany's first concentration camp, originally built to house political prisoners and those considered 'enemies of the state'. Over time, the camp's population grew to include Jehovah's Witnesses, Roma and Sinti, gay men and Jews. In 1969, Captain Beefheart & His Magic Band recorded the unsettling, erratic 'Dachau Blues' which singled out 'those poor Jews' and the six million 'burned during the war' because of 'one mad man'. The song urged the world not to forget the 'misery', the 'rained death 'n' showers 'n' skeletons' and the 'dancin' 'n' screamin' 'n' dyin' in the ovens cough 'n' smoke 'n' dyin' by the dozens'. Born Don Van Vliet, the American singer-songwriter ended the song by beseeching the Lord to prevent such horrors in a Third World War.

An operational gas chamber, known as Baracke X, existed at Dachau but there is no credible evidence it was used to murder people, nor any clear reason why the SS chose not to use it. Nonetheless 40,000 prisoners perished at the camp before it was liberated in 1945, among those liberated being the father of Geddy Lee, the lead vocalist and bass player of Rush.

Born Gershon Eliezer Weinrib in Canada in 1953, Lee was named after his maternal Polish grandfather, who perished in the Holocaust. His mother, Malka Rubenstein, survived not only a labour camp but internment at Auschwitz and Bergen-Belsen. Records from the SS show that Lee's father, Moshe Weinrib, endured an astounding eleven labour and concentration camps, including Starachowice, Auschwitz, Flossenbürg, Kaufering (a sub-camp of Dachau), Buchenwald, Leipzig, Mauthausen and the final cruelty of a Death March. Unlike many survivors, Lee's parents never concealed their wartime past. 'I was fortunate that my mother wasn't afraid to talk about it,' Lee says, adding, 'it literally gave me nightmares, but I felt I understood what they had gone through.'

All the same, Lee says that it did not make him 'a kinder teenager', although, in subsequent years, he was able to 'look at his mother's life more sympathetically'. This understanding inspired the song 'Red Sector A', written by drummer Neil Peart for the 1984 album *Grace Under Pressure*. 'Neil took that sentiment' and wrote, 'Ragged lines of ragged grey skeletons, they shuffle away. Shooting guards and smoking guns will cut down the unlucky ones'. Lee adds, 'The whole album is about being on the brink and having the courage and strength to survive.'

At the end of the war Lee's parents were reunited and lived in the Displaced Persons Camp at Bergen-Belsen. On 21 November 1946 they were married in the officers' mess hall.* 'I once asked my mother her first thoughts upon being liberated,' says Lee. 'She

---

* Two thousand couples married in the camp during the first months after liberation.

didn't believe [liberation] was possible. She didn't believe that if there was a society outside the camp, how they could allow this to exist.'⁶ Aged twelve, a year before his son's bar mitzvah, Lee's father died from chronic heart damage related to his imprisonment in Dachau. Yet, incredibly, in 1978, *NME* journalist Barry Miles accused his group, Rush, of 'proto fascism', pointing to Neil Peart's regard for the Russian-American, Jewish-born author Ayn Rand, who rejected religion in favour of libertarianism and radical capitalism. 'It's amazing how long that mud stuck,' Lee told *Mojo* in 2023. 'Part of the way we used Rand's inspiration was definitely anti-totalitarian, as played out in the sci-fi plot of *2112*. And, fairly obviously, we were never fascists.'⁷

As a child, Leonard Cohen saw a photograph showing people wearing striped pyjamas playing violins and, beside them, 'a smokestack and the smoke was made out of gypsies and children'. The image, he told an audience in Cologne in 1988, inspired him to write the melancholy tango 'Dance Me To The End Of Love' to convey the horror of those to be 'killed and burnt' as a string quartet played by order of the SS. 'Pressed into performance while this horror was going on, those were the people whose fate was this horror also. And they would be playing classical music while their fellow prisoners were being killed and burnt.' 'So, that music, "Dance me to your beauty with a burning violin,"' Cohen later explained, 'meaning the beauty thereof being the consummation of life, the end of this existence and of the passionate element in that consummation. But it is the same language that we use for surrender to the beloved.'

In 1972, the thirty-eight-year-old Canadian-born singer confronted a rowdy crowd 'on the edge of anarchy' at the Sportpalast indoor arena. 'The Berlin audiences, then and now, like to be mastered,' Cohen told *Melody Maker*. 'This was the same place where Goebbels had made his famous speech where he'd asked the famous question of the German people, "Wollt Ihr totalen Krieg?" ("Do you want total war?") and they all stood for twenty-five minutes cheering. This crowd was getting out of hand. So, I shouted out of the microphone "Wollt lhr den totalen Krieg?" and they went completely crazy. They thought I was deeply insulting them or something.'[8]

British documentary maker Tony Palmer filmed the incident. However, when Cohen watched the edited footage, he was not pleased. 'Tony had it intercut with that speech of Goebbels. I thought that was a little too heavy. It was just fooling around with something far too sacred to be treated so casually. Then it cut to Hitler riding in Nuremberg. That was one of the main reasons I didn't want this film . . . it was a little Grand Guignol,' Cohen objected, invoking the gruesome stage show performed in 1890s Paris.

The macabre notion of a prison camp orchestra accompanying labourers to and from work – or even as they entered the gas chamber – defies comprehension. In a place of unimaginable horror filled with terror, hate, fear, dogs barking and the brutal mauling of prisoners, musicians performed the works of composers like Mozart and Chopin. At Auschwitz, there were as many as nine orchestras made up of semi-starved women and men, who survived another day by playing the ad-hoc combination of accordions, clarinets, recorders, guitars, saxophones, cellos or violins. In the secrecy of their barracks, many inmates composed original scores and wrote songs. Aleksander Kulisiewicz at the US Holocaust Memorial Museum has assembled a collection of seventeen songbooks and over seventy original songs written in German, Yiddish and Polish, originating from multiple concentration camps. This was not music to accompany death, but to offer hope – a belief that, despite the burning pyres around them, music could somehow prolong life. This optimism, this faith in music when confronted with death, would echo in the songwriting of pop musicians in the years to come.

The setting: a love story in a concentration camp. The backdrop: a haunting portrait of unimaginable suffering. To a mournful tune, Paul Weller sings, 'The crab lice bite, the typhoid smells and I'm still here, handsome in rags, a trouserless man waiting helpless for dignity'. Recorded in 1984 by the Style Council, 'Ghosts Of Dachau' was inspired by *This Way for the Gas, Ladies and Gentlemen* by

Polish poet and Holocaust survivor Tadeusz Borowski.* As Weller explained in 2009, 'In amongst all this fucking degradation and disgraceful human behaviour there were still people having love affairs. There's a bit in the book where he describes a guy who's lost his trousers, he's walking around semi-naked because there was nothing else to put on, all those kinds of images. Whether it sounds right to say, but life still carried on in a strange way in those camps. I thought it was unbelievable, whether it was a strength or a stupidity of human behaviour, whichever way you look at it, I thought it was fascinating.'

As a non-Jewish political prisoner, Borowski endured two years in Auschwitz before being forced onto the infamous Death March to Dachau. A year after his liberation, he published a harrowing collection of short stories (published in English in 1967) documenting the daily realities of camp life. Borowski writes of a Red Cross ambulance transporting victims to the gas chamber and witnessing the 'selection' process as new transports arrived at the station ramp. What Paul Weller achieved in song, so Borowski conjured in text, describing moments of unexpected sensuality and life-affirming tales in the most incomprehensible of circumstances. In the collection *Farewell to Maria*, Borowski writes, 'A girl emerges, her luxuriant blonde hair tumbles onto her shoulders in a soft wave . . .' When their eyes meet, the author is mesmerised. 'There, standing before me, is a girl with wondrous blond hair, beautiful breasts wearing a batiste summer blouse, with a wise, mature gaze . . . And over there is the gas chamber . . . "Tell me, where are they taking us?" I remain silent. "I already know," she says and walks off bravely in the direction of the trucks.'[9]

In 1977, journalist Barry Cain travelled with Paul Weller and his group, the Jam, to Europe. The *Record Mirror* feature – 'Prussian Roulette' – resulted in an unexpected collation of facts acquired from a visit to Dachau.

---

* The song was originally presented to Tracey Thorn from Everything But the Girl to sing on the debut Style Council album.

The Totenkammer (morgue) was permanently crammed with corpses. According to the files of the International Tracing Service 31,951 prisoners died in the Dachau concentration camp. An additional few thousand prisoners who had not been registered at all were shot dead. The experimental station of Dr Rascher was set up in Block 5 where high pressure and exposure experiments were practised on defenceless prisoners. Prof. Schilling had prisoners infected with malaria agents. Bio-chemical experiments were also conducted in Dachau. Many of these experiments resulted in death, at times, four hundred prisoners to each room. If a bed had been badly made the culprit would be hanged by his wrists for an hour. The Wirtschaftsgebäude contained the notorious shower baths where the SS tortured prisoners by flogging and hanging them at the stake.[10]

In the shadow of the watchtower, Weller stood uneasily with his girlfriend, Gill, while bassist Bruce Foxton and drummer Rick Buckler examined the crematorium. The inclusion of historical detail in Cain's report was unusual for a rock paper, amplified by John Weller adding a disturbing sexual element to the story. Recalling a newspaper article he read at the end of the war, the Jam's manager (Weller's father) described the surreal sex life of a female SS commandant, possibly Ilse Koch. According to the report, when admitting a new batch of prisoners to the camp, she would pick the most virile-looking man and 'lay him' that night, only to have the helpless victim whipped to death the following morning, penis cut off and pickled in a jar. When American soldiers raided her home, they discovered a room full of incriminating artefacts.

Articles such as this balanced fact with gory detail and contributed to a growing narrative where artists, and indeed journalists, expressed revulsion at the crimes of the Third Reich.

On 5 May 1985, President Ronald Reagan participated in a joint German-American military ceremony at Bitburg Air Base. Intended as a gesture of reconciliation with the former Axis power and in recognition of the victims of Nazism, Reagan visited a nearby

German war cemetery where forty-eight members of the military Waffen-SS lay buried. His visit sparked worldwide condemnation. 'The crimes of the SS must rank among the most heinous in human history,' Reagan commented shortly after the visit, adding that many of those buried at Bitburg were 'simply soldiers in the German army. How many were fanatical followers of a dictator and wilfully carried out his cruel orders? And how many were conscripts, forced into service during the death throes of the Nazi war machine? We do not know. There were thousands of such soldiers for whom Nazism meant no more than a brutal end to a short life,' the president concluded.[11]

A month later, the Ramones released their new single, 'Bonzo Goes To Bitburg', inspired, in name, by some protestors' epithet for the president. The sleeve featured a photograph of Reagan at Bergen-Belsen, just hours before his speech at Bitburg. 'We had watched him going to visit the SS cemetery on TV and were disgusted,' said Jewish-born Joey Ramone. 'We're all good Americans, but Reagan's thing was like forgive and forget. How can you forget six million people being gassed and roasted?'

Formed in 1980, No Swastikas – later known as Redskins – were vehemently anti-fascist. A fervent trio of York-based Marxist-Leninist skinheads, they were staunch members of the Socialist Workers Party. Their music tackled issues like class war, Thatcherism and right-wing activism. In June 1984, during a performance at London's South Bank, the group was attacked by far-right skinheads, who then turned on the audience, triggering a fierce response and chants of 'Nazis out!' from the crowd. 'The misconception has always been that skinheads were all right-wing, which they were not,' singer Chris Dean told Eva Kowalski in 1986. 'If you look at the Specials' audiences, the 2 Tone bands, Madness, there were a lot of skinheads, a lot of anti-racist skinheads and left-wing skinheads and socialist skinheads.'[12]

The challenge was in discerning a skinhead's political views, as their uniform – braces, shaved head and eighteen-hole Dr. Martens boots – was shared across factions. Partisan alignment often only became clear when it manifested in physical action – a punch or a Nazi salute. In November 1982, at London's 100 Club, the editor of Woolwich's *Skins* fanzine expressed frustration with the ever-present violence at gigs. 'I'm writing to *Sounds* so I can get a message to the few stupid idiots at the 4-Skins gig on the 18th,' his letter began.

> Firstly, why don't all you mugs just piss off, the 4-Skins are a brilliant band and it's hard enough for bands to get gigs as it is without all you scruffy bastards fighting and giving it 'Sieg Heil' all the time. When will you grow up, half of you weren't old enough to be in there anyway! What's the matter, can't you take a pint or two without going mad? It's embarrassing to call yourself a skin with all you 14-year-old, dirty, scruffy glue bags fighting just because a German film crew were there. You're just saps, all of us genuine skins can just wait till you lot are all inside or dead from glue-sniffing, then there might be a decent, clean firm of skinheads and birds about.

The letter was signed, 'Norm, Woolwich, "get clean and get smart!"'[13]

The angry tirade highlighted not only a growing neo-Nazi infiltration at concerts but also a disturbing new trend appearing on UK high streets. In London, a T-shirt emblazoned with 'Adolf Hitler European Tour 1939–45' hung from vendors' stalls on Oxford Street, Carnaby Street, in Camden and Kensington markets, and outside football grounds, notably at West Ham United in the East End.* The shirts displayed a stencilled colour portrait of Adolf Hitler, and on the back, conquered countries during the Second World War:

September 1939 Poland
April 1940 Norway
May 1940 Luxembourg
May 1940 Holland
May 1940 Belgium

---

* In 2004, Christie's acquired an 'Adolf Hitler European Tour' T-shirt (with a Boy label) belonging to Vivienne Westwood's private collection.

June 1940 France
September 1940 ~~England~~ Cancelled
April 1941 Yugoslavia
May 1941 Greece
June 1941 Crete
August 1942 ~~Russia~~ Cancelled
July 1945 Berlin Bunker

Wayne Morris, the owner of European Son, based on Gosford Street in Coventry, designed the shirt. According to *Graffiti Magazine*, Morris, who also managed the Primitives, 'helped finance the band by opening a T-shirt emporium' that became known for its hugely successful (and controversial) 'tour' T-shirt.[14] Morris admitted to the *NME*, 'It probably was a bit unsound, though no politics were meant to be implied. But it did make a lot of money for us, which was then pumped into the band.' Profiting from the sales of the T-shirt, the Primitives crashed into the top 10. A similar range of controversial items was also sold at Merc M & Cutdown, located at 19 Ganton Street, near Carnaby Street, which specialised in Third Reich memorabilia including swastikas, armbands, SS badges, rings, magazines and T-shirts. However, by 1989, both shops had shut down.

Similarly, the Dead Kennedys capitalised on provocative fashion when they released their fifth single, 'Nazi Punks Fuck Off', which came with a free armband featuring a crossed-out swastika. Red-printed lyrics on the sleeve included the line, 'You still think the swastika look kool? The real Nazis run your schools'. Singling out coaches, businesspeople and the police, the Dead Kennedys warned them, 'In a real fourth Reich you'll be the first to go'. Thirty years later, the Dead Kennedys are still fighting to keep punk free from right-wing infiltration. On 22 February 2025, the band shared a provocative collage on social media under the same bold heading: 'Nazi Punks Fuck off!' The image featured masked men making Nazi salutes, swastikas and Donald Trump's face. At its centre was Elon Musk – owner of X (formerly Twitter) and, at the time, a special government employee – his right-arm outstretched in a clear Sieg Heil. The accompanying text read: 'Punks that support

Trump. Fuck off. It's time to take a stand against this fascist regime! Stand up and kick these Nazis out of our scene!'

Enter Phranc, the self-styled all-American folksinger, who told journalist Denise Sullivan, 'People were wearing the swastika, and it pissed me off.'15 Opening for the Smiths on their 1985 Meat is Murder tour, Phranc encountered fans saluting her while wearing Nazi emblems. 'I don't buy any of the crap about the swastika being shock value. Half the people that are wearing them that I've talked to don't know what fascism is.'16 In response, she wrote the song 'Take Off Your Swastikas', which included the chorus, 'You say, "Phranc, it's just a symbol", "It's just an emblem", "It's just a righteous decoration." Well, it means a little more to me, cause I'm a Jewish lesbian, ya see.'

The 1980s represented a significant period in rock 'n' roll with numerous musicians explicitly expressing their opposition to fascist ideologies and symbols associated with the Third Reich. However, as the new decade approached, the Stone Roses were 'shocked to discover' that the artwork for their new single, 'One Love', inadvertently included a swastika. John Squire, the group's guitarist and artist, immediately ordered the sleeve and all related materials be withdrawn. 'If you looked at it in a certain way you could see the suggestion of a swastika in the painting,' a spokesperson for the band told the NME in June 1990. 'When he realised, John just tore up the proofs.' This act of destruction signalled a shift in the music scene, where for some, the moment had arrived to use their platform to directly address the horrors of the Holocaust.

Arbeit Macht Frei

MANIC STREET PREACHERS. JANIS IAN. INDIGO GIRLS

At university, Richey Edwards focused on Holocaust studies and Nazi/Soviet foreign policy. In a conversation with *NME*, the Manic Street Preachers' guitarist remarked on how alarming it was that, in such a short time, the Holocaust had been 'rendered almost obsolete'. 'I find it really frightening,' he admitted.

> We've actually been to places like Dachau. I spent all my life in education studying it, and when you actually go there it means nothing. It's only when you come back, and you realise that there are books by people like Arthur Buntz and *The Hoax of the 20th Century* that suggest it's all a lie; it's somehow a Jewish-Christian conspiracy. This is being seriously debated by intelligent people. They suggest that some of the death camps were built after the war by the Americans to basically put the blame on Germany, to make them feel bad, when nothing actually happened. That's being debated in universities now, and I feel that's really, really frightening. Six million lives are worth nothing.[1]

In 1993, the Manic Street Preachers visited two concentration camps: Dachau, located twelve miles north-west of Munich, and known for its extreme brutality and sadistic 'kapos', who became feared figures within the camp network, and Bergen-Belsen, about 160 miles east of Berlin. The experience had a lasting impact on the band. 'Dachau is such an evil, quiet place,' bassist

Nicky Wire told *Melody Maker*. 'There's no grass, and you don't even see a worm, let alone any birds. All you can hear is this humming of nothing.'

Experiencing a similar atmosphere at Bergen-Belsen, Wire returned to his hotel and began writing down ideas for a song. 'I was struck by the lack of creatures and the silence,' he said. 'There's greenery and trees, but it seemed to me even nature couldn't face touching that horror.'[2] The resulting track, 'The Intense Humming Of Evil' opens with a voice sampled from the English version of *Judgement of the Nations* (*The Nuremberg Trials*), directed in 1947 by the pioneering Russian film-makers Elizaveta Svilova and Roman Karmen. The voiceover reads, 'The court had come, the court of the Nations. And into the courtroom will come the martyrs of Majdanek and Oświęcim [Auschwitz]. From the ditch of Kerch, the dead will rise. They will rise from the graves. They will rise from the flames bringing with them the acrid smoke and the deathly odour of scorched and martyred Europe. And the children, they too will come. Stern and merciless. The butchers had no pity on them.'

Underpinning the stark narrative, an unyielding industrial noise created an unsettling soundtrack evoking the purpose of an extermination camp: a factory of death. 'Now the victims will judge the butchers. Today the tear of a child is the judge. The grief of a mother is the prosecutor. Suddenly, a wail of feedback unleashes a menacing combination of deep bass notes and an ominous drumbeat. 'You were what you were,' sings James Dean Bradfield, 'Clean cut, and unbecoming. Recreation for the masses. You always mistook fists for flowers'.

'The Intense Humming Of Evil' was one of a pair of songs on *The Holy Bible* that addressed the Holocaust. The album came with an illustrated booklet, featuring a photograph of the entrance to Dachau, with the words 'Arbeit Macht Frei' ('Work Sets You Free') inscribed above the wrought-iron gate, along with a technical diagram of the camp crematorium, known as Baracke X. 'Welcome, welcome,' Bradfield sings, voicing the camp commandant. 'Arbeit Macht Frei. Transport of invalids. Hartheim Castle breathes us in. In Block 5 we worship malaria . . . Rascher surveys us.' This was a reference to SS doctor Sigmund Rascher, infamous for conducting inhumane medical experiments, infecting prisoners with malaria and testing euthanasia gasses at Hartheim Castle near Linz, Austria. This was one of five castle-hospitals throughout the Reich – the others were Sonnestein, Grafeneck, Hadamar and Brandenburg – where around 30,000 people, considered 'feeble-minded', sick or disabled, were gassed under the T4 Euthanasia programme, named for its Berlin headquarters at Tiergartenstraße 4. Many of the doctors from these 'eugenics' hospitals would later be posted to extermination camps at Bełżec, Sobibór, Treblinka and Majdanek.

The song continues, invoking 'six million screaming souls' and the 'transport of invalids'. The final couplet – 'Churchill no different. Wish the workers bled to a machine' – alludes to intelligence the British prime minister received as early as August 1941 from Bletchley Park about mass shootings conducted by the *Einsatzgruppen* as the German army advanced eastwards. Churchill argued that defeating Hitler was the quickest and most effective way to end the war and save Jewish lives. In fact, Hitler's belief that the Allied nations didn't care deeply about the Jews helped fuel his drive to exterminate them. While the Allied powers were not fighting an ideological war, Nazi Germany was waging both a military and genocidal racial crusade. Historians agree that for Hitler, the war presented an opportunity to fulfil his promise and eradicate the Jewish population of Europe. In his speech to the Reichstag on 30 January 1939, Hitler could not have been more explicit: 'If the international Jewish financiers . . . should again succeed in plunging the nations into a world war the result will be . . . the annihilation of the Jewish race throughout Europe.'*

---

* It is important to note that 'annihilation' is understood by many historians to mean 'expulsion' not 'extermination' and therefore not a foreshadowing of the Holocaust. However, Hitler repeated his intention five times, stating on 30 January 1942, 'And we say,' he told the party faithful on the ninth anniversary of the Nazis seizing power, 'that the war will not end as the Jews imagine it

Britain, on the other hand, entered the war to liberate occupied territories, not to defeat anti-Semitism. When General Dwight D. Eisenhower visited a liberated Buchenwald on 12 April 1945 he famously declared, 'We are told that the American soldier does not know what he is fighting for. Now, at least, he will know what he is fighting against.'

The destruction of Europe's Jews and those labelled 'inferior' by the Nazi regime thematically screamed across *The Holy Bible*. It is evident in songs like 'Mausoleum' with its aching lines – 'Wherever you go I will be carcass. Whatever you see will be rotting flesh', and in 'Of Walking Abortion' with the phrase, 'Hitler reprised in the worm of your soul'. There is also a reference to the anti-Semitic Hungarian military dictator, Miklós Horthy – 'Horthy's corpse screened to a million'. Even so, James Dean Bradfield expressed concern to the group that the songs were too 'ambivalent'. 'Do the lyrics condemn the innocent victims for succumbing to the Nazis?' he asked. 'I didn't think the first draft of "Intense Humming Of Evil" was judgemental enough. It's a song about the Holocaust and you cannot be ambivalent about a subject like that. Not even we are stupid enough to be contentious about that.'[3] Bradfield's reservations spoke to the group's righteous approach and deep respect for the victims of the Nazi extermination programme. To rock music, they delivered what historian William L. Shirer described as 'the darkest chapter of all in the history of the Third Reich'.[4]

In 1993, American composer and producer David Axelrod approached *Requiem: The Holocaust* with similar conviction.

will, namely with the uprooting of the Aryans, but the result of this war will be the complete annihilation of the Jews.' Ten days earlier, at a conference at a villa in the Berlin suburb of Wannsee, fifteen high-ranking Nazi Party officials agreed a 'Final Solution to the Jewish question'. The minutes taken by Adolf Eichmann, Chief of the RSHA Department IV B 4 (Jewish Affairs), discovered after the war, detailed a list of European Jews totalling eleven million and the phrase *Sonderbehandlung 14f13* introduced by Reinhard Heydrich as a coded euphemism meaning 'special treatment, death by gassing'.

Responding to Tom Metzger, a white supremacist who denied the Holocaust during a television broadcast, Axelrod conceived an opera centred on four arias – 'Krystallnacht', 'Trains', 'Auschwitz', and 'Gas Chambers' – which charted the journey of Jewish lives under Nazi rule, from pogroms to the so-called Final Solution.

Nine-time Grammy nominee Janis Ian grew up hearing stories about the Holocaust. As a Jewish songwriter, she felt compelled to write 'Tattoo' for her 1992 album *Breaking Silence*, saying, 'someone had to'. Her motivation came after Nashville songwriter Larry Cowan performed his own Holocaust-themed song. Ian was struck by the irony, saying, 'I thought, "Here you are, a Jew, and it takes a blond, blue-eyed guy from a strip-mining town in West Virginia to write a song about it." I felt ashamed in front of my grandparents' memories.'[5]

Ian spent three months at the Santa Monica Library, reading 'obsessively about the Holocaust'. She also discussed the song she wanted to write with Rabbi Beth Davidson, who shared a poignant insight: 'You've met survivors [of concentration camps]. There's a part of them that is never coming back.' According to the rabbi, while survivors could rebuild their lives and families, a part of them remained forever scarred. 'It's like a survivor of any kind of serious abuse,' Ian said. 'I think a part of your life is taken, your faith in humanity is taken – at least among the survivors I've known.'

The finished song examined the dehumanising experience of a Jewish woman's arrival at a death camp. From the selection process that determined life or death to the extraction of gold teeth, and the 'mountains of jewellery and toys piled in the corners'. Even after liberation, when the survivor had the tattooed number surgically removed from her wrist, it stayed on 'her empty heart'. Ian explained, 'I don't think [the song's ending] is downbeat so much as true. Life isn't over for this person, but some things are cut into you that can't be cut out.'

Recorded live at Schouwburg Concordia in Breda, the Netherlands, 'Tattoo' was chosen by the Dutch government to represent their country in European celebrations marking the 50th anniversary of the Second World War. 'My family knew a lot of concentration camp survivors and I really felt it should be written,' Ian said. 'It's part of the reason I went back into recording. I had no idea it would have the kind of impact it did.' Reflecting on her Jewish background, she added, 'Being an outsider forms you as a writer.'[6]

A similar understanding inspired Amy Ray of the Indigo Girls to invoke Woody Guthrie's spiritual, 'This Train (Is Bound for Glory)' when describing a cattle car en route to 'resettlement' in the East. 'It's a fish-white-belly, lump-in-the-throat, razor-on-the-wire, skin-and-bone, piss-and-blood in a railroad car, 100 people – gypsies, queers and David's star, this train is bound for glory', she sang. 'I was always really struck by the train imagery of [the Holocaust],' Ray says of her song, 'This Train Revised'. 'In the South, where I grew up, the train image is one of going to a better place. That irony and cruelty resonated with me . . . I wanted the song to feel harsh and show cruelty. I felt angry when I wrote it. I was so angry about what happened.'

Although not Jewish, Ray first learned about the Holocaust after attending a guest lecture by a survivor during a comparative religion class at Emory University in 1986. Embarrassed by her lack of knowledge, Ray says, 'I was shocked by a lot of what I learned about the human capacity for evil.' Ray's visit to the Holocaust Museum in Washington DC further expanded her understanding of the Nazi Aryan vision. 'There's a lot now being uncovered about the homosexual experience of the Holocaust,' she wrote in a press release for the Indigo Girls' 1994 album *Swamp Ophelia*, 'and how it affected those survivors who'd been listed as what they called a "175-er" [German statute that criminalised sexual relations between men but not women]. At the museum it's made very clear that although Jews were by far the main victims of the Holocaust, there were many others too.'

Indeed, the scale of Nazi persecution during the Third Reich is estimated to have resulted in the deaths of eleven million non-Jews, including Slavs, Roma and Sinti people, homosexuals, the mentally or physically disabled, Soviet prisoners of war, Jehovah's Witnesses, political dissidents such as Communists and trade unionists, as well as other minorities like Afro-Germans and those considered outside of the 'master race'.

Sound of Drums

SKUNK ANANSIE. KULA SHAKER. U2. MICHAEL JACKSON

In the early nineties, under the leadership of the young and dynamic Tony Blair, New Labour adopted the Union Jack, a flag long associated with the Conservative Party and, more controversially, far-right nationalism. Around the same time, a clutch of musicians began incorporating the Union Jack into their image – sometimes independently, sometimes through media portrayal – ushering in what the press came to call Britpop, centred around bands like Suede, Blur, Oasis, Elastica and Pulp. Then, ahead of a much-hyped men's semi-final football match between England and Germany, the *Daily Mirror* stirred up xenophobic passions by featuring a front-page image of two players, Stuart Pearce and Paul Gascoigne, wearing Second World War helmets, with the caption, 'ACHTUNG! SURRENDER, For you Fritz, ze Euro 96 Championship is over'. The whiff of xenophobia appalled many, among them the lead singer of Skunk Anansie, whose feelings towards the national flag would inform the group's debut single, 'Little Baby Swastikkka'. 'The Union Jack meant something different to us,' she wrote in her memoir *It Takes Blood and Guts*. 'Our first rehearsal space was run by a British Movement guy, and there was a massive British flag positioned just as you walked through the entrance.'

Deborah Anne Dyer, known as Skin, was born in 1967 to Jamaican parents. She recalls inspiration striking when she saw a small 'wobbly' swastika scrawled on a wall, a foot above ground, as though drawn by a four-year-old. Contemplating the idea of a child being taught 'to be racist when they are too young to know otherwise', Skin wrote, 'You rope them in young, so small, so innocent. So delicately done, grown up in your poison'. She then combined 'swastika' with 'KKK' (Ku Klux Klan) to create the neologism 'Swastikkka' and sang about the corrupting influence of Nazism. 'It started off as a whisper, low, over Cass [Lewis'] bassline', she said, 'and then I spoke the lines that came into my head: "Who put the little baby swastikkka on the wall . . . who put the little baby nigga-head on the wall."'

Music impresario Jonathan King campaigned for 'Little Baby Swastikkka' to be the UK entry in the Eurovision Song Contest, convinced it would win. Skin disagreed, stating, 'I don't think I represent Britain in anything to be quite honest. Waving the British flag is not my thing.'[1] However, just as it seemed that British musicians were becoming more aware of the dangers of nationalism and the swastika, Kula Shaker came onto the scene, flaunting the ancient symbol and making misjudged comments about Hitler and the Third Reich.

Fronted by the blue-eyed, blond Crispian Mills, Kula Shaker caused a stir during a March 1997 interview with *NME* in which Mills made an eyebrow-raising statement: 'Hitler knew a lot more than he made out. The Nazis studied the Vedas, the scriptures, the Holy Grail . . . they were into magic and all that. I'd love to have great big flaming swastikas onstage just for the fuck of it.'[2] The band's debut album had recently exceeded a million sales, and naturally the observation ignited media uproar. In response, Mills faxed a four-page letter to the *Independent on Sunday*, expressing regret while also admitting his past dabbling with Nazism. 'This has justifiably upset many people for which I am deeply sorry', he wrote. 'There is no better example of my naivety and insensitivity than the swastika comments.' The problem was, Mills had a history of similarly shocking remarks. In November 1996, he had said, 'You can see why Hitler got support. It was probably the uniforms that swung it.' Two months later, he speculated, 'Well, we know that democracy doesn't work. If we had a non-elected body that set the right standards . . .'[3]

This ill-judged analysis echoed David Bowie's controversial remark from two decades earlier, when he had described Hitler as 'the first rock star'. Now, sniffing the odour of scandal, the press exhumed long-buried stories from Mills' past. They discovered that in his former band, Objects of Desire, co-founder Marcus Maclaine was a member of the National Front and had also been the partner of Mills' mother, the actor Hayley Mills, for twelve years, The group motto was 'England will rise again'. In 1993, Objects of Desire had even performed at the Global Deception Conference at Wembley Arena, where far-right conspiracy theorists, including the notorious anti-Semitic propagandist Eustace Mullins and US conspiracy theorist William Cooper were featured speakers. To make matters worse, Mills thanked Cooper in the credits of Kula Shaker's number 1 album, *K*.

Next, Mills formed the Kays, a band whose name, some speculated, was an abbreviation of the Ku Klux Klan. As co-editor of the political magazine *Open Eye*, John Murray noted, 'The symbols and texts of fascism were consigned to history after the horrors of the Second World War but now there is a disturbing cultural trend towards resurrecting them which Kula Shaker seems to have become part of.'

Mills defended his use of the swastika, describing it as an ancient Indian symbol of spirituality, a view that aligned with the mystical themes woven throughout Kula Shaker's debut album. Of their 1996 top 10 singles, 'Govinda' evoked the Vishnu deity accompanied by a soundtrack of sitars and Eastern-inspired scales. 'Tattva', with its Sanskrit chorus *acintya bheda abheda Tattva*, explored the concept of the 'reality' or 'truth' of human experience. The press remained sceptical. So, Mills issued a renewed assurance in 1998, ahead of the group's post-album single 'Sound of Drums' (which peaked at number 3). He said, 'I apologise to those who have been offended and humbly ask that they accept that I am completely against the Nazis and any other latter-day form of totalitarianism.' In a follow-up interview with *Vox* magazine titled 'Cool, Karma & Collected', Mills clarified his stance, saying, 'I have *never* been anti-Semitic . . . my dear grandmother was Jewish. I loathe far-right thinking, and stand for peace, love, generosity, and learning. The truth is, there is a lot of old, hidden knowledge the Nazis took and abused. The swastika is a beautiful Hindu symbol that was perverted. For millions of people in the East, it's a sign of faith'[4]

Like Crispian Mills, U2's singer Bono understood the rules of engagement but rejected the protocols. 'There are three things you can't do in Germany,' he told *Melody Maker's* Paul Lester after U2's multimedia extravaganza at Munich's Olympiastadion. 'You can't goose-step, you can't show a swastika, and you can't do a Hitler salute.'

Bono does all three.

The Zooropa tour, 1993. Flashing images of the Hitler Youth banging drums at a Nazi rally. Bono, clad in patent black leather, stands 'against a mile-high TV image of himself to an almost deafening roar'. He goose-steps. Unfurls a swastika. Gives a Nazi salute. 'They reckon there might not be any rock 'n' roll in this country in five years' time,' the singer baits the audience, leaving Lester to wonder if Bono was very brave or very, very stupid.

As his devilish alter ego, Mister MacPhisto, Bono channels the themes of globalisation and cultural identity against the backdrop of a resurgent neo-fascism in Europe, where reports of skinhead gangs brutalising immigrants in Germany have become more frequent. U2's recent song 'Numb' includes a sample from *Triumph of the Will* where a member of the Hitler Youth beats a drum. 'We [started] playing around with ideas from the Leni Riefenstahl film footage of Nazi Germany that we used on Zoo TV,' elaborated guitarist the Edge. '[We were] really trying to ask the question of ourselves, as well as everyone else in Europe: "What do you want?" That seemed to be the question that kept coming back to us during the making of the album. Suddenly we were back on the road, touring in Germany, and the whole racist xenophobia issue exploded while we were there.'[5]

U2 used footage from Riefenstahl's film in an anti-fascist video collage, complete with turning crosses and swastikas. During the song 'Bullet The Blue Sky', one report described how three Nazi swastikas in flames were displayed across the 60-foot video screens on either side of the stage. As Bono sang, 'See the flames higher and higher', the giant screens behind him transformed burning crosses into blazing swastikas. 'The result was daunting, frightening and at the very least, provocative, and not only to those of right wing persuasion. Later, Beethoven's Ode To Joy seeped even more eerily out of the colossal amp stacks on either side of the stage. Above it the words "Tomorrow Belongs To Me" flashed terrifyingly across the screens before it was superseded by fascist-friendly shots from *Triumph of the Will*. "I think it's important to go to these places," Bono explained. "We had the sense that if there had been any demons, music had driven them out. I think fear of the devil leads to devil worship. And I don't want to give fascists power to the extent that you might be afraid to go into a building where they once were."'[6]

In Australia, Bono ad-libbed a line at the end of 'Daddy's Gonna Pay For Your Crashed Car': 'Goodbye all you neo-Nazis. I hope they give you Auschwitz'.[7] Just two years later, Michael Jackson would controversially sing the words, 'Jew me, sue me, kick me, kike me', which seemed to inadvertently validate Bono's controversial critique of modern Germany.

In 1995, Michael Jackson unveiled his new album with an extravagant four-minute trailer costing $6 million. Drawing inspiration from Leni Riefenstahl's Nazi propaganda films, Jackson's fans dubbed it the '*HIStory* teaser'. Images flash of monolithic eagles mounted on Grecian columns, soldiers march in jackboots, red flags hang from stone buildings, dome lights beam across open skies and, centre stage, stands the messiah-like Prince of Pop. 'What could Jackson have been thinking, using something like *Triumph of the Will* as a model?' asked Professor Susan Tavernetti, documentary film lecturer at San Francisco State University. 'Riefenstahl caressed Hitler's face with her camera. Jackson goes beyond this. Many more close-ups of his smiling, angelic face, followed by goose-stepping Nazi look-alikes and screaming followers.'[8]

The Simon Wiesenthal Center, an organisation established by Jewish human rights activists to confront anti-Semitism and teach the lessons of the Holocaust for future generations, was shocked by *HIStory*. Of equal concern were the anti-Semitic stereotypes portrayed on the track 'They Don't Care About Us,' – 'Jew me, sue me, everybody do me, kick me, kike me, don't you black or white me' – and highlighted in a critical review by the *New York Times*. Jackson issued an immediate response.

> The idea that these lyrics could be deemed objectionable is extremely hurtful to me, and misleading. The song in fact is about the pain of prejudice and hate and is a way to draw attention to social and political problems. I am the voice of the accused and the attacked. I am the voice of everyone. I am the skinhead, I am the Jew, I am the black man, I am the white man. I am not the one who was attacking. It is about the injustices to young people and how the system can wrongfully accuse them. I am angry and outraged that I could be so misinterpreted.

Jackson further explained on ABC News that his closest friends and employees were Jewish, asserting, 'It's not anti-Semitic because I'm not a racist person . . . I could never be a racist. I love all races.'

While some Jewish community leaders, including Rabbi Hier and Rabbi Abraham Cooper, accepted his explanation, they expressed concerns that the song's ambiguous message could mislead listeners. They urged Jackson to clarify his stance on the album's lyric sheet. In an effort to mollify the growing backlash, Jackson publicly reaffirmed his commitment to combating racism, anti-Semitism and stereotyping, and apologised for unintentionally hurting the very people he wanted to 'stand in solidarity with. I intend to include in all albums that have not been shipped as of this date [an estimated two million copies], the paragraphs above so that no one can listen to my music and misconstrue my intentions. I just want you all to know how strongly I am committed to tolerance, peace, and love, and I apologize to anyone who might have been hurt.'

Jackson later re-recorded the song, omitting the offensive lyrics, and visited the newly unveiled Museum of Tolerance in Los Angeles, dedicated to the Holocaust and confronting all forms of prejudice and discrimination in the world today. His actions, followed by a public apology, marked a new way for public figures to engage with controversy.

In 1999, James Brown, editor of *GQ* magazine and former features editor at *NME* and founder of lads' mag *Loaded*, was accused of glorying Nazism when Field Marshal Erwin Rommel was named on a list of the top 200 stylish men in *GQ*. Described as one of 'the sharpest men of the twentieth century', Rommel was placed alongside iconic figures like Al Pacino, Sean Connery, Robert De Niro, Humphrey Bogart, John Coltrane and Zico, who were said to 'epitomise our notions of style'. The inclusion of Rommel, pictured in a uniform chosen by Hitler, and the generic addition of 'the Nazis' would prove costly for Brown. 'The shit hit the fan,' he conceded in 2022, drawing attention to 'a big half-page news story' in the *Observer* 'with a load of goose-steeping soldiers alongside a picture of me.' [9]

In 1944, after the failure of the Africa campaign, Rommel assumed command of Army Group B in occupied France. Had Claus von Stauffenberg's assassination attempt on Adolf Hitler on 20 April succeeded, Rommel, his former commanding officer, would have been appointed President of the Reich. Hitler survived, suffering only minor injuries from the bomb blast, and ruthlessly pursued the conspirators. Rommel was soon implicated and given a choice by Hitler: take a vial of poison or face trail by the People's Court. 'I would not be afraid to be tried in public for I can defend everything I have done,' Rommel told his wife. 'But I know that I should never reach Berlin alive.' [10]

In 1951, James Mason played Rommel in the British film *The Desert Fox*, portraying him as a kind and honourable man attired in a gleaming knee-length leather coat and spotless uniform, in stark contrast to the pervasive image of Nazis as war criminals. While some pointed to Rommel's involvement in the assassination plot against Hitler – to prevent Germany's military collapse – his estrangement from the Führer, particularly after he predicted defeat in the west post D-Day, and his injures from an Allied airstrike in July 1944, complicated his legacy. Nonetheless, Lord Janner of Braunstone, chair of the Holocaust Education Trust and former president of the Board of Deputies of British Jews, was unequivocal in his damnation of GQ. 'The image of this General alongside some of the world's most gifted actors, musicians and designers makes decent people want to vomit. Rommel was a Nazi responsible for some of the worst crimes of the 20th century, not a hero.' [11] Rabbi Barry Marcus of the London Central Synagogue also condemned the feature, calling it 'offensive and disgraceful' to use 'the Holocaust and Nazi symbols as icons'.

As a teenager, James Brown marched against the National Front and his great-grandparents fled Germany due to their Anglo-German marriage. The suggestion that he was a 'fucking Nazi' made him 'feel sick'. 'I was embarrassed that something like this could have appeared,' he said. 'I understood the offence it had caused.' Accepting responsibility for his staff's actions, Brown called the incident 'sloppy' adding that, 'it just didn't sit right when in the intro we were describing those on the list as "cool" and "movers and shakers"'. Peter Stuart, the publisher of GQ, commented, 'This will be the best-selling issue ever, but we don't want to buy circulation this way. The magazine has suffered from a lapse in taste, and the Nazis list was the straw that broke the camel's back.'

Just a month later, Brown departed from GQ.

Swastika Eyes

PRIMAL SCREAM. FAT WHITE FAMILY. INTERPOL. BRYAN FERRY

By the turn of the millennium, five decades had passed since the end of the Second World War and, as survivors and perpetrators passed away, there was a realistic danger that Holocaust history might be marginalised. Meanwhile, however, the behaviour of many prominent rock 'n' roll artists seemed to be increasingly provocative. In 2000, the British guitar-dance band Primal Scream considered replacing the fifty stars on the US flag with swastikas for the cover of 'Swastika Eyes' from their album *XTRMNTR*. Although they abandoned the plan, fearing retail pushback[1], the song 'Swastika Eyes' remained, with singer Bobby Gillespie explaining it as a diatribe against international capitalism. 'The swastika is a really powerful symbol of totalitarianism, a good image, a great insult applicable to any authoritarian figure,' he told the *NME*, adding, 'The song's about modern fascism, multinational militarism, the United States, international fucking terrorism.'

Gillespie clearly relishes making bold statements and courting controversy. Nonetheless, his series of remarks against Israel, coupled with his intended use of swastika imagery and references to the Third Reich, has raised concerns and underscores a deeper issue within the music industry. In 1985, Primal Scream advertised a gig at Splash One in Glasgow, where Gillespie was part of the eight-strong committee who ran the night, using a poster featuring a Hitler Youth member. This image was later reproduced in his memoir, *Tenement Kid*, four decades later. The intervening years produced a litany of similarly controversial acts.

The use of provocative Third Reich language was evident in the 1997 dub track 'Stuka,' later remixed into 'Ju-87', a haunting five-and-half minute cacophony of ethereal noise with Bobby Gillespie's cautioning vocal, 'If you play with fire, you're gonna get burnt'. The song was named after the German dive bomber, the Junkers Ju 87 *Sturzkampfflugzeug*, which sounded a tormenting siren designed to screech and instil terror in its enemy targets during the early stages of the Second World War. Known as 'the Jericho Trumpet' because of its shrill fear-inducing wail, the Stuka was a key part of the blitzkrieg strategy that brought rapid victories across Europe and North Africa.

The term 'Stuka', like other wartime phrases such as 'blitzkrieg' and 'holocaust', often found its way into the lexicon of music criticism. For instance, in 1975 the music of Roy Harper was compared to a sound 'like a diving Stuka; no nervous energy, just a dynamite band blowing the roof off';[2] a year later, John Marshall, drummer with Soft Machine, 'zooming in like a Stuka diving out of the sun, made repeated attacks on the kit, roaring round and round them like a Dervish.[3] In 1981, Motörhead and Ozzy Osbourne headlined 'Heavy Metal Holocaust' at Port Vale Football Stadium. And in 2002, Tanya Donelly of Beautysleep referred to a guitar sound as 'that Stuka guitar scratch.[4] In the same year, Primal Scream released 'Miss Lucifer' from their seventh studio album *Evil Heat*, featuring the lyrics 'Skinny girl, dressed in black, leather boots, Nazi hat'. The video, which depicted a woman matching a similar description, furthered the band's visual flirtation with fascist imagery.

The controversy deepened at the Glastonbury Festival when Primal Scream were invited to sign a 'Make Poverty History' banner, but Gillespie altered the wording to read, 'Make Israel History'. Later, during their performance, he was accused of making a Nazi salute during the song 'Swastika Eyes'. When questioned about the incident, Gillespie responded, 'Did I give a Nazi salute? I don't know, you tell me! If you look at the things we've done in the past like benefits for Satpal Ram [jailed for life after defending himself in Birmingham against a racist attack], the Liverpool dockers, the

Palestine refugee children, you'll know what my politics are. I'm no fuckin' Nazi.'⁵ *

The theme resurfaced in 2013 when Gillespie spoke to *Electronic Beats* magazine about the group's new songs, 'Culturecide' and '2013'. Asked about the use of Nazi-related references in the lyrics, including phrases like 'You need a will to power, a triumph of the will', and 'the final solution to the teenage revolution', he responded,

> I think that politicians use archetypes and know how to touch people at their core. Politicians and advertisers have studied Sigmund Freud, and I think they understand psychology, needs, and fears in a kind of occult way. I threw these Nazi things in because I think that the media and the politicians use them in the same way as the Nazis. And 'the final solution to the teenage revolution' just sounds like a good rhyme to me, but I was also saying that there's no fire or danger in rock 'n' roll anymore.⁶

In 2019, Gillespie faced further backlash after criticising Madonna for agreeing to perform at the Eurovision Song Contest in Tel Aviv, Israel. During an interview with Kirsty Wark on *Newsnight*, he said, 'Madonna would do anything for money, you know, she's a total prostitute. I've got nothing against prostitutes. The whole thing is set up to normalise the state of Israel, and its disgraceful treatment of the Palestinian people. By going to perform in Israel

---

* The Glastonbury Festival found itself at the centre of fresh controversy in June 2025, after the Secretary of State for Culture, Media and Sport, Lisa Nandy, told the House of Commons on 30 June that she was 'concerned to hear reports of imagery associated with Hamas – a proscribed terrorist organisation operating in Gaza – as well as Nazi imagery' at the event. Reports also indicated that some Jewish attendees felt compelled to create their own 'safe space' in response. Tensions deepened following the performance of English punk-rap duo Bob Vylan, during which onstage rhetoric and audience chants included calls of 'Death to the IDF' (Israel's conscripted defence force, compulsory for Jews and Druze, both men and women, and for Circassian men). The head of the Simon Wiesenthal Center condemned the scenes, describing them as 'sickening, dangerous, and chillingly reminiscent of a modern-day Nazi rally.'

what you do is you normalise that. Primal Scream would never perform in Israel.' When asked if he believed in the country's right to exist, he replied, ambiguously, 'I believe in the rights of the Palestinian people.'

'And the right of Israelis.' Wark pressed.

'Stolen land,' Gillespie replied.

'If you do not believe in the right of Israel to exist, you understand then why you're seen as being anti-Semitic?'

'I'm not anti-Semitic at all,' Gillespie retorted. 'All my heroes are Jews. Karl Marx, Bob Dylan . . .'[7]

The cycle of flirtation followed by protested innocence was a routine familiar to south London's Fat White Family. The group's biographer, Adelle Stripe, described its founding members – Lias and Nathan Saoud, of Algerian-English heritage – as having an 'acerbic approach to life'. As a teenager, Nathan once designed a birthday card to his mother adorned with 'rotating red swastikas rendered in felt tip pen'. Gripped by an obsession with the Second World War, he spent much of his youth watching *The World at War*. 'He then discovered the story of Hitler's bunker around the same time as he discovered masturbation and swung between these twin obsessions.'[8]

Fat White Family's debut album *Champagne Holocaust* (2013), passed off as a 'sardonic adaptation of Oasis' 'Champagne Supernova', was followed three years later by *Songs for Our Mothers* described by guitarist, singer, songwriter and producer Saul Adamczewski as 'Nazi disco'. Adamczewski's family history was marked by contradiction: his paternal grandfather, originally a Polish milliner, was conscripted into the Waffen-SS as a teenager, while his maternal grandfather, living in Israel, converted to Judaism and was circumcised at forty. These themes of conflict and identity run through the album while brazenly invoking fascist imagery. Tracks like 'Duce' evoke Mussolini's Italy with references to the 'gene pool', 'black shirts', and 'hanging from a meat hook', while 'Lebensraum' borrowed its title from Hitler's expansionist doctrine of Aryan living space. Most striking is 'Goodbye Goebbels', a sombre ballad co-written with frontman Lias Saoudi – whose fiancé and daughter are Jewish – that imagines a poignant farewell between Hitler and Josef Goebbels in the Berlin bunker before their suicides in April 1945.

At a live performance at Cardiff's Tramshed in 2019, Colin Bond caught a moment that felt as uncomfortable as it was revealing. 'At one point, the line "So here's to the Fourth Reich (I bid you a Jew)" is greeted with whoops and cheers from the guy next to me, and somewhere down the front, I see the unmistakable silhouette of a Nazi salute. It's weird.'[9] Pressed on their repeated return to Nazi Germany as a subject matter, Saoudi explained, 'I'm obsessed with that period in history. I can't understand anybody who isn't obsessed by the Nazis. I can't watch a film unless it's got Nazis in it.'[10]

In another interview with *Fanzine*, he continued, 'Hitler's reign didn't happen very long ago. I think we're experiencing a kind of swerve to the right. So it's an interesting axis point, and that's about it. We don't rule out any subject matter. We happen to have an interest in that period of history, so that's what shows up.' Reiterating their interest in Hitler's bunker, Adamczewski chimed in, 'It's basically where we were all given birth. It birthed the world we live in now, and if you don't see that, you're dead.'

'Yeah,' Saoudi agreed. 'We crawled out of that catastrophe – the Potsdam agreement, the set-up of the welfare state, stuff like that. It all came out of that period. So we want to dismantle that. I think it's relevant, in a way. Not directly, but loosely.'

Picking up on the theme, they are asked, 'Is that why you wanted to find tenderness in Hitler's suicide [in the song 'Goodbye Goebbels']?' Saoudi responds: 'There's tenderness in all things. I think it's your job as an artist to explore whatever you feel like exploring. There was probably some love in that bunker, so why not sing about it? Why sing about one type of love and not the other?'[11]

In contrast to Fat White Family and Bobby Gillespie, whose professed socialist values were shaped by his upbringing in a Scottish trade unionist family, Carlos Dengler, the bass player for the American alternative rock band Interpol (until 2010), had a more direct and personal connection to Third Reich ideology. Onstage, he would often don Nazi-influenced uniforms. In 2002, the *Guardian* remarked that Dengler, then known as Carlos D., 'looked like he was ready to be shot in close-up by Leni Riefenstahl. Aside from giving the impression that he might at any moment put down his guitar and order the immediate annexation of the Sudetenland, the severe side parting, armbands and jackboots encapsulated something about Interpol's sound: indebted to Joy Division, another band who dabbled in Nazi imagery.'[12] *Rolling Stone* went as far as calling them 'goth Nazi', while *NME* bluntly asked, 'Why is Carlos from Interpol dressing like a Nazi?'

A *Spin* magazine cover displayed Dengler's bold stage attire, including a long black jacket, striped trousers and tall boots, with Brian Raftery commenting that 'any sane person would think he looks like an SS guard who fell into a time portal'. An accompanying feature offered a timeline of the '66.6 Greatest Moments in Goth' with an image of Dengler pictured alongside Siouxsie Sioux who, readers are reminded, 'toyed with Nazi imagery in 1976 . . . and inspires the entire aesthetic of Carlos D'. Quoted in the article, Dengler said, 'Expressions of irony through clothing are very important. I didn't wake up and go, "I'm gonna dress like a Nazi." But when I start thinking about how I want to make myself look cool, it starts to take shape along those lines.'

Descriptions of Dengler were often flippant and disregarded the deeper implications of his attire. By 2010, the *Guardian* happily described him as Interpol's 'secret weapon', stating that 'no other band could match' the bass player's style that was equal parts Lower East Side night vulture, Hitler Youth member, vampiric Crispin Glover [American actor], and *Sesame Street*'s Count von Count. Dengler took every goth-rock cliché and added a touch of Leni Riefenstahl. Clumpy black jackboots? Check. Playing bass at knee level? Check. Wearing, er, a gun holster? Check.'[13] Even German magazine *Visions* joined in the linguistic gymnastics that Third Reich glamour inspired by pitching Dengler somewhere between 'a style icon of dark coolness or as a bird with a Nazi look'. Nowhere was Dengler held accountable or accused of promoting fascism. Nowhere was there outrage or sympathy for the victims of Nazism. And, to make matters more troubling, Interpol's guitarist Daniel Kessler was Jewish. However all that changed on 6 June 2023 when an extraordinary online admission altered the narrative completely.

In an article titled 'A Farewell to Arms: A Rock Star's Taste for Fascist Drag', Dengler explained to the *Tablet*, the influential online magazine about Jewish life and identity, that his attraction to army-style uniforms stemmed from a fascination with their 'clean lines and militaristic sheen'. He vividly remembered first seeing an army-style holster draped over a mannequin in a tailor's shop, sparking a dopamine rush that led to the development of his new, pseudo-military look: a black armband, twelve-hole combat boots and 'a frozen sweep of hair combed in the Hitlerjugend style'. Dengler clarified that the inspiration for this look was not rooted in admiration for high-ranking SS officers, but rather in a 'streetwise, brownshirt pamphleteer' aesthetic. His mind would race with 'lurid images' of conquest, and he became consumed with the desire to embody 'The Ambiguous Nazi', a character blending punk's aftermath with the fascist demagogue Pink from Pink Floyd's *The Wall*. Dengler emphasised that his intention was never to glorify Nazi ideology but to celebrate the eroticism tied to clothing and S&M culture. Quoting Susan Sontag, he summed up his world view. 'The colour is black, the material is leather, the seduction is beauty, the justification is honesty, the aim is ecstasy, the fantasy is death.'

Dengler then revealed a shocking detail about his background: he was the son of a Bavarian-born, card-carrying member of the Hitler Youth. Family rumours suggested that his Nazi grandfather had chauffeured Hitler and other high-ranking Third Reich officials. After moving to the United States at the end of the war, Dengler's father would play cassette recordings of military singing and goose-step around the family dinner table, shouting phrases in German, such as 'Jewish propaganda', 'Stalin killed more' and 'the genius of Goebbels'. Nevertheless, when Dengler showed his father a photo of his stage outfit, the response was one of shock. It was then that

Dengler admitted that wearing Third Reich-inspired uniforms was a deliberate act of sadism—a way to confront and expose both his father's Nazi past and his own need to make sense of it.

Out of nowhere, here was an artist in the rock world condemning his own actions – a groundbreaking moment in music history – where the music press and the record industry had failed. Yet, despite his explanation and measured remorse, Dengler ultimately concluded that elevating 'an aesthetic to the level of camp can neutralise its original sincerity, its original content'.[14] He is wrong. The victims of the Holocaust do not need symbols of Nazism 'neutralised'; they need to remain tied to the crimes the Nazis committed, ensuring they are neither forgotten nor repeated. This message, unfortunately, was one that rock 'n' roll history overlooked – and one that was about to be further obscured by one of its most celebrated stars.

'My God, the Nazis knew how to put themselves in the limelight and present themselves,' Bryan Ferry, the former Roxy Music singer, told the German newspaper *Welt Am Sonntag* in March 2007. 'I'm talking about the films of Leni Riefenstahl and the buildings of Albert Speer and the mass marches and the flags – just fantastic. Really beautiful.'[15] Once again, here was a rock star treading in the footsteps of Mick Jagger, Lemmy and David Bowie, beguiled by the dramatic art of the Third Reich, wantonly separating fashion – its style – from belief system – its content. On one hand, it's easy to see the parallel between Hitler's control of massed rallies like those at Nuremburg, and rock stars performing for tens of thousands of adoring fans, each movement and utterance closely studied.

However, Albert Speer, Hitler's architect and later Minister of Armaments and War, was far from the self-styled 'good Nazi' he often claimed to be. After the 1938 *Kristallnacht* pogrom, Speer drove through the 'still smouldering ruins of the Berlin synagogues', affronted by the 'disorder: charred beams, collapsed facades, burned-out walls . . . the smashed panes of shop windows'. He noted how it 'offended' his 'sense of middle-class order'. Reflecting on this, he mused, 'Did I sense that this outburst of hoodlumism was changing my moral substance? I do not know. Hitler's hatred for the Jews seemed to me so much a matter of course that I gave it no serious thought.'[16]

Speer brutally exploited Jews, forcing them to work and live in squalid conditions, half-starved and treated as expendable. At the Nuremburg war trials, the charge stated: '[Speer] used his position and his personal influence in such a manner that . . . he authorised, directed and participated in the War Crimes against humanity . . . particularly the abuse and exploitation of human beings for forced labour in the conduct of aggressive war.' Speer denied knowledge of the extermination camps.* But by accepting 'common responsibility' he was able to avoid the death penalty. After serving twenty-years at Spandau Prison, Speer reinvented himself as a media personality, appearing on a never-ending carousel of chat shows and political interviews. In later years, historians discovered evidence that Speer approved finance and building resources for the expansion of Auschwitz, that he visited Mauthausen concentration camp and, on 4 October 1943, attended Himmler's speech in Posen confirming the implementation of the so-called 'Final Solution of the Jewish question, despite claiming that he left early.' None of this seemingly affected Speer's public standing. And so, his Third Reich theatrical creativity continued to influence the rock world.

Regarded worldwide as both a man of style and a successful songwriter and performer, Bryan Ferry has always stood out as a unique star. Typically dressed in beautifully tailored clothes, he often surrounds himself with fashionable female models and speaks about how books and art influence his creative approach. In 2007,

---

*   In 1944, Karl Hanke, *Gauleiter* of Lower Silesia, advised Speer to never accept an invitation to inspect a concentration camp because what he had seen could not be described. In hindsight, Speer believed this was Auschwitz, and wrote, 'I did not query him. I did not query Himmler or Hitler. I did not want to know what was happening there . . . as an important member of the leadership of the Reich I had to share the total responsibility for all that has happened. I was inescapably contaminated morally . . . I had closed my eyes . . . I still feel to this day responsible for Auschwitz in a wholly personal sense.'

when asked if he considered himself someone with a 'German work ethic', Ferry revealed perhaps more than he intended. 'Yes. I want to look back on a life where I've accomplished things,' he said to *Welt am Sonntag*. 'That's why I call my studio in west London . . . but wait, as a German I'm not allowed to tell you that.' When the interviewer jokingly suggested the name 'Führerbunker' – the Berlin air raid shelter where Hitler spent his last days – Ferry laughed, 'That's where you caught me. I usually tell German journalists that I call my studio my "headquarters". That's less catchy.' The conversation then turned to David Bowie, rumoured to have modelled his body language on Hitler standing in front of a mirror.

'I have heard of that,' Ferry replied.

'Do you also pose in front of the mirror?' *Welt* pushed.

'Not that I would tell you or anyone else anything like that,' Ferry enigmatically responded.

Having already praised the artistry of Leni Riefenstahl and Albert Speer, Ferry then found himself at the centre of a media storm. In response, he issued a statement apologising unreservedly, expressing regret 'for any offence caused by my comments on Nazi iconography'. He clarified that his remarks were 'solely made from an art history perspective. I, like every right-minded individual find the Nazi regime, and all it stood for, evil and abhorrent.'

Lord Greville Janner, vice-president of the World Jewish Congress, accepted the apology, calling it 'total, appropriate, and absolutely necessary' while hoping that 'he will never make the same mistake again'. However, some Jewish leaders were not as forgiving, questioning whether the Marks & Spencer retail chain should terminate his contract as a model. Jeremy Newmark, chief executive of the Jewish Leadership Council, acknowledged Ferry's swift clarification but noted that his language was 'deeply insensitive'. In Parliament, Labour MP Andrew Dismore tabled a motion, supported by twenty-seven signatories – including future Labour leader Jeremy Corbyn and Shadow Chancellor John McDonnell – that expressed 'complete abhorrence' of Ferry's remarks and 'behaviour in admiration of the Nazis'. Noting that his remarks 'add injury to insult in that they were published at the time of

Yom HaShoah, when Jews commemorate their six million dead in the Holocaust', it called for a boycott of Marks & Spencer's stores and Ferry's recordings and performances, urging the retail giant to reconsider its decision to continue his role.[17]

A month later, M&S ended its contract with Ferry.

Pretty as a Swastika

SLAYER. MARILYN MANSON. OZZY OSBOURNE. NICKI MINAJ. LIBERTINES. NICO

There is a peculiar phenomenon within the world of popular music whereby hard rock and metal artists are permitted to operate outside of conventional social boundaries. They are the apostates of rock. Traditionally, the media would be the gatekeepers of accountability, but in today's digital age, social media gives everyone a platform. While this opens the door to more diverse opinions, the fear of online harassment and trolling often leads to silence in the face of extreme views, which has unfortunately allowed certain elements, including Third Reich extremism, to thrive in certain music subcultures.

Paul Di'Anno, former singer of Iron Maiden, describes in his memoir, *The Beast*, wearing a long leather trench coat adorned with a swastika on its back. Similarly, Slayer, a group formed in 1981, incorporates Nazi imagery into their identity. The band's logo bears a striking resemblance to the Nazi Party eagle (*Parteiadler*), and the design is in the same font as that used by Himmler's SS. The band's guitarist adorned his instrument with a Waffen-SS sticker while their 'Slaytanic Wehrmacht' fan club pays homage to the German army, and their merchandise is steeped in Third Reich symbolism. Their late founding member Jeff Hanneman owned a collection of Nazi artefacts, gifts from his German-American father who had fought alongside the Allies in the Second World War. Hanneman said, 'I'd read a lot about the Third Reich and was absolutely fascinated by the extremity of it all, the way Hitler had been able to hypnotise a nation and do whatever he wanted, a situation where Mengele could evolve from being a doctor to being a butcher.'[1]

Slayer's 1986 album *Reign in Blood* opens with the controversial track 'Angel Of Death', named after Josef Mengele, the Nazi doctor infamous for conducting inhumane medical experiments on prisoners at Auschwitz. A year earlier, on 7 June 1985, Brazilian police discovered the corpse of Mengele, who had escaped capture after the war, first by working as a farm stableman in Bavaria and then fleeing to South America, initially to Uruguay, then Paraguay, and eventually Brazil, where he died from a stroke while swimming. The song depicted in unflinching detail the process 'patients' were subjected to in Block 11, from cleansing to 'surgery with no anaesthesia', torture, the smell of death and burning flesh, and cracked limbs. 'Pumped with fluid, inside your brain pressure in your skull begins pushing through your eyes', Hanneman writes, 'Sewn together, joining heads just a matter of time 'til you rip yourselves apart'. Although mostly incomprehensible, the repeated chorus 'Angel of Death, Angel of Death, Angel of Death' is screamed back by fanatical fans at live shows, often to the visual accompaniment of Nazi-era archival film.

Walter Yetnikoff, the president of Columbia Records, was so outraged by the track he exclaimed, 'My shareholders are all Jewish!' demanding that the track be removed. Producer Rick Rubin refused, and the band took the album to Geffen. Hanneman later told the *NME*, 'I feel you should be able to write about whatever you want. "Angel Of Death" is like a history lesson but as soon as we released it everybody was calling us Nazis. Our singer's a dark-skinned Chilean, there's no way we're fascists.'

Watain, a Swedish metal band formed in 1998, found themselves under similar fire when guitarist Set Teitan (born Davide Totaro) stepped down in 2018 following the publication of a photo of him performing a Nazi salute. Reports also suggested he made a similar gesture at a concert in Stockholm. In response, the band issued a statement, aiming to put an end to what they called 'tiresome speculation'. They stressed that none of their members had 'ties to Nazi ideology'. They pointed out that their lyrics and themes were the antithesis of right-wing ideologies and noted the diversity of their fans and crew as proof of their inclusive values, condemning the accusations as both misplaced and regrettable.[2]

In stark contrast, National Socialist black metal (NSBM) emerged from the Norwegian black metal scene in the early 1990s, promoting neo-Nazi and white supremacist beliefs. Bands like Burzum, led by Varg Vikernes, along with Mayhem, Taake, the German-based Absurd, and American band Grand Belial's Key have all made explicit statements supporting Nazi ideology. While NSBM has spread across Europe, particularly in countries that were complicit in Nazi Germany's atrocities, the genre's popularity remains relatively small. Still, where the controversy surrounding NSBM, Slayer and Watain remains a divisive issue among their fans, it pales in comparison to the vilified immoral influence attributed to Marilyn Manson.

Born Brian Hugh Warner in 1969 in Canton, Ohio, Manson's career has frequently incorporated elements of Nazi imagery, using it as a provocative theme throughout his work, glorifying violence and making inflammatory statements. He once heard a fan quip that 'if the ancient Egyptians and the Nazis created a rock star in outer space and sent him back in time to destroy the world it would be Marilyn Manson'. The singer's reaction? 'I thought that was quite amusing.'[3] In 2003, Manson told *Der Spiegel* that 'the current mood in the USA' reminded him of 'the way in which so-called degenerate art was dealt with in Germany not so long ago'.[4]

This was a reference to 'degenerate art' (*Entartete Kunst*), a term employed by the Nazi Party to justify banning works considered 'an insult to German feeling'. As a result, the state seized, and often destroyed, collections created by Salvador Dalí, Pablo Picasso, Paul Klee, Max Ernst and Edvard Munch. In 1937, Joseph Goebbels, Minister of Propaganda, arranged an exhibition in Munich of *Entartete Kunst* to 'educate' the public on the 'art of decay' and to highlight genetic inferiority and moral decline. In a badly lit gallery, accompanied by slogans such as 'nature as seen by sick minds', 'revelation of the Jewish racial soul', and 'the ideal – cretin and whore', over two million people visited the show (an average of 20,000 people per day). Later, the exhibition toured major cities throughout Germany and, according to *Artland* magazine, is still the most popular modern art show of all time.

Goebbels' campaign to eradicate moral decline from German society faced significant challenges, particularly when it came to the cabaret and burlesque scenes that had thrived in 1920s Berlin. Marilyn Manson, however, drew inspiration from these rebellious cultural movements. Discussing his fifth studio album, *The Golden Age of Grotesque* (2003) – also the title of his first art exhibition staged in Los Angeles a year earlier – Manson hailed 'the lengths that people there went to in order to live their lives to the fullest and to make their entertainment', adding that it was 'as imaginative and extreme as possible'.

The release of *The Golden Age of Grotesque* and its accompanying stage show, the Grotesk Burlesk Tour, saw Manson turn to Nazism as a provocative tool – using its imagery to deliver biting, exaggerated satire. The show fused vaudeville and burlesque with costumes designed by Jean-Paul Gaultier, along with elements of Third Reich theatrics. His jacket, photographed for the album booklet, featured insignia reminiscent of Nazi military clothing, including lyre-shaped collar badges and swallow's nest (*Schwalbennester*) shoulder decorations worn by the Luftwaffe. During the performance of 'Doll-Dagga Buzz-Buzz Ziggety-Zag', Manson mocked the Nazi Party's ban on jazz, singing, 'All the goose-step girlies with their cursive faces' followed by the mantra, 'swing heil, swing heil, swing heil'. Then, during 'Ka-Boom Ka-Boom', the stage transformed into a pseudo-Nuremburg rally, complete with SS uniforms, painted Hitler Youth drums with death's head insignia, and SS-style drapes. The festivities ended with the chorus, 'We're a death marching band'. For Manson, this was 'a comedy form of fascism', enlightening *InRock* journalist Evie Sullivan that 'it sounds very American to me. It sounds like a Happy Meal.'

The Golden Age of Grotesque topped charts across Europe, including the former Axis countries: Germany, Austria and Italy, and reached number 1 in the US, a country Manson believed resembled Nazi Germany under George W. Bush's leadership. In 2009, Manson wrote the song 'Pretty As A Swastika' for *The High End of Low*, a phrase originally coined by American columnist Walter Winchell to describe film-maker Leni Riefenstahl. To promote the album, an advertising campaign swapped images of Adolf Hitler and President Bush flanked by swastika dollar bills and the American flag. The message was clear: money equals fascism. Fearing a backlash, the record company subtly altered the title of the song to 'Pretty As A ($)' – a decision, according to Manson, made to protect the label's financial interests.

> Their censorship choice was made purely because of money. They [Interscope Records] said, 'Take that song off your record because there are two things you can't do in music – you can never say anything anti-Semitic, and you can never say anything about paedophilia.' I said, 'Thanks for telling me that. I'm going to go ahead and combine them for you on a song and then I'm going to shave a swastika into my girlfriend's pubic hair and make her wear pigtails.'[5]

When asked to explain the meaning behind 'Pretty As A Swastika,' Manson told *Time* magazine that the phrase was 'something' he had said to 'a girl', admiring her complexion – black hair, red lips and pale skin. He described it as a 'complex and poetic comment that soon led to intercourse', making him feel that there was 'no reason for it to be seen' as 'confusing, hateful, or destructive'.[6] In a later interview with German *Metal Hammer*, he addressed the song's opening line: 'When I see you in the sun you're as pretty as a swastika', saying, 'Look, art is a question mark, but in the song, I say, "Let me show you where it hurts." I say, "You're as pretty as a swastika" . . . is that a compliment or an insult? I don't even know. I see it as a romantic song and almost a discussion between two people, on who controls and who is being controlled in a relationship.'*

The most powerful criticism often comes from within the community being critiqued. Thus, when American heavy metal music-themed news website MetalSucks published an editorial denouncing Manson's 'Nazi chic' aesthetic as harmful and irrespon-

---

* Since 2021, more than a dozen women have accused Manson of sexual assault.

sible, the weight of the condemnation was especially impactful. 'I understand that in the metal world, for some artists and fans, shock value and making people feel discomfort may be point enough,' Axl Rosenberg wrote in 2018.

> I would still argue that none of this stuff was ever really okay. That's true for many reasons, not least of which being that the Holocaust is not distant history – many of us are related to or have known people who lived through it. And as is the case with slavery in America, its lasting effects are still readily visible today. You can totally freak people out and still not portray yourself as being in favour of genocide. In fact, if you're being honest with yourself, you'll quickly realize that shocking people with Nazism shows a real lack of creativity.[7]

The online backlash was predictably swift, with a flood of responses condemning Rosenberg and inundating MetalSucks' comment section with a stream of uninformed vitriol.

'I own Nazi memorabilia, and I offer no explanation or apologies. Fuck off,' read one representative post.

'Naziphobia is the real problem here,' read another.

This was further illustration of the ongoing online media conundrum: is it a platform for free expression or a breeding ground for bigotry, hatred and anti-Semitism? The matter is amplified when the artist in question enjoys worldwide adoration. Take, for instance Ozzy Osbourne and Nicki Minaj.

In 2011, the documentary *God Bless Ozzy Osbourne* explored the emotionally fraught journey to sobriety for one of rock's most iconic figures, the lead singer of Black Sabbath. Directed by Mike Fleiss and Mike Piscitelli, the film offers a raw look at the rock star's tumultuous forty-year career, featuring star-studded contributions from the likes of Tommy Lee, Henry Rollins and Sir Paul McCartney. Yet, despite the widespread praise for Osbourne, or perhaps because of it, the film-makers chose not to explore his documented fascination with Nazism.

In a 1982 interview with the US late-night cable television programme *Night Flight*, Osbourne was asked about the influences on his stage persona and surprisingly named Adolf Hitler. While assuring listeners that Hitler was a 'freak' and a 'lunatic', and that it was 'terrible what that guy did killing all those people and whatever', he added, 'But he had something about him. I admired *him* . . . I suddenly thought, "If someone put that in a positive way, for the good of mankind . . ."' Here was the familiar attempt to separate the crimes of a totalitarian state from the charisma of its leader. However, in his memoir, *I Am Ozzy*, Osbourne elaborated, 'I think war is just part of human nature. And I'm fascinated by human nature – especially the dark side. I always have been. It doesn't make me a Devil worshipper, no more than being interested in Hitler makes me a Nazi. I mean, if I'm a Nazi, how come I married a woman who's half Jewish?'

Sharon Osbourne's father, Harry Levy, was Jewish and served in the British army during the Second World War. Born in Cheetham, Manchester to émigrés from Russia and Poland, Levy reinvented himself as Don Arden and managed iconic artists such as Jerry Lee Lewis, Little Richard, Gene Vincent, the Small Faces, ELO and Black Sabbath. His unorthodox methods earned him the nickname the 'Al Capone of pop'. In a conversation about anti-Semitism, Sharon explained to the *Sun*, 'They knew he was a Jew. There he was fighting for his country, and everybody was torturing him. People from his own country were torturing him.' On one occasion, Levy was woken up in the middle of the night, forced to dig holes in the rain by fellow soldiers, who yelled, 'You're a fucking Jew and this war is over you, and this is why we have to fight and you're going to dig a fucking hole.'[8]

While performing with Black Sabbath at the Star Club, Hamburg in 1969, Ozzy Osbourne stayed in an apartment with a young woman, explaining, 'just to get a bed for the night. We weren't fussy what they looked like, as long as they had somewhere to stay. There was one bird I spent the night with, we called her the Witch. Big old hooter.' The next morning, the woman warned Osbourne not to go through her belongings, but, as he put it,

Now that's like a red rag to a bull, isn't it? So, the minute she's out, I'm going through her cupboards and, fuck me, there's a Nazi uniform at the back, probably her dad's. So, I put it on, start goose-stepping around the flat. Of course, she comes back that afternoon and finds me barking out orders in a cod-German accent and going through her drinks cabinet. The relationship didn't last long after that.[9]

So here it was: Osbourne separating a murderous regime from its theatrical facade, a position that echoes across the history of popular music, where musicians eye the Third Reich's staged parades, choreographed marches and sharp tailoring with an almost childlike awe. But as the penumbra of the Second World War fades, pop stars' engagement with the swastika persists.

In 1975, Jethro Tull relocated to Monte Carlo to record *Minstrel in the Gallery* in a radio station formerly used by the Nazi Party for propaganda broadcasts. The choice of location was coincidental. However, four decades later, frontman Ian Anderson's exploration of Norse mythology and the concept of 'an underlying cosmic force, creator spirit' resulted in the sleeve cover of 'Ginnungagap' – from Jethro Tull's album *RökFlöte* – featuring a 'black sun' motif. Widely adopted by white nationalist and neo-fascist groups, the controversial symbol was prominently featured in a dark-green mosaic on the marble floor of the *Obergruppenführersaal* (General's Hall) at Wewelsburg in North Rhine-Westphalia. Reichsführer-SS Heinrich Himmler acquired this castle in June 1934 to serve as a centre for SS scientific research.

Believing in an ancient Aryan master race that originated from a collision between a large frozen comet and the sun, Himmler assigned professionals from the *Ahnenerbe*, an SS research society, to search for the lost civilisation believed to be preserved since ancient times on the mythical island of Atlantis. The expedition to rewrite the history of the world and prove the existence of a Germanic religion to replace Christianity led SS anthropologists to the ancient kingdom of Tibet. Here, profiling took place to define racial types. The practice was subsequently continued by doctors at concentration camps across the Third Reich. In the relentless search to define 'Jewishness' and to support the fictitious belief in racial hierarchies – i.e. Jews (inferior), Aryans (superior) – Himmler sanctioned inhumane medical experimentation to find justification for the so-called Final Solution.

'It's a subject I had utterly no fascination with,' Ian Anderson insisted when controversy arose regarding Jethro Tull's use of the black sun design. 'I probably steered clear of it because it's a fertile ground for those heavy metal and hard rock freak musicians who fantasise about that world. And having been aware of that mythology attracting the likes of Heinrich Himmler, I thought it was something I'd keep a distance from.'[10]

The polar opposite could be said of Nicki Minaj's 2014 video for 'Only' which included animated images evocative of Leni Riefenstahl's *Triumph of the Will*. With five hundred million views on YouTube, the video depicted Minaj as a military dictator, surrounded by swastikas subtly altered to display her label's initials, YM, flanked by storm troopers, tanks and Speer-style Roman architecture, while she basked in the adoration of an audience organised like an army in ranks. In the resulting media outcry, Minaj posted an apology on Twitter: 'I didn't come up w/ the concept, but I'm very sorry & take full responsibility if it has offended anyone. I'd never condone Nazism in my art.' In a follow-up post, Minaj mentioned that both the producer and the person overseeing the video 'happen to be Jewish.'

The inherent contradiction of Jewish producers promoting Nazi-like imagery deepens with the involvement of co-star Drake, who appeared in the video dressed as the Pope.* Raised by a Jewish mother (his father was African American) Drake was bar

---

* In 1980, a Killing Joke concert poster – later also to feature on the sleeve of the compilation album, *Laugh? I Nearly Bought One* – appeared to show Pope Pius XI saluting a parade of Nazi soldiers. In fact, the image was of German abbot Alban Schachleiter, a known Third Reich sympathiser.

In 1995, Black Grape's Shaun Ryder wrote about the Vatican's collaboration with fleeing Nazis at the end of the Second World War on the group's debut single 'Reverend Black Grape': 'Pope, he got the Nazis to clean up their messes. He exchanged the gold and paintings; he gave them new addresses'. The verse ended with two rounds of 'Heil, heil Führer!'

mitzvah at thirteen. In 2014, *Rolling Stone* described him as 'the biggest Jewish rapper since the Beastie Boys'. Yet Drake chose not to publicly comment on 'Only'. Meanwhile, just hours after Minaj's statement, director Jeffrey Osborne refused to apologise for the video content, saying, 'I think it's actually important to remind younger generations of atrocities that occurred in the past as a way to prevent them from happening in the future.' He did acknowledge that the use of 'flags, armbands, and gas mask (and perhaps my use of symmetry?) are all representative of Nazis', but sarcastically added, 'if my work is misinterpreted because it's not a sappy tearjerker, sorry I'm not sorry. What else is trending?'[11]

The video did not condemn Nazism. Nor did anyone on Minaj's team – managers, producers or publicists – object to the content ahead of its release. Rather, Osborne's defence echoed the view of artists like Lemmy and Throbbing Gristle, who argue that displaying Third Reich insignia serves to prevent the rise of Nazism from the ashes of history. How this will be achieved is never explained. Artists often claim to invoke Nazi imagery to make a broader point about the modern world, but this justification typically comes only after an artist has been accused. If the intent is to use art as a warning from history, the argument should be inherent in the work itself, rather than an after-the-fact explanation.

Abraham H. Foxman, National Director of the Anti-Defamation League and a Holocaust survivor, condemned Minaj's video as a new low for pop culture's exploitation of Nazi symbolism. He wrote: 'The irony should be lost on no one that this video debuted on the 76th anniversary of *Kristallnacht*, the "night of broken glass" pogrom that signalled the beginning of the Final Solution and the Holocaust. This video is insensitive to Holocaust survivors and a trivialisation of the history of that era. The abuse of Nazi imagery is deeply disturbing and offensive to Jews and all those who can recall the sacrifices Americans and many others had to make as a result of Hitler's Nazi juggernaut.'[12]

*

Musicians often walk a fine line between oxygenating neo-Nazism and indulging their artistic whims, with Pete Doherty of the Libertines straddling both. Using the infamous slogan 'Arbeit Macht Frei' ('Work Sets You Free') from Auschwitz (and Dachau), the band delivered a blistering seventy-second rockabilly thrash evoking images of burning bodies in the death camp. The song concludes with the line, 'He don't like blacks or queers yet he's proud we beat the Nazis', and Doherty's ironic, 'How queer'. Upon its release, guitarist Carl Barât suggested, 'It's got nothing to do with Germany or the Germans. The song's about something that in history stands for hypocrisy and dissimulation'[13]

At the same time, Doherty and Barât rewarded a German girl who donated fifty pence to power the electricity during a 'guerrilla' house gig by both dressing as Adolf Hitler. According to their flatmate and founding member of the band, Steve Bedlow, they then 'grabbed her in the toilets and really freaked her out'.[14] The fact that Doherty, whose maternal grandfather was of Russian Jewish descent, would reference Auschwitz in a song and playfully frolic in a Nazi uniform only deepens the unease surrounding his actions five years later.

On 28 November 2009, during a show at the Munich On3-Festival, broadcast live on Bavarian radio, Doherty sang the banned verse of the German national anthem 'Deutschlandlied' ('Song of Germany') during an acoustic rendition of 'Hit The Road Jack'. Originally written as a rallying call for a unified Germany, the opening verse – *Deutschland, Deutschland, über alles* (Germany, Germany above everything. Above everything in the world) – took on a sinister tone under the Nazis' expansionist policies and was banned after the war. The performance ended with Doherty being ushered offstage as boos rang out from the audience.

A spokesperson later clarified on Sky News that Doherty 'was unaware of the controversy surrounding the German national anthem and he deeply apologises if he has caused any offence'. In a more detailed explanation on the On3 festival website, Doherty's manager stated that,

Pete wanted to celebrate his appearance in Munich by assimi-
lating and integrating with the crowd, something he tries to do
wherever he goes. Pete himself is from Jewish descent and has
fought against racism and fascism with numerous organisations
including Love Music Hate Racism. This is a subject he feels very
strongly about. Pete therefore deeply regrets if any other band,
musician, team-member, visitor, or the listeners of the broadcast
felt offended by his performance. This was not intended. Pete is
an active participant in anti-fascist and anti-racist organisations
and would like to take this opportunity to encourage anyone of
any race or creed to unite and actively fight against the resurgence of the far right's hateful doctrine in any way they can.

Artistic misunderstanding could not however be claimed by the
enigmatic Christa Päffgen, better known as Nico, the chanteuse
on the first Velvet Underground album who had a cameo role in
Federico Fellini's *La Dolce Vita*. In 1974, during a London performance, Nico delivered a discomforting rendition of 'Das Lied Der
Deutschen' (also known as 'Deutschlandlied') from her album *The
End*. Introducing the song, she described it as a 'harmless little song'.
Journalist Peter Hogan disagreed. 'Truly chilling,' he wrote, 'though
probably intended as camp cabaret . . . today it's just plain sinister . . . as it turned out, this wasn't the end, but maybe it should have
been.' In Berlin, the audience hurled plastic objects at the singer,
and as Richard Williams recalled, 'Brian Eno made air-raid noises
on his synthesiser, John Cale pounded his piano and Nico intoned
"Deutschland, über alles," cushions flying.' 'It was quite something.'[15]
   Nico performed the song until her death in 1988, after suffering a
brain haemorrhage while riding her bicycle. Despite describing herself
as a 'Nazi anarchist', *NME*'s Don Watson observed, 'Nico knew she
was playing with fire . . . later her spark was caught by DAF [Deutsch
Amerikanische Freundschaft] and Siouxsie & the Banshees.'[16]
   In 2007, Simon Reynolds reflected that Nico's

birthplace and birth date were either Cologne in 1938 or Budapest in 1943, while her father is variously said to have died in a

concentration camp or [conscripted into the *Wehrmacht*] faded away after suffering shellshock during the war. Nico herself experienced the Second World War as a primal trauma, spending her earliest years sheltering from British bombing raids and witnessing the conquest of Germany by Soviet troops. She grew up as a rootless cosmopolitan (her passport read 'ohne festen Wohnsitz,' meaning no fixed address).[17]

While her mother worked in an armaments factory, Nico spent time in an orphanage where Hitler Youth boys paraded in uniforms, and swastika flags hung outside the building. The director, Friedrich Tillman, was a member of the Nazi Party and the office manager of the T4 Euthanasia programme. By the time Nico was four, she was living with her mother and grandparents on the outskirts of Berlin, in the picturesque Spreewald forest. In her diary, Nico later recalled that in 1942 'the trains passed our house to take the Jews to Auschwitz'. Her grandfather, a railway pointsman, was responsible for directing freight to Germany, Czechoslovakia or Upper Silesia in Poland, with one of the destinations being Auschwitz. 'My family and neighbours waited by the railroad to give them food and water,' Nico wrote, 'but the guards whipped them away from our reach. I remember very clearly how many hungry people I saw when the trains came to a halt.' She also remembered imagining the rail line as a 'ribbon of death' and visualising barbed wire on the window.

Nico was however schooled in Nazi racial theory and 'Aryan supremacy', despite her youthful, innocent appearance. Danny Fields, the former Ramones manager who signed Nico to Elektra Records, described her as 'Nazi-esque' and having 'a definite Nordic Aryan streak and [the belief] that she was physically, spiritually, and creatively superior. Every once in a while,' Fields complained, 'there'd be something about Jews and I'd be, "But Nico, I'm Jewish," and she was like, "Yes, yes, I don't mean you."'[18] After a brief affair with Bob Dylan, Nico dated Lou Reed. The relationship ended with Nico telling the singer of the Velvet Underground, 'I cannot make love to Jews anymore.'

Another Brick in the Wall

PINK FLOYD. ICE CUBE. KANYE WEST. K-POP

In 1979, Pink Floyd constructed a conceptual wall with an accompanying record and film symbolising the growing divide between rock stars and audience. This monolithic barrier served as a representation of the emotional and societal barriers that exist between people, as well as a metaphor for insanity. Initially, the show was staged as an ambitious theatrical experience, with giant inflatable puppets, projections and graphics designed and animated by Gerald Scarfe, which flooded a white-brick fortification constructed at the front of the stage. By the end of the first act, the band were isolated behind this garrisoned wall, metaphorically segregated from society and the audience. In the second act, singer Roger Waters confronted his inner fears, encased by a psychological wall. In discussing the relationship between the artist and the audience, Waters rejected the idea of 'genuine' communication at concerts, arguing that rock stars are more likely to be mythologised. 'My belief is that fundamentally they owe more to Nuremburg rallies, if you like, than to art,' Waters declared. 'Hence, Pink's transformation into a fascist demagogue.'[1]

The narrative of *The Wall* was loosely autobiographical, detailing Waters' journey through marriage, infidelity, divorce, rock star excess, drugs and mental illness. Much like the character Pink played by musician Bob Geldof,* Waters experienced the loss

---

* In 1978, Geldof wrote '(I Never Loved) Eva Braun' for his group, the Boomtown Rats. The song described Hitler's relationship with his mistress alongside the cynical view that he 'never heard the screams', saw 'the blood and dirt and gore', and that underneath he was 'really gentle' and 'a little too ambitious, maybe'.

of his father, who was killed in action at Anzio, southern Italy, in February 1944. 'In terms of the internal conflicts involved in becoming the fascist swine,' he opined, 'I would own a lot of that. I'd have to; otherwise, I couldn't have written all that stuff without acknowledging my own dark side.'[2]

In 1982, Waters wrote the screenplay for a film adaptation of *The Wall*, which tells the story of a demigod spiralling into depression and the delusion of becoming a fascist dictator – a possibility, he said, 'for anyone who ever gets power in any situation'.[3] The film mirrors the Third Reich, beginning with a rally where flags decorated with insignia featuring two hammers crossed over a circle divided horizontally in red and white are displayed. This is followed by a neo-fascist convention that erupts into mob violence, set to a soundtrack of 'Run Like Hell', as properties are vandalised, windows smashed and innocent bystanders attacked by rabid dogs and rampaging gangs.

Director Alan Parker employed 380 'real-life' skinheads to re-enact the Nazi-styled rally. When asked to wear neutral facemasks, many of them instead sported 'White Power' and Union Jack T-shirts and made Nazi salutes during filming, blurring the lines between fiction and reality. Parker later admitted that maintaining order on set was a challenge. 'It was kind of hairy particularly when we did some of the more violent scenes with these skinheads. Because in the end, to them, it's not an illusion which in the film it is. They started thinking it was real. It was difficult to control them in some of the more excessive, uglier scenes.'

As the spectacle unfolds, the fanatical crowd move as a single, amorphous entity, saluting, rampaging and lynching. This was a clear reference to the November 1938 *Kristallnacht* pogrom, when the Nazis orchestrated a wave of anti-Jewish violence in retaliation for the murder of a junior diplomat in the German embassy in Paris. Across the country, Jewish properties were systemically vandalised and destroyed, including over a thousand synagogues and tens of thousands of shops and homes; women were raped, over 30,000 men were rounded up and sent to concentration camps, and as many as 800 murdered. When the music transitions into 'Waiting

For The Worms', driven by a hard staccato beat, the parallel becomes more reminiscent of the neo-Nazi marches through British towns and cities in the late 1970s. The screen fills with animated marching hammers possessed of human-like characteristics, goose-stepping in unison as an oppressive and relentless force. 'It had this onward, unthinking, crushing Nazi-like quality,' Gerald Scarfe commented.[4] A lone voice sings, 'Waiting for the final solution to strengthen the strain', and the crowd join in. 'Waiting to turn on the showers and fire the ovens . . . waiting for the queens and the coons and the reds and the Jews.'

Eric Clapton had only recently sparked controversy with his inflammatory comments at a concert in Birmingham, triggering the formation of Rock Against Racism. Echoing similar racist rhetoric, Roger Waters, as the character Pink (under the delusion that he is a fascist dictator), asked, 'Are there any queers in the theatre tonight?' When 'a Jew' and a 'coon' are singled out – one 'smoking a joint and another with spots' – the crowd are instructed to 'get them up against the wall!' The scene culminates in Pink's unsettling statement, 'If I had my way, I'd have all of you shot!' The final sequence shows an animated dove morphing into a German eagle, set to the soundtrack of 'Goodbye Blue Sky'. The bird casts a dark shadow, leaving behind a trail of waste and destruction as Pink frees himself of his inhibitions to live outside of the wall.

The Wall deals in obfuscation; neither satirical nor clearly opposing Nazism. The overtly fascist sentiment driving the narrative and the revelling in pseudo-Nazi pageantry is unexplained. To promote the film, Neal Preston photographed Pink Floyd against a wall at the Los Angeles Memorial Sports Arena, where guitarist David Gilmour, wearing a black top displaying a crossed-hammer logo, stood upright and gave a Nazi salute.

A decade after its release, on 21 July 1990, 250,000 people attended a stage version of The Wall to commemorate the fall of the Berlin Wall. The televised event attracted an estimated half a billion viewers across thirty-five countries. When Roger Waters revived the performance in 2010–13, it became the seventh-highest-grossing tour in history. However, in May 2023, he provoked an international storm when he appeared onstage at the Mercedes-Benz Arena in Berlin wearing an outfit resembling that of an SS officer – complete with a long black coat, a red armband and brandishing a mock firearm. Behind him, a projection displayed the names of Anne Frank and Palestinian-American Al Jazeera journalist Shireen Abu Akleh who had been killed on an assignment in the West Bank the previous year. The imagery seemed to suggest that Israel was behaving like Nazi Germany.

When Waters performed *The Wall* in Munich, German police launched an investigation after accusations were made that his stage costume violated laws by potentially glorifying, justifying or condoning Nazi rule and disturbing the public peace. Waters defended his position online, stating: 'The elements of my performance that have been questioned are quite clearly a statement in opposition to fascism, injustice, and bigotry in all its forms . . . attempts to portray those elements as something else are disingenuous and politically motivated.' The next show took place at the Festhalle, Frankfurt, a venue historically linked to Nazi propaganda rallies.

On 8–9 November 1938, it housed 3,000 Jews who had been beaten and abused during the *Kristallnacht* pogrom. The hall later became an assembly point for Jewish deportation to death camps, euphemistically called 'resettlement in the East'. On the evening of 28 May 2023, protesters gathered outside Festhalle, and inside, one activist waved an Israeli flag while attempting to mount the stage. 'Against this historical background, the concert should not have taken place under any circumstances,' said Sacha Stawski, a member of the Frankfurt Jewish community and head of the group Honestly Concerned, which helped organise the protest.

In February 2023, Polly Samson, author and wife of Pink Floyd guitarist David Gilmour, whose father came to London in 1938 on the *Kindertransport*, publicly criticised Roger Waters, stating, 'Sadly you are antisemitic to your rotten core. Also a Putin apologist and a lying, thieving, hypocritical, tax-avoiding, lip-synching, misogynistic, sick-with-envy, megalomaniac. Enough of your nonsense.' Gilmour retweeted this statement, adding, 'Every word demonstrably true.'

The accusation of anti-Semitism was investigated in *The Dark Side of Roger Waters*, a 2023 film by John Ware. In the documentary, several of Waters' close friends and colleagues speak out. Producer Bob Ezrin, who is Jewish, describes Waters as 'rock 'n' roll's Donald Trump', stating that despite his professed opposition to totalitarianism and racism, Waters is naive and unaware of the harm his actions cause. Norbert Stachel, a saxophonist whose family perished in the Holocaust, accuses Waters of anti-Semitism, recalling an incident in which Waters complained about 'Jew-food' at a restaurant.

Waters has been an outspoken critic of the state of Israel, even likening it to Nazi Germany, and has incited fury by floating at his concerts an inflatable pig emblazoned with the Star of David and the phrases 'dirty kyke' and 'follow the money'. Waters defended the imagery, explaining that it represented 'dogma' and further explained on his website,

> The offensive words I referenced in quotes in an email 13 years ago, were my brainstorming ideas on how to make the evils and horrors of fascism and extremism apparent and shocking to a generation that may not fully appreciate the ever-present threat. They are not the manifestation of any underlying bigotry as the film suggests. Quite the opposite. I have been trying to expose the evils of fascism ever since learning of my father's death fighting fascists in World War II.[5]

Nevertheless, in Kraków, Poland, a show was cancelled after Waters expressed support for Russia's invasion of Ukraine. Then, at London's O2 Arena, he addressed the audience, with the words appearing on a giant screen, saying, 'If you're one of those "I love Pink Floyd, but I can't stand Roger's politics" people. Then you might do well to fuck off to the bar.'

As we approach the centenary of Adolf Hitler's accession to power on 30 January 1933, Roger Waters is one of the few musicians who continues to unapologetically flirt with Third Reich-related imagery. For some, this is a form of artistic provocation, for others, it is a dangerous practice that promotes religious and race hatred. Take, for example, Phil Anselmo, the former lead singer of Pantera, who on 22 January 2016 appeared to perform a Nazi salute and shout 'White Power' during a tribute concert for former band member Dimebag Darrell in California.[6] In another controversial incident, in June 2020, rap artist Ice Cube posted online the message, 'FUCK THE NEW NORMAL UNTIL THEY FIX THE OLD NORMAL!' above a mural entitled 'Freedom for Humanity' by American artist Mear One. The image depicted Jewish bankers with hooked noses and beards seated around a Monopoly board, propped up on the backs of naked Black men. To its side a banner proclaims, 'The New World Order is the Enemy of Humanity'. The stereotype of Jewish people as excessively materialistic and money-oriented is rooted in the notorious 1903 anti-Semitic forgery *The Protocols of the Elders of Zion*, which was introduced to Hitler by the ideologue Alfred Rosen and circulated in German schools to suggest that Jewish people controlled the global financial system.

Fans of Ice Cube would not have been surprised by the anti-Semitic rhetoric. In 1991, following the break-up of N.W.A (Niggaz Wit Attitudes), he released 'No Vaseline', in which he made scathing remarks about his former bandmate Eazy-E: 'You let a Jew break up my crew' – referring to the group's former manager, Jerry Heller. He continued, 'Get rid of that devil real simple. Put a bullet in his temple. Cause you can't be the Nigga 4 Life crew. With a white Jew tellin' you what to do'. Rabbi Abraham Cooper, Associate Dean of the Los Angeles Simon Wiesenthal Center, responded with controlled outrage.

> We're not asking Ice Cube to mask the reality of the streets. By all means flag the social problems, but don't exploit them by turning a professional spat between a former manager and an artist into a racial dispute. I know that recording artists these days like to use the excuse that their music reflects reality, but this record is dangerous. Ice Cube is advocating violence against other ethnic minorities and given the climate of bigotry in the 1990s, we consider this kind of material a real threat.

Ice Cube, however, rejected the accusation, claiming, 'It's wrong for the rabbi to call me anti-Semitic,' despite the controversial language in his lyrics. 'I respect Jewish people because they're unified. I wish black people were as unified. I'm not against Jews in either of those songs. I'm just doing what they do in the media. When they describe someone, they often say he's black, Korean, or Muslim. That's all I'm doing. Saying he's a Jew doesn't mean I don't like Jews or I'm using a negative. I don't like (Heller), but it's not because he's Jewish.'[7] While some may have accepted the explanation, in 2022, rapper Kanye West remarked on the *Drink Champs* podcast that Ice Cube's lyrics had 'really influenced' him to 'get on this anti-Semite vibe'. Cube responded, 'I don't know what Ye meant by his statements. You're gonna have to ask him. I didn't put the batteries in his back. Please leave my name out of all the antisemitic talk. I'm not antisemitic and never have been.'[8]

Kanye West (also known as Ye) has described himself as 'the most influential Black person in the world'. With twenty-four Grammy Awards to his name and millions of records sold, his online following is staggering. Yet, despite all this, West has openly praised Adolf Hitler, publicly discussed *Mein Kampf* and expressed 'admiration' for the Nazis' use of propaganda. One close source claimed that West even considered naming his 2018 album after Hitler. An unnamed business executive working for West told *CNN*, 'He would praise Hitler by saying how incredible it was that he was able to accumulate so much power and would talk about all the great things he and the Nazi Party achieved for the German people.'

In 2020, West ran for president, aligning himself with the right-wing group America First. He wore a Confederate badge on his fur jacket; a symbol linked to slavery. He repeatedly espoused anti-Semitic views. He has denied the Holocaust and attacked the so-called 'Jewish media'. In 2022 he posted an image of a swastika inside the Star of David. When Twitter suspended his account, West turned to online fake-news media, where he appeared on Infowars with right-wing conspiracy theorist Alex Jones, and openly praised Nazism. The exchange makes for startling reading.

WEST: I see good things about Hitler. Every human being has something of value that they brought to the table, especially Hitler.

JONES: The Nazis were thugs.

WEST: But they did good things too. We gotta stop dissing the Nazis all the time.

JONES: Oh, my goodness! Just because you don't like one group doesn't mean . . .

WEST: I love Jewish people, but I also love Nazis.

JONES: I don't think Hitler was a good guy . . .

WEST: There's a lot of things that I love about Hitler. A lot of things.

Following the interview, Adidas relinquished all advertising ties with West. President Biden posted on Twitter, 'I just want to make a few things clear: the Holocaust happened. Hitler was a demonic figure. And instead of giving it a platform, our political leaders should be calling out and rejecting antisemitism wherever it hides. Silence is complicity.'[9] The Los Angeles Holocaust Museum issued a statement: 'Words have consequences. We see students from all over LA and most of them don't know what anti-Semitism is and to learn it from someone like Kanye West that's a serious problem.'[10]

Then, in February 2025, West advertised a new website during a Super Bowl commercial break. It sold one item: a $20 white shirt with a black swastika. Within days, the site was taken offline, replaced by a message from Shopify, the platform responsible for processing the store's orders, which read, 'This store is unavailable.' A Shopify spokesperson clarified that West's store 'did not engage in authentic commerce practices and violated our terms', leading to its removal. The Anti-Defamation League also condemned his actions in a statement that read, 'The swastika is the symbol adopted by Hitler as the primary emblem of the Nazis. It galvanized his followers in the 20th century and continues to threaten and instil fear in those targeted by antisemitism and white supremacy. There's no excuse for this kind of behaviour.'

West was later seen wearing the T-shirt in Los Angeles and tweeted, 'It was always a dream of mine to walk around with a Swastika T on.' He also made an online request for jewellers to manufacture a swastika chain design. His inflammatory tweets, including, 'I love Hitler', 'Hitler was sooooo fresh', 'IM A NAZI' and in apparent reference to companies that have relinquished links with the artist, 'I LOVE WHEN JEWISH PEOPLE COME TO ME AND SAY THEY CANT WORK WITH ME ANYMORE ITS MY FAV' drew further criticism.[11]

Three months later, West issued a new record: 'Heil Hitler'. It was immediately banned on multiple streaming platforms including Spotify, YouTube and Apple Music. Nevertheless, despite containing the lyric 'so I became a Nazi' and the repeated refrain 'Heil Hitler', the album continues to spread, shared freely by supporters online.

West's blatant and public anti-Semitism has provoked a fury of criticism, sending a clear message from fans that they are not impressed by the offensive rhetoric. In July 2025, the Australian government cancelled West's visa, preventing him from performing in the country. And yet, despite the backlash, his albums *Vultures 1* and *Vultures 2* reached number 1 and number 2 on the US charts in 2024 – highlighting how, even in the twenty-first century, pop music continues to wrestle with separating the artist's personal beliefs from their artistic output.

Social media has increasingly become a platform where the music industry's complex relationship with the Third Reich can be observed, highlighting issues about the diminishing seriousness with which its historical atrocities are regarded. Take, for instance, the all-conquering rise of K-pop, which has brought the journey of the swastika – from glam and punk rockers who wore it to 'shock' in the 1970s – to a new generation who seemingly value sartorial messaging over historical knowledge.

In 2023, Chaeyoung, a member of the girl group Twice, attracted international news headlines when she shared a photo with her 8.6 million Instagram followers in which she wore a 'Sid Vicious Something Else Action Man' T-shirt featuring a Nazi symbol at its centre. Condemnation was instant. Acting swiftly, the twenty-three-year-old singer deleted the offensive image and issued a sincere apology, 'I didn't correctly recognise the meaning of the tilted swastika in the T-shirt I wore. I deeply apologise for not thoroughly reviewing it, causing concern. I will pay absolute attention in the future to prevent any situation similar from happening again.'[12]

Born in 2000 in South Korea, Chaeyoung's admission points to a wider issue regarding education and the apparent absence of teaching on the Third Reich in South Korean schools. Are we to believe that Southeast Asian school curricula do not cover Nazism? Korea, under Japanese colonial rule until the Second World War ended, experienced atrocities like the forced sexual slavery of women, known as 'comfort women', for the military. Additionally, after the fall of Shanghai, the Korean Provisional Government declared war against the Axis forces. Moreover, why did no one in the team supporting Chaeyoung – the back-room personnel who guide stars like her – not object when she shared a swastika online? Fashion statements play a crucial role in maintaining a strong media profile, but where were the more experienced voices within her management or record company warning her about the controversial nature of Third Reich symbols?

A similar controversy erupted in 2014 when the Korean girl group Pritz performed wearing Nazi-style emblems and white armbands. While the group claimed they were unaware of the symbol's association with the Third Reich, their management team explained that the logo was inspired by traffic signage. In 2018, a member of BTS, the world's biggest K-pop band, sparked indignation wearing an SS officer's hat featuring a swastika and a *Parteiadler* logo. Then, in 2021, Sowon, from GFriend, was photographed hugging and caressing a Nazi mannequin. A year later, a member of the boy band Epex caused more hullabaloo by wearing an SS-style military uniform for a video shoot. Matters escalated when it emerged that their song 'Anthem Of Teen Spirit' made explicit reference to *Kristallnacht*, forcing the group to remove the phrases 'crystal night', 'the night in the crystal' and 'burning raw'. Meanwhile, in Japan, the all-male pop group Kishidan ignited anger among Jewish rights groups by wearing replica SS uniforms including the death's head insignia, the Iron Cross and swastikas during an appearance on MTV Japan's *Mega Vector*. The Simon Wiesenthal Center expressed 'shock and dismay', recognising 'that many young Japanese are woefully uneducated about the crimes against humanity committed by Nazi Germany and Japan during World War Two – but global entities like MTV and Sony Music should know better.'[13]

And so it goes on . . .

Ghosts

TRUPA TRUPA

The history of rock 'n' roll has seen the swastika used in various contexts, including humour, resistance, provocation and expressions of anti-Semitism. However, this narrative ends in a story of hope from modern-day Poland – the very country where Nazi Germany established extermination camps and where humanity endured its darkest moments. On 4 October 1943, in Posen, German-occupied Poland, Heinrich Himmler, Reichsführer-SS, delivered a speech on 'the Final Solution of the Jewish question', to high-ranking SS officers. 'I want to talk to you quite frankly on a very grave matter,' he began. 'Among ourselves it should be mentioned quite frankly, and yet we will never speak of it publicly . . . I mean . . . the extermination of the Jewish race . . . This is a chapter of glory in our history, which has never been written, and which shall never be written.' Had the Nazis been victorious, Himmler's vision would have prevailed. In defeat, there was no glory – instead only a history of mass extermination that Himmler tried to conceal.

Today, Grzegorz Kwiatkowski, a musician, poet, scholar and activist, is a leading voice in the struggle against Holocaust denial and the resurgence of far-right-populism. He asserts that the biggest genocide in the history of the world took place in his country, Poland. 'It still reverberates. It affects us all in a big way,' he says.

In some ways Poland is a cemetery full of ghosts. Ghosts under the ground, on the ground, in the air. So many tragedies that need sharing and remembrance. I believe that discussing these tragedies and remembering the victims can have an impact on the future and on future generations. The watchword 'never forget' is a powerful guiding principle for anti-war activism. But what I didn't know as a teenager was that many Polish people were also perpetrators.

Kwiatkowski lives in Gdansk, just thirty kilometres from Stutthof concentration camp where an estimated 65,000 prisoners died during the Second World War. 'My grandfather Józef and great-aunt Marta were prisoners at Stutthof,' he explains. 'Józef was imprisoned for studying illegally and refusing to work as slave labour for the Germans. Later, he was forced to become a *Wehrmacht* soldier, like most Polish men from the region. He was in Hamburg and Dresden when the Allies were bombing these cities. My grandfather was responsible for transporting dead bodies. He survived the war a traumatised and broken man.'

Aged nine, Kwiatkowski accompanied his grandfather to Stutthof and vividly remembers the sound of him screaming and crying. The experience left a deep impression on him. 'I didn't know what to do,' he recalls. This moment led him to ask the simplest yet most difficult questions: Why do people kill? Why do people hate? Why did people build gas chambers? 'These were the first ethical questions in my life,' he says, 'and, in some ways; they were the most important. It wasn't just history to me but reality.'

The journey to honouring his grandparents' incarceration began in 2015, when Kwiatkowski and his friend Rafał Wojczal began researching a film about Albin Ossowski – an actor, resistance fighter and former inmate of both Auschwitz-Birkenau and Buchenwald. Kwiatkowski explains: 'After the war, Ossowski moved to London and ran a famous antiques shop, where even the Queen was a customer. He agreed to participate in the documentary because he was afraid of the rise of Holocaust denial movements.'

During his research, Kwiatkowski discovered vast quantities of shoes, buried and rotting in a forest on the outer perimeter of the former Stutthof camp. These shoes had once belonged to women, men and children. During the Nazi occupation, Stutthof served as a central repair facility for footwear and leather, much of it sourced from prisoners exterminated at Auschwitz. These items were repurposed to create goods for the *Wehrmacht* and German civilians, including belts, rucksacks and holsters. When the camp was liberated on 9 May 1945, the Red Army photographed and catalogued a 'huge cone-like pile of shoes' numbering no fewer than 410,000 pairs, which weighed an estimated 490 tonnes. However, when a memorial museum was opened on the grounds in 1963, only a small fraction of the discarded footwear – between 30,000 and 50,000 pairs – was collected and housed in a large glass casket within a former canteen building. The rest was discarded beyond the camp's perimeter fence and 'left to nature'.[1]

Kwiatkowski launched a public campaign to not only have the rejected shoes displayed at Stutthof but also to have historians examine them to trace their former owners. He met significant resistance. 'The museum said it was trash and that the shoes held no historic value. But for us, these were artefacts of the Holocaust,' he says.

> In 1944, Jews were transported to Stutthof because Auschwitz was overcrowded. The wagons were moving gas chambers. Almost half of the victims were women. Yet, in Polish narratives, Stutthof is a camp of teachers, priests and intelligentsia. They don't want a mountain of Jewish shoes in the museum for fear the numbers will change the camp story. Most Polish people don't like Jews. For years, I didn't understand. Now I do. It was anti-Semitism.

Kwiatkowski continues, 'Then, during the campaign, I visited my wife's maternal family, who are of Jewish heritage. On the way, my car broke down and I had to wait in a local village for a new part. The manager of the repair centre was a proud anti-Semite who told me about the history of the region. He said, 'You know what happened a few weeks ago? A big truck with the shoes from Stutthof arrived at the city rubbish. They were afraid to bury the shoes, so they burnt them in a field nearby.'

In 2013, Kwiatkowski's group Trupa Trupa recorded their second album, ++, in the only synagogue in Gdansk not destroyed during the war. 'It had great sound,' he says. 'PJ Harvey recorded *Let England Shake* in a church and we thought, "We want that kind of sound. What church will open the door for us?" We thought, "No church. But the Jewish community will."' Like many of their subsequent recordings, ++ was an anti-war statement, blending a postpunk aesthetic with 'off-kilter melodies, dense instrumentation, and lyrical explorations of the darkest side of the human condition.'[2] A later album track, 'Never Forget', was inspired by Claude Lanzmann's film *Shoah*, and conveys the brutality the Nazis unleashed in Poland. 'We never forget humiliation', Kwiatkowski sings. 'We never forget those ghetto deaths. They sound like a midnight choir'. In 'Remainder', written and sung by bassist Woytek Juchniewicz, he chants, 'It did not take place!' 'This song,' Kwiatkowski says in his opinion, 'is a warning to Holocaust deniers.'

Through both song and poetry, Kwiatkowski confronts the rising tide of fascism and the legacy of Nazism, including Richard Wagner's missives on anti-Semitism, devoured by Adolf Hitler, and the complicity of Polish nationals in the Holocaust. 'We still have anti-Semitism,' Kwiatkowski reflects, 'I think that's because we didn't have the chance to confront history because everything was so fucked up after communism when the Allies divided Europe at the end of the war and the Soviet Union claimed Poland for the Eastern bloc. History is being distorted, and hate is becoming normalized. But I refuse to be cynical. I believe in art as an act of defiance, music as a force for truth, and solidarity as the only way forward.'

For five years, Kwiatkowski's battle with Stutthof raged on. Until, finally, in the face of mounting international pressure from media outlets like the *Guardian* and NBC, the museum relented, and the discarded shoes were reburied at the former concentration camp site. It was a small victory. 'These artefacts should be visible,' Kwiatkowski says. 'As we say in our song, "we must never forget so that this bloody history never returns".'

Then, in 2024, Kwiatkowski received an unexpected and long-awaited message. 'A moment I'd been hoping for,' he recalls. Stutthof

Museum confirmed that several hundred kilograms of shoes collected from outside the campgrounds would be displayed in the
new Visitor Service Building. They also committed to regularly
collecting shoes from the surrounding forest, monitoring the area
as the earth shifts, and properly marking the area outside the
museum so that tourists know what they might encounter and what
to do if such a situation arises. However, Kwiatkowski subsequently
discovered that tens of thousands of shoes were still lying in the
ground near the fence. 'The museum took only a portion,' he says
regretfully. 'The history is still present in the forest. I'm not giving
up – but the situation remains unresolved. Still, we almost have a
happy ending,' Kwiatkowski says with reservation. 'So, what can I
say? Hooray!'

Seven-year-old Jewish boy Sieg Maandag (1937–2013), photographed
by George Rodger, the first British photographer to enter the liberated
Bergen-Belsen in April 1945.

Epilogue

For over seventy-five years, musicians have been drawn to the language and provocative imagery of Nazism, fascinated by its power, menace and underlying sexuality. They have flirted with the theatrical spectacle of the Third Reich, displayed the swastika, flaunted memorabilia, worn Nazi uniforms and marvelled at the grandiose rallies of 1930s Germany. The figureheads of this dark era have been parodied, and some have even hailed Adolf Hitler as rock 'n' roll's first superstar. This complex and often uncomfortable history remains largely undocumented – a taboo in the world of music, reflecting its deep and troubled relationship with itself. It is also perversely thrilling.

My fascination with the Third Reich dates back to childhood. Raised in a Jewish family – a religion I rejected shortly after bar mitzvah – I happily sang along to 'Belsen Was A Gas' by the Sex Pistols and saw humour in Sid Vicious walking through the Jewish quarter of Paris in a swastika T-shirt. And yet, at the same time, I was outraged when I discovered that the post-punk band Joy Division had taken their name from the brothel in Auschwitz where SS officers raped women. This cultural paradox – pop music using dark humour as provocation while trivialising Nazism – was at the heart of my teenage awakening as both a passionate music fan and an amateur historian.

In the early 1980s, my mother briefly worked at the Board of Deputies of British Jews. One day, she mentioned that *Searchlight*, the magazine of an organisation monitoring fascist and neo-Nazi activity in the UK, had flagged a couple of my favourite bands – Madness and the Specials. My initial reaction was one of shock and concern. However, as I looked deeper into the lyrics, read about neo-Nazi infiltration at 2 Tone gigs and understood the political positions of both bands, I was reassured to learn that they were, in fact, outspoken against fascism. This experience taught me the importance of researching and verifying facts. I came to understand that both fans and artists bear a responsibility to history. The atrocities of the Third Reich are not to be used lightly as creative inspiration but must be treated with the respect due to their victims.

Then, on another occasion, my mother returned home with a video labelled 'Holocaust film footage'. The VHS tape was promptly hidden on the top shelf of a bookcase with a strict warning not to watch it without her permission. Naturally, I viewed the hour-long documentary at the first unmonitored opportunity and was deeply disturbed by the harrowing images of dead bodies – starved, mutilated, shot and gassed. Those pictures were indelibly printed on my mind, and I've since wrestled with humanity's capacity for violence and killing, alongside rock 'n' roll's cheap theatrics. *This Ain't Rock 'n' Roll* is, in many ways, an attempt to reconcile my adolescent political awakening with my love of pop music.

The central question of this book concerns the extent to which artists have commented on their flirtation with the swastika and the Third Reich, and whether rock 'n' roll – that is musicians, the media and the record industry – has ever taken responsibility for it. Early on, I reached out to musicians, inviting them to explain or even justify their behaviour. I made it clear that I wasn't looking to accuse or excuse anyone, but simply to understand. Yet the only responses I received came from those who campaign against modern fascism. It seems clear that musicians would rather these types of enquiries disappeared and would prefer not to discuss their past behaviour. This led me to realise that the more important task was to examine rock 'n' roll's documented history and its connection to the Third Reich. For almost eighty years, the stories and images have been in plain sight, providing ample opportunity for reflection by all concerned. However, the notable absence of significant archival documentation underscores rock 'n' roll's failure to confront its past.

Writing this book has been far from easy. In my effort to avoid casting myself as the Simon Wiesenthal of rock 'n' roll, I have tried to strike a delicate balance between explanation and not attributing blame – a challenging task – but simply to say: Here is what happened; here is the evidence. There was no attempt to compile a list of artists to denounce; this story is much broader than my own likes or dislikes. But when confronted with groups that have used Nazi symbolism in their work, how are we supposed to feel? That's a difficult question to answer. I am not advocating for the censorship of their music. But I do believe that using history creatively carries consequences. Holocaust-related language or Nazi symbols in popular music should be aligned with their historical context. My hope is that the book provokes critical discussion and challenges us to consider whether pop music's embrace of Third Reich imagery is a fitting way to honour the memory of the six million Jews and the lesser-known victims of the Nazi Aryan vision.

In 2023, I was awarded an Authors' Foundation grant by the Society of Authors, enabling me to embark on an 800-mile round trip across Poland to visit the remains of Nazi ghettoes and extermination camps: Auschwitz I and II, Bełżec, Majdanek, Sobibór, Treblinka and Chelmno. My aim was to witness first-hand the evidence of the Holocaust and pay respect to lives lost to Nazism. The following year, I used the remainder of the grant for a short tour of Germany to visit Bergen-Belsen, Ravensbrück and Buchenwald. This journey to see first-hand evidence of the horrors of the so-called Final Solution began thirty years earlier when I explored various sites connected to the Third Reich, including Dachau, Hitler's mountaintop retreat, the Berlin Olympic Stadium, Room 600 at the Palace of Justice at Nuremberg where post-war trials took place, the Zeppelin Field where Leni Riefenstahl filmed the Nazi Party rally, Theresienstadt concentration camp in the former Czechoslovakia and Westermarkt 20 in Amsterdam where Anne Frank's family hid from Nazi perse-cution. After years of reading and watching films about the Third Reich, the opportunity to make real that which is almost impossible to imagine proved an emotionally overwhelming experience.

While staying in Lublin in 2023, I stumbled upon a former school building where the SS had murdered the pupils. A plaque

on the outside wall commemorated the brutal act, but what troubled me most was the thought that such historical markers might
only attract the attention of an older generation. Do young people
just pass by, as I did in my teenage years living in Birmingham,
oblivious of buildings like those bombed by the Luftwaffe? This
made me think of the average English person's unfamiliarity with
Nazi extermination camps. Reichsführer-SS Heinrich Himmler
had once foretold that the history of the Jewish race's annihilation
would never be written, and though his prophecy did not come
true, the finer details of the Holocaust are not common knowledge.
Perhaps it is because many of the lesser-known camps – without gas
chambers, barracks, or gates adorned with ironic mottos for tourists
to photograph – offer little in comparison to the more visible and
grisly theatre of Auschwitz.

Rock 'n' roll has a proud history of challenging societal injustices,
from the war in Vietnam to religious and sexual oppression. By
its very nature, it is rebellious and boundary-pushing. It speaks
up for minorities and increasingly takes on issues of racism and
misogyny, even while at times perpetuating those same problems.
But let it be clear:

Rock groups do not name themselves after monuments to
slavery – but they do choose to name themselves after memorials
and locations associated with the Third Reich.

Rock groups do not celebrate the hoods and robes of the Ku
Klux Klan or admire the elegant clothing of a slave overseer – but
they do flaunt Nazi regalia, whether in album artwork, photo shoots
or in front of documentary cameras.

As the conversation around racism and misogyny in music continues to evolve, we must also confront the issue of anti-Semitism
and the persistent use of Nazi imagery. The #MeToo movement
in 2017 and the protests following George Floyd's murder in 2020
empowered a new generation to challenge systemic racism and
misogyny, rejecting them as an inevitable part of history. Yet,
despite this growing social consciousness, anti-Semitism remains a
confusing and divisive issue, often conflated with the debate around

Zionism. When a musician wears a swastika, we must remember its historical context: Hitler adopted it as a symbol of his extreme hatred of Jews. Displaying the swastika, by its very nature, signifies ideological endorsement. The symbol cannot be separated from its original meaning, no matter whether the intent is to demystify, reclaim or destroy it. As Hitler explicitly stated, the political foundation of the Third Reich was 'the annihilation of all eleven million European Jews . . . once and for all'.

Today, the Holocaust is embedded in our collective consciousness through a flood of films, books and images that serve as a constant reminder of the atrocities committed by the Nazi regime. Yet, immediately after the war, and for many more years, detailed knowledge of the Nazi camp network was scarce. While newsreels initially revealed the horrors of National Socialism, over time much of the footage was either withdrawn or censored, as the world focused more on rebuilding post-war Europe and forging economic and diplomatic relationships than on educating people about the Nazis' systematic extermination programme. Events like the trial of Adolf Eichmann in 1961 briefly reignited interest in the Holocaust, but increasingly, the conversation became more specialised and academic, with survivor testimonies often falling out of print. It was not until 2001 in the UK and 2005 in the US that the United Nations designated 27 January – to commemorate the liberation of Auschwitz – as International Holocaust Remembrance Day.

The failure of the wider world to properly address the Holocaust helps explain the music press and record industry's culpability in the narrative. The tropes of Nazism have been normalised simply because they have not been called out. Over the decades, there has been a significant lack of rigorous condemnation and a failure to recognise when discrimination shifts from racism based on skin colour to invoking Nazism and, by extension, anti-Semitism. By separating hate crime from its theatrical elements, the music industry at large becomes complicit. All the incidents described in this book are public knowledge, and although they have not historically been woven into a single narrative, they are well known among fans of the artists discussed. This largely unquestioned facet of pop culture where the swastika is routinely reproduced and celebrated without reproach is often dismissed with vague excuses like, 'It was punk' or 'It was of the time.'

With each passing decade, it's increasingly important to reconnect the symbols and names associated with the Third Reich away from popular culture to their historical context. Across Europe, and with Donald Trump's second term as president of the United States, fascism is on the rise. Now more than ever, voices must be heard to combat bigotry, racism and anti-Semitism – not just to push back against negativity but to promote positive change. In 2017, fifty years after the murder of George Lincoln Rockwell, the world was shocked by footage of neo-Nazis and white nationalists marching through Charlottesville, chanting, 'Jews will not replace us'. While the swastika and Third Reich references may have been downplayed, the movement was still closely aligned with Rockwell's memory and the American Nazi Party he founded. History teaches us the dangers of right-wing attitudes, where simple, everyday ideas gain traction and evolve into tools of intolerance. Whenever there is an opportunity, these attitudes must be challenged and questioned. We must own our mistakes, acknowledge our misjudgements and redefine what has surreptitiously slipped into the mainstream. Power manifests itself in many conflicting arenas, but it is our responsibility to expose neo-fascism and anti-Semitism wherever and in whatever form it appears. The hope is that this book acts as a literary reminder to those values: to ensure that the Holocaust is never forgotten and never repeated. Never again!

Acknowledgements

To the Authors' Foundation grant from the Society of Authors that enabled me to embark on an 800-mile round trip across Poland and then northern Germany, to visit the remains of Nazi ghettoes and extermination camps – thank you. Making a living as an author is challenging, to say the least, so this financial boost to pursue my ambition was magnificent.

I am extremely grateful to the handful of people who contributed their thoughts and took the time to talk with me. They are Lucy Adlington, Caroline Coon, Tony Drayton, Simon Holland, Grzegorz Kwiatkowski, Andrew Loog Oldham, Bernard Rhodes and Lucy 'Toothpaste' Whitman. Also Jake Burns, Chalkie Davies, Andrew Kent, Bryan Ferry, Paul Holborow, John Lydon and Paul Weller for material I have used from previous conservations we shared.

Access to an archive, a photograph, some translations are among the wonderful contributions friends have made that make all the difference, so thank you Ray Meade, Matthew Worley, Kieron Tyler, Marc Goldberg and Keith Feldman at Community Service Trust, Julian Marszalek, Martin Kelly, Ian Trowell, Jeremy Deller and Marc Olivier.

Billy Bragg has been a touchstone during my writing and then wrote a wonderful introduction – thank you for your incisive and towering strength.

To Lee Brackstone for the immense support, encouragement, editorial input and positivity. And of course to the team at White Rabbit: Lily McIlwain, Sophie Nevrkla, Tara Hiatt, Steve Marking, Tom Noble, Harry Taylor, Natalie Dawkins, Seán Costello and Sarah Fortune.

Each book I finish demands greater superlatives for my literary agent, Carrie Kania. This was by no means an easy book to clinch a deal for, but we did it. You've supported and influenced the writing and most of all offered hope and friendship. And to Susie, Lily, Eleanor and Lottie, the greatest loves of my life – and for putting up with relentless Nazi documentaries – may there always be love in your worlds. xxxx

References

Madalf Heatlump

1 Maureen Cleave, 'Well, he's come back – the man who really started it all', *Evening Standard*, 6 July 1953

2 Peter Guralnick, *Last Train to Memphis* (Abacus, 1995), p. 438

3 Maureen Cleave, 'The boys who put OOOOHHHH! into Pop', *Evening Standard*, 24 October 1964

4 http://www.mourningtheancient.com/truth-14.htm

5 https://www.alexautographs.com/auction-lot/john-lennon-signed-self-portrait-heil-john-wh_45546C1B14 said

6 *The Beatles Anthology* (Chronicle Books, 2000)

7 *Beatles Anthology*

8 Albert Speer, *Inside the Third Reich* (W&N, 2009), p. 388

9 Mark Lewisohn, *Tune In: Extended* (Little Brown, 2013)

10 'Hamburg's Heady Days of Rock & Roll', *Spiegel Online*, 2006

11 *Beatles Anthology*, p. 144

12 *Beatles Anthology*, p. 201

13 https://www.independent.co.uk/arts-entertainment/music/news/where-s-adolf-the-mystery-of-sgt-pepper-is-solved-434995.html

14 *Beatles Anthology*, p. 297

15 Brian Epstein, *A Cellarful of Noise* (Souvenir Press, 1964)

16 https://www.tabletmag.com/sections/arts-letters/articles/beatles-meet-the-chosen

Shouting the Blues

1 https://www.hollywoodsoapbox.com/interview-eric-burdon-still-not-misunderstood-after-so-many-years/

2 Keith Altham, 'Hell-Raisers of Pop', *New Musical Express Annual*, December 1965

3   Genya Ravan, *Lollipop Lounge, Memoirs of a Rock and Roll Refugee* (Billboard Books, 2004)

4   Andrew Loog Oldham, *2Stoned* (Vintage, 2003), p. 307

5   Tony Norman, 'Behind the Shades – The Stones, and Other Stories', *New Musical Express*, 17 June 1972

6   Oldham, *2Stoned*, p. 4

7   Mikko Kapanen, Andy Ellison interview, September 2000, http://johnschildren.info/interviews.html

8   *NME*, 4 February 1967

9   https://www.france24.com/en/20170614-anita-pallenberg-actress-stones-muse-dead-73

10 https://www.express.co.uk/entertainment/music/1241940/Rolling-Stones-Brian-Jones-Nazi-uniform-Germany-Sex-Pistols-Mick-Jagger-Keith-Richards

11 https://www.agenteprovocador.es/publicaciones/herr-brian-jones-paseando-por-munich-con-uniforme-nazi

12 http://www.agenteprovocador.es/publicaciones/herr-brian-jones-paseando-por-munich-con-uniforme-nazi

13 Oldham, *2Stoned*, p. 299

14 'Teen Fantasies as Art', Andrew Bailey, *Rolling Stone*, 11 April 1974

15 http://bluesonline.weebly.com/rock-dreams-beatles-and-stones.htm

16 https://www.iconicriviera.com/rolling-stones-keith-richards-house-france/

17 Philip Norman, 'The Rolling Stones in Exile', *Sunday Times*, 2001

18 https://www.standard.co.uk/showbiz/sex-drugs-and-guns-as-rocker-keith-richards-releases-his-memoirs-how-much-can-the-hellraiser-really-remember-7241554.html

19 Michael Uslan and Solomon Uslan, *Dick Clark's the First 25 Years of Rock & Roll* (Outlet, 1981), p. 181

20 Victor Bockris, *Keith Richards, the Unauthorised Biography* (Omnibus, 2002), p. 1

21 Bockris, *Keith Richards*, p. 2

22 Bockris, *Keith Richards*, p. 129

23 Keith Richards, *Life* (Weidenfeld & Nicolson, 2011), p. 375

24 Sam Cutler, *You Can't Always Get What You Want: My Life with the Rolling Stones, the Grateful Dead and Other Wonderful Reprobates* (ECW Press, 2010)

25 From the National Archives file entitled 'The use of Hyde Park for pop concerts' https://media.nationalarchives.gov.uk/index.php/summer-of-69/

26 Book review: *Hell's Angel: The Life and Times of Sonny Barger and the Hell's Angel's Motorcycle Club* https://www.theguardian.com/g2/story/0,3604,331676,00.html; http://theartofexmouth.blogspot.com/2018/01/hells-angel-ralph-sonny-barger.html; https://www.reuters.com/article/us-jagger-idUSSP22492920030303

27 Gitta Sereny, *Speer: His Battle with Truth* (Picador, 1995), p. 132

28 Jürgen Trimborn, *Leni Riefenstahl: A Life* (I.B. Tauris, 2008), pp. 40, 67

29 Trimborn, *Leni Riefenstahl*, p. 179

30 Sereny, *Speer*, p. 134

31 https://www.theguardian.com/film/2025/apr/27/leni-riefenstahl-nazi-hitler-film-maker-documentary

32 Paul Gorman, *The Life And Times of Malcolm McLaren: The Biography* (Constable, 2021), p. 354

33 Sebastian Haffner, *Defying Hitler: A Memoir* (W&N, 2012)

34 Adolf Hitler, *Mein Kampf* (Hutchinson, 1969), pp. 332, 452

35 Hitler, *Mein Kampf*, p. 450

A Lousy Publicist

1 https://sfi.usc.edu/news/2024/04/36256-hogan%E2%80%99s-heroes-actor-robert-clary-96-survived-holocaust-and-committed-himself

2 Viktor E. Frankl, *Man's Search For Meaning*, (Penguin, 1959), pp. 52–4

3 Charlie Chaplin, *My Autobiography* (Bodley Head, 1964)

4 'The Who', *NME* Originals, 2004, p. 46

5 Dougal Butler, *Moon the Loon, The Amazing Rock and Roll Life of Keith Moon* (Star, 1981)

6 Tony Fletcher, *Dear Boy: The Life of Keith Moon* (Omnibus, 1998), p. 41

7 *NME*, 8 July 1972

8 Pamela Des Barres, *I'm With the Band* (Omnibus, 2018), p. 239

9 Barney Hoskyns, *Trampled Under Foot* (Faber, 2013), pp. 327, 378, 380; Sam Aizer, *Led Zeppelin – Photographs by Neal Preston* (Omnibus, 2009), p. 146

Colour Me Pop

1 Keith Altham, 'Keith Altham Planes West to Cover America's Monterey Pop Festival and Cables This Day-By-Day Report', *New Musical Express*, 24 June 1967

2 Legs McNeil and Gillian McCain, *Please Kill Me* (Abacus, 1997), p. 40

3   McNeil and McCain, *Please Kill Me*, p. 64

4   https://thehoundnyc.com/2009/01/10/ron-asheton-3-danny-fields-on-ron-asheton/

5   Marc Spitz and Brendan Mullen, *We Got the Neutron Bomb: The Untold Story of L.A. Punk* (Three Rivers Press, 2001), pp. 30–31 https://radicalarchives.org/tag/skinhead/

6   McNeil and McCain, *Please Kill Me*, p. 84

7   'Tyranny and Mutations!', *Uncut*, February 2025, p. 75

8   https://geirmykl.wordpress.com/2015/08/16/article-about-blue-oyster-cult-from-new-musical-express-february-15-1975/

9   Chris Charlesworth, 'Cult Heroes', *Melody Maker*, 16 February 1974

10 'Tyranny and Mutations!', *Uncut*

11 Victor Bockris, *Beat Punks: New York's Underground Culture from the Beat Generation to the Punk Explosion* (Open Road Media, 2016)

12 https://forward.com/culture/music/322628/patti-smith-and-her-religious-influence/

13 Letter to Jem Shotts, 21 February 1972 http://www.vandergraafgenerator.co.uk/pawnhts.htm

14 *Mju:zik* magazine, February 1998

15 https://www.bbc.co.uk/news/entertainment-arts-52933584

16 *Q* magazine, date unknown

17 https://www.independent.co.uk/arts-entertainment/music/features/sparks-ron-and-russell-mael-franz-ferdinand-hippopotamus-top-of-the-pops-seventies-a7930641.html

Rock Around the Bunker

1   https://odysee.com/@Aminuitlesoleil:e/Rock-around-the-bunker---Le-nazi-rock-de-Gainsbourg-Interviews,-analyses-+-album-complet-(odysee):1

2   Sylvie Simmons, *Serge Gainsbourg: A Fistful of Gitanes* (Da Capo, 2002)

3   https://www.mistergainsbarre.com/1975-rock-around-the-bunker/

4   Nick Kent, Ian MacDonald and Charles Shaar Murray, 'The Man Who Put Sequins into Middle Eights', *New Musical Express*, 20 January 1973

5   Simon Reynolds *Shock And Awe: Glam Rock and Its Legacy, From the Seventies to the Twenty-First Century* (Faber, 2016)

6   Richard Cromelin, 'Snapshots of a Shy Coxcomb', *Creem*, June 1975

For Those About to Rock

1   Interview with Eric Spitznagel on MTV Hive, 2011.Reproduced here: https://www.logodesignlove.com/kiss-logo
2   Paul Stanley, *Face the Music: A Life Exposed*, (HarperOne, 2014)
3   Colin Irwin, 'Joe Walsh: Lonely Leader', *Melody Maker*, 2 August 1975
4   Mick Wall, *Lemmy: the Definitive Biography* (Orion, 2016), p. 231
5   Wall, *Lemmy*, p. 229
6   Lemmy Kilmister *White Line Fever: Lemmy: The Autobiography* (Simon & Schuster, 2016) p. 224
7   https://www.theguardian.com/music/2007/apr/16/news.joydivision
8   https://www.theguardian.com/music/2008/jul/11/news.culture
9   https://discover.hubpages.com/entertainment/Germanic-Iconography-in-Hard-Rock-Heavy-Metal
10 https://blabbermouth.net/news/ian-anderson-says-motorhead-and-motley-crues-spurious-use-of-the-umlaut-was-silly
11 *Hound Dog: The Leiber and Stoller Autobiography*, David Ritz (Omnibus Press, 2010)
12 Mick Brown, 'Alex the friendly Führer', *Sounds*, 15 May 1976
13 Mick Brown, 'The Monsters in Alex Harvey', *Rolling Stone*, 24 February 1977
14 https://www.uncut.co.uk/reviews/alex-harvey-last-teenage-idols-73468/
15 Reynolds, *Shock and Awe*

Visions of Swastikas

1   *Melody Maker*, 14 September 1974
2   https://helendonlonagency.wordpress.com/wp-content/uploads/2016/10/1974_apr2016.pdf; Thobias Rüther, *Heroes, David Bowie and Berlin* (Reaktion Books. 2014)
3   Speer, *Inside the Third Reich*, p. 102
4   Speer, *Inside the Third Reich*, p. 61
5   Speer, *Inside the Third Reich*, p. 130
6   *The German Trauma, Experiences and Reflections 1938–2001*, Gitta Sereny (Penguin, 2001), p. 1
7   Speer, *Inside the Third Reich*, p. 88
8   *BBC Breakfast Time*, 9 February 1984
9   David Quantick, 'Inside the royal family', *NME*, 9 August 1986, pp. 26, 27
10 Gitta Sereny, *Albert Speer: His Battle with Truth* (Picador, 1995) p. 350

11 Laurence Rees, *Auschwitz: the Nazis and the 'Final Solution'* (BBC Books, 2005) p. 40

12 'That Old Black and White Magic', David Buckley and Danny Eccleston, *Mojo*, September 2016

13 David Hancock, 'Punk, Politics, Religion and War . . . By A Superstar', *Evening News*, 20 September 1977

14 https://www.muhistory.com/from-the-archive-2-mu-response-to-david-bowies-nazi-salute/

15 Tim Lott, 'The Thin White Duke Has Gone. Here's The New David Bowie', *Record Mirror*, 24 September 1977

16 Bowie Meets The Press: Plastic Man or Godhead of the Seventies? Ben Edmonds, *Circus*, 27 April 1976

17 David Bowie and Brett Anderson, 'One Day, Son, All this Could Be Yours (Part One)' *NME*, 20 March 1993

18 https://welcomebackbowie.wordpress.com/articles/david-bowie-interview-in-arena-springsummer-1993/

Rivers of Blood

1 *International Times* no. 94, 1970

2 *New Musical Express*, February 4, 1967

3 Keith Altham, 'Nice, Abnormal Spoonful!', *NME*, 22 April 1966

4 Harry Shapiro, *Eric Clapton: Lost in the Blues* (Da Capo, 1992), p. 145

5 Speer, *Inside the Third Reich*, p. 152

6 Dave Renton, *When We Touched the Sky: The Anti-Nazi League 1977–1981* (New Clarion Press, 2006)

Too Fast to Live Too Young to Die

1 https://museum-collection.hackney.gov.uk/object-2013-119

2 Paul Gorman, *The Life And Times of Malcolm McLaren: The Biography* (Constable, 2020), p. 32

3 Gorman, *Malcolm McLaren*, p. 49

4 Jon Savage, *England's Dreaming* (Faber & Faber, 1992), p.40

5 Savage, *England's Dreaming*, pp. 188–9; Jon Savage, *The England's Dreaming Tapes* (Faber & Faber, 2001), p. 41

6 Savage, *England's Dreaming*, p. 56

7   Gorman, *Malcolm McLaren*, p. 203

8   Gorman, *Malcolm McLaren*, p. 305

9   Savage, *England's Dreaming Tapes*, p. 431

10 Fred and Judy Vermorel, *The Sex Pistols* (Universal, 1978)

11 Savage, *England's Dreaming Tapes*, p. 478

12 Savage, *England's Dreaming*, p.188

13 Cathi Unsworth and Jordan Mooney, *Defying Gravity: Jordan's Story* (Omnibus, 2019), pp. 169, 170

14 Savage, *England's Dreaming*, p. 55

15 '10 Questions for Vivienne Westwood', 14 January 2009, http://content.time.com/time/arts/article/0,8599,1871537,00.html

16 Vivienne Westwood and Ian Kelly, *Vivienne Westwood* (Picador, 2014), p. 59

17 Westwood and Kelly, *Vivienne Westwood*, pp. 150, 174

18 Westwood and Kelly, *Vivienne Westwood*, p. 189

19 *Punk and the Pistols*, dir. Paul Tickell (BBC, 1995)

20 Savage, *England's Dreaming Tapes*, p. 41

21 Savage, *England's Dreaming Tapes*, p. 40

22 Ed Jones, 'The Sex Pistols: The 100 Club, London', *New Society*, 7 October 1976

23 Rees, *Auschwitz*, p. 236

24 Rees, *Auschwitz*, p. 373

25 Anita Lasker-Wallfisch and Giles de la Mare, *Inherit the Truth 1939–1945: The Documented Experiences of a Survivor of Auschwitz and Belsen* (Giles de la Mare, 1996), p. 122

26 *Daily Express*, 22 August 1945, p. 3

27 Greil Marcus, ed., *Psychotic Reactions and Carburetor Dung* (Anchor Books, 1988)

28 Gorman, *Malcolm McLaren*, p. 356

29 *Record Mirror*, 15 July 1978

30 Steve Jones, *Lonely Boy: Tales from a Sex Pistol* (William Heinemann, 2016) p. 221

31 Peter Brummund with Chris Farlowe, 12 October 2017 https://www.music2stay.de/wp-content/uploads/2020/04/4iWUx20Y.pdf

32 Allan Jones, *Melody Maker*, August 1975

33 Jones, *Lonely Boy*, pp. 221, 231

34 Q, June 1996

35 Savage, *England's Dreaming Tapes*, pp. 289, 291

36 Rosalind Russell, 'Sex, Drugs and Rock 'N' Roll', *Record Mirror*, 8 April 1978

Deutschland Über Alles

1   Savage, *England's Dreaming*, p. 209

2   John Lydon, *Rotten: No Irish, No Blacks, No Dogs* (Plexus, 2003)

3   Caroline Coon, *1988: The New Wave Punk Rock Explosion* (Omnibus, 1982)

4   https://fromtheothersideofthemirror.com/2009/06/13/unpub-lished-joe-strummer-interview-part-2/

5   Savage, *England's Dreaming*, p. 219

6   Jonh Ingham, 'The Rock Special (#2): The Audience', *Sounds*, 9 October 1976

7   John Lydon, *Rotten: No Irish, No Blacks, No Dogs – The Authorised Autobiography of Johnny Rotten of the Sex Pistols* (Hodder & Stoughton, 1994), p. 185

8   'The Life & Loves of a She-Devil', *Uncut*, Simon Goddard, January 2005

9   'The Life & Loves of a She-Devil', *Uncut*, January 2005

10 Ian Birch, 'The Giraffe Looked at Siouxsie', *Melody Maker*, 17 February 1979

11 (Steve) Jane Suck, 'What's "nihilism"?', *NME*, 25 June 1977

12 Tickell, *Punk & the Pistols*

13 https://magnetmagazine.com/2007/10/06/qa-with-siouxsie-sioux/

14 *NME*, 15 December 1979

15 Chris Salewicz, *Redemption Song: the Definitive Biography of Joe Strummer* (Harper Collins, 2006)

16 Andrew Matheson, *Sick On You: The Disastrous Story of The Hollywood Brats, The Greatest Band You've Never Heard Of* (Ebury Press, 2016)

17 Martin Hayman, 'Guy's Out For Glory', *Sounds*, 30 March 1974

18 Savage, *England's Dreaming*, pp. 241–2

Blitzkrieg Bop

1   Nick Kent, *The Dark Stuff* (Faber & Faber, 2007), p. 169

2   Kris Needs, 'Make-up America!', *Mojo*, June 2006; Pamela Des Barres, *Rock Bottom: Dark Moments In Music Babylon* (St Martin's Press, 1996)

3   McNeil and McCain, *Please Kill Me*

4   McNeil and McCain, *Please Kill Me*, p. 293

5   McNeil and McCain, *Please Kill Me*, p. 293

6   McNeil and McCain, *Please Kill Me*, p. 294

7   Lester Bangs, 'Ramones Go Depresso', *New Musical Express*, 23 September 1978

8   Lester Bangs, 'The White Noise Supremacists', *Village Voice*, 30 April 1979

9   https://www.vice.com/en/article/65zmv3/electric-eels-interview

10 https://www.vice.com/en/article/65zmv3/electric-eels-interview

Fascist in the Bedroom

1   Lasker-Wallfisch and De la Mare, *Inherit the Truth*, p. 94

2   *NME*, January 1977

3   'The page you are looking at takes no responsibility for your sanity or well-being', *NME*, Mick Farren, 19 March 1977, p28

4   John Coldstream, *Dirk Bogarde: The Authorised Biography* (Orion, 2004)

5   Gitta Sereny, *Into That Darkness: An Examination of Conscience* (Vintage, 1983), p. 158-160

6   Graham K. Smith, 'I wanted to be a nun . . . then I discovered boys', *Record Mirror*, 19 May 1984

7   https://www.latimes.com/archives/la-xpm-1991-01-04-ca-7949-story.html

8   https://www.independent.co.uk/arts-entertainment/music/features/lady-gaga-fashion-is-everything-to-me-1380270.html

9   https://www.express.co.uk/celebrity-news/729899/US-Election-2016-Lady-Gaga-futuristic-Nazi-Hillary-Clinton-rally-North-Carolina; https://www.cbsnews.com/news/lady-gagas-jacket-draws-nazi-comparisons-from-alt-right/

Fascinating Fascism

1   Hauptmann A. D. Freiherr von Getting, *Die Uniformen der Braun-hemden*, (Naval & Military Press, 1934), p. 82

2   Fania Fénelon, *Playing For Time* (Syracuse University Press, 1997), pp. 62, 99

3   Lasker-Wallfisch and De la Mare, *Inherit the Truth*, pp. 93, 123, 184

4   Sarah Helm, *If This Is a Woman* (Abacus, 2016), p. 310

5   Primo Levi, *If This Is a Man* (Penguin, 1987), p. 57

6   Rees, *Auschwitz*, p. 262

7   Wilhelm Reich, *The Mass Psychology of Fascism* (Pelican, 1975) p. 66

8   Reich, *Mass Psychology of Fascism*, pp. 133–5

9   Sereny, *Speer*, p. 138

10 Speer, *Inside the Third Reich*, p. 196

11 'Well, whatever would Edvard Munch have said', Julie Burchill, *NME*, 18 November 1978

12 *Sounds*, 3 December 1977

13 'Siouxsie and the Banshees', Steve Walsh, *ZigZag* No. 77, October 1977, p. 10

14 *Sounds*, 28 February 1981

15 http://www.untiedundone.com/12802d.html

16 Ian Birch, 'The Giraffe Looked at Siouxsie', *Melody Maker*, 17 February 1979

17 Savage, *England's Dreaming Tapes*, p. 340

18 Savage, *England's Dreaming Tapes*, p. 485

19 'Siouxsie and the Banshees', Steve Walsh , *ZigZag* No. 77, October 1977, p. 10

Deutscher Girls

1 https://www.punk77.co.uk/groups/models_marco_pirroni_interview_2.htm

2 *Sniffin' Glue*, 9

3 https://www.theguardian.com/music/2014/feb/27/never-mind-swastikas-se-cret-history-punky-jews

4 Roger Huddle and Red Saunders, *Reminisces of RAR: Rocking Against Racism 1976–1979* (Redwords, 2016)

5 Vivien Goldman, *Sounds*, 2 April 1977

6 Tim Lott, *Record Mirror*, 24 September 1977

7 Ian Kershaw, *Hitler 1889–1936: Hubris* (Penguin, 1998), p. 354

8 *Sounds*, 11 October 1978

9 *Ripped & Torn*, issue 12

10 William L. Shirer, *The Rise And Fall of the Third Reich* (Pan, 1960), p. 1170

11 *Time*, 25 August 1947

12 Richard Evans, *Hitler's People: The Faces of the Third Reich* (Allen Lane, 2024), p. 405

13 'Jordan: The Kid Who Wouldn't Wear Clarke's Sandals', *NME*, 15 April 1978, pp. 7–8

14 *Temporary Hoarding* 6, p. 17

15 *Apathy for the Devil*, dir. Simon Holland (1977)

16 *New Musical Express*, 3 December 1977

Master-Racial Masturbation

1 *Guttersnipe* 7, 1979, p. 3

An Ideal for Living

1   'Harry Doherty reports from West Berlin', *Melody Maker*, 4 March 1979, p. 10

2   Julie Burchill, *NME*, 14 October 1978

3   https://www.theguardian.com/theguardian/2010/sep/21/punk-sham69-fare-well-concert

4   Simon Spence, *What Have We Got? The Turbulent Story of Oi!*, (Omnibus Press, 2023), p. 37

5   *Sounds*, November 1978

6   Bernard Sumner, *Chapter and Verse – New Order, Joy Division and Me* (Bantam Press, 2014)

7   Speer, *Inside the Third Reich*, p. 252

8   David Nolan, *Bernard Sumner: Confusion* (Independent Music Press, 2007), p. 46

9   Peter Hook, *Unknown Pleasures: Inside Joy Division* (Simon & Schuster, 2013), p. 70

10 Jon Savage, *This Searing Light, the Sun and Everything Else. Joy Division: The Oral History* (Faber & Faber, 2019), p. 91

11 Tony Wilson, *24 Hour Party People: What the Sleeve Notes Never Tell You* (Channel 4 Books, 2002), p. 61

12 Peter Hook, *Unknown Pleasures*, p. xiv

13 David Nolan, *Tony Wilson – You're Entitled to an Opinion* (John Blake, 2010), p. 50

14 Sumner, *Chapter and Verse*, p. 83

15 Simon Reynolds, *Rip It Up and Start Again: Postpunk 1978–1984*, (Faber, 2005) p. 181

16 *Trials of War Criminals, Before the Nuernberg Military Tribunals*, Vol. 1 'The Medical Case', p. 278

17 https://www.spiegel.de/international/nazi-sex-slaves-new-exhibition-docu-ments-forced-prostitution-in-concentration-camps-a-459704.html

18 Sumner, *Chapter and Verse*, p. 85

19 Savage, *Searing Light*, p. 92

20 Alan Lewis, *Sounds*, 24 June 1978

21 Hook, *Unknown Pleasures*, p. 81

22 https://www.musiclikedirt.com/2018/03/21/joy-division-and-sx-waltham-stow-youth-centre-march-30th-1979/

23 Deborah Curtis, *Touching from a Distance: Ian Curtis & Joy Division* (Faber & Faber, 2005) p. 54

24 https://worldradiohistory.com/UK/Music-Week/1991/MW-1991-02-02.pdf

Zyklon B Zombie

1 Sumner, *Chapter and Verse*, pp. 147–8

2 Peter Hook, *Substance: Inside New Order* (Simon & Schuster, 2016)

3 'Leader of the FAC', *NME*, 31 May 1986

4 'Leader of the FAC', *NME*, 31 May 1986

5 Rees, *Auschwitz*, p. 90

6 https://factoryrecords.org/cerysmatic/leader_of_the_fac_nme_310586.php

7 https://factoryrecords.org/cerysmatic/leader_of_the_fac_nme_310586.php

8 https://www.theguardian.com/culture/2012/jul/02/how-we-made-hacienda-club

9 https://www.youtube.com/watch?v=lT-yRnHzAyg

10 *Sounds*, 3 June 1978

11 *Sounds*, 3 June 1978

12 *NME*, 22 July 1978

13 Cosey Fanni Tutti, *Art Sex Music* (Faber & Faber, 2017), p. 191

14 Tutti, *Art Sex Music*, p. 155

15 Tutti, *Art Sex Music*, p. 216

16 Tutti, *Art Sex Music*, p. 216

17 https://idwalfisher.blogspot.com/2014/01/coum-transmissions-and-throb-bing.html

18 https://www.throbbing-gristle.com/tg-files/tg-files/tg_symbol.html

19 Rees, *Auschwitz*, p. 89

20 Jon Savage, 'Industrial Paranoia: The Very Dangerous Visions Of Throb-bing Gristle', *Sounds*, 3 June 1978

21 https://en.wikipedia.org/wiki/Death_in_June

22 https://thequietus.com/articles/25682-fascism-underground-music-rac-ism-industrial-black-metal-noise

23 Michael Goldberg, *Rolling Stone*, 10 December 1981

24 https://eu.news-press.com/story/entertainment/2016/02/04/devo-devo-lution-fsw-florida-southwestern-state-college-bob-rauschenberg-gal-lery-whip-it/79641674/

25 Reynolds, *Rip it Up*, p. 340

Welcome to the Cabaret

1 Simon Reynolds, *Totally Wired: Postpunk Interviews and Overviews* (Faber, 2009) p. 282

2 Victor Bockris, *Transformer: The Lou Reed Story* (Simon & Schuster, 1995) p. 224

3 *New York Times*, 1998

4 Dave Marsh, *Newsday*, 24 December 1973

5 https://www.3ammagazine com/litarchives/oct2001/bertie_marshall/ bertie_marshall.html

6 https://killyourpetpuppy.co.uk/news/the-pack-ss-label-1979/

7 https://killyourpetpuppy.co.uk/news/theatre-of-hate-ss-label-1980/com-ment-page-1/

Olympia

1 Speer, *Inside the Third Reich*, p. 119

2 *Sounds*, 9 February 1980

3 *Sounds*, 9 February 1980

4 https://www.the-skids.com/apps/blog/show/42748430

5 https://gradesfixer.com/free-essay-examples/the-controversies-around-skids-album-days-in-europa /

6 http://www.garry-bushell.co.uk/storyofoi.htm#

7 Simon Spence, *What Have We Got? The Turbulent Story of Oi!* (Omnibus, 2023) p. 59

8 Jeff Turner, *Cockney Reject* (John Blake, 2010), p. 71.

9 *40 Minutes*, BBC, 1981

10 Don Watson, 'If This Is Heaven I'm Bailing Out', *NME*, 12 May 1984

11 Ian Johnston, *Bad Seed: The Biography of Nick Cave* (Abacus, 1996), p. 126

Who Makes the Nazis?

1 Ronnie Gurr, *Record Mirror*, 31 October 1981

2 'Heroes and Villains', *NME*, 11 December 1993

3 *Melody Maker* interview with Taylor Parkes, January 1997 http://thefall.org/news/980118.html

4 Barney Hoskyns, 'Hip Priest: The Mark Smith Interview', *NME*, 14 November 1981

5   https://thefall.org/news/jamming.html; https://thefall.org/news/jamming.html%20

6   https://forward.com/culture/348928/the-surprising-jewish-story-behind-indie-rock-legend-brix-smith-start/

7   Mark E. Smith, 'Hot dog's in the far-out zone', *NME*, 30 July 1988

8   Stephen Dalton, 'Not Falling, Soaring', *Vox*, June 1991

9   'Cash for Questions', *Q* interview with David Cavanagh, February 2001

10 *Q*, April 2018 https://thefall.org/news/pics/2018-04%20Q%20-%20Mark%20E%20Smith%201957-2018%20[scan].pdf

This Way for the Gas, Ladies and Gentlemen

1   Hannah Arendt, *Eichmann in Jerusalem: A Report on the Banality of Evil* (Penguin, 1977)

2   https://www.nytimes.com/1978/04/16/archives/tv-view-trivializing-the-holocaust-semifact-and-semifiction-tv-view.html

3   https://www.jta.org/archive/fania-fenel-on-raps-cbs-for-having-red-grave-portray-her-in-tv-movie

4   Woody Guthrie Personal Papers: Merchant Marine and Military, Military Service, 28 September 1944

5   Sereny, *Speer*, p. 345

6   https://jweekly.com/2004/06/25/how-the-holocaust-rocked-rush-front-man-geddy-lee/

7   https://jweekly.com/2004/06/25/how-the-holocaust-rocked-rush-front-man-geddy-lee/

8   Chris Bohn, 'Haunted by Spector: Leonard Cohen', *Melody Maker*, 5 January 1980

9   Tadeusz Borowski, *Here in Our Auschwitz and Other Stories* (Yale University Press, 2021)

10 Barry Cain, *Record Mirror*, 5 November 1977

11 https://www.reaganlibrary.gov/archives/speech/remarks-joint-german-american-military-ceremony-bitburg-air-base-federal-republic

12 http://www.sozialismus-von-unten.de/archiv/text/redskins.htm

13 *Sounds*, 11 December 1982

14 Perry Stern, 'Nice to Cats!' *Graffiti* magazine, vol. 4, no. 8 (circa June 88)

15 https://denisesullivan.com/2014/06/02/phranc-your-basic-average-all-american-jewish-lesbian-folksinger/

16 *Surfpunks*, dir. Frans Bromet (VPRO Television, 1981)

Arbeit Macht Frei

1   *NME*, 1 October 1994

2   *Quarterly*, 2014

3   Q, December 1994

4   Shirer, *Rise and Fall of the Third Reich*

5   https://www.latimes.com/archives/la-xpm-1993-06-03-ol-42694-story.html

6   https://jewishstandard.timesofisrael.com/janis-ian-celebrates-her-jewish-ness-local-roots/

Sound of Drums

1   *Hard Report*, 3 February 1995

2   *NME*, 1 March 1997

3   Stuart Maconie, 'Smile, It Might Never Happen', Q, December 1994

4   Chris Roberts, 'Cool, Karma & Collected', *Vox*, May 1998

5   https://www.independent.ie/entertainment/music/you-dont-have-to-be-a-jew-to-be-anti-nazi/37892850.html

6   https://www.independent.ie/entertainment/music/you-dont-have-to-be-a-jew-to-be-anti-nazi/37892850.html

7   https://www.u2songs.com/songs/daddys_gonna_pay_for_your_crashed_car_live_from_sydney_november_27_1993_edi

8   https://archive.seattletimes.com/archive/?date=19950619&slug=2127154

9   https://www.theguardian.com/uk/1999/feb/14/johnarlidge.theobserver

10 Danny Orbach, *The Plots Against Hitler* (Houghton Mifflin Harcourt, 2016), p. 259

11 https://www.theguardian.com/uk/1999/feb/14/johnarlidge.theobserver

Swastika Eyes

1   Primal Scream: 'I Am A Drug Addict', Dorian Lynskey, *Select*, February 2000

2   Jonh Ingham, 'Poetry In Motion With The One Eyed Giant', *Sounds*, 14 June 1975

3   Miles, review of Soft Machine at Hammersmith Palais, London, *New Musical Express*, 3 July 1976

4   Chris Roberts, *Uncut*, March 2002

5   https://www.nme.com/news/music/primal-scream-138-1362350

6   https://www.electronicbeats.net/primal-scream-bobby-gillespie/

7   https://www.youtube.com/watch?v=xUJhlsZSSoM

8   Adelle Stripe & Lias Saoudi, *Ten Thousand Apologies: Fat White Family and the Miracle of Failure* (White Rabbit, 2022), p. 50

9   https://www.godisinthetvzine.co.uk/2019/11/29/fat-white-family-tram-shed-cardiff-27-11-2019/

10 https://drownedinsound.com/in_depth/4149623-i-can-t-watch-a-film-unless-its-got-nazis-in-it---fat-white-familys-lias-saoudi-speaks-to-dis

11 http://thefanzine.com/fat-white-family-gets-to-the-meat-of-the-matter/

12 https://www.theguardian.com/music/2007/may/17/popandrock.alexispetridis

13 https://www.theguardian.com/music/musicblog/2010/may/10/farewell-interpol-carlos-d

14 https://www.tabletmag.com/sections/arts-letters/articles/a-farewell-to-armbands-interpol-carlos-dengler

15 https://www.welt.de/wams_print/article744996/Ich-waere-gern-ein-Amateur.html https://www.theguardian.com/uk/2007/apr/17/musicnews.secondworldwar

16 Speer, *Inside the Third Reich*, p. 169

17 https://edm.parliament.uk/early-day-motion/33035/bryan-ferrys-praise-of-nazis-and-his-marks-and-spencer-contract

Pretty as a Swastika

1   Simon Witter, 'To Hell And Back, Slayer', *NME*, 21 March 1987

2   https://metalinjection.net/news/drama/waitain-part-ways-with-guitarist-after-nazi-salute-photo-surfaces?fbclid=IwAR3c4u8Nfd4jHhLVP75lEET76g-Dx6BND-qH5Wx1CEtRiHha8zOmyZejHDf4

3   *Spin*, April 2005

4   https://www.derstandard.at/story/1289559/marilyn-manson-ueber-stimmung-in-usa-und-entartete-kunst

5   John Doran, 'God of Fucking About', *Stool Pigeon*, June 2009

6   *Time* magazine, 26 May 2009

7   https://www.metalsucks.net/2018/04/11/nazi-imagery-why-watain-and-marduk-dont-get-a-pass-while-slayer-and-metallica-do/

8   https://forward.com/schmooze/430692/sharon-osbourne-opens-up-about-trauma-anti-semitism-had-on-her-family/

9   https://www.uncut.co.uk/features/an-audience-with-ozzy-osbourne-22452/

10 https://www.loudersound.com/features/ian-anderson-jethro-tull-rok-flote-interview

11 https://www.theguardian.com/music/2014/nov/12/nicki-minaj-apologises-nazi-video-only

12 https://www.rollingstone.com/music/music-news/nicki-minaj-video-director-admits-using-nazi-inspired-imagery-230895/
    https://www.adl.org/resources/press-release/adl-deeply-disturbed-nazi-imagery-nicki-minaj-video#.VGECuvTF-Io

13 https://thelibs-daily.livejournal.com/61478.html

14 Pete Welsh, *Kids in the Riot: High and Low with the Libertines* (Omnibus, 2005), p. 18

15 http://theextricate.blogspot.com/2018/01/nicos-recording-of-das-lied-der.html

16 Don Watson, 'Watch Out, the World's Behind You', *NME*, 3 August 1985

17 https://www.theguardian.com/music/2007/mar/16/popandrock3; Nico, *Cible mouvante* (Pauvert, 2001)

18 https://www.theguardian.com/music/2007/mar/16/popandrock3

Another Brick in the Wall

1   Gerald Scarfe, *The Making of Pink Floyd The Wall* (Weidenfeld & Nicolson, 2010), p. 211

2   *Pink Floyd Behind the Wall*, dir. Sonia Anderson (2011)

3   *Retrospective: Looking Back at The Wall*

4   *Pink Floyd Behind the Wall*, dir. Sonia Anderson (2011)

5   https://blabbermouth.net/news/roger-waters-rips-newly-released-documentary-as-flimsy-unapologetic-piece-of-propaganda

6   https://www.theguardian.com/music/video/2016/feb/01/phil-anselmo-ends-gig-with-nazi-salute-and-shout-of-white-power-video

7   https://www.thedailybeast.com/ice-cubes-long-disturbing-history-of-anti-semitism

8   https://www.nme.com/news/music/ice-cube-refute-kanye-west-claim-influenced-antisemitism-333155

9 https://www.theguardian.com/music/2022/dec/02/kanye-west-suspended-from-twitter-after-posting-swastika-inside-the-star-of-david?utm_term=Autofeed&CMP=twt_gu&utm_medium&utm_source=Twitter

10 *The Trouble With Kanye*, dir. Stefan Mattison (BBC, 2023)

11 https://www.forbes.com/sites/conormurray/2025/02/28/kanye-west-wears-swastika-t-shirt-around-los-angeles-report-says/

12 https://www.theguardian.com/music/2023/mar/22/k-pop-star-chaeyoung-apologises-for-wearing-swastika-logo-twice

13 https://www.theguardian.com/world/2011/mar/02/kishidan-nazi-uniforms-japan-aplogy

Ghosts

1 https://www.theguardian.com/world/2024/apr/24/people-would-never-forget-these-shoes-the-fight-to-preserve-soles-of-stutthof-nazi-camp

2 https://www.theguardian.com/music/2019/nov/29/trupa-trupa-the-polish-post-punk-band-confronting-the-holocaust

Image Credits

Index

2 Tone 189

A Certain Ratio 212–13

Albertine, Viv 124, 171

Alex Harvey Band, the 72, 127

Altham, Keith 18, 93

Anderson, Brett 89

Animals, the 18

Ant, Adam 154, 165, 172–78, 180, 182–83

Anti-Nazi League (ANL) 91, 101–03

Asheton, Ron 45–47, 144

Auschwitz-Birkenau 14, 30, 34, 44

Baker, Ginger 92, 93

Bangs, Lester 118, 143–44, 223

Barker, Simon 114, 128

Beatles, The 2, 8, 11–16

Belsen 115–18

Biggs, Ronnie 120–121

Blake, Peter 15

Blondie 194

Bloom, Eric 49, 51

Blue Öyster Cult 48–51

Bogarde, Dirk 153–54, 155

Bono 275–76

Bormann, Martin 29, 120–21, 174

Boss, Hugo 161

Bouchard, Joe 48–51

Bowie, David 75–8, 82, 84–90, 96, 127, 226, 228

Bragg, Billy 1–4

Brandon, Kirk 231–32

Branson, Richard 134

Braun, Eva 59, 72, 120

British Movement 99, 195, 237, 238

Brooks, Mel 176

Brothels 201–04

Brown, James (editor of *GQ*) 278–79

Burchill, Julie 132, 165-66, 177, 180, 195

Burdon, Eric 18–19

Cabaret 61, 73, 227, 228

Cave, Nick 239

Chaplin, Charlie 35–37

Clapton, Eric 92–95, 96

Clash, the 128, 129, 136–38

Cleave, Maureen 7, 8, 15

Cohen, Leonard 258–59

Cohn, Nik 24–5

Communism 17, 84

Cook, Paul 120, 121

Coon, Caroline 37, 109, 129, 137, 171

Cooper Clarke, John 98

Costello, Elvis 195, 223

Cream 92–93

Crowe, Cameron 78

Curtis, Ian 206–10

Damned, the 148–50

Dead Boys, the 145–6

Dead Kennedys 264–5

Dengler, Carlos 284–7

Des Barres, Pamela 41

Doherty, Pete 301–2

Donaldson, Ian Stewart 73–4

Drayton, Tony 119, 184–86, 232

Dylan, Bob 256

Eagles, the 65

Electric Eels 144–45

Eno, Brian 60

Epstein, Brian 16

Exploited, the 241–2

Fall, the 242–6

Farlowe, Chris 122

Fat White Family 283–4

Fawlty Towers 54

Ferry, Bryan 61–2, 287–90

Fields, Danny 46, 303

final solution 33, 38, 82, 100, 193, 221–23, 251, 252, 270, 288, 299, 300, 315, 323

Frehley, Ace 63–65

Gabinete Caligari 23

Gainsbourg, Serge 56–59

Goebbels, Josef 29, 82–83, 120, 237, 293

Goldman, Vivien 137, 166, 170, 171

Göring, Hermann 29, 33, 70

Guthrie, Woody 179, 255

Hall, Terry 190, 192

Hamburg 11–12, 19, 140, 297, 316

Harrison, George 11, 14, 15

Harry, Debbie 19 4

Hell's Angels 27–28

Hepworth, David 24, 26

Hess, Rudolf 196–97

Heydrich, Reinhard 38, 151

Himmler, Heinrich 76, 201, 298, 315

Hitler, Adolf 1, 7, 9, 15, 17, 28–29, 32, 78, 97, 120, 165, 174, 197, 233, 268

Hitler, Adolf – impersonation 12, 13, 19, 20, 72, 141

Holocaust 44, 249, 252, 325

Holocaust denial 56, 101

Hook, Peter 208–09, 211, 214

House of Dolls 204–05, 211

Human League 226–27

Ian, Janis 270–71

Ice Cube 309–10

Iron Cross 12, 20, 26, 45, 54, 68, 92, 93, 135, 136, 185, 228

Irwin, Colin 65–66

Israel 140, 192–93, 280, 281, 282

Jackson, Michael 95, 277–78

Jagger, Mick 19, 21, 22, 24, 25, 28, 30–31

James, Tony 135–36

Jethro Tull 298–99

Johansen, David 112, 140–41

John's Children 20

Jones, Mick 135, 137, 138

Jones, Steve 120, 121–23

Jones, Brian 20–23, 45

Jordan 108, 112–114, 180

Joy Division 2, 196–201, 205–10, 214–15, 221

KISS 63–4, 65

Koch, Ilse 178–82

K-pop 312–14

Kraftwerk 87, 223–25

Kula Shaker 273–75

Kwiatkowski, Grzegorz 315–19

Lady Gaga 157–59

Lasker-Wallfisch, Anita 117, 163, 253

Le Pen, Jean-Marie 56
Led Zeppelin 41–43
Lee, Geddy 257–58
Lemmy 66–71, 130
Lennon, John 2, 8–17, 21, 55
Levi, Primo 52, 153
London SS 135–36
Lydon, John see Rotten, Johnny
Madness 189–92
Madonna 154–56, 282
Manic Street Preachers 268–69
Manson, Charles 48
Manson, Marilyn 157, 293–96
McCartney, Paul 11, 13, 15, 21, 48, 55
McLaren, Malcolm 107–11, 124, 129
Mein Kampf 29, 32, 95, 196, 233
Melody Maker 49, 65, 194
Mercury, Freddie 81
Metropolis 77, 81
Milligan, Spike 37
Minaj, Nicki 299–300
Models, the 170
Monty Python 40, 54, 94, 132
Moon, Keith 20, 33, 38–41
Morrissey 95
Mosley, Oswald 77
Mötley Crüe 71
Motörhead 66–71, 130
Olympics, Berlin 233–34, 236
National Front, the 56, 88, 100, 137, 138, 184, 191, 235
Nazi imagery, eroticised 150, 160, 180
Nazi memorabilia 12, 18, 27, 45, 63, 68, 108, 135
New Order (Bernard Sumner) 211–15
New York Dolls 111–112, 140–141

Nico 302–03
Niemöller, Martin 101–02
Night Porter, The 60, 152–57, 182
NME, the 39, 75, 85, 89, 127, 134, 140, 148, 216, 232, 239
Numan, Gary 85
Nuremburg rally 7, 69, 78–79, 81
Nuremburg Trials 77, 196
Oi! 238–39, 243
Oldham, Andrew Loog 19–20, 24
Ono, Yoko 17
Osbourne, Ozzy 296–98
Page, Jimmy 41–43
Pallenberg, Anita 20, 31
Parsons, Tony 100-01, 143
Pearlman, Sandy 49–50
Peellaert, Guy 23–25
Pink Floyd 304–08
Pop, Iggy 45, 47, 84
pornography 151, 181
Powell, Enoch 91, 94
Presley, Elvis 8, 38
Priest, Steve 53–54
Primal Scream 280–83
punk 127–139, 184
Queen 81–82
Ramones, the 141, 142–44, 262
Ravan, Genya 18, 146
Ray, Amy 271
Reagan, Ronald 261–62
Reed, Lou 227
Rees, Laurence 32, 83, 116, 164, 212, 219
Reid, Jamie 109, 134
Residents, the 146–47
Rhodes, Bernie 128–30, 135
Richards, Keith 21, 23, 25–27, 31

Riefenstahl, Leni 1, 3–4, 28–30, 78, 82, 173, 275, 277, 299

Rock Against Racism 91, 96, 118, 133, 182, 196, 206

Rolling Stones, the 19, 20, 21, 24–27

Rommel, Erwin 278–79

Roosevelt, Franklin D., 36

Rotten, Johnny 115, 118, 119, 123, 128, 138

Roxy Music 60

Russell, Ken 108

Salon Kitty 132, 151–52, 156, 167, 182

Saunders, Red 95–98

Sereny, Gitta 28–29, 30, 79–80, 159, 165, 256

Sessler, Freddie 26–27

Severin, Steven 130, 131, 166, 169

Sex Pistols, the 109, 113, 114–119, 121, 123, 126, 127, 133–34

Sham 69 195–96

Simmons, Gene 63–65

Sioux, Siouxsie 124, 127–133, 165–69

Siouxsie and the Banshees 130–133, 165–69

Sixx, Nikki 71

Skids, the 233–38

Skrewdriver 73

Skunk Anansie 272–73

Slayer 291–92

Smith, Mark E., 242–46

Smith, Patti 51

Sontag, Susan 160, 161

Spandau Ballet 228–30

Sparks 55

Specials, the 189, 190, 192

Speer, Albert 11, 77, 79–80, 165, 174, 234, 237, 287–88

Spungen, Nancy 124–125

SS uniform 20–23, 26, 41, 53, 161–62, 164, 217, 245

Stanley, Paul 63–65

Stanshall, Vivian 38–40

Starr, Freddie 54

Starr, Ringo 13, 55

Stewart, Rod 92

Stone Roses 265

storm trooper 42–43

Strange, Steve 228, 230, 231

Strummer, Joe 130, 136, 138

Suggs 189–90

Sumner, Bernard 207–08, 211

swastika symbol 3, 14, 31–33, 45, 48, 49, 67, 84, 91, 107, 110, 114–115, 126, 130, 164, 315, 325

Sweet 53–54

Taylor, Roger 81

Thatcher, Margaret 103

Third Reich aesthetics 8, 25, 31, 45, 49, 56, 71, 132, 141, 287

Three Stooges 35

Throbbing Gristle 215–221

Thunders, Johnny 140–141

Toothpaste, Lucy *see* Whitman, Lucy

Top of the Pops 53, 55, 118, 176

Townshend, Pete 20

Van der Graaf Generator 52

Vicious, Sid 123, 124–126, 130, 133, 171

Walsh, Joe 65–66

Waters, Roger 304–08

Weller, Paul 259–61

West, Kanye 310–12

Westwood, Vivienne 30, 108, 109, 111–112, 124

Whitman, Lucy, 98–99, 1c9, 118–119, 180, 182

Who, the 20, 72

Wilson, Tony 3, 199–200, 2:2–15

World at War, the 2, 244, 252, 283

Zyklon B 218–220